T0197979

Get the eBooks FREE!
(PDF, ePub, Kindle, and liveBook all included)

We believe that once you buy a book from us, you should be able to read it in any format we have available. To get electronic versions of this book at no additional cost to you, purchase and then register this book at the Manning website.

Go to https://www.manning.com/freebook and follow the instructions to complete your pBook registration.

That's it!
Thanks from Manning!

API Design Patterns

API Design
Patterns

JJ GEEWAX
FOREWORD BY JON SKEET

MANNING
SHELTER ISLAND

For online information and ordering of this and other Manning books, please visit
www.manning.com. The publisher offers discounts on this book when ordered in quantity.
For more information, please contact

> Special Sales Department
> Manning Publications Co.
> 20 Baldwin Road
> PO Box 761
> Shelter Island, NY 11964
> Email: orders@manning.com

Manning Publications Co.
20 Baldwin Road
PO Box 761
Shelter Island, NY 11964

Development editor:	Christina Taylor
Technical development editor:	Al Krinker
Review editor:	Ivan Martinović
Production editor:	Deirdre S. Hiam
Copy editor:	Michele Mitchell
Proofreader:	Keri Hales
Technical proofreader:	Karsten Strøbæk
Typesetter:	Dennis Dalinnik
Cover designer:	Marija Tudor

ISBN: 9781617295850
Printed in the United States of America

To Kai and Luca. You are awesome.

brief contents

contents

ix

foreword

It started with a drum kit. In the summer of 2019, a friend of mine got me into drumming with an electronic kit, and I embraced it wholeheartedly. Sometimes I would actually play the drums, but I spent a rather larger proportion of my time writing code to interact with my drum kit's configuration using MIDI SysEx commands.

When the COVID-19 pandemic hit, I suddenly had rather different priorities in terms of considering the audio/visual needs of my local church, both while we were worshiping remotely and considering how we might meet in person again. This involved learning about protocols such as VISCA, NDI, and OSC (for cameras and audio mixers) as well as more software-oriented integration with Zoom, VLC, Power-Point, Stream Deck, and more.

These projects don't have huge amounts of business logic. Almost all the code is integration code, which is at once frustrating and hugely empowering. It's frustrating because of protocols that are obscurely documented or aren't really designed for the kind of usage I'm trying to achieve, or are just inconsistent with each other. It's empowering because once you've cracked the integration aspect, you can write useful apps really easily, standing on the shoulders of multiple giants.

While my experience over the past couple of years has been primarily local integration, the same balance of frustration and empowerment applies with web APIs. Every experience I've had of picking up a new web API has had a curve of emotional responses, including some mix of excitement, bewilderment, annoyance, acceptance, and eventual uneasy peace. Once you thoroughly understand a powerful API, it feels like you're the conductor of a magnificent orchestra, ready to play whatever music you provide—even if the violin players' notes are only eventually consistent and you have to use a different color of baton for the brass section for no obvious reason.

This book won't change that on its own. It's only a book. But if you read it and follow its guidance, you can help to change the experience for your users. If lots of people read it and follow its guidance, together we might move the needle toward a more consistent and less frustrating web API experience.

It's important to understand the value of this book as more than the sum of its parts. For any one of the aspects JJ dives into, any given team could make a reasonable choice (albeit one that might miss some of the corner cases pointed out here). That choice may even be better for that specific situation than the recommendation provided in this book due to the limited requirements of the context. That approach achieves lots of local optimal decisions but a highly fragmented bigger picture, with potentially several different approaches being taken, even by APIs within the same company.

Beyond consistency for any given problem, this book provides a consistent approach across multiple areas of API design. It's rare for API designers to be given the space to think deeply about this, and I count myself as very lucky to have worked with JJ and others (notably Luke Sneeringer) in discussing many of the topics within the book. I'm thrilled that the investment Google has made in API design can pay dividends to other developers through this book and through the AIP system at https://aip.dev.

While I have great confidence in the value of this book, it doesn't make it easy to design a great API. Instead, it takes away a lot of the incidental complexity that comes with API design, allowing you to focus on the aspects that are truly unique to the API you want to build. You should still expect to have to think, and think hard, but with confidence that the result of that thinking can be an API that is a joy to work with. Your users may never explicitly thank you for it; a well-designed API often feels obvious despite being the result of huge amounts of toil. But you can sleep well at night knowing that they won't have experienced the frustrations of an API that doesn't quite feel right, even when it works.

Use this book as a footstool to help your API be a giant that provides shoulders for others to stand on.

—Jon Skeet, Staff Developer Relations Engineer, Google

preface

In school, we learned about computer science in the same way that we might learn about the laws of physics. We analyzed run-time and space complexity using Big-O notation, learned how a variety of sorting algorithms worked, and explored the different ways of traversing binary trees. So as you might imagine, after graduating, I expected my day job to be primarily scientific and mathematical in nature. But imagine my surprise when I found that wasn't the case at all.

It turned out that most of the work I had to do was more about design, structure, and aesthetics than about mathematics and algorithms. I never needed to think about which sorting algorithm to use because there was a library for that (usually something like array.sort()). I did, however, have to think long and hard about the classes I'd create, the functions that would exist on those classes, and what parameters each function would accept. And this was far more difficult than I expected.

In the real world, I learned how perfectly-optimized code is not nearly as valuable as well-designed code. And this turned out to be doubly true for web APIs, as they generally have a far broader audience with a wider variety of use cases.

But this begs the question: what does it mean for software to be "well-designed"? What is a "well-designed web API"? For quite some time I had to rely on a mostly haphazard collection of resources to answer these questions. For some topics there might be interesting blog posts that explored some of the popular alternatives in use today. For others there might be a particularly useful answer on Stack Overflow that could guide me in the right direction. But in many scenarios, there was relatively little material on the topic in question, and I was left trying to come up with an answer on my own and hoping my colleagues didn't hate it too much.

After many years of this (and carrying around a notebook with "Scary API Problems" written on the cover), I finally decided that it was time to write down all the information I'd collected and had seen to work first-hand. At first, this was a set of rules for Google that Luke Sneeringer and I codified, which ultimately became AIP.dev. But these rules read sort of like a book of laws; they said what you should do, but didn't say why you should do it that way. After lots of research and asking myself this exact question over and over, this book is here to present these rules, but also to explain why.

As great as it would be for this book to be the ultimate solution to the world's API design problems, I sadly don't think this is the case. The reason for this is simple: much like architecture, any sort of design is generally a matter of opinion. This means that some of you may think these guidelines are beautiful and elegant and use them for all of your projects going forward. At the same time, some of you may think that this book presents designs that are hideous and overly restrictive and use it as an example of what not to do when building a web API. Since I can't make everyone happy, my only goal is to provide a set of battle-tested guidelines, along with logical explanations for why they look the way they do.

Whether you use them as examples to follow or avoid is up to you. At the very least, I hope the topics covered in this book spark many conversations and quite a lot of future work on this fascinating, complex, and intricate world of API design.

acknowledgments

As with most of my work, this book is the result of many contributions from many different people. First, I have to thank my wife, Ka-el, for listening to me rant and complain while struggling with the finishing touches of this manuscript. There's a good chance that this book may have been abandoned had it not been for her unwavering support. Additionally, many others have played a similar role, including Kristen Ranieri, Becky Susel, Janette Clarke, Norris Clarke, Tahj Clarke, Sheryn Chan, Asfia Fazal, and Adama Diallo, to whom I'm very grateful.

A core team of API enthusiasts were instrumental in reviewing and debating the topics covered in this book, as well as providing high-level guidance. In particular, I want to thank Eric Brewer, Hong Zhang, Luke Sneeringer, Jon Skeet, Alfred Fuller, Angie Lin, Thibaud Hottelier, Garrett Jones, Tim Burks, Mak Ahmad, Carlos O'Ryan, Marsh Gardiner, Mike Kistler, Eric Wheeler, Max Ross, Marc Jacobs, Jason Woodard, Michael Rubin, Milo Martin, Brad Meyers, Sam McVeety, Rob Clevenger, Mike Schwartz, Lewis Daly, Michael Richards, and Brian Grant for all of their help over the years.

Many others contributed to this book indirectly with their own independent work, and for that I must thank Roy Fielding, the "gang of four" (Erich Gamma, Richard Helm, Ralph Johnson, and John Vlissides), Sanjay Ghemawatt, Urs Hoelzle, Andrew Fikes, Sean Quinlan, and Larry Greenfield. I'd also like to thank Stu Feldman, Ari Balogh, Rich Sanzi, Joerg Heilig, Eyal Manor, Yury Izrailevsky, Walt Drummond, Caesar Sengupta, and Patrick Teo for their support and guidance while exploring these topics at Google.

A special thanks to Dave Nagle for being a champion for all my work in ads, the cloud, APIs, and beyond and for encouraging me to push myself beyond my comfort zone. And thanks to Mark Chadwick who, over 10 years ago, helped me get past my imposter syndrome in API design. His constructive feedback and kind words are a big part of why I decided to dive deeper into this interesting area of computer science. Additionally, a special thank you is owed to Mark Hammond, who first taught me to question everything, even when it's uncomfortable.

This project would not have been possible without the editorial team at Manning, in particular Mike Stephens and Marjan Bace who okay'd the initial idea for this book, and Christina Taylor who stuck with me for another long-term project. I am also grateful for the detailed chapter reviews by Al Krinker; my project editor, Deirdre Hiam; copyeditor, Michele Mitchell; proofreader, Keri Hales; and reviewer editor, Ivan Martinović. Thank you to all those at Manning who helped make this happen.

To all the reviewers: Akshat Paul, Anthony Cramp, Brian Daley, Chris Heneghan, Daniel Bretoi, David J. Biesack, Deniz Vehbi, Gerardo Lecaros, Jean Lazarou, John C. Gunvaldson, Jorge Ezequiel Bo, Jort Rodenburg, Luke Kupka, Mark Nenadov, Rahul Rai, Richard Young, Roger Dowell, Ruben Vandeginste, Satej Kumar Sahu, Steven Smith, Yul Williams, Yurii Bodarev, and Zoheb Ainapore, your suggestions helped make this a better book.

about this book

API Design Patterns was written to provide a collection of safe, flexible, reusable patterns for building web APIs. It starts by covering some general design principles and builds on these to showcase a set of design patterns that aim to provide simple solutions to common scenarios when building APIs.

Who should read this book

API Design Patterns is for anyone who is building or plans to build a web API, particularly when that API will be exposed to the public. Familiarity with some serialization formats (e.g., JSON, Google Protocol Buffers, or Apache Thrift) or common storage paradigms (e.g., relational database schemas) is certainly nice to have but is in no way required. It's also a nice bonus if you're already familiar with HTTP and its various methods (e.g., GET and POST), as it is the transport of choice throughout the examples in this book. If you find yourself designing an API and running into problems and thinking, "I'm sure someone must have figured this out already," this book is for you.

How this book is organized: A roadmap

This book is divided into six parts, with the first two parts covering more general topics in API design and the next four dedicated to the design patterns themselves. Part 1 opens by setting the stage for the rest of the book and providing some definitions and evaluative frameworks for web APIs themselves and the design patterns that we'll apply to those web APIs in the future.

- Chapter 1 starts by defining what we mean by an API and why APIs are important. It also provides a framework of sorts for how we can evaluate how good an API really is.
- Chapter 2 expands on chapter 1 by looking at how design patterns can be applied to APIs and explaining how they can be useful to anyone building them. It covers the anatomy of an API design pattern as well as a short case study of how using one of these design patterns can lead to an overall better API.

Part 2 aims to further build on the stage established in part 1 by outlining some general design principles that should be considered when building any API.

- Chapter 3 looks at all the different components we might need to name in an API and what to take into consideration when choosing names for them. It also shows how naming is critically important despite seeming like something superficial.
- Chapter 4 digs deeper into larger APIs, where we might have multiple resources that relate to one another. After going through some questions to ask when deciding on the resources and their relationships, it finishes by covering some examples of things to avoid.
- Chapter 5 explores how different data types and the default values for these data types should be used in an API. It covers the most common data types such as strings and numbers, as well as the more complex possibilities like maps and lists.

Part 3 marks the beginning of the design pattern catalog, starting with the fundamental patterns that should apply to almost all APIs.

- Chapter 6 looks closely at how resources can be identified by users of an API, digging into the low-level details of identifiers such as tombstoning, character set and encodings, and using checksums to distinguish between missing versus invalid IDs.
- Chapter 7 outlines in great detail how the different standard methods of web APIs (get, list, create, update, and delete) should work. It also explains why it's so important that each standard method behave in exactly the same way across all the resources rather than varying to accommodate the unique aspects of each resource.
- Chapter 8 expands on two specific standard methods (get and update) to address how users can interact with parts of a resource rather than the entire thing. It explains why this is necessary and useful (for both users and the API), as well as how to keep support for this functionality as minimally intrusive as possible.
- Chapter 9 pushes past standard methods and opens the door to any sort of action we might want in an API using custom methods. Special emphasis is given to explain when custom methods make sense (and when they don't), as well as how to make this decision in your own API.

- Chapter 10 explores the unique scenario where API methods may not be instantaneous and how to support this in a convenient way for users with long-running operations (LROs). It explores how LROs work and all the methods that can be supported by LROs, including pausing, resuming, and canceling the long-running work.

- Chapter 11 covers the concept of work that gets executed over and over, sort of like cron jobs for web APIs. It explains how to use Execution resources and run these on either a schedule or on demand.

Part 4 focuses on resources and how they relate to one another, sort of like a more expansive exploration of chapter 4.

- Chapter 12 explains how small, isolated bits of related data might be segregated into singleton sub-resources. It goes into detail about the circumstances for when this is a good idea as well as when it's not.

- Chapter 13 outlines how resources in a web API should store references to other resources with either reference pointers or in-lined values. It also explains how to handle edge-case behaviors such as cascading deletes or updates as referenced data changes over time.

- Chapter 14 expands on one-to-one relationships between resources and explains how to use association resources to represent many-to-many relationships. It also covers how metadata can be stored about these relationships.

- Chapter 15 looks at using add and remove shortcut methods as an alternative to relying on association resources when handling many-to-many relationships. It also covers some of the trade-offs when using these methods and why they might not always be the ideal fit.

- Chapter 16 looks at the complex concept of polymorphism, where variables can take on a variety of different types. It covers how to handle polymorphic fields on API resources as well as why polymorphic methods should be avoided.

Part 5 moves beyond interactions involving a single API resource at a time and begins looking at API design patterns targeted at interacting with entire collections of resources.

- Chapter 17 explains how resources can be copied or moved in an API. It addresses the nuanced complications such as handling external data, inherited metadata from a different parent, and how child resources should be treated.

- Chapter 18 explores how to adapt the standard methods (get, create, update, and delete) to operate on a collection of resources rather than a single resource at a time. It also covers some of the tricky pieces, such as how results should be returned and how to handle partial failures.

- Chapter 19 expands on the idea of the batch delete method from chapter 17 to remove resources that match a specific filter rather than just a specific identifier. It also explores how to address issues of consistency and best practices to avoid accidental destruction of data.

- Chapter 20 looks closely at ingestion of non-resource data that, itself, is not directly addressable. It covers how to use anonymous writes as well as topics of consistency and the trade-offs of when this type of anonymous data ingestion is a good fit for an API.

- Chapter 21 explains how to handle browsing large data sets using pagination, relying on opaque page tokens to iterate through data. It also demonstrates how to use pagination inside single large resources.

- Chapter 22 looks at how to handle applying filter criteria to listing resources and the best way to represent these filters in APIs. This applies directly to the topics covered in chapter 19.

- Chapter 23 explores how to handle importing and exporting resources in and out of an API. It also dives into the nuanced differences between import and export operations as compared to backup and restore.

Part 6 focuses on the somewhat less exciting areas of safety and security in APIs. This means ensuring that APIs are safe from attackers but also that the API methods provided are made safe from users' own mistakes.

- Chapter 24 explores the topic of versioning and what it means for different versions to be compatible with one another. It digs into the idea of compatibility as a spectrum and the importance of a compatibility policy definition that is consistent across an API.

- Chapter 25 begins the work of protecting users from themselves by providing a pattern (soft deletion) for allowing resources to be removed from view while not being completely deleted from the system.

- Chapter 26 attempts to protect the system from duplicate actions using request identifiers. It explores the pitfalls of using request IDs as well as an algorithm to ensure that these IDs are handled properly in large-scale systems.

- Chapter 27 focuses on validation requests that allow users to get a preview of an action in an API without executing the underlying operation. It also explores how to handle more advanced topics such as side effects during both live requests and validation requests.

- Chapter 28 introduces the idea of resource revisions as a way of tracking changes over time. It also covers the basic operations, such as restoring to previous revisions, and more advanced topics, such as how to apply revisions to child resources in the hierarchy.

- Chapter 29 presents a pattern for informing users when API requests should be retried. It also includes guidelines about different HTTP response codes and whether they are safe to be retried.

- Chapter 30 explores the topic of authenticating individual requests and the different security criteria to be considered when authenticating users in an API. It presents a specification for digitally signing API requests that adheres to security best practices to ensure API requests have verifiable origin and integrity and are not able to be repudiated later.

About the code

This book contains many examples of source code both in numbered listings and in line with normal text. In both cases, source code is formatted in a `fixed-width font like this` to separate it from ordinary text. Sometimes code is also in **bold** to highlight code that has changed from previous steps in the chapter, such as when a new feature adds to an existing line of code.

In many cases, the original source code has been reformatted; we've added line breaks and reworked indentation to accommodate the available page space in the book. In rare cases, even this was not enough, and listings include line-continuation markers (➡). Additionally, comments in the source code have often been removed from the listings when the code is described in the text. Code annotations accompany many of the listings, highlighting important concepts.

After quite a bit of discussion with our early readers and review team, I've decided to use TypeScript as the standard language for a variety of reasons. First, TypeScript is easy to follow for anyone familiar with both dynamic languages (like JavaScript or Python) as well as static languages (like Java or C++). Additionally, while it might not be everyone's favorite, and not all readers will be able to write their own TypeScript code right away, the code snippets can be treated as pseudo code, and most software developers should be able to discern the meaning.

When it comes to defining APIs using TypeScript, there are two pieces to address: resources and methods. For the former, TypeScript's primitives (e.g., interfaces) are quite expressive when defining schemas for API resources, keeping the API definitions short enough that they almost always fit in just a few lines. As a result, all API resources are defined as TypeScript interfaces, which has the added bonus of making the JSON representation quite obvious.

For API methods, the problem is a bit more complicated. In this case, I've opted to use TypeScript abstract classes to represent the overarching API itself, with abstract functions to define the API methods, following a convention commonly used with Google's Protocol Buffers' RPCs. This provides the ability to define just the API methods without having to worry about the underlying implementations.

When considering the inputs and outputs of API methods, I've decided to rely again on Protocol Buffers for inspiration, thinking in terms of request and response interfaces. This means that in most cases there will be interfaces representing these inputs and outputs, named as the API method with a `-Request` or `-Response` suffix (e.g., `CreateChatRoomRequest` for a `CreateChatRooom` API method).

Finally, since this book relies quite a lot on RESTful concepts, there had to be a way of mapping these RPCs to a URL (and HTTP method). For this, I've chosen to use TypeScript decorators as annotations on the various API methods, with one decorator for each of the different HTTP methods (e.g., `@get`, `@post`, `@delete`). To indicate the

URL path that the API method should map to, each decorator accepts a template string, which also supports wildcards for variables in the request interface. For example, `@get("/{id=chatRooms/*}")` would populate an ID field on the request. In this case, the asterisk indicates a placeholder for any value excluding a forward slash character.

As great as it would have been to rely on OpenAPI specifications for all these design patterns, there are a few issues that tended to do a disservice to readers of this book. First, OpenAPI specifications are intended for consumption primarily by computers (e.g., code generators, documentation renders, etc.). Since the goal of this book is to communicate complicated API design topics to other API designers, OpenAPI just didn't seem like the best option available for that goal.

Secondly, while OpenAPI is an amazing project, it is quite verbose regardless of whether we represent APIs in YAML or JSON format. Unfortunately, representing these complicated topics using OpenAPI would have been completely possible, but not the most concise choice, leading to quite a lot of extra content without adding as much value.

In the end, between OpenAPI, Protocol Buffers, and TypeScript, the early readers and reviewers gave pretty clear feedback that the TypeScript option was the best fit for this particular use case. Keep in mind that I'm not at all advocating people use TypeScript for defining their APIs. It was just a very good fit for this project.

Live book discussion forum

Purchase of *API Design Patterns* includes free access to a private web forum run by Manning Publications where you can make comments about the book, ask technical questions, and receive help from the author and from other users. To access the forum, go to https://livebook.manning.com/book/api-design-patterns/welcome/v-7. You can also learn more about Manning's forums and the rules of conduct at https://livebook.manning.com/#!/discussion.

Manning's commitment to our readers is to provide a venue where a meaningful dialogue between individual readers and between readers and the author can take place. It is not a commitment to any specific amount of participation on the part of the author, whose contribution to the forum remains voluntary (and unpaid). We suggest you try asking the author some challenging questions lest his interest stray! The forum and the archives of previous discussions will be accessible from the publisher's website as long as the book is in print.

Other online resources

For further reading on API design topics, see https://aip.dev, which covers many similar topics in quite a lot of detail.

about the author

JJ Geewax is a software engineer at Google, focusing on real-time payment systems, cloud infrastructure, and API design. He is also the author of *Google Cloud Platform in Action* and the cofounder of AIP.dev, an industry-wide collaboration on API design standards started at Google. He lives in Singapore with his wife, Ka-el, and son, Luca.

about the cover illustration

The figure on the cover of *API Design Patterns* is captioned *Marchand d'Estampes à Vienne*, or "Merchant of Prints in Vienna." The illustration is taken from a collection of dress costumes from various countries by Jacques Grasset de Saint-Sauveur (1757–1810), titled *Costumes de Différents Pays*, published in France in 1797. Each illustration is finely drawn and colored by hand. The rich variety of Grasset de Saint-Sauveur's collection reminds us vividly of how culturally apart the world's towns and regions were just 200 years ago. Isolated from each other, people spoke different dialects and languages. In the streets or in the countryside, it was easy to identify where they lived and what their trade or station in life was just by their dress.

The way we dress has changed since then, and the diversity by region, so rich at the time, has faded away. It is now hard to tell apart the inhabitants of different continents, let alone different towns, regions, or countries. Perhaps we have traded cultural diversity for a more varied personal life—certainly for a more varied and fast-paced technological life.

At a time when it is hard to tell one computer book from another, Manning celebrates the inventiveness and initiative of the computer business with book covers based on the rich diversity of regional life of two centuries ago, brought back to life by Grasset de Saint-Sauveur's pictures.

Part 1

Introduction

API design is complicated. After all, if it were easy there would probably be little need for this book at all. But before we start exploring the tools and patterns to make API design a bit more manageable, we first have to agree on some fundamental terminology and what to expect from this book. In the next two chapters, we'll cover some of the introductory material that will act as a platform for us to build on throughout the rest of the book.

We'll start in chapter 1 by defining in detail what we mean by an API. More importantly, we'll investigate what good APIs look like and how to distinguish them from bad APIs. Then in chapter 2, we'll look more closely at what we mean by a design pattern and the anatomy of the patterns outlined in the rest of the book, with the end goal of relying on these design patterns to build consistently good APIs.

Introduction to APIs

This chapter covers

- What are interfaces?
- What are APIs?
- What is resource orientation?
- What makes an API "good"?

Chances are that by picking up this book you're already familiar with the high-level concept of an API. Additionally, you probably already know that API stands for application programming interface, so the focus of this chapter will cover what these basics actually mean in more detail, as well as why they matter. Let's start by looking more closely at this idea of an API.

1.1 What are web APIs?

An API defines the way in which computer systems interact. And since an exceptionally small number of systems live in a vacuum, it should come as no surprise that APIs are everywhere. We can find APIs in the libraries we use from language package managers (e.g., an encryption library that provides a method like `function encrypt(input: string): string`) and technically in the code we write ourselves, even if it's never intended for use by anyone else. But there's one special type of

API that is built to be exposed over a network and used remotely by lots of different people, and it's these types that are the focus of this book, often called "web APIs."

Web APIs are interesting in many ways, but the most interesting aspect of this special category is arguably the fact that those building the API have so much control while those using web APIs have relatively little. When we use a library, we deal in local copies of the library itself, meaning those building the API can do whatever they want, whenever they want without the possibility of harming users. Web APIs are different because there are no copies. Instead, when the builders of a web API make changes, these changes are forced on users whether they ask for them or not.

For example, imagine a web API call that allows you to encrypt data. If the team that works on this API decides to use a different algorithm when encrypting your data, you don't really have a choice in the matter. When calling the encryption method, your data will be encrypted with the latest algorithm. In a more extreme example, the team could decide to shut off the API entirely and ignore your requests. At that point, your application will suddenly stop working and there's not much you can do about it. Both of these scenarios are shown in figure 1.1.

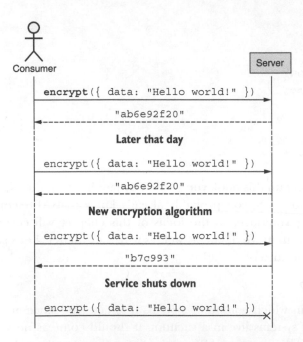

Figure 1.1   **Possible consumer-facing experiences when dealing with a web API**

However, the drawbacks of a web API for consumers are often the primary benefits for those building the APIs: they're able to maintain complete control of the API. For example, if the encryption API used a super-secret new algorithm, the team that built it would probably not want to just give that code away to the world in the form of a library. Instead, they'd probably prefer to use a web API, which would allow them to expose the *functionality* of the super-secret algorithm without giving away their valuable intellectual property. Other times, a system might require extraordinary computational power, which would take way too long to run if it was deployed as a library and run on a home computer or laptop. In those cases, such as with many machine learning APIs, building a web API allows you to expose the powerful functionality while hiding the computational requirements from consumers, shown in figure 1.2.

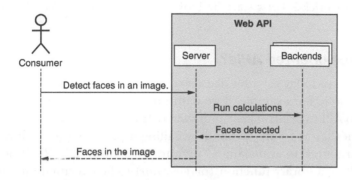

Figure 1.2 An example of a web API hiding the computational power needed

Now that we understand what APIs (and specifically web APIs) are, this raises the question: why do they matter?

1.2 Why do APIs matter?

It's not uncommon for software to be designed and built for human use exclusively, and there's nothing fundamentally wrong with this. However, over the past several years we've seen more and more focus on automation, where we aim to build computer programs that do what we humans do, only faster. Unfortunately, it's at this point that the "human-only" software becomes a bit of a problem.

When we design something exclusively for human use, where our interactions involve a mouse and keyboard, we tend to conflate the system's layout and visual aspects with the raw data and functional aspects. This is a problem because it can be difficult to explain to a computer how to interact with a graphical interface. And this problem gets worse because changing the visual aspects of a program may also require us to reteach the computer how to interact with this *new* graphical interface. In effect, while changes may simply be cosmetic to us, they're completely unrecognizable to a computer. Put differently, to a computer there is no such thing as "cosmetic only."

APIs are interfaces specifically for computers with important properties to make it easy for computers to use them. For example, these interfaces have no visual aspects, so there's no need to worry about superficial changes. And these interfaces generally evolve in only "compatible" ways (see chapter 24), so there's no need to reteach the computer anything in the face of new changes. In short, APIs provide a way to speak the language computers need to interact in a safe and stable way.

But this doesn't stop at simple automation. APIs also open the door to composition, which allows us to treat functionality like Lego building blocks, assembling pieces together in novel ways to build things that are much larger than the sum of their parts. To complete the cycle, these new compositions of APIs can likewise join the ranks of reusable building blocks, enabling even more complex and extraordinary future projects.

But this leads to an important question: how can we make sure the APIs we build fit together like Lego bricks? Let's start by looking at one strategy for this, called *resource orientation.*

1.3   *What are resource-oriented APIs?*

Many web APIs that exist today act a bit like servants: you ask them to do something and they go off and do it. For example, if we want the weather for our hometown we might order the web API to `predictWeather(postalCode=10011)` like a servant. This style of ordering another computer around by calling a preconfigured subroutine or method is often referred to as making a "remote procedure call" (RPC) because we're effectively *call*ing a library function (or *procedure*) to be executed on another computer that is somewhere potentially far away (or *remote*). The critical aspect of APIs like this is the primary focus on the actions being performed. That is, we think about calculating the weather (`predictWeather(postalCode=...)`) or encrypting data (`encrypt(data=...)`) or sending an email (`sendEmail(to=...)`), each with an emphasis on "doing" something.

So why aren't all APIs RPC-oriented? One of the main reasons has to do with the idea of "statefulness," where API calls can either be "stateful" or "stateless." An API call is considered stateless when it can be made independently from all other API requests, with no additional context or data whatsoever. For example, a web API call to predict the weather involves only one independent input (the postal code) and would therefore be considered stateless. On the other hand, a web API that stores a user's favorite cities and provides weather forecasts for those cities has no runtime inputs but requires a user to already have stored the cities they're interested in. As a result, this kind of API request, involving other prior requests or previously stored data, would be considered stateful. It turns out that RPC-style APIs are great for stateless functionality, but they tend to be a much poorer fit when we introduce stateful API methods.

> **NOTE** If you happen to be familiar with REST, now might be a good time to point out that this section is not about REST and RESTful APIs specifically, but more generally about APIs that emphasize "resources" (as most RESTful APIs do). In other words, while there will be a lot of overlap with the topic of REST, this section is a bit more general than just REST.

To see why this is, let's consider an example of a stateful API for booking airline flights. In table 1.1, we can see a list of RPCs for interacting with airline travel plans, covering actions such as scheduling new bookings, viewing existing bookings, and canceling unwanted travel.

Table 1.1 Summary of methods for an example flight-booking API

Method	Description
ScheduleFlight()	Schedules a new flight
GetFlightDetails()	Shows information about a specific flight
ShowAllBookings()	Shows all travel plans currently booked
CancelReservation()	Cancels an existing flight reservation
RescheduleFlight()	Reschedules an existing flight to another date or time
UpgradeTrip()	Upgrades from economy class to first class

Each of these RPCs is pretty descriptive, but there's no escaping the requirement that we memorize these API methods, each of which is subtly different from the others. For example, sometimes a method talks about a "flight" (e.g., RescheduleFlight()) and other times operates on a "reservation" (e.g., CancelReservation()). We also have to remember which of the many synonymous forms of the action were used. For example, we need to remember whether the way to see all of our bookings is Show-Flights(), ShowAllFlights(), ListFlights(), or ListAllFlights() (in this case, it's ShowAllFlights()). But what can we do to solve this? The answer comes in the form of standardization.

Resource orientation aims to help with this problem by providing a standard set of building blocks to use when designing an API in two areas. First, resource-oriented APIs rely on the idea of "resources," which are the key concepts we store and interact with, standardizing the "things" that the API manages. Second, rather than using arbitrary RPC names for any action we can think of, resource-oriented APIs limit actions to a small standard set (described in table 1.2), which apply to each of the resources to form useful actions in the API. Thinking of this a bit differently, resource-oriented APIs are really just a special type of RPC-style APIs where each RPC follows a clear and standardized pattern: <StandardMethod><Resource>().

Table 1.2 Summary of standard methods and their meanings

RPC	Description
Create<Resource>()	Creates a new <Resource>
Get<Resource>()	Shows information about a specific <Resource>
List<Resources>()	Shows a list of all existing <Resources>
Delete<Resource>()	Deletes an existing <Resource>
Update<Resource>()	Updates an existing <Resource> in place

If we go down this route of special, limited RPCs, this means that instead of the variety of different RPC methods shown in table 1.1, we could come up with a single resource (e.g., `FlightReservation`) and get equivalent functionality with the set of standard methods, shown in table 1.3.

Table 1.3   Summary of standard methods applied to the flight resource

Method		Resource		Methods
Create				`CreateFlightReservation()`
Get				`GetFlightReservation()`
List	×	`FlightReservation`	=	`ListFlightReservations()`
Delete				`DeleteFlightReservation()`
Update				`UpdateFlightReservation()`

Standardization is clearly more organized, but does that mean that all resource-oriented APIs are strictly better than RPC-oriented APIs? Actually, no. For some scenarios RPC-oriented APIs will be a better fit (particularly in the case where the API method is stateless). In many other cases however, resource-oriented APIs will be much easier for users to learn, understand, and remember. This is because the standardization provided by resource-oriented APIs makes it easy to combine what you already know (e.g., the set of standard methods) with what you can easily learn (e.g., the name of a new resource) to start interacting with the API right away. Put a bit more numerically, if you are familiar with, say, five standard methods, then, thanks to the power of a reliable pattern, learning about one new resource is actually the same as learning five new RPCs.

Obviously, it's important to note that not every API is the same, and it's a bit crude to define the complexity of an API in terms of the size of a to-do list of "stuff to learn." On the other hand, there is an important principle at work here: the power of patterns. It seems that learning about composable pieces and combining them into more complex things that follow a set pattern tends to be easier than learning about pre-built complex things that follow a custom design every time. Since resource-oriented APIs exploit the power of battle-tested design patterns, they are often easier to learn and therefore "better" than their RPC-oriented equivalents. But this brings us to an important question: What does "better" mean here? How do we know if an API is "good"? What does "good" even mean?

1.4   *What makes an API "good"?*

Before we explore a few of the different aspects that tend to make APIs "good," we first need to dig into why we have an API at all. In other words, what is the purpose of building an API in the first place? Often this comes down to two simple reasons:

1 We have some functionality that some users want.
2 Those users want to use this functionality programmatically.

For example, we might have a system that is amazing at translating text from one language to another. There are probably lots of people in the world who want this ability, but that alone isn't enough. After all, we could launch a translation mobile app that exposes this amazing translation system instead of an API. To merit an API at all, the people who want this functionality must also want to write a program that uses it. Given these two criteria, where does this lead us when thinking about the desirable qualities of an API?

1.4.1 Operational

Starting with the most important piece, no matter what the final interface looks like, the system as a whole must be **operational**. In other words, it must do the thing users actually want. If this is a system that intends to translate text from one language to another, it must actually be able to do so. Additionally, most systems are likely to have many **nonoperational** requirements. For example, if our system translates text from one language to another, there may be nonoperational requirements related to things like latency (e.g., the translation task should take a few milliseconds, not a few days) or accuracy (e.g., translations should not be misleading). It's these two aspects together that we say constitute the operational aspects of a system.

1.4.2 Expressive

If it's important that a system is able to do something, it's just as important that the interface to that system allows users to express the thing they want to do clearly and simply. In other words, if the system translates text from one language to another, the API should be designed such that there is a clear and simple way to do so. In this case, it might be an RPC called `TranslateText()`. This type of thing might sound obvious, but it can actually be more complicated than it seems.

One example of this hidden complication is the case where an API supports some functionality already but, due to an oversight on our part, we didn't realize that users wanted it and therefore didn't build an expressive way for users to access that functionality. Scenarios like these tend to manifest as *workarounds*, where users do unusual things to access hidden functionality. For example, if an API provides the ability to translate text from one language to another, then it's possible a user could coerce the API into acting as a language detector even if they're not really interested in translating anything, as shown in listing 1.1. As you might imagine, it would be far better if users had an RPC called `DetectLanguage()` rather than making lots of API calls guessing at the language.

> **Listing 1.1 Functionality to detect language using only a TranslateText API method**

```
function detectLanguage(inputText: string): string {
  const supportedLanguages: string[] = ['en', 'es', ... ];
  for (let language of supportedLanguages) {
    let translatedText = TranslateApi.TranslateText({
      text: inputText,
```

This assumes the API in question defines a TranslateText method that takes some input text and a target language to translate into.

```
        targetLanguage: language
    });
    if (translatedText === inputText) {       ←┤
      return language;
    }
  }
  return null;       ←┤
}
```

If the translated text is the same as the input text, we know that the two languages are the same.

If we don't find translated text that is the same as the input text, we return null, indicating we can't detect the language of the input text.

As this example shows, APIs that support certain functionality but don't make it easy for users to access that functionality would be not very good. On the other hand, APIs that are expressive provide the ability for users to clearly dictate exactly what they want (e.g., translate text) and even how they want it done (e.g., "within 150 milliseconds, with 95% accuracy").

1.4.3   Simple

One of the most important things related to the usability of any system is *simplicity*. While it's easy to argue that something being simple is reducing the number of *things* (e.g., RPCs, resources, etc.) in an API, unfortunately this is rarely the case. For example, an API could rely on a single ExecuteAction() method that handles all functionality; however, that's not really simplifying anything. Instead, it shifts complexity from one place (lots of different RPCs) to another (lots of configuration in a single RPC). So what exactly does a simple API look like?

Rather than trying to excessively reduce the number of RPCs, APIs should aim to expose the functionality that users want in the most straightforward way possible, making the API as simple as possible, but no simpler. For example, imagine a translation API wanted to add the ability to detect the language of some input text. We could do this by returning the detected source text on the response of a translation; however, this still obfuscates the functionality by hiding it inside a method designed for another purpose. Instead, it would make more sense to create a new method that is designed specifically for this purpose, such as DetectLanguage(). (Note that we might also include the detected language when translating content, but that's for another purpose entirely.)

Another common position on simplicity takes the old saying about the "common case" ("Make the common case fast") but focuses instead on usability while leaving room for edge cases. This restatement is to "make the common case awesome and the advanced case possible." This means that whenever you add something that might complicate an API for the benefit of an advanced user, it's best to keep this complication sufficiently hidden from a typical user only interested in the common case. This keeps the more frequent scenarios simple and easy, while still enabling more advanced features for those who want them.

For example, let's imagine that our translation API includes the concept of a machine learning model to be used when translating text, where instead of specifying the target language, we choose a model based on the target language and use that model as the "translating engine." While this functionality provides much more flexibility and control to users, it is also much more complex, with the new common case shown in figure 1.3.

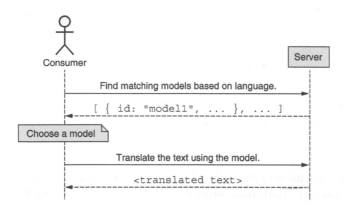

Figure 1.3 Translating text after choosing a model

As we can see, we've effectively made it much more difficult to translate some text in exchange for supporting the more advanced functionality. To see this more clearly, compare the code shown in listing 1.2 to the simplicity of calling `Translate-Text("Hello world", "es")`.

Listing 1.2 Translating text after choosing a model

```
function translateText(inputText: string,
                       targetLanguage: string): string {
  let sourceLanguage =
      TranslateAPI.DetectLanguage(inputText);
  let model = TranslateApi.ListModels({
    filter: `sourceLanguage:${sourceLanguage}
             targetLanguage:${targetLanguage}`,
  })[0];
  return TranslateApi.TranslateText({
    text: inputText,
    modelId: model.id
  });
}
```

Since we need to choose a model, we first need to know the language of the input text. To determine this we could rely on the hypothetical DetectLanguage() method provided by the API.

Once we know both the source and destination languages, we can choose any of the matching models provided by the API.

Now that we finally have all the required inputs, we can get back to our original goal of translating text into a target language.

How could we design this API to be as simple as possible, but no simpler as well as make the common case awesome and the advanced case possible? Since the common case involves users who don't really care about a specific model, we could do this by designing the API so that it accepts either a `targetLanguage` or a `modelId`. The advanced case would still work (in fact, the code shown in listing 1.2 would continue to work), but the common case would look far simpler, relying on just a `target-Language` parameter (and expecting the `modelId` parameter to be left undefined).

Listing 1.3   Translating text to a target language (the common case)

```
function translateText(inputText: string,
                       targetLanguage: string,
                       modelId?: string): string {
  return TranslateApi.TranslateText({
    text: inputText,
    targetLanguage: targetLanguage,
    modelId: modelId,
  });
}
```

Now that we have some background on how simplicity is an important attribute of a "good" API, let's look at the final piece: predictability.

1.4.4   *Predictable*

While surprises in our lives can sometimes be fun, one place surprises do not belong is in APIs, either in the interface definition or underlying behavior. This is a bit like the old adage about investing: "If it's exciting, you're doing it wrong." So what do we mean by "unsurprising" APIs?

Unsurprising APIs rely on repeated patterns applied to both the API surface definition and the behavior. For example, if an API that translates text has a `Translate-Text()` method that takes as a parameter the input content as a field called `text`, then when we add a `DetectLanguage()` method, the input content should be called `text` as well (not `inputText` or `content` or `textContent`). While this might seem obvious now, keep in mind that many APIs are built by multiple teams and the choice of what to call fields when presented a set of options is often arbitrary. This means that when two different people are responsible for these two different fields, it's certainly possible that they'll make different arbitrary choices. When this happens, we end up with an inconsistent (and therefore surprising) API.

Even though this inconsistency might seem insignificant, it turns out that issues like these are much more important than they appear. This is because it's actually pretty rare that users of an API learn each and every detail by thoroughly reading all the API documentation. Instead, users read just enough to accomplish what they want to do. This means that if someone learns that a field is called `text` in one request message, they're almost certainly going to assume it's named the same way in another, effectively building on what they've already learned to make an educated guess about things they haven't yet learned. If this process fails (e.g., because another message named that field `inputText`), their productivity hits a brick wall and they have to stop what they're doing to go figure out why their assumptions failed.

The obvious conclusion is that APIs that rely on repeated, predictable patterns (e.g., naming fields consistently) are easier and faster to learn and therefore better. And similar benefits arise from more complex patterns, such as the standard actions we saw in our exploration of resource-oriented APIs. This brings us to the entire purpose of this book: APIs built using well-known, well-defined, clear, and (hopefully) simple patterns will lead to APIs that are predictable and easy to learn, which should lead to overall "better" APIs. Now that we have a good grasp on APIs and what makes them good, let's start thinking about higher-level patterns we can follow when designing them.

Summary

- Interfaces are contracts that define how two systems should interact with one another.
- APIs are special types of interfaces that define how two computer systems interact with one another, coming in many forms, such as downloadable libraries and web APIs.
- Web APIs are special because they expose functionality over a network, hiding the specific implementation or computational requirements needed for that functionality.
- Resource-oriented APIs are a way of designing APIs to reduce complexity by relying on a standard set of actions, called *methods*, across a limited set of things, called *resources*.
- What makes APIs "good" is a bit ambiguous, but generally good APIs are operational, expressive, simple, and predictable.

Introduction to
API design patterns

2

This chapter covers

- What an API design pattern is
- Why API design patterns are important
- The anatomy and structure of an API design pattern
- Designing an API with and without design patterns

Now that we have a grasp of what APIs are and what makes them "good," we can explore how we might apply different patterns when building an API. We'll start by exploring what API design patterns are, why they matter, and how they'll be described in later chapters. Finally, we'll look at an example API and see how using pre-built API design patterns can save lots of time and future headaches.

2.1 What are API design patterns?

Before we start exploring API design patterns we have to lay a bit of groundwork, starting with a simple question: what is a design pattern? If we note that software design refers to the structure or layout of some code written in order to solve a problem, then a software design *pattern* is what happens when a particular design

14

can be applied over and over to lots of similar software problems, with only minor adjustments to suit different scenarios. This means that the pattern isn't some pre-built library we use to solve an individual problem, but instead more of a blueprint for solving similarly structured problems.

If this seems too abstract, let's firm it up and imagine that we want to put a shed in our backyard. There are a few different options to choose from, ranging from what we did a few hundred years ago to what we do today thanks to the magic of companies like Lowe's and Home Depot. There are lots of options, but four common ones are as follows:

1 Buy a pre-built shed and put it in the backyard.
2 Buy a shed kit (blueprints and materials) and assemble it ourselves.
3 Buy a set of shed blueprints, modify the design as necessary, then build it ourselves.
4 Design and build the entire shed from scratch.

If we think of these in terms of their software equivalent, they would range from using a pre-built off-the-shelf software package all the way through writing an entirely custom system to solve our problem. In table 2.1 we see that these options get more and more difficult as we move through the list, but also add more and more flexibility from one option to the next. In other words, the least difficult has the least flexibility, and the most difficult has the most flexibility.

Table 2.1 Comparison of ways to build a shed with ways to build software

Option	Difficulty	Flexibility	Software equivalent
Buy pre-built	Simple	None	Use a pre-built software package
Assemble from a kit	Easy	Very little	Build by customizing existing software
Build from blueprints	Moderate	Some	Build from a design document
Build from scratch	Difficult	Most	Write completely custom software

Software engineers tend to choose the "build from scratch" option most of the time. Sometimes this is necessary, particularly in cases where the problems we're solving are new. Other times this choice wins out in a cost-benefit analysis because our problem is just different enough to prevent us from relying on one of the easier options. And still other times we know of a library that happens to solve our problem exactly (or close enough), and we choose to rely on someone else having already solved the problem at hand. It turns out that choosing one of the in-between options (customizing existing software or building from a design document) is much less common but could probably be used more often with great results. And this is where design patterns fit in.

At a high level, design patterns are the "build from blueprints" option applied to software. Just like blueprints for a shed come with the dimensions, locations of doors and windows, and the materials for the roof, design patterns come with some set of specifications and details for the code that we write. In software this often means specifying a high-level layout of the code as well as the nuances of relying on the layout to solve a particular design problem. However, it's rare that a design pattern is made to be used entirely on its own. Most often, design patterns focus on specific components rather than entire systems. In other words, the blueprints focus on the shape of a single aspect (like the roof shape) or component (like a window design) rather than the entire shed. This might seem like a downside at first glance, but that's only the case if the goal is exactly to build a shed. If you're trying to build something sort of like a shed, but not quite a shed, then having blueprints for each individual component means you can mix and match lots of them together into exactly what you want to build, choosing roof shape A and window design B. This carries over into our discussion of design patterns, since each one tends to focus on a single component or problem type of your system, helping you build exactly what you want by assembling lots of pre-designed pieces.

For example, if you want to add debug logging to your system, you'll likely want one and only one way to log messages. There are lots of ways you could do this (for example, using a single shared global variable), but there happens to be a design pattern aimed at solving this software problem. This pattern, described in the seminal work *Design Patterns* (Gamma et al., 1994), is called the singleton pattern, and it ensures that only a single instance of a class is created. This "blueprint" calls for a class with a private constructor and a single static method called `getInstance()`, which always returns a single instance of the class (it handles creating that single instance if and only if it doesn't exist yet). This pattern is not at all complete (after all, what good is it to have a singleton class that does nothing?); however, it's a well-defined and well-tested pattern to follow when you need to solve this small compartmentalized problem of always having a single instance of a class.

Now that we know what software design patterns are generally, we have to ask the question: what are API design patterns? Using the definition of an API as described in chapter 1, an API design pattern is simply a software design pattern applied to an API rather than all software generally. This means that API design patterns, just like regular design patterns, are simply blueprints for ways of designing and structuring APIs. Since the focus is on the interface rather than the implementation, in most cases an API design pattern will focus on the interface exclusively, without necessarily building out the implementation. While most API design patterns will often remain silent on the underlying implementation of those interfaces, sometimes they dictate certain aspects of the *API*'s behavior. For example, an API design pattern might specify that a certain RPC can be *eventually consistent*, meaning that the data returned from that RPC could be slightly stale (for example, it could be read from a cache rather than the authoritative storage system).

We'll get into a more formal explanation of how we plan to document API patterns in a later section, but first let's take a quick look at why we should care about API design patterns at all.

2.2   *Why are API design patterns important?*

As we already learned, API design patterns are useful in building APIs, just like blue-prints are when building a shed: they act as pre-designed building blocks we can use in our projects. What we didn't dig into is why we need these pre-designed blueprints in the first place. Aren't we all smart enough to build good APIs? Don't we know our business and technical problems best? While this is often the case, it turns out that some of the techniques we use to build really well-designed software don't work as well when building APIs. More specifically, the iterative approach, advocated in particular by the agile development process, is difficult to apply when designing APIs. To see why, we have to look at two aspects of software systems. First, we have to explore the flexibil-ity (or rigidity) of the various interfaces generally, and then we must understand what effect the audience of the interface has on our ability to make changes and iterate on the overall design. Let's start by looking at flexibility.

As we saw in chapter 1, APIs are special kinds of interfaces that are made primarily so computing systems can interact with one another. While having programmatic access to a system is very valuable, it's also much more fragile and brittle in that changes to the interface can easily cause failures for those using the interface. For example, changing the name of a field in an API would cause a failure for any code written by users before the name change occurred. From the perspective of the API server, the old code is asking for something using a name that no longer exists. This is a very different scenario from other kinds of interfaces, such as *graphical user-interfaces* (GUIs), which are used primarily by humans rather than computers and as a result are much more resilient to change. This means that even though a change might be frus-trating or aesthetically displeasing, it typically won't cause a catastrophic failure where we can no longer use the interface at all. For example, changing the color or location of a button on a web page might be ugly and inconvenient, but we can still figure out how to accomplish what we need to do with the interface.

We often refer to this aspect of an interface as its *flexibility*, saying that interfaces where users can easily accommodate changes are *flexible* and those where even small changes (like renaming fields) cause complete failures are *rigid*. This distinction is important because the ability to make lots and lots of changes is determined in large part by the flexibility of the interface. Most importantly we can see that rigid inter-faces make it much more difficult for us to iterate toward a great design like we would in other software projects. This means that we often end up stuck with all design deci-sions, both good and bad. This might lead you to think that the rigidity of APIs implies we'll never be able to use an iterative development process, but this is not always the case thanks to another important aspect of interfaces: visibility.

Generally, we can put most interfaces into two different categories: those that your users can see and interact with (in software usually called the *frontend*) and those that they can't (usually called the *backend*). For example, we can easily see the graphical user interface for Facebook when we open a browser; however, we don't have the abil-ity to see how Facebook stores our social graph and other data. To use more formal terms for this aspect of visibility, we can say that the frontend (the part that all users see and interact with) is usually considered *public* and the backend (only visible to a smaller internal group) is considered *private*. This distinction is important because it partly determines our ability to make changes to different kinds of interfaces, particularly rigid ones like APIs.

If we make a change to a public interface, the whole world will see it and may be affected by it. Since the audience is so large, carelessly making changes could result in angry or frustrated users. While this certainly applies to rigid interfaces like APIs, it also applies to flexible interfaces just the same. For example, in the early days of Facebook most major functional or design changes caused outrage among college students for a few weeks. But what if the interface isn't public? Is it a big deal to make changes to backend interfaces that are only seen by members of some private internal group of people? In this scenario the number of users affected by a change is much smaller, possibly even limited to people on the same team or in the same office, so it seems we have gained back a bit more freedom to make changes. This is great news because it means we should be able to iterate quickly toward an ideal design, applying agile principles along the way.

So why are APIs special? It turns out that when we design many APIs (which are rigid by definition) and share them with the world, we really have a worst-case scenario for both aspects. This means that making changes is much more difficult than any other combination of these two properties (as summarized in table 2.2).

Table 2.2   **Difficulty of changing various interfaces**

Flexibility	Audience	Example interface	Change difficulty
Flexible	Private	Internal monitoring console	Very easy
Flexible	Public	Facebook.com	Moderate
Rigid	Private	Internal photo storage API	Difficult
Rigid	Public	Public Facebook API	Very difficult

Put simply, this "worst of both worlds" scenario (both rigid and difficult to change) makes reusable and proven design patterns even more important for building APIs than other types of software. While code is often private and out of sight in most software projects, design decisions in an API are front and center, shown to all of the users of the service. Since this seriously limits our ability to make incremental improvements on our designs, relying on existing patterns that have survived the tests of time are very valuable in getting things right the first time rather than just eventually as in most software.

Now that we've explored some of the reasons these design patterns are important, let's get into an API design pattern by dissecting it and exploring its various components.

2.3 Anatomy of an API design pattern

Like most pieces in software design, API design patterns are made up of several different components, each one responsible for a different aspect of consuming the pattern itself. Obviously the primary component focuses on how the pattern itself works, but there are other components targeted at the less technical aspects of consuming a design pattern. These are things like figuring out that a pattern exists for a given set of problems, understanding whether the pattern is a good fit for the problem you're dealing with, and understanding why the pattern does things in one way rather than using a (possibly simpler) alternative.

Since this anatomy lesson could get a bit complicated, let's imagine that we're building a service that stores data and that the customers of that service want an API where they can get their data out of the service. We'll rely on this example scenario to guide our discussion through each of the pattern components that we'll explore next, starting with the beginning: the name.

2.3.1 Name and synopsis

Each design pattern in the catalog has a name, given to uniquely identify the pattern in the catalog. The name will be descriptive enough to convey what the pattern is doing, but not so long-winded that it's not easy to shout across a noisy room. For example, when describing a pattern that solves our example scenario of exporting data, we could call it "Import, export, back-up, restore, snapshot, and rollback pattern," but it's probably better named as "Input/Output pattern" or "IO pattern" for short.

While the name itself is usually enough to understand and identify the pattern, it's sometimes not quite verbose enough to sufficiently explain the problem that the pattern addresses. To ensure there is a short and simple introduction to the pattern itself, there will also be a short summary of the pattern following the name, which will have a brief description of the problem it is aiming to solve. For example, we might say that the input/output pattern "offers a structured way of moving data to or from a variety of different storage sources and destinations." In short, the overall goal of this section is to make it easy to quickly identify whether any particular pattern is worth further investigation as a potential fit for solving a given problem.

2.3.2 Motivation

Since the goal of an API design pattern is to provide a solution for a category of problems, a good place to start is a definition of the problem space the pattern aims to cover. This section aims to explain the fundamental problem so that it's easy to understand why we need a pattern for it in the first place. This means we first need a detailed problem statement, which often comes in the form of a user-focused objective. In the case of our data export example, we might have a scenario where a user "wants to export some data from the service into another external storage system."

After that, we must dig a bit deeper into the details of what users want to accomplish. For example, we might find that users need to export their data to a variety of storage systems, not just Amazon's S3. They also may need to apply further constraints on how the data is exported, such as whether it's compressed or encrypted before transmission. These requirements will have a direct impact on the design pattern itself, so it's important that we articulate these details of the problem we're addressing with this particular pattern.

Next, once we understand the user objectives more fully, we need to explore the edge cases that are likely to arise in the normal course of actual implementation. For example, we should understand how the system should behave when the data is too large (and how large is too large, since those words often mean different numbers to different people). We also must explore how the system should react in failure scenarios. For example, when an export job fails we should describe whether it should be retried. These unusual scenarios are likely to be much more common than we typically expect, and even though we might not have to decide how to address each scenario right away, it's critical that the pattern take note of these blanks so that they can eventually be filled in by an implementation.

2.3.3 *Overview*

Now we're getting closer to the fun part: explaining what the design pattern recommends as a solution to the problem space. At this point, we're no longer focused on defining the problem, but on offering a high-level description of the solution. This means that we get to start exploring the tactics we'll employ to address the problem and the methods we'll use to do so. For example, in our exporting data scenario, this section would outline the various components and their responsibilities, such as a component for describing the details of what data to export, another for describing the storage system that acts as a destination for the exported data, and still another for describing encryption and compression settings applied before sending the data to that destination.

In many cases the problem definition and list of solution requirements will dictate a general outline of a solution. In those cases, the goal of the overview is to explicitly articulate this outline rather than leaving it to be inferred from the problem description, regardless of how obvious a solution may seem. For example, if we're defining a pattern for searching through a list of resources, it seems pretty obvious to have a query parameter; however, other aspects (such as the format of that parameter or the consistency guarantees of the search) might not be so obvious and merit further discussion. After all, even obvious solutions may have subtle implications that are worth addressing, and, as they say, the devil is often in the details.

Other times, while the problem is well-defined, there may not be a single obvious solution, but instead several different options that may each have their own trade-offs. For example, there are many different ways to model many-to-many relationships in an API, each with its different benefits and drawbacks; however, it's important that an API choose one option and apply it consistently. In cases like this, the overview will discuss each of the different options and the strategy employed by the recommended pattern. This section might contain a brief discussion of the benefits and drawbacks of the other possible options mentioned, but the bulk of that discussion will be left for the trade-offs section at the end of the pattern description.

2.3.4 Implementation

We've gotten to the most important piece of every design pattern: how we go about implementing it. At this point, we should thoroughly understand the problem space that we're trying to address and have an idea of the high-level tactics and strategy we'll be employing to solve it. The most important piece of this section will be interface definitions defined as code, which explain what an API using this pattern to solve a problem would look like. The API definitions will focus on the structure of resources and the various specific ways to interact with those resources. This will include a variety of things such as the fields present on resources or requests, the format of the data that could go into those fields (e.g., Base64 encoded strings), as well as how the resources relate to one another (e.g., hierarchical relationships).

In many cases, the API surface and field definitions themselves may not be sufficient to explain how the API actually works. In other words, while the structure and list of fields may seem clear, the behavior of those structures and interaction between different fields may be much more complex rather than simple and obvious. In those cases, we'll need a more detailed discussion of these non-obvious aspects of the design. For example, when exporting data we may specify a way to compress it on the way to the storage service using a string field to specify the compression algorithm. In this situation, the pattern might discuss the various possible values of this field (it might use the same format used by the Accept-Encoding HTTP header), what to do when an invalid option is supplied (it might return an error), and what it means when a request leaves the field blank (it might default to gzip compression).

Finally, this section will include an example API definition, with comments explaining what an API that correctly implements this pattern should look like. This will be defined in code, with comments explaining the behaviors of the various fields, and will rely on a specific example of a scenario illustrating the problem that's addressed by the pattern. This section will almost certainly be the longest and have the most detail.

2.3.5 Trade-offs

At this point we understand what a design pattern gives us, but we've yet to discuss what it takes away, which is actually pretty important. Put bluntly, there may simply be things that are not possible if the design pattern is implemented as designed. In these cases it's very important to understand what sacrifices are necessary in order to achieve the benefits that come from relying on a design pattern. The possibilities here are quite varied, ranging from functional limitations (e.g., it's impossible to export data directly as a download to the user in a web browser) to increased complexity (e.g., it's much more typing to describe where you want to send your data), and even to more technical aspects like data consistency (e.g., you can see data that might be a bit stale, but you can't know for sure), so the discussion can range from simple explanations to detailed exploration of the subtle limitations when relying on a particular design pattern.

Additionally, while a given design pattern may often fit the problem space perfectly, there will certainly be scenarios where it is a close enough fit but not quite perfect. In these cases it's important to understand what consequences will arise by relying on a design pattern that is in this unique spot: not the wrong pattern, but not quite a perfect pattern either. This section will discuss the consequences of slight misalignments like this.

Now that we've gotten a better grasp on how API design patterns will be structured and explained, let's switch gears and look at the difference these patterns can make when building a supposedly simple API.

2.4   *Case study: Twapi, a Twitter-like API*

If you're unfamiliar with Twitter, think of it like a place where you can share short messages with others—that's it. It's a little scary to think that an entire business is built on everyone creating tiny messages, but apparently that's enough to merit a multibillion dollar technology company. What's not mentioned here is that even with an extremely simple concept, there happens to be quite a lot of complexity hiding underneath the surface. To better understand this, let's begin by exploring what an API for Twitter might look like, which we'll call Twapi.

2.4.1   *Overview*

With Twapi, our primary responsibility is to allow people to post new messages and view messages posted by other people. On the surface this looks pretty simple, but as you might guess, there are a few hidden pitfalls for us to be aware of. Let's start by assuming that we have a simple API call to create a Twapi message. After that, we'll look at two additional actions this API might need: listing lots of messages and exporting all messages to a different storage system.

Before we get moving, there are two important things to consider. First, this will be an example API only. That means that the focus will remain on the way in which we define the interface and not on how the implementation actually works. In programming terms, it's a bit like saying we'll only talk about the function definition and leave the body of the function to be filled in later. Second, this will be our first foray into looking at an API definition. If you haven't looked through the "About this book" section, now might be a good time to do that so the TypeScript-style format isn't too surprising.

Now that those things are out of the way, let's look at how we're going to be listing some Twapi messages.

2.4.2 Listing messages

If we can create messages, it seems pretty reasonable that we'll want to list those messages we created. Additionally, we'll want to see the messages created by our friends, and taking this a step further, we might want to see a long list of messages that is a prioritized collection of our friends' popular messages (sort of like a news feed). Let's start by defining a simple API method to do this, relying on no design patterns at all.

WITH NO DESIGN PATTERNS

Starting from the beginning, we need to send a request asking to list a bunch of messages. To do this, we need to know whose messages we want, which we'll call a "parent." In response, we want our API to send back a simple list of messages. This interaction is outlined in figure 2.1.

Figure 2.1   Simple flow of requesting Twapi messages

Now that we understand the flow involved in listing these messages, let's formalize it into an actual API definition.

Listing 2.1   Example API that lists Twapi messages

First, we define the API service as an abstract class. This is simply a collection of API methods defined as TypeScript functions.

We can use TypeScript static variables to store metadata about the API, such as the name or version.

Here we rely on special wrapper functions to define the HTTP method (GET) and URL pattern (/users/<user-id>/messages) that should map to this function.

```typescript
abstract class Twapi {
  static version = "v1";
  static title = "Twapi API";

  @get("/{parent=users/*}/messages")
  ListMessages(req: ListMessagesRequest): ListMessagesResponse;
}

interface ListMessagesRequest {
  parent: string;
}

interface ListMessagesResponse {
  results: Message[];
}
```

The ListMessagesRequest takes a single parameter: the parent. This is the owner of the messages that we're trying to list.

Here the ListMessages function accepts a ListMessagesRequest and returns a ListMessagesResponse.

The ListMessagesResponse returns a simple list of the messages the provided user owns.

As you can see, this API definition is pretty simple. It accepts a single parameter and returns a list of matching messages. But let's imagine that we deploy it as our API and consider one of the biggest problems that will likely arise as time goes on: large amounts of data.

As more and more people use the service, this list of messages can start to get pretty long. This might not be a big deal as responses start having tens or hundreds of messages, but what about when you start getting into the thousands, hundreds of thousands, or even millions? A single HTTP response carrying 500,000 messages, with each message up to 140 characters, means that this could be up to 70 megabytes of data! That seems pretty cumbersome for a regular API user to deal with, not to mention the fact that a single HTTP request will cause the Twapi database servers to send down 70 megabytes of data.

So what can we do? The obvious answer is to allow the API to break what could become very large responses into smaller pieces and allow users to request all the messages one chunk at a time. To do that, we can rely on the pagination pattern (see chapter 26).

PAGINATION PATTERN

As we'll learn in chapter 26, the pagination pattern is a way of retrieving a long list of items in smaller, more manageable chunks of data rather than the entire list being sent at once. The pattern relies on extra fields on both the request and response; however, these should seem pretty simple. The general flow of this pattern is shown in figure 2.2.

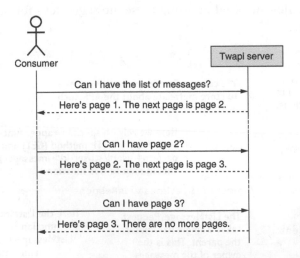

Figure 2.2 Example flow of the pagination pattern to retrieve Twapi messages

Here's what this looks like in an actual API definition.

Listing 2.2 Example API that lists Twapi messages with pagination

```
abstract class Twapi {
  static version = "v1";
  static title = "Twapi API";
```

```
    @get("/{parent=users/*}/messages")
    ListMessages(req: ListMessagesRequest): ListMessagesResponse;
}

interface ListMessagesRequest {
    parent: string;
    pageToken: string;
    maxPageSize?: number;
}

interface ListMessagesResponse {
    results: Message[];
    nextPageToken: string;
}
```

Notice that the method definition stays the same; no changes necessary here.

To clarify which chunk (or page) of data we're asking for, we include a page token parameter to the request.

We also include a way to specify the maximum number of messages that the Twapi server should return to us in a single chunk.

The response from the Twapi server will include a way to fetch the next chunk of messages.

WHAT HAPPENS IF WE DON'T START WITH THE PATTERN?

With these small changes to the API service, we've actually put together an API method that is able to survive a surge in growth in the number of Twapi messages posted, but this leaves an obvious question unanswered: Why should I bother following this pattern from the start? Why not just add these fields later on when it becomes a problem? In other words, why should we bother to fix something that isn't broken yet? As we'll learn later when we explore backward compatibility, the reason is simply to avoid causing existing software to break.

In this case, changing from our more simple original design (sending back all the data in a single response) to relying on the pagination pattern (splitting the data into smaller chunks) might look like an innocuous change, but it would actually cause any previously existing software to function incorrectly. In this scenario, existing code would expect a single response to contain all the data requested rather than a portion of it. As a result, there are two big problems.

First, because the previously written software expects all data to come back in a single request, it has no way of finding data that shows up on subsequent pages. As a result, code written before the change is effectively cut off from all but the first chunk of data, which leads us to the second problem.

Since existing consumers have no idea how to get additional chunks of data, they are left with the impression that they've been given all the data despite having only a small piece. This misunderstanding can lead to mistakes that can be very difficult to detect. For example, consumers trying to compute an average value of some data may end up with a value that might look accurate but is actually only an average of the first chunk of data returned. This, obviously, will likely lead to an incorrect value but won't create an obvious error. As a result, this bug could go undetected for quite some time.

Now that we've looked at the example of listing messages, let's explore why we might want to use a design pattern when exporting data.

2.4.3   *Exporting data*

At some point, users of the Twapi service may want the ability to export all of their messages. Similar to listing messages, we first must consider that the amount of data we need to export might become pretty large (possibly hundreds of MB). Additionally, and unlike listing messages, we should take into account that there may be lots of different storage systems on the receiving end of this data, and ideally we'd have a way to integrate with new ones as they become popular. Further, there could be lots of different transformations we may want to apply to the data before exporting it, such as encrypting it, compressing it, or anonymizing some pieces of it as needed. Finally, all of this is unlikely to work well in a synchronous fashion, meaning we need a way of expressing that there is some pending work (i.e., the actual exporting of the data) that is running in the background for the consumer to monitor the progress.

Let's start by coming up with a simple implementation for this API and look at some of the various issues that might arise in the future.

WITH NO DESIGN PATTERN

As noted, we have a few main concerns: large amounts of data, the final destination of the data, the various transformations or configurations of the data (e.g., compression or encryption), and finally the asynchronous nature of the API. Since we're just trying to get out a basic API for exporting our Twapi messages, the simplest option that covers the majority of these factors is to trigger the generation of a compressed file to be downloaded in the future. In short, when someone makes a request to this API, the response doesn't actually contain the data itself. Instead, it contains a pointer to where the data might be downloaded at some point in the future.

Listing 2.3   Simple API to export messages

```
abstract class Twapi {
  static version = "v1";
  static title = "Twapi API";

  @post("/{parent=users/*}/messages:export")
  ExportMessages(req: ExportMessagesRequest):
      ExportMessagesResponse;
}

interface ExportMessagesRequest {
  // The parent user of the messages to be exported.
  parent: string;
}

interface ExportMessagesResponse {
  // The location of a compressed file
  // containing the messages requested.
  exportDownloadUri: string;
}
```

> The URI that we map to uses the POST HTTP verb, as well as a special syntax to convey that this is a special action being performed, not one of the standard REST actions.

> Just like our previous examples, we rely on an ExportMessages function, which takes a request and returns a response.

> We only want to allow exporting data for one single user at a time, so the export method is scoped to a single parent (user).

> The response from the Twapi server specifies the location of the compressed file to be downloaded later on from a simple file server rather than this API service.

This API does accomplish the primary task (exporting the data) and several of the secondary tasks (asynchronous retrieval) but misses a few important aspects. First, we have no way to define extra configuration about the data involved. For example, we didn't get a chance to choose the compression format or the keys and algorithm to use when encrypting the data. Next, we weren't able to choose the final destination of the data. Instead, we were simply told where we might go looking for it later. Finally, if we look more closely, it becomes clear that the asynchronous nature of the interface is only partially useful: while the service does asynchronously return a location from which we can download the data, we have no way to monitor the progress of the export operation, nor a way to abort the operation in the case that we're no longer interested in the data.

Let's see if we can improve on this design by using a few of the design patterns later defined in our catalog of design patterns, primarily focusing on the import/export pattern.

IMPORT/EXPORT PATTERN

As we'll learn in chapter 28, the import/export pattern is aimed at problems just like this one: we have some amount of data in our API service and consumers want a way of getting it out (or in). However, unlike the pagination pattern we discussed earlier, this pattern will rely on others, such as the long-running operations pattern (discussed in chapter 13), to get the job done. Let's start by defining the API and then looking more closely at how each piece works together. Just like before, keep in mind that we won't go into all the details of every aspect of the pattern, but instead will try to give a high-level view of the relevant pieces.

Listing 2.4   API to export messages using a design pattern

```
abstract class Twapi {
    static version = "v1";
    static title = "Twapi API";

    @post("/{parent=users/*}/messages:export")
    ExportMessages(req: ExportMessagesRequest) :
        Operation<ExportMessagesResponse,
                ExportMessagesMetadata>;
}

interface ExportMessagesRequest {
    // The parent user of the messages to be exported.
    parent: string;
    outputConfig: MessageOutputConfig;
}

interface MessageOutputConfig {
    destination: Destination;
```

Unlike the previous examples, the return type of our ExportMessages method is a long-running operation, which returns an ExportMessagesResponse upon completion and reports metadata about the operation using the ExportMessagesMetadata interface.

In addition to the parent (user), the ExportMessagesRequest also accepts some extra configuration about the resulting output data.

Here we define the "destination," which says where the data should end up when the operation completes.

```
  compressionConfig?: CompressionConfig;
  encryptionConfig?: EncryptionConfig;
}
```

← **Additionally, we can tweak the way in which the data is compressed or encrypted using separate configuration objects.**

```
interface ExportMessagesResponse {
  outputConfig: MessageOutputConfig;
}
```

← **The result will echo the configuration used when outputting the data to the resulting destination.**

```
interface ExportMessagesMetadata {
  // An integer between 0 and 100
  // representing the progress of the operation.
  progressPercent: number;
}
```

← **The ExportMessagesMetadata will contain information about the operation, such as the progress (as a percentage).**

What's so great about this pattern? First, by relying on an encapsulated output configuration interface, we're able to accept the various parameters at request-time and then reuse this same content in our response back as confirmation to the consumer. Next, inside this configuration we're able to define several different configuration options, which we'll look at in more detail in listing 2.5. Finally, we're able to keep track of the progress of the export operation using the long-running operation's metadata information, which stores the progress of the operation as a percentage (0% being "not started" and 100% being "complete").

All that said, you may have noticed that a few of the building blocks we used in the previous API definition weren't defined. Let's define exactly how those look while offering a few example configurations.

Listing 2.5   Interfaces for configuring the destinations and configurations

```
interface Destination {
  typeId: string;
}
```

Just like the original example, here we can define a file destination, which puts the output on a file server to be downloaded later.

```
interface FileDestination extends Destination {
  // The uploaded file will be hosted on our servers.
  fileName: string;
}
```
←

```
interface AmazonS3Destination extends Destination {
  // This requires write access to the bucket
  // and object prefix granted to
  // AWS Account ID 1234-5678-1234.
  uriPrefix: string;
}
```

← **In addition to the file download example, we can also request that data be stored in a location on Amazon's Simple Storage Service (S3).**

```
interface CompressionConfig {
  typeId: string;
}
```

Here we define the various compression options offered and the configuration values for each.

```
interface GzipCompressionConfig {
  // An integer value between 1 and 9.
```
←

```
    compressionLevel: number;
}

interface EncryptionConfig {
    // All sorts of encryption configuration here
    // can go here, or this can be
    // extended as CompressionConfig is.
}
```

> **We can either define all encryption configuration options in a single interface or use the same sub-classing structure (as shown with compression) for the various choices.**

Here we can see the various ways of defining the configuration options such as destinations for data or how the data should be compressed. The only thing left is to understand how exactly this long-running operation stuff actually works. We'll explore this pattern in much more detail in chapter 28, but for now, let's just throw out a simple API definition of these interfaces so that we have at least a high-level understanding of what they're doing.

Listing 2.6 Definition of common error and long-running operation interfaces

```
interface OperationError {
    code: string;
    message: string;
    details?: any;
}
```

> **One basic component we'll need is a concept of an error, which is (at least) an error code and a message. It may also include an optional field with lots more detail about the error.**

```
interface Operation<ResultT, MetadataT> {
    id: string;
    done: boolean;
    result?: ResultT | OperationError;
    metadata?: MetadataT;
}
```

> **A long-running operation is a promise-like structure, parameterized based on the result and metadata types (just like Java Generics).**

Unlike the other interfaces that are specific to exporting messages, these (`Error` and `Operation`) are more general and can be shared across the entire API. In other words, it's safe to think of these more like common building blocks than specific to a particular function.

WHAT HAPPENS IF WE DON'T START WITH THE PATTERN?

Unlike our previous example where the pattern-driven and non-pattern-driven options look pretty close to one another, in this scenario the two options differ significantly in the resulting API surface. As a result, the answer to this question is clear: if you find yourself needing the functionality provided (different export destinations, separate configurations, etc.) then starting in a non-pattern-driven approach will result in breaking changes for consumers. By starting with a pattern-driven approach for this problem, the API will evolve gracefully as new functionality is needed.

Summary

- API design patterns are sort of like adaptable blueprints for designing and structuring APIs.
- API design patterns are important because APIs are generally very "rigid" and therefore not easy to change, so design patterns help minimize the need for large structural changes.
- Throughout this book, API design patterns will have several sections, including the name and summary, suggested rules, motivation, overview, implementation, and trade-offs of using the provided pattern over custom alternatives.

Part 2

Design principles

Not all tools in our API design toolbox will be design patterns. In the next few chapters, we'll look at some topics in API design that don't quite qualify as design patterns (as defined in chapter 2), but are still important and helpful for guiding us on our journey toward building good APIs (as defined in chapter 1).

In chapter 3, we'll look at guidelines for naming the different components of our APIs. Next, in chapter 4, we'll cover how to logically arrange these components and define their relationships with one another. Finally, in chapter 5, we'll look at how to decide between the many data types available for the different fields we might need in our APIs.

Naming 3

Whether we like it or not, names follow us everywhere. In every software system we build, and every API we design or use, there are names hiding around each corner that will live far longer than we ever intend them to. Because of this, it should seem obvious that it's important to choose great names (even if we don't always give our naming choices as much thought as we should). In this chapter, we'll explore the different components of an API that we'll have to name, some strategies we can employ to choose good names, the high-level attributes that distinguish good names from bad ones, and finally some general principles to help guide us when making tough naming decisions that we'll inevitably run into.

3.1   *Why do names matter?*

In the world of software engineering generally, it's practically impossible to avoid choosing names for things. If that were possible, we'd need to be able to write chunks of code that used only language keywords (e.g., class, for, or if), which would be unreadable at best. With that in mind, compiled software is a special case. This is because with traditional compiled code, the names of our functions and variables are only important to those who have access to the source code, as the name itself generally disappears during compilation (or minification) and deployment.

On the other hand, when designing and building an API, the names we choose are much more important, as they're what all the users of the API will see and interact with. In other words, these names won't simply get compiled away and hidden from the world. This means we need to put an extraordinary amount of thought and consideration into the names we choose for an API.

The obvious question here becomes, "Can't we just change the names if they turn out to be bad choices?" As we'll learn in chapter 24, changing names in an API can be quite challenging. Imagine changing the name of a frequently used function in your source code and then realizing you need to do a big find-and-replace to make sure you updated all references to that function name. While inconvenient (and even easy in some IDEs), this is certainly possible. However, consider if this source code was available to the public to build into their own projects. Even if you could somehow update all references for all public source code available, there is always going to be private source code that you don't have access to and therefore cannot possibly update.

Put a bit differently, changing public-facing names in an API is a bit like changing your address or phone number. To successfully change this number everywhere, you'd have to contact everyone who ever had your phone number, including your grandmother (who might use a paper address book) and every marketing company that ever had access to it. Even if you have a way to get in touch with everyone who has your number, you'd still need them to do the work of updating the contact information, which they might be too busy to do.

Now that we've seen the importance of choosing good names (and avoiding changing them), this leads us to an important question: What makes a name "good"?

3.2   *What makes a name "good"?*

As we learned in chapter 1, APIs are "good" when they are operational, expressive, simple, and predictable. Names, on the other hand, are quite similar except for the fact that they aren't necessarily operational (in other words, a name doesn't actually do anything). Let's look at this subset of attributes and a few examples of naming choices, starting with being expressive.

3.2.1 *Expressive*

More important than anything else, it's critical that a name clearly convey the thing that it's naming. This thing might be a function or RPC (e.g., `CreateAccount`), a resource or message (e.g., `WeatherReading`), a field or property (e.g., `postal_address`), or something else entirely, such as an enumeration value (e.g., `Color.BLUE`), but it should be clear to the reader exactly what the thing represents. This might sound easy, but it's often very difficult to see a name with fresh eyes, forgetting all the context that we've built by working in a particular area over time. This context is a huge asset generally, but in this case it's more of a liability: it makes us bad at naming things.

For example, the term *topic* is often used in the context of asynchronous messaging (e.g., Apache Kafka or RabbitMQ); however, it's also used in a specific area of machine learning and natural language processing called *topic modeling*. If you were to use the term *topic* in your machine learning API, it wouldn't be all that surprising that users might be confused about which type of topic you're referring to. If that's a real possibility (perhaps your API uses both asynchronous messaging and topic modeling), you might want to choose a more expressive name than `topic`, such as `model_topic` or `messaging_topic` to prevent user confusion.

3.2.2 *Simple*

While an expressive name is certainly important, it can also become burdensome if the name is excessively long without adding additional clarity. Using the example from before (`topic`, referring to multiple different areas of computer science), if an API only ever refers to asynchronous messaging (e.g., an Apache Kafka–like API) and has nothing to do with machine learning, then `topic` is sufficiently clear and simple, while `messaging_topic` wouldn't add much value. In short, names should be expressive but only to the extent that each additional part of a name adds value to justify its presence.

On the other hand, names shouldn't be oversimplified either. For example, imagine we have an API that needs to store some user-specified preferences. The resource might be called `UserSpecifiedPreferences`; however, the `Specified` isn't adding very much to the name. On the other hand, if we simply called the resource `Preferences`, it's unclear whose preferences they are and could cause confusion down the line when there are system- or administrator-level preferences that need to be stored and managed. In this case, `UserPreferences` seems to be the sweet spot between an expressive name and a simple name, summarized in table 3.1.

Table 3.1   Choosing between simple and expressive names

Name	Notes
`UserSpecifiedPreferences`	Expressive, but not simple enough
`UserPreferences`	Simple enough and expressive enough
`Preferences`	Too simple

3.2.3   *Predictable*

Now that we've gone through the balance between expressive and simple, there's one final and very important aspect of choosing a good name: predictability. Imagine an API that uses the name `topic` to group together similar asynchronous messages (similar to Apache Kafka). Then imagine that the API uses the name `messaging_topic` in other places, without much reason for choosing one or the other. This leads to some pretty frustrating and unusual circumstances.

Listing 3.1   Example frustrating code due to inconsistent naming

```
function handleMessage(message: Message): void {        Here we use the name topic to
  if (message.topic === "budget.purge") {               read the topic of a given message.
    client.PurgeTopic({
      messagingTopic: "budget.update"                   Here we use the name messagingTopic
    });                                                  to represent the same concept.
  }
}
```

In the odd case that this doesn't seem frustrating, consider an important principle we're violating here. In general, we should use the same name to represent the same thing and different names to represent different things. If we take that principle as axiomatic, this leads to an important question: how is `topic` different from `messagingTopic`? After all, we used different names, so they must represent different concepts, right?

The basic underlying goal is to allow users of an API to learn one name and continue building on that knowledge to be able to predict what future names (e.g., if they represent the same concept) would look like. By using `topic` consistently throughout an API when we mean "the topic for a given message" (and something else when we mean something different), we're allowing users of an API to build on what they've already learned rather than confusing them and forcing them to research every single name to ensure it means what they would assume.

Now that we have an idea of some of the characteristics of good names, let's explore some general guidelines that can act as guard rails when naming things in an API, starting with the fundamental aspects of language, grammar, and syntax.

3.3   *Language, grammar, and syntax*

While code is all about ones and zeros, fundamentally stored as numbers, naming is a primarily subjective construct we express using language. Unlike programming languages, which have very firm rules about what's valid and what's not, language has evolved to serve people more than computers, making the rules much less firm. This allows our naming choices to be a bit more flexible and ambiguous, which can be both a good and bad thing.

On the one hand, ambiguity allows us to name things to be general enough to support future work. For example, naming a field `image_uri` rather than `jpeg_uri` prevents us from limiting ourselves to a single image format (JPEG). On the other hand, when there are multiple ways to express the same thing, we often tend to use them interchangeably, which ultimately makes our naming choices unpredictable (see section 3.2.3) and results in a frustrating and cumbersome API. To avoid some of this, even though "language" has quite a bit of flexibility, by imposing some rules of our own, we can avoid losing the predictability we value so highly in a good API. In this section, we'll explore some of the simple rules related to language that can help minimize some of the arbitrary choices we'll have to make when naming things.

3.3.1 Language

While there are many languages spoken in the world, if we had to choose a single language that was used the most in software engineering, currently American English is the leading contender. This isn't to say that American English is any better or worse than other languages; however, if our goal is maximum interoperability across the world, using anything other than American English is likely to be a hindrance rather than a benefit.

This means that English language concepts should be used (e.g., `BookStore` rather than `Librería`) and common American-style spellings should generally be preferred (e.g., *color* rather than *colour*). This also has the added benefit of almost always fitting comfortably into the ASCII character set, with a few exceptions where American English has borrowed from other languages (e.g., *café*).

This doesn't mean that API comments must be in American English. If the audience of an API is based exclusively in France, it might make sense to provide documentation (which may or may not be automatically generated from API specification comments) in French. However, the team of software engineers consuming the API is likely to use other APIs, which are unlikely to be exclusively targeted toward customers in France. As a result, it still holds that even if the audience of an API doesn't use American English as their primary language, the API itself should still rely on American English as a shared common language across all parties using lots of different APIs together.

3.3.2 Grammar

Given that an API will use American English as the standard language, this opens quite a few complicated cans of worms as English is not exactly the simplest of languages with many different tenses and moods. Luckily, pronunciation won't be an issue as source code is a written rather than spoken language, but this doesn't necessarily alleviate all the potential problems.

Rather than attempt to dictate every single aspect of American English grammar as it applies to naming things in an API, this section will touch on a few of the most common issues. Let's start by looking at actions (e.g., RPC methods or RESTful verbs).

IMPERATIVE ACTIONS

In any API, there will be something equivalent to a programming language's "functions," which do the actual work expected of the API. This might be a purely RESTful API, which relies only on a specific preset list of actions (Get, Create, Delete, etc.), then you don't have all that much to do here as all actions will take the form of `<StandardVerb><Noun>` (e.g., `CreateBook`). In the case of non-RESTful or resource-oriented APIs that permit nonstandard verbs, we have more choices for how we name these actions.

There is one important aspect that the REST standard verbs have in common: they all use the imperative mood. In other words, they are all commands or orders of the verb. If this isn't making a lot of sense, imagine a drill sergeant in the Army shouting at you to do something: "Create that book!" "Delete that weather reading!" "Archive that log entry!" As ridiculous as these commands are for the Army, you know exactly what you're supposed to do.

On the other hand, sometimes the names of the functions we write can take on the indicative mood. One common example is when a function is investigating something, such as `String.IsNullOrEmpty()` in C#. In this case, the verb "to be" takes on the indicative mood (asking a question about a resource) rather than the imperative mood (commanding a service to do something).

While there's nothing fundamentally wrong with our functions taking on this mood, when used in a web API it leaves a few important questions unanswered. First, with something that looks like it can be handled without asking a remote service, "Does `isValid()` actually result in a remote call or is it handled locally?" While we hope that users assume all method calls are going over the network, it's a bit misleading to have what appears to be a stateless call do so.

Secondly, what should the response look like? Take the case of an RPC called `isValid()`. Should it return a simple Boolean field stating whether the input was valid? Should it return a list of errors if that input wasn't valid? On the other hand, `GetValidationErrors()` is more clear: either it returns an empty list if the input is completely valid or a list of errors if it isn't. There's no real confusion about the shape the response will take.

PREPOSITIONS

Another area of confusion when choosing names centers on prepositions, such as "with," "to," or "for." While these words are very useful in everyday conversation, when used in the context of a web API, particularly in resource names, they can be indicative of more complicated underlying problems with the API.

For example, a Library API might have a way to list `Book` resources. If this API needed a way to list `Book` resources and include the `Author` resources responsible for that book, it may be tempting to create a new resource for this combination: `BookWithAuthor` (which would then be listed by calling `ListBooksWithAuthors` or something similar). This might seem fine at first glance, but what about when we need to list `Book` resources with the `Publisher` resources embedded? Or both `Author` and

`Publisher` resources? Before we know it, we'll have 30 different RPCs to call depending on the different related resources we want.

In this case, the preposition we want to use in the name ("with") is indicative of a more fundamental problem: we want a way to list resources and include different attributes in the response. We might instead solve this using a field mask or a view (see chapter 8) and avoid this oddly-named resource at the same time. In this case, the preposition was an indication that sometimes wasn't quite right. So even though prepositions probably shouldn't be forbidden entirely (e.g., maybe a field would be called `bits_per_second`), these tricky little words act a bit like a *code smell*, hinting at something being not quite right and worth further investigation.

PLURALIZATION

Most often, we'll choose the names for things in our APIs to be the singular form, such as `Book`, `Publisher`, and `Author` (rather than `Books`, `Publishers`, or `Authors`). Further, these name choices tend to take on new meanings and purposes through the API. For example, a `Book` resource might be referenced somewhere by a field called `Author.favoriteBook` (see chapter 13). However, things can sometimes get messy when we need to talk about multiples of these resources. To make things more complicated, if an API uses RESTful URLs, the collection name of a bunch of resources is almost always plural. For example, when we request a single `Book` resource, the collection name in the URL will almost certainly be something like `/books/1234`.

In the case of the names we've used as examples (e.g., `Book`), this isn't much of an issue; after all, mentioning multiple `Book` resources just involves adding an "s" to pluralize the name into `Books`. However, some names are not so simple. For example, imagine we're making an API for a podiatrist's office (a foot doctor). When we have a `Foot` resource, we'll need to break this pattern of just adding an "s," leading to a `feet` collection.

This example certainly breaks the pattern, but at least it's clear and unambiguous. What if our API deals with people and therefore has a `Person` resource. Is the collection `persons`? Or `people`? In other words, should `Person(id=1234)` be retrieved by visiting a URL that looks like `/persons/1234` or `/people/1234`? Luckily our guidelines about using American-style English prescribes an answer: use `people`.

Other cases are more frustrating still. For example, imagine we are working on an API for the aquarium. What is the collection for an `Octopus` resource? As you can see, our choice of American English sometimes comes back to bite us. What's most important though is that we choose a pattern and stick to it, which often involves a quick search for what the grammarians say is correct (in this case, "octopuses" is perfectly fine). This also means that we should never assume the plural of a resource can be created simply by adding an "s"—a common temptation for software engineers looking for patterns.

3.3.3 *Syntax*

We've reached the more technical aspects of naming. As with the previous aspects we've looked at, when it comes to syntax the same guidelines are in place. First, pick something and stick to it. Second, if there's an existing standard (e.g., American English spellings), use that. So what does this mean in a practical sense? Let's start with case.

CASE

When we define an API, we need to name the various components, which are things like resources, RPCs, and fields. For each of these, we tend to use a different case, which is sort of like a format in which the name is rendered. Most often, this rendering is only apparent in how multiple words are strung together to make a single lexical unit. For example, if we had a field that represents a person's given name, we might need to call that field "first name." However, in almost all programming languages, spaces are the lexical separation character, so we need to combine "first name" into a single unit, which opens the door for lots of different options, such as "camel case," "snake case," or "kebab case."

In camel case, the words are joined by capitalizing the letters of all words after the first, so "first name" would render as `firstName` (which has capital letters as humps like a camel). In snake case, words are joined using underscore characters, as in `first_name` (which is meant to look a bit like a snake). In kebab case, words are joined with hyphen characters, as in `first-name` (which looks a bit like a kebab skewering the different words). Depending on the language used to represent an API specification, different components are rendered in different cases. For example, in Google's Protocol Buffer language, the standard is for messages (like TypeScript interfaces) to use upper camel case, as in `UserSettings` (note the uppercase "U") and snake case for field names, as in `first_name`. On the other hand, in open API specification standards, field names take on camel case, as in `firstName`.

As noted earlier, the specific choice isn't all that important so long as the choices are used consistently throughout. For example, if you were to use the name `user_settings` for a protocol buffer (https://developers.google.com/protocol-buffers) message, it would be very easy to think that this is actually a field name and not a message. As a result, this is likely to cause confusion to anyone using the API. Speaking of types, let's take a brief moment to look at reserved words.

RESERVED KEYWORDS

In most API definition languages, there will be a way to specify the type of the data being stored in a particular attribute. For example, we might say `firstName: string` to express in TypeScript that the field called `firstName` contains a primitive string value. This also implies that term *string* has some special meaning, even if used in a different position in code. As a result, it can be dangerous to use restricted keywords as names in your API and should be avoided whenever possible.

If this seems difficult, it can be worthwhile to spend some time thinking about what a field or message truly represents and not what the easiest option is. For example, rather than "to" and "from" (from being those special reserved keywords in languages like Python), you might want to try using more specific terminology such as "sender" and "recipient" (if the API is about messages) or maybe "payer" and "payee" (if the API is about payments).

It's also important to consider the target audience of your API. For example, if the API will only ever be used in JavaScript (perhaps it's intended to be used exclusively in a web browser), then keywords in other languages (e.g., Python or Ruby) may not be worth worrying about. That said, if it's not much work, it's a good idea to avoid keywords in other languages. After all, you never know when your API might end up being used by one of these languages.

Now that we've gone through some of these technical aspects, let's jump up a level and talk about how the context in which our API lives and operates might affect the names we choose.

3.4   Context

While names on their own can sometimes convey all the information necessary to be useful, more often than not we rely on the context in which a name is used to discern its meaning and intended use. For example, when we use the term *book* in an API, we might be referring to a resource that lives in a Library API; however, we might also be referring to an action to be taken in a Flight Reservation API. As you can imagine, the same words and terminology can mean completely different things depending on the context in which they're used. What this means is that we need to keep the context in which our API lives in mind when choosing names for it.

It's important to remember that this goes both ways. On the one hand, context can impart additional value to a name that might otherwise lack specific meaning. On the other hand, context can lead us astray when we use names that have a very specific meaning but don't quite make sense in the given context. For example, the name "record" might not be very useful without any context nearby, but in the context of an audio recording API, this term absorbs the extra meaning imparted from the API's general context.

In short, while there are no strict rules about how to name things in a given context, the important thing to remember is that all the names we choose in an API are inextricably linked to the context provided by that API. As a result, we should be cognizant of that context and the meaning it might impart (for better or worse) when choosing names.

Let's change direction a bit and talk about data types and units, specifically how they should be involved in the names we choose.

3.5   Data types and units

While many field names are descriptive without units (e.g., `firstName: string`), others can be extraordinarily confusing without units. For example, imagine a field called "size." Depending on the context (see section 3.4), this field could have entirely different meanings but also entirely different units. We can see the same field (`size`) that would have entirely different and, in many cases, confusing meaning and units.

Listing 3.2   An audio clip and image using size fields

This might contain Base64-encoded binary audio content.

```
interface AudioClip {
  content: string;
  size: number;
}

interface Image {
  content: string;
  size: number;
}
```

The units of this field are confusing. Is it the size in bytes? Or the duration in seconds of the audio? Or dimensions of the image? Or something else?

In this example, the size field could mean multiple things, but those different meanings also would lead to very different units (e.g., bytes, seconds, pixels, etc.). Luckily this relationship goes both ways, meaning that if the units were present somewhere the meaning would become more clear. In other words, `sizeBytes` and `sizeMegapixels` are much more clear and obvious than just `size`.

Listing 3.3   An audio clip and image using clearer size fields with units

```
interface AudioClip {
  content: string;
  sizeBytes: number;
}

interface Image {
  content: string;
  sizeMegapixels: number;
}
```

Now the meaning of these size fields is much more clear because the units are provided.

Does this mean that we should always simply include the unit or format for any given field in all scenarios? After all, that would certainly minimize any confusion in cases like those shown. For example, imagine that we wanted to store the dimensions of the image in pixels resource along with the size in bytes. We might have two fields called `sizeBytes` and `dimensionsPixels`. But the dimensions are actually more than one number: we need both the length and the width. One option is to use a string field and have the dimensions in some well-known format.

Listing 3.4   An image storing the dimensions in pixels using a string field

```
interface Image {
  content: string;
  sizeBytes: number;

  // The dimensions (in pixels). E.g., "1024x768".
  dimensionsPixels: string;
}
```

The format of the field is expressed in a leading comment on the field itself.

The units of the field are clear (pixels), but the primitive data type can be confusing.

While this option is technically valid and is certainly clear, it displays a bit of an obsession toward using primitive data types always, even when they might not make sense. In other words, just like sometimes names become more clear and usable when a unit is included in the name, other times a name can become more clear when using a richer data type. In this case, rather than using a string type that combines two numbers, we can use a Dimensions interface that has length and width numeric values, with the unit (pixels) included in the name.

Listing 3.5   An image with dimensions relying on a richer data type

```
interface Image {
   content: string;
   sizeBytes: number;
   dimensions: Dimensions;
}
```
In this case, the dimensions field name doesn't need a unit in the name as the richer data type conveys the meaning.

```
interface Dimensions {
   lengthPixels: number;
   widthPixels: number;
}
```
The units of the field are clear (pixels) without any special string formatting.

In this case, the meaning of the dimensions field is clear and obvious. Further, we don't have to unpack some special structural details of the field itself because the Dimensions interface has done this for us. Let's wrap up this topic of naming by looking at some case studies of what can go wrong when we don't take the proper caution when choosing names in an API.

3.6   Case study: What happens when you choose bad names?

These guidelines about how to choose good names and the various aspects worth considering during that choosing process are all well and good, but it might be worthwhile to look at a couple of real-world examples using names that aren't quite right. Further, we can see the end consequences of these naming choices and the potential issues they might cause. Let's start by looking at a naming issue where a subtle but important piece is left out.

SUBTLE MEANING

If you were to walk into a Krispy Kreme donut shop and ask for 10 donuts, you'd expect 10 donuts, right? And you'd be surprised if you only got 8 donuts? Maybe if you got 8 donuts you'd assume that the store must be completely out of donuts. It certainly wouldn't seem right that you'd get 8 donuts right away, then have to ask for 2 more donuts to get your desired 10.

What if, instead, you only had a way to ask for a maximum of N donuts. In other words, you could only ask the cashier "Can I have up to 10 donuts?" You'd get back any number of donuts, but never more than 10. (And keep in mind that this might result in you getting zero donuts!) Suddenly the weird behavior in the first donut shop example makes sense. It's still inconvenient (I've not yet seen a donut shop with this kind of ordering system), but at least it's not baffling and surprising.

In chapter 21, we'll learn about a design pattern that demonstrates how to page through a bunch of resources during a list standard method operation in a way that's safe, clear, and scales nicely to lots and lots of resources. And it turns out that this exclusive ability to ask only for the maximum (and not an exact amount) is exactly how the pagination pattern works (using a `maxPageSize` field).

The folks over at Google (for historical reasons) follow the pagination pattern as described except for one important difference: instead of specifying a `maxPageSize` to say "give me a maximum of N items," requests specify a `pageSize`. These three missing characters lead to an extraordinarily large amount of confusion, just like the person ordering donuts: they think they're asking for an exact number, but they actually are only able to ask for a maximum number.

The most common scenario is when someone asks for 10 items, gets back 8, and thinks that there must be no more items (just like we might assume the donut shop is out of donuts). In fact, this isn't the case: just because we got 8 back doesn't mean the shop is out of donuts; it just means that they have to go find more in the back. This ultimately results in API users to miss out on lots of items because they stop paging through the results before the actual end of the list.

While this might be frustrating and lead to some inconvenience, let's look at a more serious mistake made by mixing up units for a field.

UNITS

Back in 1999, NASA planned to maneuver the Mars Climate Orbiter into an orbit about 140 miles above the surface. They did a bunch of calculations to figure out exactly what impulse forces to apply in order to get the orbiter into the right position and then executed the maneuver. Unfortunately, soon after that the team noticed that the orbiter was not quite where it was supposed to be. Instead of being at 140 miles above the surface, it was far lower than that. In fact, calculations made later seemed to show that the orbiter would've been within 35 miles of the surface. Sadly, the minimum altitude the orbiter could survive was 50 miles. As you'd expect, going below that floor means that the orbiter was likely destroyed in Mars's atmosphere.

In the investigation that followed, it was discovered that the Lockheed Martin team produced output in US standard units (specifically, lbf-s or pound-force seconds) whereas the NASA teams worked in SI units (specifically, N-s or Newton seconds). A quick calculation shows that 1 lbf-s is equivalent to 4.45 N-s, which ultimately resulted in the orbiter getting more than four times the amount of impulse force needed, which ultimately sent it below its minimum altitude.

Listing 3.6   A (very simplified) example of the API for calculations on the MCO

```
abstract class MarsClimateOrbiter {
  CalculateImpulse(req: CalculateImpulseRequest):
```

```
        CalculateImpulseResponse;
    CalculateManeuver(req: CalculateManeuverRequest):
        CalculateManeuverResponse;
}
```

The CalculateImpulseRequest and CalculateManeuverResponse interfaces are omitted for brevity.

```
interface CalculateImpulseResponse {
    impulse: number;
}

interface CalculateManeuverRequest {
    impulse: number;
}
```

Here we have the impulse calculated, but there are no units! This implies we can feed the previous output as the next input.

If, on the other hand, the integration point had included the units in the names of the fields, the error would've been far more obvious.

Listing 3.7 Alterations to the example interfaces to include units

```
interface CalculateImpulseResponse {
    impulsePoundForceSeconds: number;
}

interface CalculateManeuverRequest {
    impulseNewtonSeconds: number;
}
```

Here it becomes obvious that you can't just take the output of one API method and feed it into the next method due to the different units.

Obviously the Mars Climate Orbiter was a far more complicated piece of software and machinery than portrayed here, and it's unlikely that this exact scenario (https://en .wikipedia.org/wiki/Mars_Climate_Orbiter#Cause_of_failure) could have been avoided simply by using more descriptive names. That said, it's a good illustration of why descriptive names are valuable and can help highlight differences in assumptions, particularly when coordinating between different teams.

3.7 Exercises

1 Imagine you need to create an API for managing recurring schedules ("This event happens once per month"). A senior engineer argues that storing a value for seconds between events is sufficient for all the use cases. Another engineer thinks that the API should provide different fields for various time units (e.g., seconds, minutes, hours, days, weeks, months, years). Which design covers the correct meanings of the intended functionality and is the better choice?

2 In your company, storage systems use gigabytes as the unit of measurement (10^9 bytes). For example, when creating a shared folder, you can set the size to 10 gigabytes by setting `sizeGB = 10`. A new API is launching where networking throughput is measured in Gibibits (2^{30} bits) and wants to set bandwidth limits in terms of Gibibits (e.g., `bandwidthLimitGib = 1`). Is this too subtle a difference and potentially confusing for users? Why or why not?

Summary

- Good names, like good APIs, are simple, expressive, and predictable.
- When it comes to language, grammar, and syntax (and other arbitrary choices), often the right answer is to pick something and stick to it.
- Prepositions in names are often API smells that hint at some larger underlying design problem worth fixing.
- Remember that the context in which a name is used both imparts information and can be potentially misleading. Be aware of the context in place when choosing a name.
- Include the units for primitives and rely on richer data types to help convey information not present in a name.

Resource scope and hierarchy

4

This chapter covers

- What a resource layout is
- The various types of resource relationships (reference, many-to-many, etc.)
- How entity relationship diagrams describe resource layout
- How to choose the right relationship between resources
- Resource layout anti-patterns to be avoided

As we learned in chapter 1, shifting our focus away from actions and toward resources allows us to more easily and more quickly build our familiarity of an API by leveraging simple patterns. For example, REST provides a set of standard verbs we can apply to a bunch of resources, meaning that for every resource we learn about, we also pick up five different actions that can be performed on that resource (create, get, list, delete, and update).

While this is valuable, it means that it becomes far more important to think carefully about the resources we define as part of an API. A key part of choosing the right resources is understanding how they'll fit together in the future. In this

47

chapter, we'll explore how we might lay out the various resources in an API, the options available, and general guidelines for choosing the right way to associate resources with one another. Additionally, we'll look at a couple of anti-patterns (things *not* to do) when considering how to lay out a set of resources in an API. Let's start at the beginning by looking at what we mean specifically by resource layout.

4.1   What is resource layout?

When we talk about resource layout, we generally mean the arrangement of resources (or "things") in our API, the fields that define those resources, and how those resources relate to one another through those fields. In other words, resource layout is the entity (resource) relationship model for a particular design of an API. For example, if we were to build an API for a chat room, the resource layout refers to the choices we make that might result in a ChatRoom resource along with a User resource that might associate somehow with a room. This manner, in which User and ChatRoom resources associate with one another, is what we're interested in. If you've ever designed a relational database with various tables, this should feel familiar: the database schema you design is often very similar in nature to how the API is represented.

While it might be tempting to say that the relationship is all that matters, it's actually a bit more involved than this. While the relationship itself is the only thing with a direct influence in the resource layout we end up with, there are many other factors that influence the layout indirectly. One obvious example is the resource choices themselves: if we choose to not have a User resource and instead stick to a simple list of users by name (members: string[]), then there's no other resource to lay out and the question is avoided entirely.

As the name hints, the resource layout of an API is probably easiest to understand when we look at it visually as boxes connected to one another by lines. For example, figure 4.1 shows how we might think of our chat room example with lots of users and lots of chat rooms all interconnected to one another.

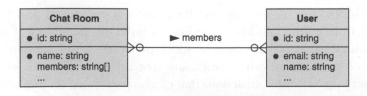

Figure 4.1   A chat room contains lots of user members.

And if we were building an online shopping API (e.g., something like Amazon), we might store User resources along with their various addresses (for shipping items bought online) and payment methods. Further, payment methods could themselves have a reference to an address for the billing address of the payment method. This layout is shown in figure 4.2.

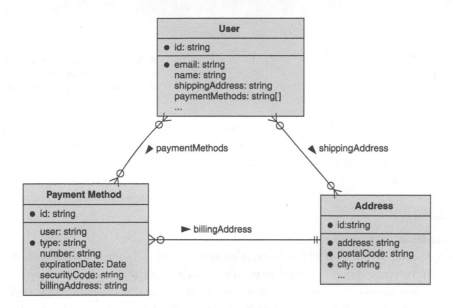

Figure 4.2   Users, payment methods, and addresses all have different relationships to one another.

In short, it's important to remember that resource layout is a broad concept that encompasses the resources we choose for an API and, most importantly, how those resources interact and relate to one another. In the next section, we'll take a brief tour of the different types of relationships and the interactions (and limitations) each type might provide.

4.1.1   Types of relationships

When thinking about the resource layout, we have to consider the variety of ways in which the resources can relate to one another. It's important to consider that all relationships we'll talk about are bidirectional in nature, meaning that even if the relationship seems one-sided (e.g., a message points to a single user as the author), the reverse relationship still exists even if it's not explicitly defined (e.g., a user is capable of authoring multiple different messages). Let's dive right in by looking at the most common form of relationship: references.

REFERENCE RELATIONSHIPS

The simplest way for two resources to relate to one another is by a simple reference. By this, we mean that one resource refers to or points at another resource. For example, in a chat room API we might have Message resources that make up the content of the chat room. In this scenario, each message would obviously be written by a single user and stored in a message's author field. This would lead to a simple reference relationship between a message and a user: a message has an author field that points at a specific user, shown in figure 4.3.

Figure 4.3 A message resource contains a reference to a specific user who authored the message.

This reference relationship is sometimes referred to as a *foreign key* relationship because each Message resource would point to exactly one User resource as an author. As noted earlier though, a User resource is obviously capable of having many different messages associated with it. As a result, this can also be considered a *many-to-one* relationship where a user might write many messages but a message always has one user as the author.

MANY-TO-MANY RELATIONSHIPS

Like a fancier version of references, a many-to-many relationship represents a scenario where resources are joined together in such a way that each resource points at multiple instances of the other. For example, if we have a ChatRoom resource for a group conversation, this will obviously contain lots of individual users as members. However, each user is also able to be a member of multiple different chat rooms. In this scenario, ChatRoom resources have a many-to-many relationship with users. A ChatRoom points at lots of User resources as the members of the room and a user are able to point at multiple chat rooms of which they might be members.

The mechanics of how this relationship works is left for future exploration (we see these in part 3), but these many-to-many relationships are very common in APIs and have several different options for how they can be represented, each with their own benefits and drawbacks.

SELF-REFERENCE RELATIONSHIPS

At this point, we can discuss what might sound strange but is in fact just another special version of a reference: self-references. As the name hints, in this relationship a resource points to another resource of the exact same type, so the self refers to the type rather than the resource itself. In fact, this is exactly like a normal reference relationship; however, we have to call this out as something different because of its typical visual representation, shown in figure 4.4, where an arrow points back at the resource itself.

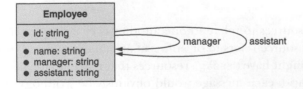

Figure 4.4 An employee resource points at other employee resources as managers and assistants.

You may be wondering why a resource would point at another resource of the exact same type. That's a reasonable question, but this type of relationship actually shows up far more often than you might expect. Self-references are most frequently seen in hierarchical relationships where the resource is a node in a tree or in network-style APIs where the data can be represented as a directed graph (like a social network).

For example, imagine an API for storing a company directory. In that scenario, employees point to one another to keep track of who reports to whom (e.g., employee 1 reports to employee 2). This API might also have further self-references for special relationships (e.g., employee 1's assistant is employee 2). In each of these cases, we can model the resource layout with a self-reference.

HIERARCHICAL RELATIONSHIPS

Finally, we need to discuss a very special type of relationship, which is another take on the standard reference relationship: hierarchies. Hierarchical relationships are sort of like one resource having a pointer to another, but that pointer generally aims upward and implies more than just one resource pointing at another. Unlike typical reference relationships, hierarchies also tend to reflect *containment* or *ownership* between resources, perhaps best explained using folder terminology on your computer. The folders (or directories for Linux users) on your computer contain a bunch of files and in that sense these files are *owned* by the folder. Folders can also contain other folders, and the cycle then repeats, sometimes indefinitely.

This might seem innocuous, but this special relationship implies some important attributes and behaviors. For example, when you delete a folder on your computer, generally all the files (and other folders) contained inside are likewise deleted. Or, if you are given access to a specific folder, that often implies access to the files (and other folders) inside. These same behaviors have come to be expected from resources that behave in this way.

Before we get too far along, let's look at what a hierarchical relationship looks like. We've actually been using examples of hierarchical relationships in previous chapters, so they shouldn't seem surprising. For example, we've talked about ChatRoom resources that are made up of a bunch of Message resources. In this case, there is an implied hierarchy of ChatRooms *containing* or *owning* Messages, shown in figure 4.5.

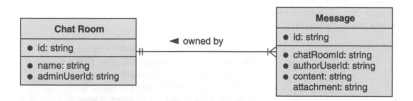

Figure 4.5 ChatRoom resources act as the owner of Message resources through hierarchical relationships.

As you can imagine, it's generally implied that having access to a ChatRoom resource would also grant access to the Message resources that constitute the body of content in the chat room. Additionally, when deleting the ChatRoom resource, it's generally assumed that this action cascades down to the Message resources based on the parent-child hierarchical relationship. In some cases, this cascading effect is a huge benefit (e.g., it's nice to be able to delete an entire folder on our computer without first deleting every individual file inside). In other cases, cascading behavior can be quite problematic (e.g., we might think we're granting access to a folder when we're actually granting access to all files inside that folder, including subfolders).

In general, hierarchical relationships are complex and lead to lots of tricky questions. For example, can resources change parents? Put differently, can we move a Message resource from one ChatRoom resource to another? (Generally, that's a bad idea.) We'll explore more about hierarchies and both their drawbacks and benefits in section 4.2.

4.1.2 *Entity relationship diagrams*

Throughout this chapter, you may have seen some interesting symbols at the ends of the lines connecting the different resources. While we don't have time to go into a full deep dive of UML (Unified Modeling Language; https://en.wikipedia.org/wiki/Unified_Modeling_Language), we can at least look at some of these arrows and explain how they work.

In short, rather than an arbitrary arrow pointing from one resource to another, we can have the arrow ends convey important information about the relationship. More specifically, each arrow end can tell us *how many* resources might be on the other end. For example, figure 4.6 shows that a school has many students, but each student attends only one school. Additionally, each student attends many classes and each class contains many students.

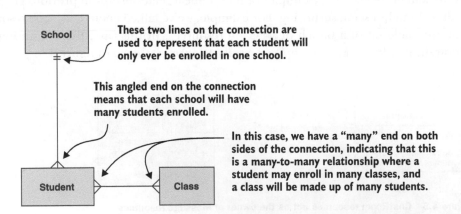

Figure 4.6   Example entity relationship diagram showing schools, students, and classes

While these two symbols are certainly the most common, there are others you may see from time to time. These are to cover the cases where any associated resources are optional. For example, technically a class may be made up of zero students (and vice versa). As a result, technically, the diagram may look more like figure 4.7.

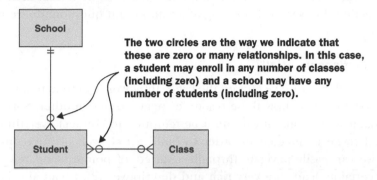

Figure 4.7 Updated diagram showing students may not enroll in classes (and classes may not have any students enrolled)

Sometimes it can be tough to get the hang of reading this type of notation, so it might help to clarify the direction in which each connector should be read. The best way to read these diagrams is to start at one resource, following the line, then look at the connector at the *end* of the line, then finish at the other resource. It's important to remember that you're skipping the connector symbol that's touching the resource you're starting with. To make that more clear, figure 4.8 shows the connection between the `School` and `Student` resources broken up into two separate diagrams, with the direction in which the connection should be read written next to the line.

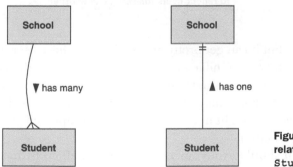

Figure 4.8 How to read entity relationships using `School` and `Student` resources as examples

As we can see, a school has many students and students have one school. For simplicity's sake we combine these two into a single diagram and single line connecting the two, as we saw in our previous examples.

Now that we have a good grasp on how to read these diagrams, let's get to the more important work of figuring out how to model our APIs by choosing the right relationships between resources.

4.2   *Choosing the right relationship*

As we learned in section 4.1, making the choice about the right type of relationship often depends on the resources we choose in the first place, so we'll treat these two as linked for this section. Let's start by looking at an important question: do we need a relationship at all?

4.2.1   *Do you need a relationship at all?*

When building an API, after we've chosen the list of things or resources that matter to us, the next step is to decide how these resources relate to one another. Sort of like normalizing a database schema, it can often be tempting to connect everything that might ever need to be connected in order to build a rich web of interconnected resources that we can easily navigate through a variety of pointers and references. While this will certainly lead to a very rich and descriptive API, it can also become untenable and run into serious performance degradation as the API receives more and more traffic and stores more and more data.

To see what we mean, let's imagine a simple API where users can follow one another (e.g., something like Instagram or Twitter). In this case, users have a many-to-many self-reference where a user follows lots of other users and each user might have lots of followers, as shown in figure 4.9.

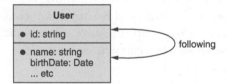

Figure 4.9   A `User` resource with a self-reference to reflect users following one another

This might seem innocuous, but it can get pretty messy when you have users with millions of followers (and users following millions of other users) because these types of relationships lead to scenarios where a single change to one resource can affect millions of other related resources. For example, if someone famous deletes their Instagram account, millions of records might need to be removed or updated (depending on the underlying database schema).

This isn't to say that you should avoid any relationships at all costs. Instead, it's important to weigh the long-term cost of any given relationship early on. In other words, the resource layout (and the relationships) is not always free of cost. And just like it's important to know how much your mortgage might cost you before you sign the paperwork, it's likewise important to recognize the true cost of a given API design during the design process rather than at the tail end. In scenarios where it's truly critical to maintain a relationship (e.g., the previous example, where storing follower relationships seems pretty important), there are ways to mitigate the performance degradation, but it's still a good idea to be judicious when defining reference relationships in any API.

Put differently, reference relationships should be purposeful and fundamental to the desired behavior. In other words, these relationships should never be accidental, nice to have, or something you might need later on. Instead, any reference relationship should be something important for the API to accomplish its primary goal.

For example, services like Twitter, Facebook, and Instagram are built around relationships between users following one another. A self-reference relationship between users is truly fundamental to the goal of these services—after all, without this relationship Instagram would become equivalent to a simple photo storage app. Compare this to something like a direct messaging service; we can see that even though this kind of API certainly involves relationships between users in the form of chats, they're certainly not critical to the application in the same way. For example, it's important to have a relationship between the two users involved in the chat but not so important to have a full collection of all relationships between potential contacts.

4.2.2 References or in-line data

Assuming that some sort of relationship is critical to the behavior and functionality of your API, we then have to explore and answer some important questions. First, we need to explore whether it makes sense to in-line the data in your API (i.e., store a duplicate copy inside a resource), or rely on a reference (i.e., keep just a pointer to the official data). Let's do this by looking at a simple scenario that relies on our chat room example.

Imagine that each chat room must have one single administrator user. We have two options: we can either point at the administrator user via a reference field (e.g., adminUserId) or we can in-line the data for this user and represent it as a part of the ChatRoom resource. To see what this looks like, look at figures 4.10 and 4.11 that show each scenario.

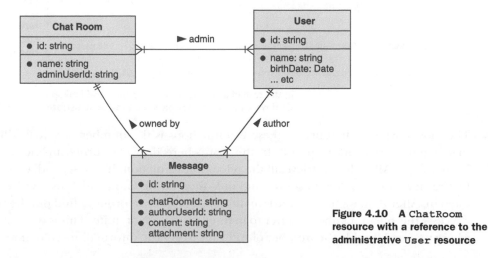

Figure 4.10 A `ChatRoom` resource with a reference to the administrative `User` resource

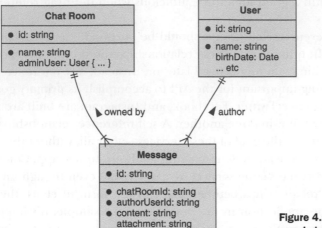

Figure 4.11   A `ChatRoom` **resource with an administrative user represented in-line**

In the first diagram (figure 4.10) we can see that the `ChatRoom` resource points at the `User` resource when specifying the administrator. On the other hand, in the second diagram (figure 4.11) we can see that the `adminUser` field actually *contains* the information about the administrator. This leads to the obvious question: which of these is best? It turns out the answer depends on the questions you're asking or the actions you're performing.

If you're trying to see the administrator's name, it's far easier to use the in-line data. To see why, let's look at what we'd have to do to get this information for each scenario.

Listing 4.1   Retrieving the administrator for both reference and in-line examples

```
function getAdminUserNameInline(chatRoomId: string): string {
  let chatRoomInline = GetChatRoomInline(chatRoomId);
  return chatRoomInline.adminUser.name;
}

function getAdminUserNameReference(chatRoomId: string): string {
  let chatRoomRef = GetChatRoomReference(chatRoomId);
  let adminUser = GetAdminUser(chatRoomRef.adminUserId);
  return adminUser.name;
}
```

In both cases, we start by retrieving the ChatRoom resource.

In the case of a reference, we have a second lookup to do if we want more information on the administrator.

The most obvious difference in these two functions is the number of actual API calls that require a network response. In the first, where data is returned in-line, we only need a single API call to retrieve all the relevant information. In the second, we have to first retrieve the `ChatRoom` resource and only then do we know which user we're interested in. After that, we have to retrieve the `User` resource in order to find out the name.

Does this mean it's always better to in-line our data? Not quite. This is one example where we need double the number of API calls to get the information we're interested in. But what if we aren't interested in that information very often? If that's the case, then we're sending down lots and lots of bytes every time someone asks for a ChatRoom resource, and those bytes are just being ignored. In other words, whenever someone asks for a ChatRoom resource, we also tell them all about the User resource that is the administrator for that room.

This might not seem like a big deal, but what if each user also stores all of their friends (other User resources) in-line as well? In that case, returning the administrator with the chat room might actually result in a whole lot of extra data. Further, there's often extra computational effort (typically coming from database queries that require joining data under the hood) involved when coming up with all of this extra in-line data. And it has the potential to grow quite fast and in unpredictable ways. So what do we do?

Unfortunately this will depend on what your API is doing, so this is a judgment call. A good rule of thumb is to optimize for the common case without compromising the feasibility of the advanced case. That means we need to take into consideration what the related resource is, how large it is now, and how large it's likely to get and decide how important it is to include the administrator's information in the response. In this scenario, the typical user probably isn't looking up who the administrator of their chat room is all that often and is instead focused on sending messages to their friends. As a result, in-lining this data is probably not all that important. On the other hand, the User resource might be quite small, so it may not be a huge problem to in-line this data if it's often used by the API.

With all that said, we've not yet addressed the other important type of relationship: hierarchy. Let's look at when it makes sense to choose a hierarchical relationship over another type.

4.2.3 Hierarchy

As we learned before, hierarchical relationships are a very special type of reference relationship between a parent resource and a child resource rather than two generally related resources. The biggest differences with this type of relationship are the cascading effect of actions and the inheritance of behaviors and properties from parent to child. For example, deleting a parent resource typically implies deletion of a child resource. Likewise, access (or lack of access) to a parent generally implies the same level of access to a child resource. These unique and potentially valuable features of this relationship mean that it has a great deal of potential, for both good and bad.

How do we decide when it makes sense to arrange our resources in a hierarchical relationship rather than a simple relationship. Assuming that we've already decided modeling this specific relationship is fundamental to our API (see section 4.2.1), we can actually rely on these behaviors as an important indicator of whether this relationship is a good fit.

For example, when we delete a chat room we almost certainly also want to delete the Message resources belonging to that chat room. Further, if someone is granted access to the `ChatRoom` resource, it wouldn't really make sense if they didn't also have access to view the `Message` resources associated with that chat room. These two indicators mean that we're almost certainly going to want to model this relationship as a proper hierarchy.

There are also some signs that you *shouldn't* use a hierarchical relationship as well. Since a child resource should only ever have a single parent, we can quickly know that a resource that already has one parent cannot have another. In other words, if you have a one-to-many relationship in mind, then hierarchy is definitely not a good fit. For example, `Message` resources should only ever belong to a single chat room. If we wanted to associate a single `Message` resource with lots of `ChatRoom` resources, hierarchy is probably not the right model.

This isn't to say that resources can point to one (and only one) resource. After all, most resources will be children of another and may still be referenced by (or reference) other resources. For example, imagine that `ChatRoom` resources belong to companies (a new resource type for this example). Companies might have retention policies (represented by `RetentionPolicy` resources) that say how long messages hang around before being deleted. These retention policies would be children of a single company but may be referenced by any of the `ChatRoom` resources in the company. If that's got you confused, look at the resource layout diagram in figure 4.12.

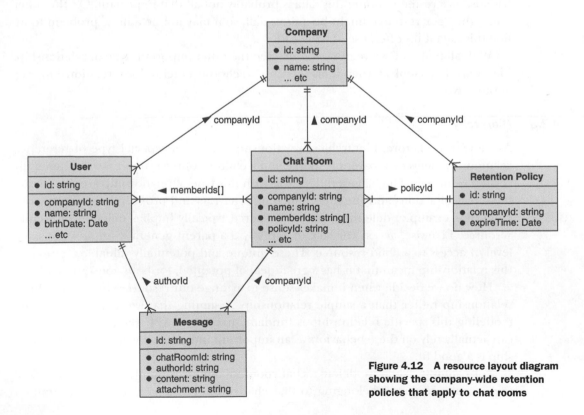

Figure 4.12 **A resource layout diagram showing the company-wide retention policies that apply to chat rooms**

As you can see here, User, ChatRoom, and RetentionPolicy resources are all children of a Company resource. Likewise, Message resources are children of the ChatRoom resource. But RetentionPolicy is reusable and can be applied to lots of different rooms.

Hopefully at this point you have a good idea of when to rely on references versus hierarchies (as well as when to in-line information rather than use a reference as a pointer). But after exploring these topics there are a couple of knee-jerk reactions we tend to fall into when designing our APIs. Let's take a moment and look at some resource layout anti-patterns and how to avoid them.

4.3   Anti-patterns

As with most topics, there are common blanket behaviors that are easy to follow under all circumstances, but these behaviors tend to lead us awry. After all, it's much easier to blindly follow a rule than to think deeply about an API design and decide on the best way to arrange resources and how they relate to one another.

4.3.1   Resources for everything

It can often be tempting to create resources for even the tiniest concept you might want to model in your API. Typically this comes up during modeling when someone decides that every single concept that becomes a data type must be a proper resource. For example, imagine we have an API where we can store annotations on images. For each annotation, we might want to store the area that's included (perhaps as some sort of bounding box), as well as a list of notes that make up the content of the actual annotation.

At this point, we have four separate concepts to consider: images, annotations, bounding boxes, and notes. The question becomes, which of these should be resources and which should end their journey at the point of becoming only data types? One knee-jerk reaction is to make everything a resource, no matter what. This might end up looking something like the resource layout diagram shown in figure 4.13.

Now we have four complete resources that have the full resource life cycle. In other words, we need to implement five different methods for each of these resources, totaling 20 different API calls. And it leaves the question: is this the right choice? After all, do we really need to give each bounding box its own identifier? And do we really need separate resources for each individual note?

If we think a bit harder about this layout, we might find two important things. First, the BoundingBox resource is one-to-one with an annotation, so we get almost no value from putting it into a separate resource. Second, it's unlikely that the list of Note resources will get exceptionally large, so we don't gain all that much by representing these as resources, either. If we take that into consideration, we have a much simpler resource layout.

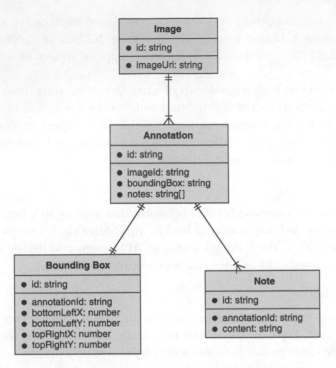

Figure 4.13   A resource layout diagram showing all concepts built as resources

Listing 4.2   Simplified interfaces relying on in-line representations

```
interface Image {
  id: string;
}

interface Annotation {
  id: string;
  boundingBox: BoundingBox;
  notes: Note[];
}

interface BoundingBox {
  bottomLeftPoint: Point;
  topRightPoint: Point;
}

interface Point {
  x: number;
  y: number;
}

interface Note {
  content: string;
  createTime: Date;
}
```

These two interfaces are actual resources (notice the identifier field).

All of these are not resources; they are just data types that are surfaced in the API inside the Annotation resource.

This means that we actually only have two resources to think about (instead of four), which is much easier both to understand and build. Figure 4.14 shows the resource layout diagram in its more simplified version.

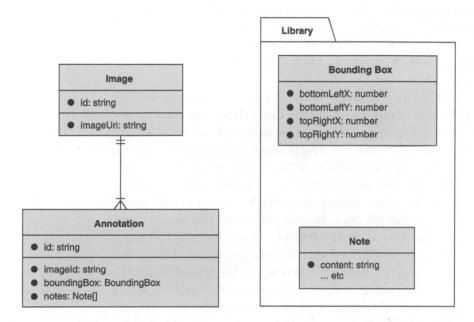

Figure 4.14   Resource layout diagram of two simple resources rather than four

A good rule of thumb here is to avoid two issues. First, if you don't need to interact with one of your proposed resources independent of a resource it's associated with, then you might be fine with it being just a data type. In this example, it's unlikely that someone would need to manipulate the bounding box outside of the context of the image itself, meaning this is probably fine as a data type.

Second, if the concept you're thinking of *is* something you might want to interact with directly (in this case, you might want to delete one single note or create new ones individually), if it's able to be in-lined (see section 4.2.2) then that might be a good choice. In this case, Note resources were sufficiently small and not expected to grow into a large collection for each annotation, meaning they're probably safe to in-line rather than represent as independent resources.

4.3.2   *Deep hierarchies*

The next common anti-pattern to avoid is specifically about hierarchies. Often hierarchical relationships can appear so incredibly powerful and useful that we try to use them everywhere we can. However, overly deep hierarchies can be confusing and difficult to manage for everyone involved.

For example, let's imagine that we're building a system to manage course catalogs for universities. We need to keep track of the different universities, the school or program in which the course exists (e.g., the nursing school or the engineering school), the courses that are available, the semester in which the course is offered, and the various course documents (e.g., the syllabus). One way to keep track of all this is to put everything together in a single hierarchy, shown in figure 4.15.

While this technically will work just fine, it's pretty difficult to reason about and keep all the different parents in our minds. It also means that we now need to know quite a lot of information in order to find a single document (see section 6.3.6 for more discussion on this topic), which can be challenging to store and recall. But the bigger problem here is that the benefits of using hierarchy here aren't really necessary to get the job done. In other words, we can probably create just as good of an API without so many levels of hierarchy.

What if we decided that the key pieces are universities, courses, and documents? In that world, the school becomes a field on the course, as does the semester. We do this by asking whether the school and semester levels of the hierarchy are really all that critical.

For example, what are we planning to use the hierarchical behavior for? Do we plan to delete schools often? (Probably not.) What about semesters? (Also, probably not.) The most likely scenario is that we'd like to see all semesters that a given course was listed. But we can do this by filtering based on a course identifier and likewise for listing courses by a given school ID.

Keep in mind that this isn't to say we should get rid of these resources entirely. In the case of a semester, it's unlikely that we need a listing of the available semesters for exploratory purposes, but schools might be something worth keeping around. The suggested change is instead to change the relationship between schools and courses from a hierarchical one to a referential one. This new (shallower) hierarchy is shown in figure 4.16.

By arranging our resources in this way (i.e., shallower), we can still do things like grant access to all documents for a given instance of a course or list all courses for a given semester, but we've whittled the hierarchy down to the pieces that really benefit from them.

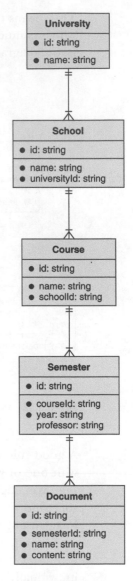

Figure 4.15 Course catalog with a deep hierarchy

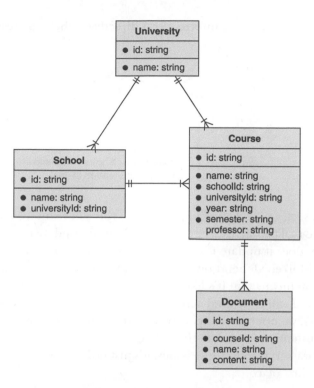

Figure 4.16   Course catalog with a shallower hierarchy

4.3.3   In-line everything

With the advent of nonrelational databases, in particular large-scale key-value storage systems, there is often the tendency to de-normalize (or in-line) all data, including that which would, in the past, have been neatly organized into individual tables to be joined with fancy SQL queries. And while sometimes it makes sense to fold information into a single resource rather than making everything its own resource (as we learned in section 4.3.2), folding too much information into a single resource can be just as detrimental as separating every piece of information apart into its own resource.

One big reason for this has to do with data integrity, which is also a common problem with de-normalized schemas in nonrelational databases. For example, let's imagine that we're building a library API that stores books written by different authors. One option would be for us to have two resources, Book and Author, where Book resources point to Author resources, shown in figure 4.17. If we were to in-line this information instead, we

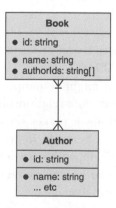

Figure 4.17   Books with Authors as a separate resource

might store the author names (and other information) directly on the `Book` resource, shown in figure 4.18.

 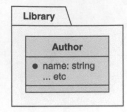

Figure 4.18   Books modeled with `Author` information in-line

As we learned before (see section 4.2.2), in-lining data like this can be quite valuable, but it also can lead to some real problems. For example, when you update the name of one of the book's authors, does it update that name across all the books they've written? The answer to this will likely depend on your implementation, but the fact that we have to ask that question means that it's likely to cause confusion. In other words, when we in-line data that will still be shared across other resources (e.g., authors who have written several books), we open the scary can of worms where we have to decide how users of the API are intended to update that shared data (e.g., authors' names). And while there are good ways to resolve those issues, it's just not a question we should have to worry about in the first place.

4.4   *Exercises*

1   Imagine you're building a bookmark API where you have bookmarks for specific URLs online and can arrange these in different folders. Do you model this as two separate resources (`Bookmark` and `Folder`) or a single resource (e.g., `Entity`), with a type in-line to say whether it's acting as a folder or a bookmark?

2   Come up with an example and draw an entity relationship diagram that involves a many-to-many relationship, a one-to-many relationship, a one-to-one relationship, and an optional one-to-many relationship. Be sure to use the proper symbols for the connectors.

Summary

- Resource layout refers to the arrangement and relationships between resources in an API.
- While it might be tempting to connect every resource in an API, fight the urge and only store relationships if they provide important functionality to the API.
- Sometimes it makes sense to store a separate resource for a concept. Other times it's better to in-line that data and leave the concept as a data type. The decision depends on whether you need to atomically interact with that concept.
- Avoid overly deep hierarchical relationships as they can be difficult to comprehend and manage.

Data types and defaults

This chapter covers

- What we mean by data types
- How a `null` value differs from one that's missing entirely
- An exploration of the various primitive and collective data types
- How to handle serialization for various data types

When designing any API, we always have to think of the types of data we want to accept as input, understand, and potentially store. Sometimes this sounds pretty straightforward: a field called "name" might just be a string of characters. Hidden in this question though is a world of complexity. For example, how should the string of characters be represented as bytes (it turns out there are lots of options for this)? What happens if the name is omitted in an API call? Is that any different from providing an empty name (e.g., { "name": "" })? In this chapter we'll explore the various data types you will almost certainly experience when designing or using APIs, how best to understand their underlying data representation, and how best to handle the default values of the various types in a sane and straightforward way.

5.1   *Introduction to data types*

Data types are an important aspect of almost every programming language, telling the program how to handle a chunk of data and how it should interact with the variety of operators provided by the language or the type itself. And even in languages with dynamic typing (where a single variable can act as lots of different data types rather than being restricted to a single one), the type information at a single point in time is still quite important, dictating how the programming language should treat the variable.

However, when designing APIs, we have to break out of the mode of thinking of a single programming language primarily because a major goal of our API is to let anyone, programming in any language, interact with the service. The standard way we do that is by relying on some serialization protocol, which takes a structured representation of data in our programming language of choice and converts it into a language-agnostic representation of serialized bytes before sending it to a client who asked for it. On the other end, the client deserializes these bytes and converts them back into an in-memory representation that they can interact with from the language they use (which may or may not be the same as ours). See figure 5.1 for an overview of this process.

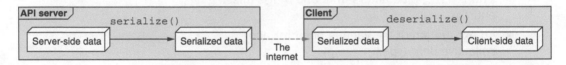

Figure 5.1   Data moving from API server to client

While this serialization process provides a huge benefit (essentially allowing an API to be used by any programming language), it's not without its downsides. The biggest one is that some information will be lost in translation due to the fact that every language acts somewhat differently. In other words, due to the difference in features and functionality of different programming languages, all serialization protocols will be "lossy" in one way or another.

This leads us back to the importance of data types and how to use them in an API. Put simply, it's fundamentally insufficient to rely on the data types provided by our programming language of choice when thinking about those who will use a web API. Instead, we have to think in terms of the data types offered by our chosen serialization format (most commonly JSON) and how we might extend that format in cases where it doesn't stack up with our needs. This means we'll need to decide on the types of the data we want to send to and receive from clients and ensure they are documented well enough so that clients are never surprised by their behavior.

This is not to say that a web API must have a strict schema along the lines of a relational database system; after all, one of the most powerful things from modern development tools is the flexibility provided by dynamic schema-less structures and data storage. However, it's important to consider the type of the data we're interacting with, clarifying it with additional annotations when necessary. Without this extra context on data, we may end up stuck, guessing about the actual intent of a client. For example, a + b might act one way for numeric values (e.g., 2 + 4 might result in 6) but may behave completely differently for text values (e.g., "2" + "4" might result in "24"). Without this type context we'd be forced to make a guess about the intent when a client uses the + operator: is it addition or concatenation? And what if one value is a number and the other is a string? This can lead to even more guesswork. But what if a value is omitted entirely?

5.1.1 *Missing vs. null*

Surprisingly, one of the most confusing aspects arises from the scenario when data is missing rather than present. First, in many serialization formats there's a null value, which is a flag indicating a non-value (e.g., a string could be value or the literal null). So how should an API behave when trying to add, for example, null and 2? Any API using a serialization format that supports a null value like this will need to decide how best to handle this type of input to their API. Should it pretend that null is mathematically equivalent to 0? What about trying to add null and "value"? In this scenario should null be interpreted as the empty string ("") and try to concatenate it?

To make things worse, dynamic data structures (e.g., a JSON object) have a new concern: what if the value is simply not present? In other words, rather than a value provided that happens to be set explicitly to null, what if the key where that value would be stored is missing entirely? Is that treated the same as an explicitly null value? To see what this means, imagine you have a Fruit resource that you expect to contain a name and a color, both string data types. Consider the following example JSON objects and the value an API might discern for the resource's color value:

```
fruit1 = { name: "Apple", color: "red" };
fruit2 = { name: "Apple", color: "" };
fruit3 = { name: "Apple", color: null };
fruit4 = { name: "Apple" };
```

As you can see, the first color value is obvious (fruit1.color == "red"). However, what should we do about the others? Is the empty color ("") treated the same as an explicit null color (is fruit2.color treated any differently from fruit3.color)? What about the fruit with the *missing* color value? Is fruit3.color treated any different from fruit4.color? These might just seem like quirks of JSON; however, they do exist in lots of other serialization formats (e.g., Google's Protocol Buffers [https://opensource.google/projects/protobuf] has some confusing behavior in this area), and they present scenarios that every API must address or risk being wildly inconsistent and confusing for those using the API. In other words, you can't simply assume that the serialization library will do the right thing because it's almost a certainty that everyone will be using different serialization libraries!

In this chapter, we'll go through all the common data types, starting with the simple ones (sometimes known as *primitives*) and moving toward the more complex (such as maps and collections). You should be already familiar with most of these concepts, so the focus will be less about the basics of each data type and more about the necessary considerations for using them with web APIs. We'll dig into the different "gotchas" to look out for with each data type and how best to address them for any API. We'll also stick to JSON as the serialization format of choice, but most of the recommendations will apply to any format that supports dynamic data structures, using both inferred and explicit type definitions. Let's start with the simplest of all: true and false values.

5.2   Booleans

In most programming languages, Booleans are the simplest data type available, representing one of two values: `true` or `false`. Due to this limited value set, we tend to rely on Boolean values for storing flags or simple yes or no questions. For example, we might store a flag on a chat room about whether the room is archived or whether chat bots are allowed in the room.

Listing 5.1   A ChatRoom resource with a Boolean flag

```
interface ChatRoom {
  id: string;
  // ...
  archived: boolean;
  allowChatbots: boolean;
}
```

Here we would have lots of other fields for the chat room.

This flag marks whether a chat room has been archived.

This makes a statement about whether chat bots are permitted in a chat room.

However, Boolean flags can be quite limiting in future cases where a yes or no question may become a more general question that requires a more nuanced answer than a Boolean field can provide. For example, there may be a future where chat rooms allow lots of different types of participants rather than just normal users and chat bots. In this scenario, our current design would lead to a long list of every type allowed (or disallowed), such as `allowChatbots`, `allowModerators`, `allowChildren`, `allowAnonymousUsers`, and so on. If this is a possibility, it may actually make more sense to avoid using a collection of Boolean flags and instead rely on a different data type or structure to define the categories of participants allowed or disallowed from a particular chat room.

Assuming a Boolean field is the right choice for a variable, there are some other interesting aspects to consider. Hidden in the name of Boolean fields is a statement of whether the field is positive or negative. In the example of `allowChatbots`, the `true` value for the field indicates that a chat bot is allowed into the chat room. But it could just as easily have been `disallowChatbots` where the `true` value would prohibit chat bots from the chat room. Why choose one or the other?

In general, positive Boolean fields are easiest for most of us to understand for a simple reason: humans have to think a bit harder about double negatives. And the false value for a negative field is just that. For example, imagine the field was `disallow-Chatbots`. How do you check whether chat bots are permitted in a given chat room?

Listing 5.2 A function to add a chatbot to a room, if permitted

```
function addChatbotToRoom(chatbot: Chatbot,
                          roomId: number): void {
  let room = getChatRoomById(roomId);
  if (room.disallowChatbots === false) {      ⟵─┐  Here we can check whether
    chatbot.join(room.id);                        │  chat bots are disallowed. If
  }                                                │  false, we can join the room.
}
```

Is this impossible to follow? Probably not. Is it a bit more cognitive load than the much simpler version (`if (room.allowChatbots) { ... }`)? For most of us, probably. Based on that alone, it's almost always a good idea to go with positive Boolean flags. But there are scenarios when it might make sense to rely on negative flags, primarily when we consider the default or unset value of the field.

For example, in some languages or serialization formats (e.g., until recently, Google's Protocol Buffers v3) many primitives, such as Boolean fields, could only ever have a zero value rather than a `null` or `missing` value. As you might guess, for Boolean values this zero value almost always equates to `false`. This means that when we consider the value of the `allowChatbots` field when a chat room is created, without any further intervention the chat room does *not* allow chatbots (`defaultChatRoom.allowChatbots == false`). But we cannot distinguish between the user saying, "I didn't set this value, so please do what you think is best" (i.e., a `null` or `missing` value) from "I don't want to allow chat bots" (i.e., an explicit `false` value). In both cases the value is simply `false`. What can we do?

While there are many solutions to this problem, one common choice is to rely on the positive or negative aspect of the Boolean field's name to land on the "right" default value. In other words, we can choose a name for a Boolean field such that the zero value provides the default we're looking for. For example, if we want anonymous users to be allowed by default, we might decide to name the field `disallowAnonymous-Users` so that a zero value (`false`) would result in the default we want (anonymous users allowed). This choice, unfortunately, locks the default into the name of the field, which prohibits future flexibility (i.e., you cannot change the default down the line), but, as they say, desperate times call for desperate measures.

5.3 *Numbers*

Getting slightly more complex from the simple yes or no questions, numerical values allow us to store all sorts of valuable information such as counts (e.g., `viewCount`), sizes and distances (e.g., `itemWeight`), or currency values (e.g., `priceUsd`). In general, anything that we might want to perform arithmetic calculations on (or even if these calculations would only make logical sense), number fields are the ideal choice of data type.

There is one notable example that is actually *not* a good fit for this data type: numeric identifiers. This might be surprising as many database systems (and almost all relational database systems) use automatically incrementing integer values as primary key identifiers for their rows. So why wouldn't we do likewise with identifiers in an API?

While we might still use a numeric field under the hood for a variety of reasons (e.g., performance or space constraints), in an API surface numeric types are best used for values that provide some form of arithmetic benefit out of the values being actual numbers. In other words, if an API exposes items that have a weight value in grams, we might conceivably add all of these values to determine the combined weight in grams of a set of these items. On the other hand, it generally doesn't make any sense to add a set of numeric identifiers and do something with that value. On the contrary, the addition of a bunch of numeric IDs is likely to be pretty useless. As a result, it's important to rely on numeric data types for their numeric or arithmetic benefit and not for the fact that they happen to be written with only the numeral characters (perhaps with a decimal point here or there). In general, values that only happen to look like numbers but behave more like tokens or symbols should probably be string values instead (see section 5.4).

With all that said, whenever using numeric values in an API, there are a few things to consider. Let's start by looking at how we define boundaries or ranges of acceptable values for these numeric fields.

5.3.1   Bounds

When defining boundaries for a numeric field, whether it's a whole number or a decimal (or some other mathematical representation such as fractions, imaginary numbers, etc.), it's important to consider the upper bound or maximum value, the lower bound or minimum value, and the zero value. Since these each have an effect on one another, let's consider the absolute value bounds and then decide whether to take advantage of both the negative and positive sides of that range.

When it comes to bounds, our main focus is their size. In other words, all numbers ultimately need to be stored somewhere, and this means we need to know how much space (in bits) to allocate for these values. For small integers, perhaps 8 bits is enough, with 256 possible values (–127 to 127). For most common number values, 32 bits is typically an acceptable size, with about 4 billion possible values (from negative 2 billion to positive 2 billion). For most things we could care about, 64 bits is a safe size, with about 18 quintillion possible values (from negative 9 quintillion to positive 9 quintillion). This range gets a bit more confusing when we introduce floating point numbers, as there are lots of different representations, ranging up to 256 bits of storage for these values, but the point is that there is typically a representation that will work for the range you have in mind for your API.

While these are all fine possibilities, you may be wondering why we're paying any mind at all to the sizes of numbers that will live in a database somewhere. After all, isn't the point of APIs to abstract away all this stuff? That is correct; however, it's important because the way different computers and different programming languages handle numbers is far from uniform. For example, JavaScript doesn't even have a proper integer value but instead only has a number type that handles all numeric values for the language. Further, many languages handle extraordinarily large numbers in very different ways. For example, in Python 2 the int type is capable of storing 32-bit integers whereas the long type can handle arbitrary large numbers, storing a minimum of 36 bits. In short this means that if an API response were to send a very large number to a consumer, there's a possibility that the language on the receiving end might not be able to properly parse and understand it. Further, those on the receiving end of these potentially huge numbers need an idea of how much space to allocate to store them. In short, the bounds are going to be quite important.

As a result, the common practice is to rely on 64-bit integer types for whole numbers internally unless there's a great reason not to. In general, even when you might not need anywhere near the 64-bit range at the moment, absolute certainties in software are rare so it's much safer to set upper and lower bounds with room for growth over time.

5.3.2 *Default values*

As we learned in section 5.1.1, with most data types we also have additional scenarios to consider, specifically a null value and a missing value where the field is simply omitted, just like Booleans (section 5.2), but in serialization formats that don't provide a mechanism for primitives to hold a null value, we'll have no way of distinguishing between a true value of 0 (or 0.0) and a default value where a user is saying, "I don't have an opinion here so you can choose what's best for me."

While it's possible to rely on the zero value as a flag for the default, this is problematic for a couple of reasons. First, a value of zero might actually be meaningful and necessary as part of the API; however, if we use it as an indicator of a default we're prevented from having an actual zero value. In other words, if we use 0 as a way of saying "Do whatever is best" (which in this case might be a value of 57), we have no way to actually specify an intentional value of 0. Second, especially in cases where a value of zero might make logical sense, using this value as a flag can be confusing and lead to unintended consequences, violating some of the key principles of good APIs (in this case, predictability). To answer the question of handling defaults for numeric values, we actually have to switch gears and talk in more detail about how these values should be serialized.

5.3.3 *Serialization*

As we learned in section 5.3.1, some programming languages handle numeric values differently from others. This is particularly apparent when we have very large numbers, at least above 32-bit numbers, but even more so with numbers past the 64-bit limit. It also comes up quite a lot when dealing with decimal numbers due to issues with floating point precision that are ubiquitous and a known drawback of the design of this format.

Ultimately though, we need to send numeric values to the API users (and accept incoming numeric values from those same users). If we intend to rely on serialization libraries without digging any deeper, then it's likely we'll be pretty disappointed.

Listing 5.3   Two numbers are different but considered equal because they're big

```
function compareJsonNumbers(): boolean {
  const a = JSON.parse('{"value":
➡    999999999999999999999999}');
  const b = JSON.parse('{"value":
➡    999999999999999999999998}');
  return a['value'] == b['value'];
}
```

These two number values are clearly not the same (they differ by 1).

However, if we parse a JSON document with them and compare, Node.JS will say they are the same!

This problem isn't only limited to large integer numbers. It also is a concern with floating point arithmetic for decimal numbers.

Listing 5.4   Adding numbers results in floating point arithmetic issues

```
function jsonAddition(): number {
  const a = JSON.parse('{"value": 0.1}');
  const b = JSON.parse('{"value": 0.2}');
  return a['value'] + b['value'];
}
```

Unfortunately, this returns 0.30000000000000004 rather than 0.3.

So what do we do? The scenario in listing 5.4 should sufficiently suggest that using numeric values and assuming they'll be the same across languages can be quite scary. The short answer might frustrate some purists, but it just happens to work pretty well: use a string of characters.

This simple strategy, where numeric values are represented as string values when serialized, is nothing more than a mechanism to avoid these primitive numeric values from being interpreted as actual numeric values. Instead, the values themselves can be interpreted by a library that might do a better job at handling these types of scenarios. In other words, rather than a JSON library parsing 0.2 as a JavaScript `Number` type, we can use a library like Decimal.js to parse the value into an arbitrary-precision decimal type.

Listing 5.5   Adding numbers correctly to avoid any floating point issues

```
const Decimal = require('decimal.js');

function jsonDecimalAddition(): number {
  const a = JSON.parse('{"value": "0.1"}');
  const b = JSON.parse('{"value": "0.2"}');
  return Decimal(a['value']).add(Decimal(b['value']));
}
```

Note that these numeric values are strings and not actual numbers.

When we add these using an arbitrary-precision library like Decimal.js, we get the right value (0.3).

Since the underpinning of this strategy relies on strings, let's take a moment to explore string fields.

5.4 Strings

In almost every programming language, strings tend to be something we take for granted without truly understanding how they work under the hood. Even those of us who spent time learning how C handles strings of characters tend to hide from character encodings and the wide world of Unicode. And while it's not imperative to become an expert on Unicode, character encoding, or other string-related topics, there are a few things that are pretty important when considering how to handle strings in an API. And since the majority of fields in an API tend to be strings, this is all the more important.

In the Western world it's pretty safe to think of strings as a collection of individual characters representing textual content. This is a pretty big generalization, but this isn't a book on Unicode, so we'll have to generalize. Since a great deal of the content we want to convey in an API is textual in nature, strings are probably the most useful of all the data types available.

Strings are also probably the most versatile data type available when building an API. They can handle simple fields like names, addresses, and summaries; they can be responsible for long blocks of text; and, in cases where a serialization format doesn't support sending raw bytes over the wire, they can represent encoded binary data (e.g., Base64 encoded bytes). Strings are also the best suited option for storing unique identifiers, even if those identifiers happen to look like numbers rather than text. We might store them as bytes under the hood (see chapter 6 for more information), but the representation in the API would almost certainly be best represented using a string of characters.

Before we start going on about how strings are the savior of the world, let's take a moment to look at a few of the potential pitfalls with string fields and how we can use them most effectively, starting with boundary conditions.

5.4.1 Bounds

As we learned in section 5.3.1, boundary conditions are important because ultimately we have to consider how much space to allocate to store the data. And just like with numerical values, we have the same aspect to consider with string values. If you've ever defined a schema for a relational database and ended up with VARCHAR(128), where the 128 was a completely arbitrary choice, you should be familiar with this sometimes unwelcome necessity.

Just as we learned with numbers, these size limits matter because those on the receiving end of the data need to have an idea of how much space to allocate to store these values. And just like with numbers, increasing sizes due to underestimation early in the life of an API is a pretty uncomfortable and unfortunate situation to be in. As a result, it's generally best to err on the side of rounding up when it comes to choosing the maximum lengths of string fields.

The next question worth addressing though is how to define maximum lengths. It turns out that our original definition of a string as a collection of characters only works in some limited circumstances, because many languages don't quite follow this concept as closely as we'd like. However, the bigger problem arises because the unit of measurement for storage space (bytes on disk) doesn't maintain a one-to-one relationship with the unit of measurement for string length (what we've called *characters*). What can we do?

With the aim of avoiding writing an entire chapter on Unicode, the simplest answer to this question is to continue thinking in terms of characters (even though these are actually Unicode *code points*) and then assume the most verbose serialization format for storage purposes: UTF-32. This means that when we store the string data, we allocate 4 bytes per character rather than the typical single byte we might expect when using ASCII.

Regardless of this storage space conundrum, there's one other aspect we'll need to consider for every string field: handing excessive input. With numerical values, a number out of range can safely be rejected by the API with a friendly error message: "Please choose a value between 0 and 10." With string values, we actually have two different choices. We can always reject the value just like a number being out of range, but, depending on the circumstances and context, this might be a bit unnecessary. Alternatively, we have the option to truncate the text if it extends past the limit defined.

While truncation might seem like a good idea, it can be misleading and surprising, neither of which is a characteristic of a good API, as we explored in chapter 1. It also introduces a new set of choices for the API (Should this field truncate or reject?), which can lead to further unpredictability as different fields exhibit different behaviors. As a result, just like numbers, it generally makes the most sense to reject any input that extends past the defined limit of the field.

5.4.2   *Default values*

Similarly to number and Boolean fields, many serialization formats don't necessarily permit a distinct null value (null) from a zero value (""). As a result, it can be difficult to determine the difference between a user specifying that a string should be the empty string rather than a user specifically asking the API to "do what's best" for the field given the rest of the context.

Luckily though, there are quite a few options available. In many cases, an empty string is simply not a valid value for a field. As a result, the empty string can indeed be used as a flag indicating that a default value should be injected and saved. In other cases, the string value might have a specific set of appropriate values, with the empty string being one of the choices. In this scenario, it's perfectly reasonable to allow a choice of "default" to act as a flag indicating that a default value should be stored instead.

5.4.3   *Serialization*

Thanks to the ubiquity of the Unicode standard, almost all serialization frameworks and languages handle strings in pretty much the same way. This means that, unlike with the numerical values we explored in section 5.3, our focus is less on precision or subtle overflow errors and more on safely handling strings that might span the entire spectrum of human language rather than just the characters used in the Western world.

Under the hood, strings are nothing more than a chunk of bytes. However, the way we interpret these bytes (the encoding) tells us how to turn them into something that looks like actual text—in whatever language we happen to be working in. Put simply, this means that when it comes time to serialize the string we're using on the API server, we can't just send it back in whatever encoding we happen to be using at the time. Instead, we should standardize on a single encoding format and use that consistently across all requests and responses.

While there are lots of encoding formats (e.g., ASCII, UTF-8 [https://tools.ietf .org/html/rfc3629], UTF-16 [https://tools.ietf.org/html/rfc2781], etc.), the world has gravitated toward UTF-8, as it's quite compact for most common characters while still flexible enough to encode all possible Unicode code points. Most string-oriented serialization formats (e.g., JSON and XML; https://www.w3.org/TR/xml/) have settled on UTF-8, while others (e.g., YAML) don't explicitly note which encoding must be used. Put simply, unless there's a great reason not to, APIs should use UTF-8 encoding for all string content.

If you're thinking that this is one place where we can simply let the library do the work, you're *almost* right, but not quite. It turns out that even after we specify an encoding, there are multiple ways to represent the same string content due to Unicode's *normalization forms* (https://unicode.org/reports/tr15/#Norm_Forms). Think of this a bit like the various ways we can represent the number 4: 4, 1+3, 2+2, 2*2, 8/2, and so on. In a UTF-8 encoded string, it's possible to do the same thing with the binary representations. For example, the character "è" can be represented as that single special character ("è" or 0x00e9) or as a combination of a base character ("e" or 0x0065) and an accent character ("`" or 0x0301). These two representations are visually and semantically identical, but they aren't represented by the same bytes on disk and, therefore, to a computer that does exact matching, completely different values.

To get around this, Unicode (http://www.unicode.org/versions/Unicode13.0.0/) supports different normalization forms and some serialization formats (e.g., XML) standardized on a specific form (in the case of XML, Normalization Form C) to avoid mixing and matching these semantically identical representations of text. While this might not matter all that much for a string representing a long-form description of an API resource, it becomes extraordinarily important when the string represents an identifier. If identifiers can have different byte representations, it's possible to have the same semantic identifier actually refer to different resources. As a result, it's a good idea for APIs to reject incoming strings that aren't UTF-8 encoded using Normalization Form C, but an absolute necessity for strings that happen to represent resource identifiers. For more on this topic of identifiers and their formats, look at chapter 6.

5.5   *Enumerations*

Enumerations, sort of like drop-down selectors for programmers, are a staple in the world of strongly typed programming languages. And while these might be wonderful things in languages like Java, their transplantation into the world of web APIs is often a mistake.

While enumerations can be very valuable, as they both act as a form of validation (only the specified values are considered valid) and compression (each value is typically represented by a number rather than the textual representation that we refer to in code), when it comes to a web API these two things are generally benefits with a cost of reduced flexibility and clarity.

Listing 5.6   Enumerations as types in an API

```
enum Color {
   Brown = 1,          ← Here we can define a
   Blue,                 bunch of possible colors.
   Green,              ←
}                          This list might go on
                           to include many more
interface Person {         options to be added later.
   id: string;
   name: string;          We can use this enumeration
   eyeColor: Color;    ← to handle a person's eye color.
}
```

For example, let's consider the enumeration in listing 5.6. If we were to use this with the true integer values, we might end up with `person.eyeColor` being set to 2. Obviously this is quite a bit more confusing than `person.eyeColor` being set to `"blue"` as the former requires me to look up what the number value actually means. In code this is usually not an issue at all; however, when looking through logs of requests it can become quite burdensome.

Further, when new enumeration values are added on the server, the client will be required to update their own copy of that local mapping (often requiring a client library update) rather than simply sending a different value. Even scarier, if an API decides to add a new enumeration value and the client hasn't been told what that value means, the client code will be left confused and unsure what to do.

For example, consider the scenario where an API adds a new `Color` value such as `Hazel` (#4). Unless the client-side code has been updated to accommodate this new value, we might end up with a pretty confusing scenario. On the other hand, if we use a different type of field (such as a string), we might end up with a similar error due to a previously unknown value, but we won't be confused by the meaning of that value (`"hazel"` is much clearer than 4).

In short, enumerations should generally be avoided when another type (such as a string) can work instead. This is particularly true when new values are expected to be added, and even more so when there's some sort of standard out there for the value in question. For example, rather than using an enumeration for the valid file types (PDF, Word document, etc.), it'd be much safer to use a string field that allows specific media types (formerly known as MIME types) such as `"application/pdf"` or `"application/msword"`.

5.6 Lists

Now that we have a grasp on the various primitive data types, we can start digging into collections of those data types, the simplest of these being a list or an array. In short, lists are nothing more than a group of some other data types, such as strings, numbers, maps (see section 5.7), or even other lists. These collections are typically address-able by the *index* or position in the list using square bracket notation (e.g., `items[2]`) and are supported by almost all serialization formats (e.g., JSON).

While not all storage systems support lists of items natively, remember that the goal of an API is to provide the interface that's most useful to a remote user, *not* to expose the exact data as it's stored in a database. That said, lists are one of the more commonly misused structures seen in web APIs today. So when should you use a list?

In general, lists are great for simple primitive collections that represent something inherent to an API resource. For example, if you have a `Book` resource, you may want to show a list of categories or tags about the book, which might be best represented as a list of strings.

Listing 5.7 Storing a list of categories on a Book resource

```
interface Book {
    id: string;
    title: string;
    categories: string[];      ⟵──  Here, books have a list of
}                                    string categories attached
                                     to them.
```

5.6.1 Atomicity

Hidden in this example is something pretty important to remember: list fields, despite containing multiple items, are best used when the items are considered an atomic piece of data to be modified and replaced entirely rather than piecemeal. In other words, if we want to update the categories on a `Book` resource, we should do so by replacing the list of items in its entirety. Put differently, there should never be a way of updating the second item in a list field. There are many excellent reasons for this, such as the fact that order becomes extraordinarily important when we address items by their position in a list or that we might not have a guarantee that a new item wasn't inserted in the meantime, pushing the item of interest into a new position.

Further, just like any other field on a resource, it's almost always a bad idea to allow data to be stored and modified from two different places, so allowing multiple methods of updating the content in a list field is something worth avoiding. This is particularly tempting because of the normalization principles we are trained to rely on with relational databases. For example, if we use something like MySQL to store this list of categories on a `Book` resource, we might actually have a separate table of `BookCategories` with a unique identifier, a foreign key to a book, and a category string with a uniqueness constraint. There is a temptation to allow this editing of categories by exposing an API to update these book categories by providing a unique ID of a book and the category we want to edit (since technically that is enough to uniquely identify the row in question).

Allowing this sort of modification opens a very scary can of worms related to consistency: it's possible that someone might set a list of categories while someone else is editing a single category using a different entry point. In that case, even relying on other mechanisms for transaction isolation (e.g., ETags; https://tools.ietf.org/html/rfc7232#section-2.3) won't be of much use, resulting in an API that is, put simply, full of surprises.

A good rule of thumb for list values is to treat them almost as though the list was actually a JSON-encoded string of items. In other words, you're not setting `book.categories = ["history", "science"]` but instead something closer to `book.categories = "[\"history\", \"science\"]"`. You wouldn't ever expect an API to allow you to modify a single character in a string, so don't expect an API to allow you to modify a single entry in a list field.

For more exploration on these topics of resources and their relationships to one another, look at part 4, particularly chapters 13, 14, and 15, all of which touch on the idea of using list fields to represent relational data in web APIs.

The next thing to consider is whether a list should permit different data types in the same list. In other words, is it a good idea to mix and match string values with number values in the same list? While it certainly isn't a total disaster to do so, it can lead to some confusion, particularly given the guidance from section 5.3.3 on handling large numbers and decimal numbers. These values might be represented as strings, so it could become difficult to untangle whether a given entry is actually a string or a numeric value that was only represented as a string. Based on this, it's generally best to stick to a single data type and keep list values homogeneous.

5.6.2   *Bounds*

Finally, one very common scenario with list values is about size: what happens when the list gets so long that it's unmanageable? To avoid this frustrating scenario, all lists should have some bound imposes specifying how many items they might have at most as well as how large each item may be (see section 5.3.1 or 5.4.1 for how to handle bounds for numeric and string data types). Additionally, inputs beyond these boundaries should be rejected rather than truncated (for the same reasons explained in section 5.4.1). This helps avoid surprise and confusion coming from exceedingly large lists of values that may accidentally grow to an unwieldy size.

If the potential size of a list is difficult to estimate or there's a good reason to suspect it may grow without a hard boundary, it's probably a good idea to rely on a sub-collection of actual resources rather than an in-line list on the resource. While it might seem cumbersome, the API will be much more manageable in the future when resources aren't enormous due to unbounded list fields. However, if you end up backed into a corner with this, look at the pagination pattern (chapter 21), which can help turn large, unwieldy resources into smaller manageable chunks.

5.6.3   *Default values*

Lists are similar to strings in that in some serialization formats and libraries there is no easy way to distinguish between the zero value (for lists, [ ]) and a null value. Unlike strings, however, it's almost always reasonable to have an empty list as a value, making it unlikely that an API could rely on an empty list value as a way of indicating a request to use some default value instead of the empty list. This leaves us with a complicated question: how do you specify in this scenario that you want the value to be whatever the default is rather than a literal empty list of items?

Unfortunately, in situations like these there doesn't seem to be any simple elegant answer. Either the default can be used at creation (with the assumption that an empty list would not be valid for a newly created resource) or a list value is simply not the right data type for this information. If the former scenario doesn't work for one reason or another, the only other safe option is to skip the list value entirely and switch over to managing this data as a proper subcollection of resources that are managed separately from the parent resource. Obviously this is not an ideal solution, but it's certainly the safest choice available given the constraints.

5.7   *Maps*

Finally, we can discuss the most versatile and interesting data type available to us: maps. In this section, we'll actually consider two similar but distinct key value–based data types: custom data types (what we've been calling *resources* or *interfaces*) and dynamic key-value maps (often what JSON calls *objects* or *maps*). While these two are not identical, the differences between them are limited, with the main distinction being the existence of a predefined schema. In other words, maps are arbitrary collections of key-value pairs, whereas custom data types or *sub-resources* might be represented in the same way; however, they have a predefined set of keys as well as specific types for the corresponding values. Let's start by looking at those with a predefined schema.

As resources evolve to represent more and more information, a typical step is to group similar pieces of information together rather than keeping everything flat. For example, as we add more and more configuration about a ChatRoom resource, we might decide instead to group some of these configuration fields together.

Listing 5.8   Storing data directly on a resource or in a separate structure

```
interface ChatRoomFlat {
  id: string;
  name: string;
  password: string;
  requirePassword: boolean;            In the flattened option, all
  allowAnonymousUsers: boolean;        fields are stored directly
  allowChatBots: boolean;              on the resource.
}

interface ChatRoomReGrouped {
  id: string;
  name: string;
  securityConfig: SecurityConfig;      Here we pull out all the information
}                                      related to accessing the ChatRoom
                                       in a separate structure.
interface SecurityConfig {
  password: string;
  requirePassword: boolean;
  allowAnonymousUsers: boolean;
  allowChatBots: boolean;
}
```

In this case, we've simply grouped several fields together based on their common theme of controlling security and access to a chat room. This level of abstraction makes sense only because we're really thinking in terms of grouping similar fields about a resource. If, on the other hand, the fields are related to the resource but fundamentally distinct and meaningful outside the context of the resource, it might be worthwhile to explore the singleton sub-resource, explained in chapter 12.

Now that we've explored custom data types with their predefined schemas, let's take a moment to look at dynamic key-value maps. While they may end up rendered in the same way, these two structures are often used in very different ways. Whereas we used a custom data type as a way of collapsing similar fields together and isolating them inside a single field, dynamic key-value maps are a better fit for storing arbitrary, dynamic data that has no expected structure. In other words, custom data types are simply a way of rearranging fields we know of and want to organize a bit better, while maps are better suited for dynamic key-value pairs with keys that are unknown at the time we define the API. Further, while there may be some overlap in these keys across resources, it's absolutely not a requirement that all resources have the same keys as they would with a custom data type field.

This kind of arbitrary structure of key-value pairs is a great fit for things like dynamic settings or configuration that depends on the details of a particular instance of a resource. To see what this means, imagine that we have an API for managing product information for items in a grocery store. We would obviously need a way of saying what ingredients were in each product and in what quantities, for example 3 grams of sugar, 5 grams of protein, 7 milligrams of calcium, and so on. It would be quite difficult to do this with a predefined schema listing all the possible ingredients, and even if we were able to do that, many of the values for these items would be zero since each item has all sorts of different ingredients. In this case, a map might make the most sense.

Listing 5.9 Tracking ingredients and amounts using a map field

```
interface GroceryItem {
  id: string;
  name: string;
  calories: number;
  ingredientAmounts: Map<string, string>;
}
```

> We can rely on a map of ingredients to the amounts.

Using the schema defined, the JSON representation of a GroceryItem might look something like listing 5.10. In this case, the ingredients are dynamic and free to vary for each different item.

Listing 5.10 Example JSON representation of an ingredients map

```
{
  "id": "514a0119-bc3f-4e3f-9a64-8ad48600c5d8",
  "name": "Pringles",
  "calories": "150",
  "ingredientAmounts": {
    "fat": "9 g",
    "sodium": "150 mg",
    "carbohydrate": "15 g",
    "sugar": "1 g",
    "fiber": "1 g",
    "protein": "1 g"
  }
}
```

It's important to note that since we can choose the data type for the keys of our map, technically we're free to choose anything under the sun. Some choices for a key type would be disastrous (e.g., some rich data type that is not easily serializable). Others might look like they're acceptable but are still a bad idea. For example, technically it might make sense to allow a number value to be the key type for a map; however, as we learned in section 5.3.3, numbers suffer from some pretty dangerous issues, particularly when they get big, but even sometimes just as small decimal values. As a result, strings are almost certainly the best choice for the data type of the keys in a map.

More importantly, since map keys are technically unique identifiers, it's also important that these string values be encoded in the UTF-8 format, and, as we learned in section 5.4.3 (and will learn more about in chapter 6) that these strings be in Normalization Form C to avoid duplicate key values due to byte representation issues.

5.7.1   Bounds

While custom data types' schemas avoid any bounding problems (instead, the schema defines its own boundary conditions), maps are very similar to lists in that they can both very easily grow out of control. As a result, maps, just like with lists, should define an upper bound on how many keys and values might be included in the field. This can become pretty important as it sets expectations on how large the field's content might grow. Beyond that, it's also important to set limits on how large each key and each value can be as string values (see section 5.4.1 for more information on string value bounding). In general this works out to specifying that a key might be up to 100 or so characters and values might be up to 500 or so characters.

On rare occasions, values' sizes might not be as evenly distributed. As a result, some APIs have opted to provide an upper bound on the total number of characters to be stored in the map field, allowing users the freedom to decide how those different characters might be represented (a few very small values and one or two very large values). While this is an acceptable strategy if absolutely necessary, it should be avoided as it tends to lead toward a slippery slope where more and more data ends up being stored in a map when it probably is better stored elsewhere.

5.7.2   Default values

Unlike lists, in almost all serialization formats and languages it's pretty easy to distinguish between an empty map value or zero value ({}) and a null value (null). In that case, it's pretty safe to let the null value indicate that the API should do whatever it thinks is best for the field given the rest of the API request. An empty map, on the other hand, is a user's way of specifying that the map should contain no data at all, which is itself a meaningful statement.

5.8   Exercises

1   A company in Japan targeting Japanese speakers only wants to use UTF-16 encoding rather than UTF-8 for the string fields in their API. What should they consider before making this decision?

2   Imagine that ChatRoom resources currently archive any messages older than 24 hours. If you want to provide a way to disable this behavior, what should you name the field that would do this? Is this the best design to provide this customization?

3   If your API is written in a language that natively supports arbitrarily large numbers (e.g., Python 3), is it still best practice to serialize these to JSON as strings? Or can you rely on the standard JSON numeric serialization?

4   If you want to represent the native language for a chat room, would it be acceptable to have an enumeration value for the supported languages? If so, what would this enumeration look like? If not, what data type is best?

5   If a specific map has a very uneven distribution of value sizes, what's the best way to place appropriate size limits on the various keys and values?

Summary

- For every value, we also need to consider both a `null` value and an `undefined` or missing value, which may or may not have the same meaning.
- Booleans are best used for flags and should be named such that a true value means the positive aspect (e.g., `enableFeature` rather than `disableFeature`).
- Numeric values should have a true numeric meaning rather than just being made up of numeric digits.
- To avoid issues with large numbers (above 32 or 64 bits) or floating point arithmetic issues, numeric values should be serialized as strings in languages that don't have appropriate native representations.
- Strings should be UTF-8 encoded, and for any string used as an identifier of any sort, normalized to Normalization Form C.
- Enumerations should generally be avoided, relying on string values instead, with validation done on the server side rather than the client side.
- Lists should be treated as atomic collections items that are individually addressable on the client side only.
- Both lists and maps should be bounded by the total number of items allowed in the collection; however, maps should further bound the sizes of both keys and values.

Part 3

Fundamentals

In the following set of design patterns, rather than looking at addressing a specific, narrowly scoped problem, we'll instead explore broader topics that are applicable to almost all APIs. These core design patterns will set the stage for designing good APIs, but we'll also rely on them as building blocks for the design patterns we'll see later on.

In chapter 6, we'll start by looking at how the resources in our APIs can be uniquely identified. Then, in chapters 7 through 9, we'll define a core set of interaction patterns with standard and custom methods (as well as learning how these apply when operating on subsets of a resource). In chapter 10, we'll learn how to handle API methods that might take a long time to complete with LROs and, finally, chapter 11 will cover how to manage repeated work in APIs with rerunnable jobs.

Resource identification

6

This chapter covers

- What an identifier is
- Attributes of good identifiers
- What good identifiers actually look like
- How to implement a system for making identifiers
- How this guidance works with UUIDs

In this chapter, we'll explore resource identifiers in-depth. This includes what they are, what makes for a good one (and a bad one), as well as how they can be used in your APIs. We'll also dig in to some of the common identifier formats in use today (such as universally unique identifiers or UUIDs; https://tools.ietf.org/html/rfc4122), as well as new custom formats targeted specifically for use in web APIs.

6.1 What is an identifier?

First, what exactly do we mean when we talk about *resource identifiers*? In short, identifiers give us a way to uniquely address and talk about individual resources in an API. In more technical terms, these identifiers are chunks of bytes (usually a string value or an integer number) that we can use as the way we point to exactly one resource in a resource collection. Almost always, these identifiers enable users of an

87

API to perform some type of lookup operation. In other words, these identifiers are used to address a single resource among some larger collection of resources.

It turns out that we often use identifiers like these in our everyday lives; however, not all identifiers are equally useful (or even equally unique). For example, many governments use a name and date of birth as an identifier for a person, but there have been plenty of cases where people are mixed up based on the assumption that no two individuals share a name and birth date. A better option, in the United States at least, is a Social Security number (a government-assigned nine-digit number), which is used to uniquely identify a person for most financial transactions (e.g., paying taxes or taking out a loan), but this number has its own set of drawbacks. For instance, SSNs are currently limited to a maximum of 1 billion people in total (nine digits), so as the population of the US grows over the years, the country may run out of numbers to give out.

It's clearly important to have identifiers for resources in an API; however, it's much less clear what exactly these identifiers should look like. Put differently, we haven't necessarily said what attributes make some identifiers good and others bad. In the next section, we'll explore these in more detail.

6.2 *What makes a good identifier?*

Since almost all resources we'll need to interact with in our API will need identifiers, it's clear that identifiers are important. And since it's up to us as API designers to choose the representation of these identifiers, this leaves one big question: what makes an identifier good? To answer this, we'll need to explore many different attributes of identifiers and the various options we'll need to decide between. For now, we'll focus exclusively on the attributes themselves and make more specific recommendations a bit later (in section 6.3).

6.2.1 *Easy to use*

The simplest place to start is one of the most obvious: identifiers should be easy to use in the most common scenarios. Perhaps the most typical scenario for an identifier is looking up an individual resource in a web API (what we learned as the standard get method in section 1.4). This means that sending a request to a server asking "Please give me resource <ID>" should be as simple and straightforward as possible while minimizing the opportunity for mistakes. In particular, this must take into consideration the fact that identifiers will often show up in URIs. This means that, for example, using a forward slash ("/") or other reserved characters in an identifier is going to be a bit tricky as they have special meaning in URIs and should probably be avoided.

6.2.2 *Unique*

Another obvious requirement of a good identifier is probably that it must be truly unique. In other words, an identifier must be, by definition, completely one of a kind or it isn't really capable of doing its job, which is to uniquely identify a single resource in an API. This might seem a bit overly simplistic, but there are some subtleties we need to address about what it means to be truly unique. One of these is that uniqueness is rarely absolute and instead usually depends on the context or scope in which the identifier is considered. For example, in the scope of computer companies, Apple is considered a unique identifier (there's only one Apple in the scope of computer companies), but in the scope of all companies Apple isn't actually unique (there's also Apple Records, Apple Bank, etc.). We'll need to decide whether identifiers need to be unique across all resources of the same type, all resources in the same API, or all resources in the world. Admittedly, true global uniqueness is theoretically impossible but should be doable in practice given sufficiently large key spaces (the possible choices for identifiers) and no intentional bad actors.

6.2.3 *Permanent*

Next, and slightly more subtle, is the idea that identifiers should probably not change once they're assigned. This is primarily because of the potential problems introduced (and therefore further decisions to be made) in scenarios where identifiers do end up changing. For example, imagine the case where `Book(id=1234, name="Becoming")` changes its identifier and becomes `Book(id=5678, name="Becoming")`. This on its own might not be a big deal, but consider then that a new book is created: `Book(id=1234, name="Design Patterns")`. In this case, this new book reuses the original identifier (`1234`), which ultimately means that depending on *when* you ask for `Book 1234`, you would get different results.

For most scenarios this might not be a big deal, but imagine that users can specify their favorite book and someone selects `Book 1234` to be their favorite (`User (favoriteBook=1234, ...)`). This leaves a very reasonable question: is their favorite book *Becoming* or *Design Patterns*? In this world where identifiers aren't permanent, to answer the question of which book we're referring to we also need to know when the favorite was selected, or more specifically when it retrieved `Book 1234`. Without that information, it's unclear what book we're actually talking about. As a result, it's best not only that identifiers are permanent, but that they're single-use, forever. In other words, once `Book 1234` exists, you should never end up using that same identifier ever again, even after the original `Book 1234` is deleted.

6.2.4 *Fast and easy to generate*

So far, we've been using simple numbers like "1234" as example identifiers, but it's unlikely these will be actual identifiers in real life. Instead, it's far more likely that these identifiers will have some element of randomness to them rather than relying on incrementing integers. Since that typically means there's more computation in choosing these identifiers, it's important to ensure that it doesn't take too long to make that choice.

For example, since we said that all identifiers must be permanent and single-use forever, that means we'll need to be certain that any ID we choose hasn't been used already. We could do this by keeping a list of all the resources and choosing IDs at random until we find one that hasn't been used before, but that's not exactly the most efficient nor the simplest option out there. It's also likely to get slower and slower over time, making it an even worse choice. Whatever option we choose, it should be fast and easy, and, most importantly, have predictable performance characteristics.

6.2.5 *Unpredictable*

While it's important that identifiers are fast and easy (and predictably so) when being chosen, it's also important that it's difficult for someone to predict what the next identifier will be. Ultimately this comes down to security and can be easily solved with a sufficiently large key space, but if the method of choosing those identifiers is as simple as choosing the next available number, it makes it easier to target and exploit potential vulnerabilities like misconfigured security rules.

For example, if an attacker were just probing around randomly checking for resources that were accidentally unprotected in a randomly allocated key space of 256-bit integers, there's a very small chance of landing on a resource that even exists, let alone one that's misconfigured. If, on the other hand, we use a far more predictable method, such as counting integers over the same key space (1, 2, 3, . . .), then an attacker is almost guaranteed to find resources that exist and can hope to land on one that's misconfigured to be open to the world rather than locked down.

6.2.6 *Readable, shareable, and verifiable*

Next, while we as engineers may hate to admit it, the identifiers we use in our APIs may at some point need to be communicated over a phone, pasted into a text message, or shared over some other noncomputational medium. This means, for example, that we don't want confusion between the digit 1, the lowercase L, uppercase I, or the pipe character (|), as writing these down on paper can be tricky (try communicating "1lI1|1I1I11I11I11I" over the phone, which is tricky even in code font!). In short, we should consider that identifiers will be interpreted and communicated by humans, so it's important that they aren't needlessly difficult in this aspect.

In addition to easy communication, a good identifier makes it easy to quickly determine if the identifier itself has been copied wrong. In other words, we should be able to tell the difference between a valid identifier that points to nothing and a completely invalid identifier that will never point to anything. One easy way to provide this is to use a simple checksum segment of the identifier. This isn't such a crazy idea and is used quite often. For example, the identifiers used for books are called ISBNs (https://en.wikipedia.org/wiki/International_Standard_Book_Number) and they work in just this way, where the last digit of a book's ISBN is used as a check digit to verify that the other digits actually make sense and haven't been mistyped.

6.2.7 Informationally dense

Finally, identifiers are going to be used all the time, so size and space efficiency are going to be important. This means we should aspire to pack as much information into as short a value as possible. This might mean choosing a more dense character set such as Base64 (https://tools.ietf.org/html/rfc4648) over a less dense one, such as simple numerals. In this example, consider that we can only store a total of 10 choices per character if we use numeric IDs, but we can store 64 per character if we use Base64-encoded text.

Optimizing for information density will be a balancing act with the other attributes that make good identifiers. For example, Base64 has many characters available, but those characters include both lowercase "i," uppercase "I," and the digit "1," which we learned can be confusing when written down or read. To see how all of this comes together, let's look at the various design considerations for how we might go about choosing a format for these identifiers.

6.3 What does a good identifier look like?

Now that we have a decent idea of what attributes to look for in a good identifier, we can try implementing a scheme to use for defining resource identifiers. First, we'll walk through the suggested implementation, and after that we'll compare it to the various criteria described in section 6.2.

6.3.1 Data type

Before we can get into much else, we'll need to first settle on the data type to use for storing these identifiers. While there are lots of reasonable options, strings, by far, are the most versatile and therefore the recommended option. They provide the highest information density (7 bits of entropy per character used over HTTP), are familiar to use, and provide lots of wiggle room in deciding how to make them easy to share, read, and copy.

While there are several other options, ranging from the common (e.g., positive integers) to the not so common (raw uninterpreted bytes), these provide artificial limitations imposed by their type (e.g., integers are limited to 10 choices per ASCII character, or ~3.3 bits of entropy per ASCII character over HTTP) or other drawbacks (e.g., raw bytes are inconvenient to work with in many programming languages).

Since we've settled on strings, we have a whole new set of questions to answer. First, what is the character set of these strings? Can we use any valid Unicode string? Or are there limitations? After that, we have to decide whether all characters are allowed. For example, in HTTP, the forward slash character ("/") is generally used to denote a separator, so we probably wouldn't want that in our identifier. Further, as we learned earlier, some characters (like the pipe character, "|") are easily confused with others (like "I", "1", or "l"). What do we do about these? Let's start by looking at the character set.

6.3.2   *Character set*

As much as I'd love to reminisce and explain Unicode and all its inner workings, not only would it take far too long, but I suspect there are still gaps in my knowledge of the standard. As a result, I'll focus on some simple examples involving character sets to clarify why this implementation will rely on ASCII (American Standard Code for Information Interchange).

ASCII is pretty simple: 7 bits of data to represent 128 different characters. This data is typically shoved into an 8-bit byte, which is used by HTTP requests when interacting with the majority of web APIs today. As you might guess, there are far more than 128 different characters, which is what the Unicode specification aims to solve. This is great; however, in the mission for ultimate backward compatibility, Unicode actually allows for more than one way to represent what we would consider the same chunk of text. For example, "á" could be represented as a single Unicode code point (U+00E1) or a composition of the "a" and the accent character code points (U+0061 and U+0301). While these both look like "á" on our screens (or on paper), when stored in a database they look very different—which is exactly the problem since computers don't see the visual "á" character; they see the bytes that make it up.

While there are certainly ways to get around this (e.g., use Normalization Form C and other Unicode wizardry), the ambiguities cause far more problems than they're worth (e.g., you must now specify how to handle data submitted that isn't in Normalization Form C, etc.). As a result, the safest bet for modern web APIs is to rely on ASCII for unique identifiers.

Now that we've settled on ASCII, we'll need to decide whether we further limit that to a subset of the 128 characters due to other concerns.

6.3.3   *Identifier format*

While it would be lovely if we could use all 128 characters provided by ASCII (or even all strings that the Unicode standard can represent), there's one important and desirable attribute of identifiers we need to consider, which we discussed in section 6.2.6: ease of reading, sharing, and copying. This means, quite simply, that we need to avoid characters in ASCII that are easily confused with others or might obfuscate the URL in the HTTP request. This leads us to a very useful serialization format: Crockford's Base32 (https://www.crockford.com/base32.html).

Crockford's Base32 encoding relies on using 32 of the available ASCII characters rather than all 128. This includes A through Z and 0 through 9 but leaves out lots of the special characters (like the forward slash) as well as I, L, O, and U. While the first three are left out due to potential confusion (I and l could be confused with 1, and O could be confused with 0), the third is left out for another interesting reason: profanity. It turns out that by leaving out the U character, it's actually less likely that you'll end up with an English-language profanity in your identifiers.

With that said, you might have noticed something else puzzling: why did we bother to leave out L? After all, the uppercase form can't be confused with anything; however, it could be confused in the lowercase form (with 1). The reason is that this format has a single canonical form, made up of the uppercase letters (less those mentioned) and 0–9, but it is more accommodating of mistakes when decoding a variety of inputs. In this case, rather than simply saying that L is an invalid character, this algorithm will assume that it was mistaken (in its lowercase form) for the digit 1 and treat it that way. This case insensitivity applies more generally (e.g., a is treated as A) and applies to other potentially confused characters such as O and o (which will be treated as 0). In other words, this format is exceedingly friendly toward mistakes and is designed so that it can do the right thing based on the assumption that those mistakes will continue to occur.

Finally, Crockford's Base32 encoding treats hyphens as optional, meaning we have the flexibility of introducing hyphens for readability purposes if we want. This means that we could have the ID abcde-12345-ghjkm-67890, which would be canonically represented as ABCDE12345GHJKM67890 in Crockford's Base32.

In short, Crockford's Base32 encoding satisfies quite a large number of the criteria outlined in section 6.2: it's easy to use, easy to make unique, provides reasonably high information density (32 choices or 5 bits per ASCII character), easy to make unpredictable, and, most importantly, very readable, copyable, and shareable thanks to its accommodating and flexible decoding process. Now we just have a few more issues to address.

6.3.4 Checksums

One of the key requirements listed in section 6.2.6 is the ability to distinguish between an identifier that is missing (e.g., it was never created or was deleted) and one that could never possibly exist, which would mean that there was clearly a mistake in the identifier. One easy way to do this is by including some form of integrity check as part of the identifier. This integrity check typically takes the form of some fixed number of checksum characters at the end of the identifier that is derived from the rest of the content of the identifier itself. Then, when parsing the identifier, we can simply recalculate the checksum characters and test whether they match. If they don't, then some part of the identifier has been corrupted and it's considered invalid.

Crockford's Base32 has a simple algorithm included based on a modulo calculation. In short, we treat the value as an integer, divide it by 37 (the smallest prime number greater than 32), and calculate the remainder of the value. Then we use a single Base37 digit (and the specification includes 5 additional characters for checksum digits) to denote the remainder value.

6.3.5 Resource type

While we've focused primarily on the unique part of the identifier, it's also very valuable to be able to know the type of the resource from its identifier. In other words, being told a resource has an ID of abcde-12345-ghjkm-67890 is not very useful unless you're also told the *type* of resource involved (so that you can decide what RPC to call or URL to visit to retrieve the resource, for example). One common solution to this is to prefix the ID with the name of the collection involved, such as `books/abcde-12345-ghjkm-67890`. By doing this, we can take that identifier, know what type of resource it's talking about, and do useful things with it. By using a forward slash as the separator, we end up with a full identifier that would fit in an HTTP request (e.g., `GET /books/abcde-12345-ghjkm-67890`). There are plenty of other options available (e.g., using a colon character, resulting in an ID like `book:abcde-12345-ghjkm-67890`); however, given the friendly relationship with HTTP and usefulness in standard URLs, a forward slash with the collection name tends to be a great fit.

6.3.6   *Hierarchy and uniqueness scope*

Now that we've decided that we'll use the collection name as part of the identifier (e.g., `books/1234` rather than just `1234`), this leads to a new question: how does hierarchy work in an identifier? For example, if we have both `Book` resources and `Page` resources (with pages belonging to books), do we express that hierarchical relationship in the identifier or do we leave each as their own top-level resource? In other words, would `Page` resources have an identifier like `pages/5678` (top-level resources) or `books/1234/pages/5678` (representing hierarchical relationships in the identifier)?

The answer is that hierarchical relationships are very useful and should be used when appropriate, but there is a specific set of scenarios in which they make sense (and many where hierarchy is *not* a good choice). Too often, API designers rely on hierarchical relationships as an expression of *association* between two resources rather than ownership, which can become problematic. For example, we might say, "Book 1 is currently on Shelf 1" and end up with resource identifiers that look like `shelves/1/books/1`. Unfortunately, since books tend to move between shelves over time, we'll want to change the identifier to reflect this move. And, as you might guess, this flies right in the face of the permanence requirements we defined in section 6.2.3.

While it might be perfectly reasonable to make it a rule that "books shall never move between shelves" (in which case this identifier would be perfectly reasonable), this kind of behavioral restriction isn't really necessary. Instead, we should simply recognize that a book's current position on a shelf is a mutable attribute of the book itself and store the `shelfId` as a property of the `Book` resource.

When exactly *does* it make sense to use hierarchical identifiers? In general, APIs should only rely on hierarchical relationships when they represent true *ownership* of one resource over another, specifically focused on the cascading characteristics of the relationship. This means that we should layer resources underneath other resources when we want things like cascading deletion (if you delete the parent, it deletes the children) or cascading security rules (set security rules on the parent and they flow downward to the children). And obviously, as we noted previously, resources should not be capable of moving from one parent to another. For example, while `Books` might move between `Shelves`, `Pages` typically won't move between `Books`. This means that we'd identify a `Page` resource as `books/1/pages/2` rather than just `pages/2`.

Additionally, in cases where we rely on hierarchical identifiers to express an owner-ship relationship, it's important to remember that the child resource (the page) only ever exists within the context of its parent (the book). That means that we can never talk about page 2 alone because it leads to the obvious question: page 2 of what book? In practical terms, this means that the identifier of a page always includes the identi-fier of the parent resource.

This leads to a slightly more subtle question, but one that's still pretty important: can we have multiple pages all with the ID "2"? For example, can we have both books/1/pages/2 and books/9/pages/2? This particular example should hopefully make the answer to this an obvious yes. After all, lots of books have a second page. Since the parent resources are different and the identifier is the combination of the two in a hierarchical relationship, while these two identifiers are *similar* (as they both end in "pages/2"), the two strings are completely different and these two pages belong to entirely different books (in this example, book 1 and book 9).

Now that we have an idea of what a good identifier might look like, let's look at some of the lower-level technical details involved in creating and working with identi-fiers that align with these expectations.

6.4 Implementation

So far we've explored characteristics of identifiers and some of the specifics, but there are quite a few of the deeper technical details we need to formalize, which is the focus of this section. Let's start by looking at something straightforward and fundamental to an identifier: how big it is.

6.4.1 Size

How long should a given identifier be? While we could simply say it varies over time (i.e., the length of the identifier might grow as more are created), that can make things quite complicated for people using the API who might be storing these identifi-ers in their databases, so it's generally a good idea to provide some predictability on the space requirements for these identifiers and simply choose a fixed size for how long they'll be.

In this case, we have a few different options depending on our needs. Addressing the simplest option first, we may only need identifiers that are unique across a single resource type. In other words, it might be perfectly fine to have both book 1 and author 1, since we have the different resource types to distinguish between the two 1's. In this case, we probably only need around 64 bits worth of storage space (similar to using a single 64-bit integer in a relational database like MySQL). Using Crockford's Base32, we have a total of 32 choices (or 5 bits) per ASCII character, which means we can probably get away with 12 total characters for the identifier (providing 60 bits for our identifier). When serializing (and de-serializing) this, we will need one more char-acter for the checksum digit, meaning 13 characters in total, leading to identifiers like books/AHM6A83HENMP~ (or books/ahm6a83henmp~ or books/ahm6-a83h-enmp~ using lowercase and potential hyphens as separators for readability).

In some other cases, we may need identifiers that are globally unique—not just across resource types or even across this single API, but across all resources everywhere. To accomplish this, we should probably aim to have at least the same number of possible identifiers as standard UUIDs (universally unique identifiers), which is a 128-bit ID represented by 32 hexadecimal digits. Since 6 of those bits are reserved for metadata about the ID, this leaves 122 bits for the identifier value. Using Crockford's Base32, we would need around 24 characters, which would give us a 120-bit identifier. Combine this with one additional checksum digit for a total of 25 characters, leading to identifiers that might look like books/64s36d-1n6rv-kge9g-c5h66~ (remember, the hyphens are optional and can technically be placed anywhere, and all the letters are case insensitive).

As we'll learn later when we talk about aliases, we may want to introduce a leading "0" character to distinguish between identifiers and aliases, which would add one extra character to our regular IDs. With all that behind us though, it's time to discuss an important but subtle (and thus far assumed) issue: who makes IDs.

6.4.2   Generation

We've talked quite a bit about the format and data type that an identifier should take; however, there's been a running assumption that these are just random identifiers, and we've said nothing about how to actually create them. Let's start by looking at an important aspect of this: origin.

ORIGIN

Before we talk about how to generate these identifiers, we should first talk about who should actually create them. In short, it's worth noting that allowing users of an API to choose their own identifiers is a very dangerous thing and should be avoided.

For starters, this can lead to frustration and confusion when the name has been used at some point in the past. Since our requirement of permanence (section 6.2.3) means identifiers must never be reused (even after being deleted), a user who wants to recreate a resource might be confused by getting an error message about an ID collision when they are certain a resource with that ID doesn't exist (and it might not exist now, but it did at some point in the past). While this can be mitigated with a sufficiently large set of available IDs, humans are particularly bad at choosing random values from a given set.

Next, when API users want to choose their own identifiers, they tend to make poor decisions, for example, by putting personally identifiable information into the identifier itself. In other words, someone might create a book with an identifier of pad(base32-Encode("harry-potter-8")) (equivalent to D1GQ4WKS5NR6YX3MCNS2TE05===), which, obviously, the author would want to keep secret from the world. However, this can be difficult because most systems don't treat IDs (even Base32-encoded ones) as secret information. Instead, identifiers are commonly treated as opaque, random pieces of data to be used however is most convenient. This means that they're generally considered safe to store in log files and share with anyone. This includes showing these IDs on big dashboards around the office, highlighting potential errors or statistics for individual resources. If an API allows user-chosen identifiers, there may come a day where a large customer (or a government) demands that some IDs be kept secret, which may be exceptionally difficult (or even impossible) to accomplish.

Finally, one of our last requirements of identifiers is that they are unpredictable (see section 6.2.5). While it's certainly possible that the users of your API will have a background in cryptography or pseudo-random number generators, as we noted before, that's generally not the case. As a result, asking users to choose their own identifiers can be problematic. In the best case, it can be annoying if required ("Why can't you just come up with an ID for me?"), but in the worst case it can be dangerous, even if this is an optional feature. In particular, this creates an opportunity for users to generate predictable identifiers, making them an easy attack target for security mistakes.

PSEUDO-RANDOM NUMBER GENERATORS

Just like with most programming problems, we have several different ways to go about generating random identifiers. One option is to use a cryptographically secure random byte generator (e.g., Node.js's `crypto.randomBytes()` function) and convert that into Crockford's Base32 (using, for example, Node.js's `base32-encode` package). Another option would be to use a random choice algorithm to choose a set number of characters from Crockford's Base32 alphabet. Neither of these is necessarily right or wrong, just different.

The former focuses on the number of bytes involved in the randomly chosen identifier (choosing an ID as it will be stored in the database) while the latter cares more about the user-facing identifier (choosing an ID as a user will actually see it). So long as you do the math ahead of time, knowing how many characters you want your bytes to represent or how many bytes your chosen characters will need reserved in your database, either one is reasonable.

The math itself is pretty simple, since we're just converting between 8-bit bytes and 5-bit characters. This means that for each byte of data in an ID, the 8 bits of each of those bytes must be represented by characters capable of holding 5 bits. In short, this means base32Length == Math.ceil(bytes * 8 / 5).

For illustration purposes, let's look at how to generate a random identifier focused on bytes-first.

Listing 6.1 Generating a random Base32-encoded identifier

```
const crypto = require('crypto');
const base32Encode = require('base32-encode');

function generateId(sizeBytes: number): string {
  const bytes = crypto.randomBytes(sizeBytes);
  return base32Encode(bytes, 'Crockford');
}
```

Here, sizeBytes is the number of bytes in the ID.

Start by generating some random bytes.

Return the Crockford Base32 encoding.

Now that we know how to generate an ID, we need to be sure that this ID isn't in use (and also wasn't ever in use in the past). Let's look briefly at how we might do this.

6.4.3   Tomb-stoning

As we learned in the section about identifier permanence, it's critical that identifiers be used no more than one time across the life span of an API. This means that even after a resource has been deleted, we can't reuse that same identifier. There are lots of ways to do this, some requiring more storage space than others.

One simple option is to rely on the idea of *soft deletion* (addressed in chapter 25). In this design pattern, rather than actually deleting a resource and its data entirely ("hard deletion"), we could simply mark the resource as deleted. Then, from the perspective of our identifier generation code, we simply continue generating random values until we come across a value that's not yet taken, checking our database along the way to ensure the ID is actually available. While this pattern can be useful regardless of whether we're concerned about tomb-stoned identifiers, it suffers from the age-old problem of unpredictable execution time that will statistically only get worse as more and more identifiers are created and the set of available IDs gets used up. That said, with a 120-bit identifier, the key space is about the same size as the number of bacterial cells in existence on the planet. This means that choosing the same one twice is sort of like picking one bacterial cell from all of those on the planet and then randomly picking that exact same one again. In other words, running into a collision should be exceptionally rare.

In cases where relying on the soft deletion pattern doesn't make sense (perhaps the data involved is significant and you must purge it for some reason, for example regulatory requirements), you have lots of other options. For example, you can store just the identifiers that have been taken in a hash-map somewhere or hold onto a Bloom filter and add IDs to that filter as they start being used. That said, collisions are still best avoided by using a sufficiently large identifier relative to the number of resources you'll be creating and using a reliable and cryptographically secure source of randomness to generate your identifiers.

6.4.4   Checksum

As noted in section 6.3.4, calculating a checksum is as simple as treating our byte value as an integer and using the modulo 37 value as the checksum value. This means we divide the number by 37 and use the remainder as the checksum. Sometimes, however, code speaks a bit louder than words. Note that we'll rely on the BigInt type for handling large integers that might result from a byte buffer of arbitrary length.

Listing 6.2   Calculating a Base32 checksum value

```
function calculateChecksum(bytes: Buffer): number {
  const intValue = BigInt(`0x${bytes.toString('hex')}`);
  return Number(intValue % BigInt(37));
}
```

Start by converting the byte buffer into a BigInt value.

Calculate the checksum value by determining the remainder after dividing by 37.

Additionally, we'll need a way to encode this checksum value as a string (rather than just the numeric value). To do this, we can build on the standard Base32 alphabet with five additional characters: *, ~, #, =, and U (this also includes u when parsing the values due to the case insensitivity of Crockford's Base32). This way, any value that results from our checksum calculation (which will range from 0 to 36) will have a character value to use in the identifier.

Listing 6.3   Using the Base37 alphabet to choose a checksum value character

```
function getChecksumCharacter(checksumValue: number): string {
  const alphabet = '0123456789ABCDEFG' +
                   'HJKMNPQRSTVWXYZ*~$=U';
  return alphabet[Math.abs(checksumValue)];
}
```

Define the alphabet (Base32 plus the five additional characters).

Return the character at position checksumValue.

At this point, you may be wondering, "Okay, so I have a checksum character. Now what?" Quite simply we can append this character to the end of our Base32-encoded identifier when displaying identifiers to users, and when identifiers are provided we can rely on this checksum character being correct. Let's start by updating the generateId function to include the checksum character.

Listing 6.4   Generating a Base32 identifier with a checksum character

```
const crypto = require('crypto');
const base32Encode = require('base32-encode');

function generateIdWithChecksum(sizeBytes: number): string {
  const bytes = crypto.randomBytes(sizeBytes);
  const checksum = calculateChecksum(bytes);
  const checksumChar = getChecksumCharacter(checksum);
  const encoded = base32Encode(bytes, 'Crockford');
  return encoded + checksumChar;
}
```

Calculate the checksum and get the correct checksum character.

Return the Base32 serialized identifier with the checksum character appended.

On the other end, we should parse all incoming identifiers as two pieces: the identifier itself and the checksum character. If we check the checksum character and it turns out to be incorrect, that doesn't mean that the checksum was calculated incorrectly. It actually means that there was probably a typo or other mistake in the identifier itself, and we should reject the identifier as invalid. To see how this might work, listing 6.5 implements a `verifyIdentifier` function that returns a Boolean value of whether a given identifier should be considered valid.

Listing 6.5   Verifying a Base32 identifier based on its checksum value

```
function verifyId(identifier: string): boolean {      Split the identifier into
  const value = identifier.substring(                 two pieces: the value and
    0, identifier.length-1);                ←─┐       the checksum character.
  const checksumChar = identifier[identifier.length-1];
  const buffer = Buffer.from(                          Decode the Base32 value
    base32Decode(value, 'Crockford'));      ←─┘       into its raw bytes.
  return (getChecksumCharacter(calculateChecksum(buffer))
    ➡    === checksumChar);                 ←──── Return whether the calculated checksum
}                                                 value is equal to the provided one.
```

Now that we've covered how to calculate and verify checksum values, let's move on to how all of this works from a data store perspective.

6.4.5   *Database storage*

For all our talk about not using auto-incrementing integers, most databases out there recommend this and have optimized quite a bit for it, which leads to the obvious question: if we use this new-fangled random Base32-encoded identifier, how should we store it so that our databases don't fall over from exhaustion or confusion?

First, we have to decide what exactly will need to get stored in the database. Obviously the identifier itself will need to be stored, but what about the checksum character? This value (and any other metadata that we may have encoded into the identifier when handing it to users) should *not* be stored in the database. Instead, we should always calculate that value on the fly as a verification step on incoming IDs (and append it dynamically on outgoing IDs). If we ever have to make changes to the algorithm used in calculating the checksum value, it'll be a great relief to know we won't have to go through and rewrite every entry in our database to reflect the new checksum character.

Now that we've decided the only piece of data to store is the actual identifier, we need to consider how exactly we'll store that. There are lots of different options for how we store this data, but we'll discuss three different ones, starting with the simplest: strings.

Many databases (particularly key-value storage systems) are very good at using string values as identifiers. If you happen to be using one of those, then storing the identifiers of your resources becomes incredibly simple: you simply store the string representation of your resource identifier as it appears to your customers (after removing the checksum character, of course). This is basically as straightforward and simple as it gets, so if you can get away with this option, go for it. Also keep in mind that Crockford's Base32 encoding preserves sorting order, which means that we shouldn't have any weirdness where sorting in the database acts differently than sorting on the client side.

Unfortunately, not all databases are as good at storing (and indexing) string values as others. Further, when storing the string representation of an identifier you're actually wasting space (since each 8-bit character only represents 5 bits of actual data). With this in mind, we can always go with the lowest level available: storing raw bytes. Many databases are quite good at using raw bytes fields as identifiers. For those types of databases, we can rely on the raw bytes data type (for example, MySQL calls this `BINARY`) for our primary key, enforcing uniqueness constraints and adding indexes that make single-key lookup queries fast and simple.

Finally, if we choose the size of an identifier properly, we can size it so that it will fit nicely inside a common integer type (e.g., 32 or 64 bits). If possible, this is probably the best option because almost all databases are exceptionally good at storing and indexing numeric values. To do this, we simply take the bytes represented by our identifier and treat them as representing an integer, which we saw how to do when learning how to calculate the checksum value for a given ID (e.g., `byteBuffer.readBigInt64BEInt(0)`). Using an integer as the underlying storage format is likely the most commonly supported option, as it will fit with almost all database systems out there.

6.5 *What about UUIDs?*

If you're not familiar with UUIDs, it's probably safe for you to skip this section. In short, UUIDs are common 128-bit identifier formats with a relatively long history (the specification, RFC-4122, is dated July 2005). UUIDs are basically a standard identifier format with quite a few handy features such as name spacing, lots of available IDs, and therefore a negligible chance of collisions. We won't get into all the details of UUIDs, but you may recognize them by their hyphenated format, where they look like the following: `123e4567-e89b-12d3-a456-426655440000`.

If you are aware of what UUIDs are and you've read this far and are thinking, "Why aren't we just using UUIDs and calling this a day?" then you're not alone (for one thing, it would've been much faster to just skip this chapter if that were the case). The short answer is that UUIDs are perfectly fine if you need them, but there are three points worth mentioning for why we didn't replace this entire chapter with the message, "Just use UUIDs."

First, UUIDs are large (122 total bits of identifier space, 128 bits of data in total), which is overkill for the most common scenarios. In cases like these, you might want to use an ID format that is shorter and easier to read if you know you won't be creating trillions of resources.

Next, UUIDs in their string format are not all that informationally dense since they rely only on hexadecimal (Base16) notation for transport. In short, this means that we're only carrying 4 bits of information per ASCII character, compared to the 5 bits per character we get by using Base32 encoding. While this might not be important for computers (after all, compression is pretty great these days), when we need to copy and share these over nontechnical means (e.g., share the identifier over the phone), high information density can certainly be a nice benefit.

Finally, UUIDs, by definition, don't come with their own checksum value. This means we don't have a great way to distinguish with certainty between a UUID that is missing versus a UUID that couldn't possibly have ever existed (and therefore likely has a typographical error present). In cases like this, it would make sense to introduce an additional checksum value to the identifier so that we can tell the difference between these two scenarios, perhaps using a similar method to how Base32 calculates a checksum character.

With all that in mind, it might make sense to use UUID values internally, but still present a Base32 string as the customer-facing identifier. This allows you to benefit from all of the features UUIDs provide, such as name spacing (UUID v3 and v5) or timestamp-based values (UUID v1 and v2), as well as the Base32 feature set, such as checksum values, readability, and higher information density.

You might generate a Base32-encoded UUID v4 (randomly generated) with a checksum character.

Listing 6.6   Generating a random Base32-encoded UUID v4

Generate the UUID (in this case, a random UUID v4) and store it in the buffer.

```
const base32Encode = require('base32-encode');       In this example, we use
const uuid4 = require('uuid/v4');                     the uuid package on NPM.

function generateBase32EncodedUuid(): string {        Start by allocating a 16-byte
  const b = Buffer.alloc(16);                         buffer to hold the UUID.
  uuid4(null, b);
  const checksum = calculateChecksum(b);              Calculate the checksum
  const checksumChar = getChecksumCharacter(checksum); and get the right Base37
  return base32Encode(b, 'Crockford') + checksumChar; checksum character.
}
             Return the Crockford Base32
             encoded value (and the checksum).
```

We might also want to do this if we have a database that is particularly good at storing and indexing UUIDs, rather than storing these as strings, raw bytes, or integers, as we noted in section 6.4.5.

6.6   *Exercises*

1 Design a new encoding and decoding scheme with a larger checksum size, chosen relative to the size of the identifier.
2 Calculate the likelihood of a collision for a randomly chosen 2-byte (16-bit) identifier. (Hint: See the birthday problem[1] as a guide.)
3 Design an algorithm to avoid collisions when using a 2-byte (16-bit) identifier that doesn't rely on a single counter. (Hint: Think about distributed allocation.)

---

[1] https://en.wikipedia.org/wiki/Birthday_problem

Summary

- Identifiers are the values used to uniquely point to specific resources in an API.
- Good identifiers are easy to use, unique, permanent, fast and easy to generate, unpredictable, readable, copyable, shareable, and informationally dense.
- From a customer's perspective, identifiers should be strings, using the ASCII character set, ideally relying on Crockford's Base32 serialization format.
- Identifiers should use a checksum character to distinguish between a resource that doesn't exist and an identifier that could never point to a resource (and is likely the result of a mistake).

Standard methods

This chapter covers

- What idempotence is and its side effects
- A tour of all standard methods (get, list, create, update, delete)
- An additional semi-standard method: replace
- Benefits and drawbacks of relying on standard methods

As we learned in chapter 1, one of the characteristics of a good API is predictability. One great way to build a predictable API is to vary only the resources available while keeping a consistent set of specific actions (often called methods) that everyone can perform on those resources. This means that each of these methods must be consistent in appearance and behavior down to the last detail; otherwise, the predictability is completely lost when the same action isn't identical when applied to multiple resources. This pattern explores the specific rules that should be followed when implementing these standard methods across the resources in an API.

7.1 Motivation

One of the most valuable aspects of a well-designed API is the ability for users to apply what they already know in order to more quickly understand how an API works. In other words, the less a user has to learn about an API, the quicker they can start using it to accomplish their own goals. One way to do this, expressed often in RESTful APIs, is to use a set of standard actions (or methods) on a variety of resources defined by the API. Users will still need to learn about the resources in the API, but once they've built up their understanding of those resources, they're already familiar with a set of standard methods that can be performed on those resources.

Unfortunately, this only works if each of the standard methods is truly standardized, both across the API as a whole as well as more generally across the majority of web APIs. Luckily, the REST standard has been around for quite some time and has laid the groundwork for this level of web API standardization. Based on that, this pattern outlines all the standard methods and the various rules that should be applied to each of them, taking quite a lot of inspiration from the REST specifications.

7.2 Overview

Since our goal is to drive more consistency and end up with a more predictable API, let's start by looking at the list of proposed standard methods and their overall goals, shown in table 7.1.

Table 7.1   Standard methods overview

Name	Behavior	Example
Get	Retrieves an existing resource	`GetChatRoom()`
List	Lists a collection of resources	`ListChatRooms()`
Create	Creates a new resource	`CreateMessage()`
Update	Updates an existing resource	`UpdateUserProfile()`
Delete	Removes an existing resource	`DeleteChatRoom()`
Replace	Replaces an entire resource	`ReplaceChatRoom()`

While these methods and their descriptions might seem quite straightforward, there is actually a large amount of information missing. And when information is missing, this leads to ambiguity. This ambiguity ultimately leads to a wide range of interpretation of how each method should act, leading to the same "standard" method acting completely different across different APIs or even different resources in the same API.

Let's look closely at a single method for an example: delete. The behavior description in table 7.1 says that this method removes an existing resource. In other words, we might expect that if a resource was created and a user deletes it, we should get the equivalent of a 200 OK HTTP response code and go on our merry way. But what if the resource doesn't exist yet? Should the response still be OK? Or should it return a 404 Not Found HTTP error?

Some might argue that the intent of the method is to remove the resource, so if the resource no longer exists, then it has done its job and should return an OK result. Others argue that it's important to distinguish between a result (the resource no longer existing when the method is executed) and the behavior (the resource was specifically removed by this method being executed), and therefore trying to remove a resource that doesn't exist should return a Not Found error, indicating that the resource does not exist now, but it also did not exist when this method was executed.

Further, what if the resource does exist but the user trying to execute the method does not have access to the resource? Should the result be a 404 Not Found HTTP error? Or a 403 Forbidden HTTP error? Should these error codes differ depending on whether the resource actually exists? Ultimately, this subtle design choice is meant to prevent an important security problem. In this case, if an unauthorized user attempts to retrieve a resource, they can determine whether the resource truly doesn't exist (by receiving a 404 Not Found response) or whether the resource does exist, but they just don't have access to it (by receiving a 403 Forbidden response). By doing so, it's possible for someone with no access permissions whatsoever to probe a system for the resources that exist and potentially target them later for attack.

There is no good reason for every API designer to re-answer these questions over and over. Instead, the guidelines in this chapter provide some standard answers that ensure consistency (and prevent security leaks or other issues) across standard methods in a way that will grow gracefully as an API expands over time. But rather than just stating a bunch of rules, let's explore these types of nuanced and subtle issues in the next section.

7.3   *Implementation*

Before we get into the specifics of each standard method, let's begin by exploring the cross-cutting aspects that apply to all standard methods, starting with an obvious question: is it a hard requirement that all resources must support all standard methods? In other words, if one of my resources is immutable, should the resource still support the update standard method? Or if it's permanent, should it still support the delete standard method?

7.3.1   *Which methods should be supported?*

Since the goal of standardizing a set of methods is all about driving consistency, it may seem a bit curious that this question is even up for discussion. In other words, it might seem hypocritical that there's an entire chapter on implementing a set of standard behaviors in the exact same way, only to then allow some resources to simply opt out of implementing the methods at all. And that's a fair point, but when it comes down to it, practicality is still a critical component of API design, and there's simply no way to escape the real-life scenarios where certain resources might not want to support all standard methods. In short, not every standard method is required for each resource type.

Some scenarios are different from others though, and it'll become important to distinguish between cases where a method shouldn't be supported entirely (e.g., returning the equivalent of a 405 Method Not Allowed HTTP error) and cases where a method is simply not permitted on this specific instance (returning the equivalent of a 403 Forbidden HTTP error). What should never happen though, is a scenario where an API simply omits a specific route (e.g., the update method) and returns a 404 Not Found HTTP error whenever someone attempts to use that method on a resource. If an API were to do this, the implication is that the *resource* doesn't exist, which isn't true: it's the method that technically doesn't exist for that resource type.

What are the rules when deciding whether to support each standard method? While there are no firm requirements, the general guideline is that each standard method should exist on each resource unless there is a good reason for it not to (and that reason should be documented and explained). For example, if a resource is actually a singleton sub-resource (see chapter 12), the resource is a singleton and exists only by virtue of its parent existing. As a result, only the get and update standard methods make any sense; the rest can be ignored entirely. This is also an example of a case where the method fundamentally doesn't make sense and as a result should return the equivalent of a 405 Method Not Allowed HTTP error.

In other cases, certain methods might not make sense for a specific instance of a resource but still make conceptual sense for the resource type. For example, if a storage system has a "write protection" flag on a specific directory that prevents modifications on resources living inside that directory, the API should still support the standard methods (e.g., update and delete) but return an error when someone attempts to perform those actions on the resource if they're not currently permitted. This scenario also covers resource types that might be considered permanent (i.e., should never be deleted) or immutable (i.e., should never be modified). Just because they are permanent and immutable now does not mean they will never be in the future. As a result, it makes the most sense to implement the complete set of standard methods and simply return a 403 Forbidden error code whenever anyone attempts to modify or delete them.

Now that we have some guidelines on when to define which methods, let's look at one of the core assumptions of standard methods: a lack of side effects.

7.3.2 *Idempotence and side effects*

Since a critical piece of standard methods is their predictability, it should come as no surprise that standard methods should do exactly what they say they'll do and nothing more. Put simply, standard methods should not have any side effects or unexpected behavior. Further, some methods have a specific property called *idempotence*, which indicates whether repeating the same request (with the same parameters) multiple times will have the same effect as a single request. Breaking the assumptions generally held about this property on specific methods can lead to disastrous consequences, such as data loss or corruption.

Determining what is acceptable and not breaking the no-side-effects rule can be complicated, as many APIs have scenarios where extra behavior is required, beyond that indicated by just a simple standard method, and often it can seem as though the standard method is the right place for that behavior to live. This can lead to even more confusion when the extra behavior is subtle or doesn't really change any meaningful state, so much so that we might still consider the method idempotent.

What constitutes a side effect? Some are obvious, for example in an email API, creating an email and storing the information in a database would not be considered a side effect. But if that standard create method also connected via SMTP to a server to send that email, this would be considered a side effect (and therefore avoided as part of the standard create method).

What about a request counter, where every time you retrieve a resource it increments a counter to keep track of how many times it has been retrieved via a standard get method? Technically, this means this method is no longer idempotent as state is changing under the hood, but is this really such a big problem? The complicated answer is it depends. Does the counter updating have a performance implication where the request will be significantly slower or vary more than it otherwise would? What happens if updating the counter fails for any reason? Is it possible to have an error response where the resource retrieval fails simply because the counter had a technical issue that prevented it from being updated?

Ultimately, as we'll learn in chapter 24 with defining a versioning policy, your judgment of what constitutes a side effect is a bit open to interpretation. While the blatant side effects (such as connecting to third-party or external services or triggering additional work that may cause the standard method to fail or result in a partially executed request) should be avoided at all costs, some of the more subtle cases might make sense for an API given consumer expectations.

Now that we've covered the general aspects of standard methods, let's dig into each method and explore some of what we'll need to consider for each one, starting with the read-only methods first and continuing with the rest.

7.3.3   Get

The goal of the standard get method is very straightforward: the service has a resource record stored somewhere and this method returns the data stored in that record. To accomplish this, the method accepts only a single input: the identifier of the resource in question. In other words, this is strictly a key-value lookup of the data stored.

Listing 7.1   An example of the standard get method

```
abstract class ChatRoomApi {
  @get("/{id=chatRooms/*}")
  GetChatRoom(req: GetChatRoomRequest): ChatRoom;
}
```

The standard get method always retrieves a resource by its unique identifier.

The result of a standard get method should always be the resource itself.

```
interface GetChatRoomRequest {
  id: string;
}
```

As with most methods that don't actively alter the underlying data, this method should be idempotent, meaning you should be free to run it multiple times and, assuming no other changes are happening concurrently, the result should be the same each time. This also means that this method, like all standard methods, should not have any noticeable side effects.

While there is plenty more to discuss about a standard get method, such as retrieving specific resource revisions, we'll leave these topics for later discussion in specific future design patterns. For now, let's move on to the next read-only standard method: list.

7.3.4 List

Since the standard get method is exclusively a key-value lookup, we obviously need another mechanism to browse the available resources, and the list standard method is just that. In a list method, you provide a specific collection that you need to browse through and the result is a listing of all the resources belonging to that collection.

It's important to note that the standard list method is different from the standard get method in its target: instead of asking for a specific resource, we instead ask for a list of resources belonging to a specific collection. This collection might itself belong to another specific resource, but that's not always the case. For example, consider the case where we might have a set of ChatRoom resources, each of which contains a collection of Message resources. Listing ChatRoom resources would require targeting the chatRooms collection, whereas listing the Message resources for a given ChatRoom would target the messages collection, belonging to the specific ChatRoom.

Listing 7.2 An example of the standard list method

```
abstract class ChatRoomApi {
  @get("/chatRooms")                                    When listing resources belonging to a
  ListChatRooms(req: ListChatRoomsRequest): ListChatRoomsResponse;    top-level collection, there is no target!

  @get("/{parent=chatRooms/*}/messages")
  ListMessages(req: ListMessagesRequest): ListMessagesResponse;
}
                                              When listing resources belonging to a
interface ListChatRoomsRequest {              subcollection of a resource, the target is
  filter: string;                             the parent resource (in this case, the
}                                             ChatRoom resource).

interface ListChatRoomsResponse {
  results: ChatRoom[];
}

interface ListMessagesRequest {
  parent: string;
```

```
    filter: string;
}

interface ListMessagesResponse {
    results: Message[];
}
```

While the concept of listing a set of resources might seem just as simple as the standard get method, it actually has quite a lot more to it than meets the eye. While we won't address everything about this method (e.g., some aspects are covered in future design patterns, such as in chapter 21), there are a few topics worth covering here, starting with access control.

ACCESS CONTROL

While it doesn't make sense to go into too much detail, there is an important aspect worth covering: how should the list method behave when different requesters have access to different resources? Put differently, what if you want to list all the available ChatRoom resources in an API but you only have access to see some of those resources? What should the API do?

It's obviously important that API methods are consistent in their behavior, but does that mean that every response must be the same for every requester? In this scenario, the answer is no. The response should only include the resources the requester has access to. This means that, as you'd expect, different people listing the same resources will get different views of the data.

If possible, resources could be laid out to minimize scenarios like these (e.g., ensure single-users resources have a separate parent), leading instead to simple 403 Forbidden error responses when listing resources that are secured from the requester; however, there is simply no avoiding the fact that there will be times when a user has access to some items in a collection but not all.

RESULT COUNTS

Next, there is often the temptation to include a count of the items along with the listing. While this might be nice for user-interface consumers to show a total number of matching results, it often adds far more headache as time goes on and the number of items in the list grows beyond what was originally projected. This is particularly complicated for distributed storage systems that are not designed to provide quick access to counts matching specific queries. In short, it's generally a bad idea to include item counts in the responses to a standard list method.

If some sort of result count is absolutely necessary, or the data involved in the collection is guaranteed to remain small enough to handle counting results without any extreme computation burden, it's almost always more efficient to use some sort of estimate and rely on that to indicate the total number of results rather than an exact count. And if the count is an estimate rather than an exact count, it's also important that the field be named for what it is (e.g., resultCountEstimate) to avoid potential confusion about the accuracy of the value. To leave breathing room for the unexpected, if you decide that result counts are both important and feasible, it's still a good idea to name the field as an estimate (even if the value is an exact count). This means that if you need to change to estimates in the future to alleviate the load on the storage system, you're free to do that without causing any confusion or difficulty for anyone. After all, an exact count is technically just a very accurate estimate.

SORTING

For similar reasons, applying ordering over a list of items is also generally discouraged. Just like showing a result count, the ability to sort the results is a common nice-to-have feature, particularly for consumers who are rendering user interfaces. Unfortunately, allowing sorting over results in a standard list method can lead to even more difficulty than displaying result counts.

While allowing sorting might be easy to do early on in the life cycle of an API, with relatively small amounts of data it will almost certainly become more and more complicated as time goes on. More items being returned in a list requires more server processing time to handle the sorting, but, most importantly, it's very difficult to apply a global sort order to a list that is assembled from several different storage backends (as is the case in distributed storage systems). For example, consider trying to consolidate and sort 1 billion items spread across 100 different storage backends. This is a complicated problem to solve with static data in an offline processing job (even if each data source sorts its smaller portion of the data first) but even more complex for a rapidly changing data set like a live API. Further, executing this type of sorting on demand each time a user wants to view their list of resources can very easily result in overloaded API servers.

All in all, this tiny little feature tends to add a significant amount of complexity in the future for relatively little value to the API consumer. As a result, just like a total result count, it is generally a bad idea.

FILTERING

While ordering and counting the items involved in a standard list method is discouraged, filtering the results of that method to be more useful is a common, and therefore encouraged, feature. This is because the alternatives to applying a filter (e.g., requesting all items and filtering the results after the fact) are exceptionally wasteful of both processing time and network bandwidth.

When it comes to implementing filtering, there is an important caveat. While it can be tempting to design a strictly typed filtering structure to support filtering (e.g., with a schema for the various conditions, as well as "and" and "or" evaluation conditions), this type of design typically does not age very well. After all, there's a good reason SQL still accepts queries as simple strings. Just like enumerations, as seen in chapter 5, as we expand the functionality or different types available for filtering, clients are required to upgrade their local schemas in order to take advantage of these changes. As a result, while filtering is encouraged, the best choice of data type for conveying the filter itself is a string, which can then be parsed by the server and applied before returning results, either by passing the parsed filter to the storage system if possible, or directly by the API service. This topic is discussed in much more detail in chapter 22.

So far, we've focused on reading data out of an API. Let's switch gears and look at how we get data into an API using the standard create method.

7.3.5 *Create*

Neither the standard get method (section 7.3.3) nor the standard list method (section 7.3.4) is of any use unless there is some data in the API. And the primary mechanism to get data into any API is to use a standard create method. The goal of the standard create method is simple: given some information about a resource, create that new resource in the API such that it can be retrieved by its identifier or discovered by listing resources. To see what this might look like, an example of creating `ChatRoom` and `Message` resources is shown in listing 7.3. As you can see, the request (sent via a HTTP `POST` method) contains the relevant information about the resource, and the resulting response is always the newly created resource. Additionally, the target is either the parent resource, if available, or nothing more than a top-level collection (e.g., `"/chatRooms"`).

Listing 7.3   An example of the standard create method

In both cases, the standard create method uses the POST HTTP verb.

```
abstract class ChatRoomApi {
  @post("/chatRooms")
  CreateChatRoom(req: CreateChatRoomRequest): ChatRoom;

  @post("/{parent=chatRooms/*}/messages")
  CreateMessage(req: CreateMessageRequest): Message;
}

interface CreateChatRoomRequest {
  resource: ChatRoom;
}

interface CreateMessageRequest {
  parent: string;
  resource: Message;
}
```

The standard create method always returns the newly created resource.

While the concept behind creating resources is simple, there are few areas worth exploring in more detail as they're a bit more complicated than meets the eye. Let's start by taking a brief look at how we identify these newly created resources.

IDENTIFIERS

As we learned in chapter 6, it's usually best to rely on server-generated identifiers for newly created resources. In other words, we should let the API itself choose the identifier for a resource rather than attempting to choose one ourselves. That said, there are many cases where it makes more sense to let the consumer of the API choose the identifier (e.g., if the API is being used by a mobile device that intends to synchronize a local versus remote set of resources). In those types of scenarios, it is perfectly acceptable to allow consumer-chosen IDs; however, they should follow the guidelines provided in chapter 6.

If you must provide a resource identifier at the time it's being created, this should be done by setting the ID field in the resource interface itself. For example, to create a ChatRoom resource with a specific identifier, we would make an HTTP request looking something like POST /chatRooms { id: 1234, ... }. As we'll see later on, there's an alternative to this with the semi-standard replace method, but since not all APIs are expected to support that method, it's probably best to focus on setting identifiers as part of a standard create method.

CONSISTENCY

Years ago, it was almost guaranteed that every bit of data you create would be stored in a single database somewhere, usually a relational database service like MySQL or PostgreSQL. Nowadays, however, there are many more storage options that scale horizontally without falling over as the data set grows. In other words, when you have too much data for the database as it's configured, you can simply turn on more storage nodes and the system will perform better with the larger data size.

These systems have been a miraculous cure for the plague (and gift) of enormous data sets and extraordinarily large numbers of requests, but they often come with their own set of trade-offs. One of the most common is related to consistency, with *eventual consistency* being a common side effect of the seemingly infinite scalability. In eventually consistent storage systems, data is replicated around the system over time, but it usually takes a while to arrive at all the available nodes, leading to a world where data is updated but hasn't been replicated everywhere right away. This means you may create a resource but it might not show up in a list request for quite some time. Even worse, depending on how routing is configured, it might be possible that you create a resource but then get an HTTP 404 Not Found error when you attempt to retrieve that same resource via a standard get method.

While this might be unavoidable depending on the technology being used, it should absolutely be avoided if at all possible. One of the most important aspects of an API is its transactional behavior, and one of the key aspects of that is *strong consistency*. This means, in short, that you should always be able to immediately read your writes. Put differently, it means that once your API says you've created a resource, it should be created in every sense of the word and available to all the other standard methods. That means you should be able to see it in a standard list method, retrieve it with a standard get method, modify it with a standard update method, and even remove it from the system with a standard delete method.

If you find yourself in a position where you have some data that cannot be managed in this way, you should seriously consider using a custom method (see chapter 9) to load the data in question. The reason is pretty simple: APIs have expectations about the consistency of standard methods but, as we'll see in chapter 9, custom methods come with none of those expectations. So rather than having an eventually consistent `CreateLogEntry` method, consider using a custom import method such as `ImportLogEntries`, which would explain to any potential users that the results are eventually consistent across the system. Another option, if you can be certain when the data replication across the system is complete, would be to rely on long-running operations, which we'll explore in more detail in chapter 10.

Now that we have some idea of the subtleties involved in creating new resources, let's look at how we modify existing resources with the standard update method.

7.3.6   *Update*

Once a new resource is loaded into an API, unless the resource is itself immutable and intended to never be changed, we'll need a straightforward way to modify the resource, which leads us to the standard update method. The goal of this method is to change some existing information about a single resource, and as a result it should avoid side effects, as noted in section 7.3.2.

The recommended way to update a resource relies on the HTTP `PATCH` method, pointing to a specific resource using its unique identifier and returning the newly modified resource. One key aspect of the `PATCH` method is that it does partial modification of a resource rather than a full replacement. We'll explore this in much more detail, as there's quite a bit to discuss on the topic (e.g., how do you distinguish between user intent of "don't update this field" versus "set this field to blank"), but for now the key takeaway is that a standard update method should update only the aspects of a resource explicitly requested by the API consumer.

Listing 7.4   **Example of the standard update method**

```
abstract class ChatRoomApi {
  @patch("/{resource.id=chatRooms/*}")          ◁──┐  The standard update method uses
  UpdateChatRoom(req: UpdateChatRoomRequest): ChatRoom;  the HTTP PATCH verb to modify only
}                                                        specific pieces of the resource.

interface UpdateChatRoomRequest {
  resource: ChatRoom;
  // ...        ◁────────┐  We'll learn how to safely
}                        │  handle partial updates of
                         │  resources in chapter 8.
```

The standard update method is the perfect place to modify an existing resource, but there are still some scenarios where updates are best done elsewhere. Scenarios like transitioning from one state to another are likely to be accomplished by some alternative action. For example, rather than setting a `ChatRoom` resource's status to archived, it's much more likely that an `ArchiveChatRoom()` custom method (see chapter 9) would be used to accomplish this. In short, while an update method is the standard mechanism to modify an existing resource, it is far from the only way to accomplish this.

7.3.7 Delete

Once a resource has outlived its purpose in an API, we'll need a way to remove it. This is exactly the purpose of the standard delete method. Listing 7.5 shows how this method might look for deleting a ChatRoom resource in an API. As you'd expect, the method relies on the HTTP DELETE method and is targeted at the resource in question via its unique identifier. Further, unlike most other standard methods, the return value type here is an empty message, expressed as void in our API definition. This is because the successful result of a standard delete method is to have the resource disappear entirely.

Listing 7.5 The standard delete method

```
abstract class ChatRoomApi {
  @delete("/{id=chatRooms/*}")
  DeleteChatRoom(req: DeleteChatRoomRequest): void;
}

interface DeleteChatRoomRequest {
  id: string;
}
```

The standard delete method uses the HTTP DELETE verb to remove the resource.

The result is an empty response message rather than an actual response interface.

IDEMPOTENCE

While this method is also very straightforward in purpose, there is a bit of potential confusion about whether this is considered idempotent and how to handle requests to delete already deleted resources. Ultimately, this comes down to a question of whether the standard delete method is more result focused (declarative) or action focused (imperative). On the one hand, it's possible to picture deleting a resource as simply making a request to declare that your intent is for the resource in question to no longer exist. In that case, deleting a resource that has already been deleted should be considered a success due to the simple fact that the resource is gone after the request finished processing. In other words, executing the standard delete method twice in a row with the same parameters would have the same successful result, therefore making the method idempotent, shown in figure 7.1.

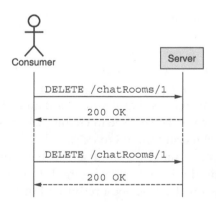

Figure 7.1 A declarative view on the standard delete method results in idempotent behavior.

On the imperative side, it's possible to picture the standard delete method as requesting that an action be taken, that action being to remove the resource. Therefore, if the resource does not exist when the request is received, the service is unable to perform the intended action and the request would result in a failure. In other words, attempting to delete the same resource twice in a row might result in a success the first time but a failure the second time, shown in Figure 7.2. As a result, a delete method behaving this way would *not* be considered idempotent. But which option is right?

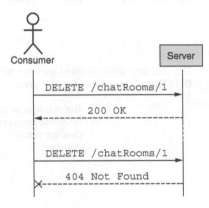

Figure 7.2   Imperative view of the standard delete method results in non-idempotent behavior.

While there are lots of declarative APIs out there (e.g., Kubernetes), resource-oriented APIs are generally imperative in nature. As a result, the standard delete method should behave in the non-idempotent manner. In other words, attempting to delete a resource that doesn't exist should result in a failure. This can lead to lots of complications when you're worried about network connections getting snapped and responses being lost, but we'll explore quite a bit more about repeatability for API requests in chapter 26.

Finally, let's look at a semi-standard method that's related to our implementation of the standard update method called the standard replace method.

7.3.8   *Replace*

As we learned in section 7.3.6, the standard update method is responsible for modifying the data about existing resources. We also noted that it relied exclusively on the HTTP PATCH method to allow updating only pieces of the resource (which we'll learn far more about in chapter 8). But what if you actually want to update the entire resource? The standard update method makes it easy to set specific fields and control which fields are set on the resource, but this means that if you're unfamiliar with a field (e.g., it was added in a future minor version, as we'll see in chapter 24), it's possible that the resource will have a value that you don't intend to exist.

For example, in figure 7.3 we can see a consumer updating a ChatRoom resource, attempting to set the description field using the HTTP PATCH method. In this case, if the consumer wanted to erase all the tags on the ChatRoom resource but the client

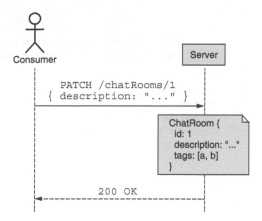

Figure 7.3 The standard update method modifies the remote resource but does not guarantee the final content.

didn't know about the tags field, there's no way for the client to accomplish this! So how do you handle it?

The semi-standard replace method's goal is exactly that: replace an entire resource with exactly the information provided in this request. This means that even if the service has additional fields that aren't known about yet by the client, these fields will be removed given that they weren't provided by the request to replace the resource, shown in figure 7.4.

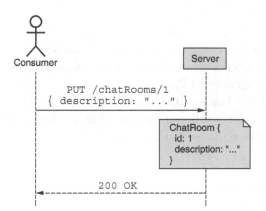

Figure 7.4 The standard replace method ensures the remote resource is identical to the request content.

To accomplish this, the replace method uses the HTTP PUT verb rather than the PATCH verb targeted at the resource itself and provides exactly (and exclusively) the information meant to be stored in the resource. This full replacement, compared to the specific targeted modification provided by the standard update method, ensures that the remote copy of a resource looks exactly as expressed, meaning clients need not worry whether there are additional fields lingering around that they weren't aware of.

Listing 7.6   Definition of the standard replace method

```
abstract class ChatRoomApi {
  @put("/{resource.id=chatRooms/*}")
  ReplaceChatRoom(req: ReplaceChatRoomRequest):
      ChatRoom;
}

interface ReplaceChatRoomRequest {
  resource: ChatRoom;
}
```

Unlike the standard update method, the replace method relies on the HTTP PUT verb.

Similar to the standard update method, the replace method returns the newly updated (or created) resource.

This leads to a potentially confusing question: if we can replace the content of a resource with exactly what we want, can't we just use that same mechanism to replace a non-existing resource? In other words, can this magical replace standard method actually be a tool for creating new resources?

The short answer is yes: this replacement tool can be used to create new resources, but it should not be a replacement itself for the standard create method because there are cases where API consumers may want to create a resource if (and only if) the resource doesn't already exist. Similarly, they may want to update a resource if (and only if) the resource already *does* exist. With the standard replace method, there's no way to know whether you're replacing (updating) an existing resource or creating a new one, despite the ultimate success of the method either way. Instead, you only know that what was once stored in the place for a specific resource is now set to the content provided when making the replace request.

Further, as you might guess, using the standard replace methods to create resources means the API must support user-chosen identifiers. As we learned in chapter 6, this is certainly possible and acceptable in some cases but should generally be avoided for a variety of reasons (see section 6.4.2).

And with that, we've explored the key standard methods that will make up the lion's share of the interaction for most resource-oriented APIs. In the next section we'll briefly review what this looks like when we put it all together.

7.3.9   *Final API definition*

Shown in listing 7.7 is a collection of all the standard methods we've talked about so far: create, get, list, update, delete, and even replace. The example follows those from earlier, with ChatRoom resources and child Message resources.

Listing 7.7   Final API definition

```
abstract class ChatRoomApi {
  @post("/chatRooms")
  CreateChatRoom(req: CreateChatRoomRequest): ChatRoom;

  @get("/{id=chatRooms/*}")
  GetChatRoom(req: GetChatRoomRequest): ChatRoom;
```

```
  @get("/chatRooms")
  ListChatRooms(req: ListChatRoomsRequest): ListChatRoomsResponse;

  @patch("/{resource.id=chatRooms/*}")
  UpdateChatRoom(req: UpdateChatRoomRequest): ChatRoom;

  @put("/{resource.id=chatRooms/*}")
  ReplaceChatRoom(req: ReplaceChatRoomRequest): ChatRoom;

  @delete("/{id=chatRooms/*}")
  DeleteChatRoom(req: DeleteChatRoomRequest): void;

  @post("/{parent=chatRooms/*}/messages")
  CreateMessage(req: CreateMessageRequest): Message;

  @get("/{parent=chatRooms/*}/messages")
  ListMessages(req: ListMessagesRequest): ListMessagesResponse;
}

interface CreateChatRoomRequest {
  resource: ChatRoom;
}

interface GetChatRoomRequest {
  id: string;
}

interface ListChatRoomsRequest {
  parent: string;
  filter: string;
}

interface ListChatRoomsResponse {
  results: ChatRoom[];
}

interface UpdateChatRoomRequest {
  resource: ChatRoom;
}

interface ReplaceChatRoomRequest {
  resource: ChatRoom;
}

interface DeleteChatRoomRequest {
  id: string;
}

interface CreateMessageRequest {
  parent: string;
  resource: Message;
}

interface ListMessagesRequest {
  parent: string;
```

```
    filter: string;
}

interface ListMessagesResponse {
  results: Message[];
}
```

7.4   *Trade-offs*

Whenever you rely on standards rather than entirely custom-designed tooling, you give up some flexibility. And unfortunately, unless your scenario happens to be an exact match for which the standard was designed, this trade-off can occasionally be painful. But in exchange for those mismatches, you almost always get quite a few benefits.

In some ways, it's a bit like shopping for clothing. That new shirt in size medium might be just a bit too big, but size small is definitely way too small, and you're left feeling like your options are either to lose weight or have a bit of a baggy shirt. But the benefit is that this shirt costs about $10 instead of $100 because it's able to be mass produced. This is sort of the scenario we find ourselves in with resource-oriented APIs and standard methods.

These standard methods are not perfect for every situation. They will have some mismatches from time to time, for example where things aren't really created but more brought about into existence. And you could absolutely design a custom method to handle these unique scenarios (see chapter 9). But in exchange for relying on standard methods rather than an entirely custom RPC-based API, you get the benefit of those using your APIs being able to quickly learn and understand the different methods without having to do much work. And even better, once they've learned how the methods work (in case they hadn't already known that from working with RESTful APIs in the past), they know how the methods work across all of the resources in your API, effectively multiplying their knowledge at the drop of a hat.

In short, standard methods should (and likely will) get an API 90% of the way there. And for the rest of the scenarios, you have custom methods to explore in the next chapter. But the standardization of using a set of common building blocks is so useful that it's almost always the best choice to try building the API using standard methods and only expanding to custom options when some unforeseen scenario makes them absolutely necessary.

7.5   *Exercises*

1   Is it acceptable to skip the standard create and update methods and instead just rely on the replace method?
2   What if your storage system isn't capable of strong consistency of newly created data? What options are available to you to create data without breaking the guidelines for the standard create method?
3   Why does the standard update method rely on the HTTP PATCH verb rather than PUT?

4 Imagine a standard get method that also updates a hit counter. Is it idempotent? What about a standard delete method? Is that idempotent?

5 Why should you avoid including result counts or supporting custom sorting in a standard list method?

Summary

- Standard methods are a tool to drive more consistency and predictability.
- It's critical that all standard methods follow the same behavioral principles (e.g., all standard create methods should behave the same way).
- Idempotency is the characteristic whereby a method can be repeatedly called with identical results on all subsequent invocations.
- Not all standard methods must be idempotent, but they should not have side effects, where invoking the method causes changes somewhere else in the API system.
- While it might seem counterintuitive, the standard delete method should not be idempotent.
- Standard methods do force a tight fit into a very narrow set of behaviors and characteristics, but this is in exchange for a much easier-to-learn API that allows users to benefit from their existing knowledge about resource-oriented APIs.

Partial updates and retrievals

This chapter covers

- Why we might want to update or retrieve only specific pieces of a resource
- How best to communicate the fields of interest to the API service
- How to handle individual items in complex fields, such as maps and interfaces
- Whether to support addressing individual items in a repeated field (e.g., arrays)
- Defining default values and handling implicit field masks
- How to deal with invalid field specifications

As we learned in chapter 7, it's important that we have the ability to update resources in piecemeal fashion rather than always relying on full replacement. In this pattern, we explore using *field masks* as a tool to update only the specific fields we're interested in for a given resource. Further, we also cover how to apply field masks to the same problem in the opposite direction: retrieving only specific fields on a resource. While slightly less common, the ability to retrieve parts of a resource rather than the entire thing is particularly important in memory-sensitive applications, such as IoT devices consuming API output.

8.1 Motivation

In this design pattern, we'll actually be exploring two sides of the same coin, both related to different views of a resource. In any API that we've discussed so far, we've only ever spoken of resources as self-contained, atomic units. Put differently, we've never considered the possibility that a resource could be broken apart into its constituent attributes and manipulated on a more granular level. Despite the fact that this makes some of the programming paradigms much simpler (e.g., you never have to worry about managing part of a resource), it can become problematic when you want to be more specific and expressive about your intent when interacting with the API. Let's look at two specific instances of new functionality prohibited by this restriction.

8.1.1 Partial retrieval

In most APIs, when you retrieve a resource you either get the entire resource or an error, all or nothing. For many of us, this isn't really a problem. After all, what else could we want? But what if the resource in this API grows to be quite large with hundreds of different fields and subfields? Or what if the computing resources available to the device making the request are significantly limited, for example on a very small IoT device? Or what if the connectivity is limited in speed or extraordinarily expensive? In these scenarios, controlling exactly how much information is returned from the API suddenly becomes quite important.

And while this might seem like something only ever needed for enormous resources or very restrictive conditions, keep in mind that while a single new field might only take up a tiny bit more space (and therefore more cost, bandwidth, and memory on the device), when listing many of these resources that little bit of space is multiplied by the number of items. As you might imagine, suddenly what was once a small number can actually grow quite large as the number of resources grows and time rolls on. Ultimately, there is quite a lot of value in providing the ability for users of an API to retrieve only the pieces of a resource (or list of resources) that they're truly interested in.

8.1.2 Partial update

The logic behind supporting partial updates is a bit more complicated—and less focused on the performance factors and issues like hardware limitations. Instead of worrying about reading specific pieces of a resource, we're more concerned with being able to do fine-grained targeting and modification of specific fields. So why exactly would we care about this type of more specific updating? Isn't it important to ensure a resource looks exactly the way we want rather than a collection of lots of little changes?

First, there's a concern about data consistency. As the user of an API, when we only have the broad brush of a standard replace method (see chapter 7) to paint with, we're forced to update all the fields on a resource rather than just the one we're interested in. Overwriting fields that don't really matter to us, without the proper consistency checks available, can potentially cause data loss, which is obviously not a good thing at all. To see how this might happen, imagine the following code snippets (shown in table 8.1) being run by two separate clients against the same resource.

Table 8.1   An example sequence of code run by two users that could present problems

User 1 API call	User 2 API call
```let chatRoom = GetChatRoom({ id: '1' });```	```let chatRoom = GetChatRoom({ id: '1' });```
```chatRoom.title = "My Chat!";```	```let desc = fetchRandomQuote();```
```chatRoom = ReplaceChatRoom({ chatRoom: chatRoom, });```	```chatRoom.description = desc;```
	```chatRoom = ReplaceChatRoom({ chatRoom: chatRoom, });```

If these two sequences were executed without any sort of consistency checks or locking, the end result is that only the final standard replace method matters. The first one, executed by user 1 might as well have never happened at all! And by looking at this, there's no great reason why these two updates should conflict at all. User 1 wanted to update the title of the ChatRoom resource, whereas user 2 only wanted to update the description field, which was completely separate. And even if we added in some consistency checks, the second standard replace method would fail and require a retry to ensure that the update was actually committed.

But there's more to this problem, and more ways to cause data loss. As we'll see in more detail in chapter 24, APIs rarely stay the same. Instead, they tend to evolve over time to support new features and fix bugs in existing ones. And one of the most common scenarios we end up relying on is the ability to add new fields to resources while still considering the new version backward compatible. But this can present quite a problem if your only mechanism to update resources is to replace them entirely and your local interfaces are not up to date with the complete (new) list of fields on a resource.

For example, let's imagine that we want to update the title of a ChatRoom resource, but in the time since we last updated our client library (when the only field we stored on the ChatRoom resource was a title field and the administrator), the service added a new description field. In this world, if someone previously set a description for the resource, it's possible that our standard replace method will end up clobbering that data and we end up, yet again, with data loss. To see what this looks like, listing 8.1

shows two different clients updating a `ChatRoom` resource. In the first, the code is up-to-date and is well aware of the new description field. In the latter, the code hasn't been updated in a while and has never heard of this description field.

Listing 8.1 Two different clients updating a single resource

```
> let chatRoom = latestClient.GetChatRoom({ id: '1' });
> chatRoom.description = 'Description!';
> ReplaceChatRoom({ chatRoom: chatRoom });
> console.log(chatRoom);
{
  id: '1',
  title: 'Old title',
  description: 'description'
}

> chatRoom = oldClient.GetChatRoom({ id: '1' });
> console.log(chatRoom);
{
  id: '1',
  title: 'Old title',
}
> chatRoom.title = 'New title';
> ReplaceChatRoom({ chatRoom: chatRoom });

> chatRoom = latestClient.GetChatRoom({ id: '1' });
> console.log(chatRoom);
{
  id: '1',
  title: 'New title',
  description: null
}
```

First, we use the "latest client" to update the description of the room.

If we use the old client to fetch the resource, the description field is entirely missing.

We then update the title with the old client without any issues.

However, now when we use the new client again, the description field has been erased!

While this might look scary and as though something is wrong, the truth is that the standard replace method is doing exactly what it's supposed to do. Recall that this method is designed specifically to make the remote resource look *exactly* like the resource specified in the request. That means removing the data from any fields that are missing, whether or not that was our intent.

In short, the goal of partial updates is to allow API consumers to be more specific about their intent. If they intend to replace the entire resource, they have the standard replace method at their disposal. If they intend to update only a single field, there should be a more fine-grained mechanism by which they can express this intent to update the resource. In this case, partial updates are a great solution.

8.2   Overview

To accomplish both of these goals (enabling partial retrievals and partial updates), we can actually rely on a single tool: the field mask. Fundamentally, a field mask is just a collection of strings, but these strings represent a list of fields that we're interested in on a given resource. When it comes time to retrieve a resource and we want to be more specific about which fields we'd like to retrieve, we can simply provide the field mask expressing which fields should be returned, shown in figure 8.1.

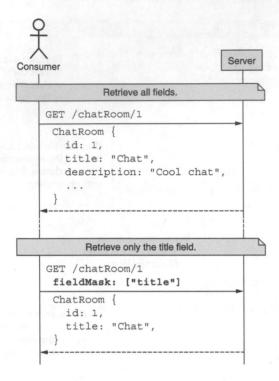

Figure 8.1   Using a field mask when retrieving a resource

And just as we can use a field mask to control which fields we're interested in retrieving, we can also rely on the same tool to control which fields a service should update on a resource. In this case, when updating a resource we can provide the list of fields we intend to update and ensure that only those specific fields are modified, shown in figure 8.2.

Further, since JSON happens to be a dynamic data structure, if the field mask itself is missing from a PATCH request, we can infer the field mask from the attributes present in the JSON object (shown in figure 8.3). While this can become far more complicated when dealing with dynamic data structures in our API, in most cases this field mask inference provides the most expected results.

This might seem simple, but there are quite a few edge cases and tricky scenarios that are far more complicated than they might seem. In the next section, we'll explore how to go about implementing support for field masks in an API.

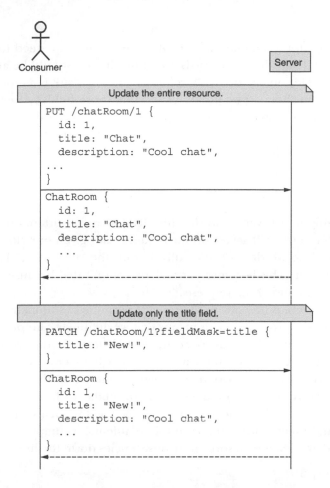

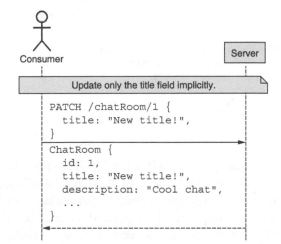

Figure 8.2 Replacing an entire resource versus updating a single field

Figure 8.3 Updating a single field using an implicit field mask, inferred from the data provided

8.3   Implementation

Now that we have a grasp on the high-level concept of field masks, we need to look at how they work in more detail. In other words, we know that we should be able to send this list of arbitrary fields on GET or PATCH requests and the result is a more specific update or retrieval. But how do we go about sending those fields? After all, a GET request doesn't accept a body, and a PATCH request should have the resource itself as the body of the request. Let's dig deeper into how we transport the field mask without causing any significant disruption to the standard requests that we defined in chapter 7.

8.3.1 Transport

While field masks certainly appear very powerful, they lead to an important question: how do we transmit them to the API server in our request? And given our close relationship with HTTP, how do we do so while still obeying the rules of HTTP and resource-oriented API design? This becomes particularly complicated because of two important constraints on GET and PATCH requests.

First, for GET requests, there is no body to the request permitted (and many HTTP servers will strip it out if one is provided). This means that we definitely cannot use the HTTP request body to indicate the fields we're interested in retrieving. Next, for PATCH requests, even though a body is obviously permitted (that's how we go about updating the resource itself), resource-oriented design dictates that the body of a PATCH request must be the resource representation being updated. In other words, while we technically *could* provide the field and the resource together in a single JSON representation, this would break quite a few of the fundamental assumptions of the standard update method and lead to all sorts of inconsistencies down the line.

Listing 8.2   Partial updates confusion caused by breaking HTTP PATCH method rules

```
PATCH /chatRooms/1 HTTP/1.1
Content-Type: application/json

{
  "chatRoom": {        ◁——   The ChatRoom resource in this case is not the
    "id": 1,                  body of the request, breaking the guidelines
    "title": "Cool Chat"      for a standard update method.
  },
  "fieldMask": ["title"]   ◁——   The FieldMask itself is alongside
}                                 the ChatRoom resource.
```

What can we do? There are two potential places besides the HTTP request body for our field masks: headers and query strings. While both of these technically work, it turns out that query parameters are quite a bit more accessible, particularly given that we can even modify these in a browser request, whereas headers are buried a bit deeper in the plumbing of HTTP, making them less accessible. As a result, query parameters are probably a better choice.

Unfortunately, there appears to be no specification for repeated query parameters, meaning how the repeated query string parameters are interpreted will depend on the HTTP server in use. For instance, consider the examples in table 8.2. As you can see, different servers handle these inputs differently, so it's important to rely on a library that will be consistent with the most common standard of using the same field multiple times, such as `?fieldMask=title&fieldMask=description`. Even though one of the alternatives (`fieldMask=a,b`) might seem more concise, this can present issues when we need to explore maps or nested interfaces (see section 8.3.5).

Table 8.2 Examples of how different systems handle multi-value query parameters

System	Expected format	Notes
PHP	`?fieldMask[]=a&fieldMask[]=b`	
Flask (Python)	`?fieldMask=a&fieldMask=b`	`request.args.to_dict(` `    flat=False)`
Spring (Java)	`?fieldMask=a&fieldMask=b`	
	`?fieldMask=a,b`	
Express (Node.js)	`?fieldMask=a&fieldMask=b`	

This means that we have to augment the request messages for both the standard update method and standard get method. As you can see, this is just a matter of adding a new `fieldMask` attribute on the request messages.

Listing 8.3 Example of standard get and update requests with field masks included

```
type FieldMask = string[];          ◁─────  A FieldMask type is nothing
                                            more than an array of paths.
interface GetChatRoomRequest {
  id: string;
  fieldMask: FieldMask;             ◁──┐
}
                                       We can simply add a
                                       fieldMask property to
interface UpdateChatRoomRequest {      the update and get
  resource: ChatRoom;                  request interfaces.
  fieldMask: FieldMask;             ◁──┘
}
```

Now that we know how to transport these field mask values in our API (while still adhering to HTTP and resource-oriented API standards), let's look more closely at the values each field mask entry contains, starting with maps and nested interfaces.

8.3.2 Maps and nested interfaces

So far, we've really only thought about flat resource data structures—that is, those with no nested value types whatsoever. As much as we might love the simplicity of that world, it's not necessarily reflective of reality, where we have values on resources that, themselves, are other interface types. Additionally, we may find ourselves in the scenario where a resource contains a field that is a map type, which is simply a collection of key-value pairs. This leads us to an interesting conundrum: does this idea of partial updates and retrievals extend inside nested structures? Or does it only apply at the very top level, effectively treating resources as completely flat structures?

The good news is that there is definitely a way to allow pointing to nested fields with field masks (both in nested static interfaces and in dynamic map-like values). The bad news is that this requires quite a lot of specificity and special escape characters in the field mask entries themselves. To see how this works, let's start with a simple list of rules that we can assemble into a powerful toolbox to address most scenarios. And don't worry, we'll look at examples in a moment.

1 Separate parts of a field specification must use a dot character (.) as a separator.
2 All fields of a nested message may be referred to using an asterisk character (*).
3 Map keys should always be strings.
4 All parts of a field specification (field names or map keys) that can't be represented as an unquoted string literal must be quoted using backtick characters (`).
5 A literal backtick character may be escaped by using two backtick characters (``).

If these rules have you terrified, just hang in there. The examples will make it much cleaner. To explore this unique problem space, let's start with an example, shown in listing 8.4. In this case, let's imagine our `ChatRoom` resource has both a `LoggingConfig` field as well as `settings` map field that might contain arbitrary key-value style data. Le's look at how we might go about addressing each of the various fields.

Listing 8.4   Adding a nested interface field and a dynamic map field

```
interface ChatRoom {
  id: string;
  title: string;
  description: string;
  loggingConfig: LoggingConfig;
  settings: Object;
}

interface LoggingConfig {
  maxSizeMb: number;
  maxMessageCount: number;
}
```

> Here we have a nested field, though it is a static structure with well-defined fields.

> The settings field is an arbitrary key-value map, with values of varying types.

To visualize how we might apply each of these rules, table 8.3 shows an example representation of the data in a `ChatRoom` resource, with an example of how we might address that single field as an entry in a field mask.

As you can see, there's a way to address each individual field in the resource using the rules. While most are pretty straightforward (e.g., `"description"` and `"settings .test.value"`, others are particularly ugly and might be confusing at first glance. For

Table 8.3 A resource representation with corresponding field mask entries for each field

ChatRoom resource	Field mask entry
{	"*"
"id": 1,	"id"
"title": "Chat Room",	"title"
"description": "Cool chat!"	"description"
"loggingConfig": {	"loggingConfig.*"
"maxSizeMb": 10,	"loggingConfig.maxSizeMb"
"maxMessageCount": 1000	"loggingConfig.maxMessageCount"
},	
"settings": {	"settings.*"
"1234": "abcd",	"settings.`1234`"
"`hello`": null,	"settings.```hello```"
"*": "star",	"settings.`*`"
"test.value": true	"settings.`test.value`"
"test": {	"settings.test.*"
"value": false	"settings.test.value"
}	
}	
}	

example, in cases where map keys might be interpreted as numeric values, we need to quote these in backticks. The same goes for cases where a dot character might be misinterpreted for a separator literal character (such as the case of "settings.test .value" and "settings.`test.value`" which could be easily confused). Finally, if backticks need to be used as literal characters, these should simply be doubled (wherever you need a `, just use ``).

By following these five rules for defining the format of a field mask, we should be able to address any nested field in a data structure, even if it has strange character literals (like dots, asterisks, or backticks).

However, this does leave out an important category of field types in resources: repeated fields or arrays. In the next section, we'll explore how we might address repeated fields in resources using field masks.

8.3.3   *Repeated fields*

We have a clear and simple way to address fields in nested interfaces and map fields, but what about repeated fields, such as lists of strings? What if the repeated field is a nested interface itself? How do we go about addressing the last name of all the authors of a given book? Luckily, there is a clear way to do this. But before we get to that, there's an important limitation that must be discussed first: addressing items in a repeated field by their index.

We're all familiar with how we address a single item in an array in our programming language of choice. Almost always, this is something like item[0] to get the first item in an array called item. While this is obviously a critical piece of functionality in a programming language, does it really make sense in a web API?

If we happen to be the only user of that API, or the resource we're addressing is completely immutable, *and* the index is a unique identifier or sorts, then maybe. But in almost every other scenario, this functionality in a web API can be misleading in more ways than one.

First, accessing an item by its index implies that this index is a unique identifier, when in most cases this is actually not the case. The index is an identifier *now*, but it's not a stable identifier in that it could very easily change over time, either by inserting an item before the item in question or by replacing the entire array value. Next, by using an index as an identifier of any sort, there's a clear implication of a stable ordering of this particular list. This means that the order of items in the list is guaranteed to remain consistent over time, even as new items are appended to the end of the list. These might seem like small implications, but maintaining them over time can become quite a burden, one that comes without much benefit.

Due to all of these issues, it really doesn't make much sense to be able to address items of a list individually by their index in a web API. If this sort of functionality is truly required, it's far more useful to rely on a map field (which has stable, true, local unique identifiers for its items) or a collection of sub-resources, each one having their own global unique identifier. And as a result, it's important that APIs do *not* support the ability to either retrieve or update a single item in a repeated field based on its index. In other words, a consumer should *never* have the ability to instruct the API to update or retrieve "the item at index 0" in a repeated field on a resource. This idea of the first item is completely meaningless unless the API guarantees all sorts of extra functionality that is incredibly burdensome to maintain over time.

Fortunately, this does not mean that we can have no interaction at all with items in repeated fields. On the contrary, there is one very useful thing we may want to do with these fields, and to accomplish this we'll certainly need a way to express that intent.

Let's imagine that our ChatRoom resource includes an administrator field of type User. We've learned how to get just the administrator's name (e.g., fieldMask=admin .name), but what if there are multiple administrators? How can we get just the names of each administrator?

Listing 8.5 Representation of a ChatRoom with multiple administrators

```
interface ChatRoom {
  id: string;
  title: string;
  description: string;
  administrators: User[];          ◄─┐  In this case, administrators
}                                     │  is a repeated field of User
                                      │  interfaces.
interface User {
  name: string;
  email: string;
  // ...
}
```

In this case we can rely, once again, on the asterisk to indicate the equivalent of a *for-each* loop of sorts. In other words, we can treat a prefix of `"administrators.*."` as a way of saying "For each administrator, provide only the fields listed." In this case, to retrieve only the name of an administrator, we could use a field mask value of `"administrators.*.name"`. However, remember that this additional function does not preclude us from asking for all of the administrators using the (simple) field mask of administrators.

Unfortunately, while this ability does enable us to select specific fields across items in a repeated field, it does not enable us to update these fields. The reason is based on the same reasons there is no way to address `"administrators[0]"`: the repeated field is not guaranteed to be stable, and it's therefore impossible to know which item in the list is intended to be updated with which value.

Listing 8.6 A (bad) example of attempting to update items in a repeated field by index

```
PATCH /chatRooms/1?fieldMask=administrators.*.name HTTP/1.1
Content-Type: application/json

{
  "administrators": [
    { "name": "New name for Index 0" },   ◄─┐  There's no guarantee that this
    { "name": "New name for Index 1" }      │  will replace the administrator
  ]                                          │  we're interested in without
}                                            │  strong consistency and
                                             │  ordering guarantees.
```

As you can see, if the order was not guaranteed or a new administrator was added and shifted the indexes around, there would be no certainty that the result would be as we intended. Rather than updating individual items in a repeated field, we instead must perform a full replacement on all repeated fields.

8.3.4 Default values

As we learned in chapter 5, the goal of a default value is to do "the right thing" for the user. This is because leaving something blank is the API user's way of expressing that they don't necessarily have an opinion on this aspect of the API and are trusting the

API to provide them with behavior that best suits most other users. In the case of field masks, the defaults differ only slightly for the standard method being used (standard get versus standard update).

In a standard get method, the default is almost always the complete list of fields available on a resource. That means that every field present on the interface for a resource should be returned unless a field mask is specified. This ensures that the standard get method that does support partial retrieval behaves in the same way as if partial retrieval wasn't supported at all (we explore this in more detail in section 8.4.1).

There is an exception to this guideline. In cases where a resource has fields which, for whatever reason, would cause a fundamentally worse user experience for API consumers, these fields should be removed from the default of the field mask being left unset. For example, let's imagine that a resource contains fields that are exceptionally large or would take so long to compute that the standard get method would take several minutes to return any results. In cases like this, it might make more sense to exclude these problematic fields from the default set of fields returned. This would mean that users who are interested in these fields would need to express their interest by explicitly specifying a field mask.

This scenario should be relatively uncommon, but it's critical that if a field does fall under this exception (that is, it will not be included by default and must be explicitly requested), the field documentation itself must include that fact. Without that indication somewhere in the documentation, it could lead to exceedingly confusing behavior and force API consumers to discover this fact only after trial and error, which is certainly not ideal.

This leads to one last scenario worth considering: what if we need to retrieve all the fields, but we'd rather not list each and every one of these? In other words, we don't want to follow the default of letting the API decide what fields we should guess. Instead, we want to specifically ask for every single field available, including those that might be large or difficult to compute. This also might include fields that have been added since we last updated our client code (see chapter 24). How can we do this?

The answer is actually pretty simple and straightforward: we should rely on a special sentinel value to indicate "everything"; in this case, that value is an asterisk ("*"). If this value is present in a field mask, all fields should be returned, regardless of whether any other fields are present as well.

Now that we've explored default values for partial *retrievals* of data, we need to switch gears a bit to decide what the default should be for partial *updates* of data via the standard update method. Unfortunately, when it comes to updating resources the default of all fields recommended for retrieval doesn't quite make sense; after all, if we provide all fields by default, then it's really more like a standard replace method than a standard update method. What should we do?

One convenient choice is to attempt to infer a field mask based on the data provided. In other words, we can go through the input data, and we only update fields if they have a value specified. In the next section, we'll explore this idea in more detail.

8.3.5 Implicit field masks

Unlike the default value for retrieving data, updating data requires a bit more thought and effort. This is because if we were to follow the same rules (default to all fields), we'd end up with a standard update method that actually behaves like a standard replace method (since it has to replace all fields). This leads us to an important question: what does an unset field mask mean on a standard update method (using an HTTP PATCH method)?

Most commonly, HTTP PATCH indicates an intent to update the resource with only the data provided in the body of the request. This brings us to an interesting option for the default value of a field mask in a standard update method: infer the field mask from the data provided. While this strategy might seem simple and obvious, this inference is incredibly powerful. So powerful, in fact, that it's likely to be the primary way in which users of an API actually benefit from field masks. How do we do this exactly?

This inference works by iterating through all the fields provided and keeping track of the path to that field. If the field itself has a value specified (in JSON or TypeScript this means that the value is not undefined), then we include that field path in the final inferred field mask.

Listing 8.7 Function to infer a field mask from a resource object

```
type FieldMask = string[];                              ←──  We begin by defining a FieldMask type
                                                              as an array of string field names.

function inferFieldMask(resource: Object): FieldMask {
  const fieldMask: FieldMask = [];                            We then iterate
                                                              through all the key-
  for (const [key, value] of Object.entries(resource)) {  ←  value pairs of the
    if (value instanceof Object) {                            resource object
      for (const field of inferFieldMask(value)) {  ←         provided.
        fieldMask.push(`${key}.${field}`);
      }                                                   We use recursion to find
    } else if (value !== undefined) {  ←                  the fields in the nested
      fieldMask.push(key);                                object and simply
    }                                                     prepend the original
  }                    If the value is set at all         field with a "." character
                       (including null), we               as a separator.
  return fieldMask;    consider it implicitly
}                      part of the field mask.
```

Using the code in listing 8.7, we can infer the user's intentions simply by looking at the data provided. In other words, if a user intends to only update a single field, they can imply that by simply providing only that field in the body of the request (e.g., PATCH /chatRooms/1 { "description": "New description" }) and we can infer that they meant to use that single field (["description"]) as the field mask.

It's important to note here that a value of null is not the same as leaving a field out of the request body. In other words, while a value of undefined in JavaScript or a missing field in JSON would indeed be left out of the inferred field mask, a value of null would actually show up in the field mask. As a result, setting a field to `null` (e.g., `PATCH /chatRooms/1 { "description": null }`) would result in the same field mask as our previous example (`["description"]`) and, similarly, end up with the value for the description field being set to the value specified, which, in this case, would be an explicit `null` value.

This is usually a perfectly acceptable pattern of behavior, but it can raise problems when we begin dealing with dynamic data structures, where the fields available on a resource can actually vary over time. Let's spend some time understanding how we can best handle dynamic data structures and the unique behavior they bring about.

8.3.6   *Updating dynamic data structures*

As we learned in chapter 5, static data structures are almost always easier to deal with. This is primarily due to the fact that they have only two different categories for values of fields: an actual value (e.g., `ChatRoom({ title: "Cool chat!" })`) and a `null` value (e.g., `ChatRoom({ title: null })`). On the other hand, dynamic data structures (such as maps) have a third category due to the fact that fields themselves may or may not be present: `undefined`. For example, as we saw in section 8.3.2, the settings field was a map that falls under this category. A key (e.g., `"test"`) could be either a value, an explicit `null`, or missing from the map entirely (which in JavaScript is considered equivalent to `undefined`).

This leads to a tricky situation. Let's imagine that the settings field is set to `{ "test": "value" }`. To change the value, we can rely on an implicit field mask: `PATCH /chatRooms/1 { "settings": { "test": "new value" } }`. Likewise, this will continue to work if we want to set the value to an explicit `null` value: `PATCH /chatRooms/1 { "settings": { "test": null } }`. But how do we go about removing the key entirely? Put differently, how do we go about setting the value to `undefined`?

Unfortunately, `undefined` is not part of the JSON specification, so using this value explicitly like we might in some JavaScript code simply won't work. Additionally, most other programming languages don't have a sentinel value for a missing key in a map. As a result, we'll need another mechanism to remove keys from dynamic data structures.

While it could be possible to use a special symbol to indicate undefined in our API, this is error prone and can introduce more complications later on. It also will either conflict with the range of JSON values or break the rules of the JSON specification. In short, this special flag to represent undefined is unlikely to be a very robust strategy.

Another option is to rely on full replacement of the field. That is, we would retrieve the resource, remove the offending key, and update the resource by replacing the entire map field. While this will certainly work (and we can avoid data consistency issues using freshness checks), it only works if we're updating a single field. If the entire resource is dynamic (as is the case in many web APIs for storage systems), this becomes more complicated as we're effectively using the standard replace method to make it function.

Instead, the next best solution is to rely on an explicit field mask with a missing value in the request body. In other words, we explicitly state that we'd like to update a specific field, but we omit that field entirely. For example, the request in listing 8.8 would ensure that the `"test"` key is removed from the settings field on a `ChatRoom` resource. Note that this isn't setting the value to `null`, but actually removing the value entirely.

> **Listing 8.8   Example method to remove a field from a dynamic data structure**

```
PATCH /chatRooms/1?fieldMask=settings.test HTTP/1.1
Content-Type: application/json

{}          ⟵┤  Since all that matters is that settings.test be equivalent to
                undefined, we don't have to provide any data at all!
```

Given this request, when it comes time to determine what to update, we will assign the input value to the resource's value (`resource["settings"]["test"] = input ["settings"]["test"]`), which in this case will be equivalent to undefined and have the desired result of removing the key from the dictionary. In other languages, it will be important to determine if the input had the indicated field present, and if not, explicitly remove the key. For example, it wouldn't be acceptable to use Python's `input.get('settings', {}).get('test')`, as this would result in a value of `None`. And setting the value to a Python `None` is not the same as removing the key from the Python dictionary.

This leads us to our final topic: what happens when you provide a field that doesn't exist?

8.3.7   *Invalid fields*

As we learned in section 8.3.6, specifying fields in a field mask that aren't present in the body of a request is a neat trick to support removing data from a dynamic data structure. However, what about cases where the underlying data structure isn't dynamic?

While it might be tempting to adopt the defensive coding strategy and throw some sort of error when a field is provided that can't possibly exist, this is unlikely to work very well. The primary reason for this is, as we'll see in chapter 24, it's quite common to add new fields and sometimes to remove them. As a result, it's not unbelievable that a requester might include a field that has existed in one version but no longer exists in the current version. In these cases, it's safer all around to simply treat all structures as though they're dynamic and never throw any sort of error when a field specified in a field mask isn't found in the request when updating or in the resource when retrieving.

In other words, whenever we have a field that isn't found, we treat its value as `undefined` and either update the data or return the result.

8.3.8   *Final API definition*

As we learned in section 8.3.1, we'll rely on the new `FieldMask` type (equivalent to a string array) to define two new fields on the standard get request and standard update request.

Listing 8.9   Final API definition

```
abstract class ChatRoomApi {
  @get("/{id=chatRooms/*}")
  GetChatRoom(req: GetChatRoomRequest): ChatRoom;

  @patch("/{resource.id=chatRooms/*}")
  UpdateChatRoom(req: UpdateChatRoomRequest): ChatRoom;
}

type FieldMask = string[];

interface GetChatRoomRequest {
  id: string;
  fieldMask: FieldMask;
}

interface UpdateChatRoomRequest {
  resource: ChatRoom;
  fieldMask: FieldMask;
}
```

8.4   *Trade-offs*

Partial updates and retrievals using field masks can be very powerful, but it's important to remember that the goal is still quite limited: to minimize unnecessary data transfer and allow fine-grained modification of API resources. Often, it can be tempting to consider field masks and partial retrievals in particular as SQL-like querying tools to fetch specific data from a resource that happens to have far more data than it otherwise should. While field masks may be used to accomplish this goal, they certainly should not.

In the cases where an API has lots of related data and needs a mechanism for users to retrieve specific data based on relationships between the different resources, field masks are an underpowered tool for the job. Instead, something like GraphQL is a far better fit, providing a powerful system for joining related data in an API, while also providing the ability to limit the resulting data using query formats that resemble field masks. And while we won't get into GraphQL in this book, if you find yourself needing this type of functionality, it's certainly worth looking at.

Let's look at a few other considerations worth exploring now that we've seen how partial retrievals and updates work using field masks.

8.4.1 *Universal support*

While it is a hard requirement to support partial updates for a standard update method (otherwise the method would really just be a standard replace method), it is not at all a requirement that every API must support partial retrieval. The reason for this is pretty simple: not every API has resources that are so large or complex that they merit supporting partial retrievals. Contrarily, even a small resource can benefit from allowing fine-grained control over what fields are updated on a resource, as that's more an issue of concurrency than resource size and complexity.

It is important to note, however, that if an API does decide to support partial retrieval, it should do so across the board rather than on a resource-by-resource basis. In other words, if an API ends up with a single resource that ends up requiring support for partial retrievals, the API should implement the functionality across all resources. The reason for this is aimed at consistency. The goal of a standard get method is to be consistent across resources, so introducing any variability that depends on which resource you're interacting with leads to surprises, resulting ultimately in a worse-off API for consumers.

8.4.2 *Alternative implementations*

It's also important to note that there are several other implementations available for supporting partial updates of resources with the HTTP PATCH method. For example, JSON Patch (RFC-6902; https://tools.ietf.org/html/rfc6902) is a fantastic option in the case where you need far more explicit and detailed control over the resource that's being modified. JSON Patch relies on a series of operations (sort of like operational transforms) that are applied sequentially to modify a JSON document. Rather than just deciding which values to set, JSON Patch provides advanced functionality such as the ability to copy values from one field to another (without first retrieving that value) or manipulating array values using indexes and the test operation to assert that the item at that index is indeed the intended item.

And JSON Patch is not the only other option. There's also JSON Merge Patch (RFC-7396; https://tools.ietf.org/html/rfc7396), which is a bit closer to the field mask implementation explored in this chapter, but it has its own list of quirks and is, itself, entirely based on an inferred or implicit field mask. As you might guess, this brings about issues with dynamic data structures when it comes time to distinguish between explicitly setting values to null and removing them from the structure entirely. Further, it's recursive for nested JSON objects (e.g., maps and nested interfaces) but not for repeated fields (e.g., arrays), leading to potential confusion for these richer data structures.

While many of these are great options, the idea of using field masks to specify the exact fields that should be retrieved or updated is simple enough for most to grasp quickly while still powerful enough to provide the necessary functionality to maintain pinpoint accuracy when retrieving or updating resources.

8.5   *Exercises*

1   Imagine a ChatRoom resource might have a collection of administrator users rather than a single administrator. What do we lose out on by using an array field to store these resources? What alternatives are available?

2   How do we go about removing a single attribute from a dynamic data structure?

3   How do we communicate which fields we're interested in with a partial retrieval?

4   How do we indicate that we'd like to retrieve (or update) all fields without listing all of them out in the field mask?

5   What field mask would we use to update a key "`hello.world`" in a map called settings?

Summary

- Partial retrieval is particularly important in cases where resources are large or clients consuming resource data have limited hardware.

- Partial updates are critical for fine-grained updates without worrying about conflicts.

- Field masks, which support ways to address fields, nested fields in interfaces, and map keys, should be used to indicate the fields that should be retrieved or updated.

- Field masks should not provide a mechanism to address items in array fields by their position or index in that field.

- By default, field masks should assume a value of *everything* for partial retrievals and an implicit field mask (where the fields specified are inferred based on their presence) for partial updates.

- If fields are invalid, they should be treated as though they do exist but have a value of undefined.

Custom methods

This chapter covers

- Why standard methods can't cover all possible scenarios
- Using custom methods for cases where side effects are necessary
- How to use stateless custom methods for computation-focused API methods
- Determining the target for a custom method (resource versus collection)

Often, there will be actions we need to perform on our API resources that won't fit nicely into one of the standard methods. And while these behaviors could technically be handled by the resource's standard update method, the behavioral requirements of many of these operations would be quite out of place for a standard method, leading to a surprising, confusing, and overly complex interface. To address this, this pattern explores how to safely support these actions on resources in a web API while maintaining a simple, predictable, and functional API using what we'll call *custom methods*.

9.1   *Motivation*

In most APIs, there will come a time when we need the ability to express a specific action that doesn't really fit very well in one of the standard methods. For example, what's the right API for sending an email or translating some text on the fly? What if you're prohibited from storing any data (perhaps you're translating text for the CIA)? While you can mash these actions into a standard method (most likely either a create action or an update action), at that point you're sort of bending the framework of these standard methods to accommodate something that doesn't quite fit. This leads to an obvious question: should we try to jam the behavior we want into the existing methods, bending the framework a bit to fit our needs? Or should we change our behavior into a form that fits a bit more cleanly within the framework? Or should we change the framework to accommodate our new scenario?

The answer to this depends on the scenario, but in this chapter we'll explore custom methods as one potential solution to this conundrum. Essentially, this goes with the third option where we change the framework to fit our new scenario, thereby ensuring that nothing is bent just to make things fit.

As you might guess, the concepts behind using custom methods are not complicated—after all, most RPC-based APIs use this idea all the time. The tricky part with custom methods lies in the details. When is it safe to use them? Are we really sure a standard method isn't an option? Can we parameterize a custom method call? The list goes on.

In this chapter, we'll explore custom methods and all of the details and nuance that they bring with them. But before we get into how custom methods work, let's take a moment to address the elephant in the room: do we really need to use custom methods?

9.1.1   *Why not just standard methods?*

While the standard methods we learned about in chapter 7 are often sufficient to do pretty much anything with an API, there are times where they feel not quite right. In these cases, it often *feels* as though we're following the letter of the law, but not the spirit of that law: having standard methods act sufficiently different from expectations, leading to surprise, and therefore not a very good API. In short, just because we *can* perform an action with a standard method doesn't mean that we *should* perform that action. But what determines this? Can we put anything more explanatory besides it feels wrong? Let's look at this by way of a concrete example: state changes.

Often, API resources can exist in one of several states. For example, an email might start out in a draft state, then move into a sent state, and possibly (if we're using some fancy email service) unsent. This is obviously one of those scenarios where we *could* use our standard update method, but it just doesn't seem quite right to do so.

Why exactly are state changes not a great fit for an update method? The first reason is pretty simple: most state changes are transitions of some sort or another, and as a result, transitioning to a new state (which happens to be stored in some state field) is fundamentally different from setting the value of a scalar field (e.g., setting the subject of the email). Because of this, setting the state to indicate this transition happening can be both confusing and surprising, neither of which makes for a good API.

Listing 9.1 Marking an email as sent using the standard update method

```
const email = GetEmail({id: 'email id here'});
UpdateEmail({id: email.id, state: 'sent'});
```

To start, an email's state is draft.

In this example, we send the email by updating its state field to sent.

As you can see, causing an email to be sent by updating a state property is a bit off-putting. This field *feels* like it should be managed by the API service itself rather than updated by the client. In short, treating a field as a mechanism by which we transition from one state to another can be pretty confusing. Further, it conflates the true purpose of the update method as it provides the ability to both update stored data as well as transition to a new state at the same time—two separate conceptual actions.

In addition to the confusion caused by updating a field to transition to a new state, we have a second potential issue having to do with side effects. As we learned in chapter 7, standard methods really should not do anything besides the specific action their name implies. In other words, a create method should create a new resource and do nothing else. Similarly, an update method should update a resource and nothing more. But often, state changes come with additional actions that need to be performed. For example, if we have an email message resource that we want to change from draft to sent, we also have to actually send the email to the recipients (otherwise, marking it as sent is effectively meaningless). And simply updating a state field to sent is a pretty subtle way to imply that you're going to talk to an SMTP server in order to send an email to some recipient.

The problem only expands from there. When we use a standard update method to perform actions with side effects such as these, we have to consider the fact that there are now potentially two different systems we need to communicate with in order to complete the update operation (shown in figure 9.1). First, for every update, no matter

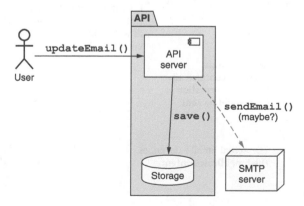

Figure 9.1 The API may need to communicate with multiple different systems for a single update.

what, we need to communicate with a storage system to update a database somewhere with the new information. Second, if the update happens to change an email resource's state from draft to sent, we also need to communicate with an email sending system (which must further communicate with a recipient's email service) to get the job done. What should be a simple "update the database" operation is now a messy chain of dependencies and potentially long-running background operations where failures could arise at any step.

To make things even worse, this means that, depending on the content being updated, the standard update method might either return a result immediately or delay awhile until the email sending has taken place. This leads to all sorts of confusion when a user is simply trying to update some content about their email.

It's important to note that there is nothing *technically* wrong with this diagram. Lots of API calls may communicate with lots of different services, and that's not necessarily a bad thing. The problem is that this diagram breaks the rules defined earlier about what standard methods should and should not do. As a result, the problem isn't about an API call that talks to multiple different systems; it's about a standard method (such as an update) talking to multiple different systems, triggering side effects, and taking on downstream dependencies. This makes an API fundamentally worse by blowing away our ability to rely on certain aspects of standard methods and instead making a standard method unpredictable and confusing.

Before we wrap this up, we have one more elephant to address in the room: why not rearrange our resources so that the actions we want to perform fit more closely with the expectations of standard methods? In this example, we might instead have `EmailDraft` resources and `Email` resources, where we don't transition between states but instead create a new `Email` resource based off an `EmailDraft` resource.

Listing 9.2   Arranging resources to fit with the standard methods

```
abstract class EmailApi {                                We always start by creating
  @post("/{parent=users/*}/emailDrafts")      <--------  mutable EmailDraft resources.
  CreateEmailDraft(req: CreateEmailDraftRequest): EmailDraft;

  @post("/{parent=users/*}/emails")           <--------  Creating an Email resource
  CreateEmail(req: CreateEmailRequest): Email;           would actually send the email
}                                                        as well. Email resources would
                                                         be immutable.
interface EmailDraft {          <--------  An EmailDraft
  id: string;                              resource contains all
  subject: string;                         the key information
  // ...                                   that would be sent.
}

interface Email {                          The actual Email references
  id: string;                              the EmailDraft content.
  content: EmailDraft;   <--------
}
```

While this is certainly acceptable, shuffles like these assume that relying only on standard methods is some sacrosanct principle of API design. In truth, standard methods are a means to an end; in this case, the goal is an operational, expressive, simple, and predictable API. When a design takes away from that, it is almost certainly better to adjust your tools to fit the needs of the API rather than the other way around.

What do we do instead? The obvious answer is to rely on a separate API call that is not a standard method (and therefore can have side effects) to isolate the functionality into a single place rather than overloading the existing standard methods. While this might seem pretty simple, as with most things in API design, the devil is in the details. Now that we've gone through why custom methods are necessary, in the next section we'll briefly go through what custom methods are and some common uses.

9.2 Overview

Custom methods are nothing more than API calls that fall outside the scope of a standard method and therefore aren't subject to the strict requirements that we impose on standard methods. They might look a bit different, as we'll see in the next section, but from a purely technical standpoint there is really nothing special about custom methods.

Standard methods offer us some fantastic building blocks to use with our APIs, but the cost for this very broad scope is the extensive collection of guidelines, rules, and restrictions of standard methods. Custom methods, on the other hand, have almost no restrictions whatsoever, meaning they are free to do whatever is best for the scenario rather than forcing the scenario to fit the structure and rules of a standard method.

This also comes with some downsides, particularly the fact that users of an API can't make as many assumptions about a custom method as they might with the list of standard methods. This is not to say that custom methods in an API should all be contradictory or inconsistent. On the contrary, custom methods should be consistent across an API. However, the point is that there are generally no hard and fast rules for custom methods out of the box. Instead, the choice is left to the API designer to decide on a set of rules and precedents, and then those rules should be consistent across that API.

While the concept of this pattern is simple (see listing 9.3 for an example custom method), the pattern becomes complicated quickly as we have to work through quite a few different scenarios and the nuance behind them. For example, if state changes require extra context or parameterization, how should that extra information be provided? What if the method operates on a collection of resources rather than a single resource? What about the case where there's no state involved at all?

Listing 9.3 **Example custom method launching a rocket**

```
abstract class RocketApi {
  @post("/{id=rockets/*}:launch")
```

Custom methods use the POST HTTP verb and a special ":" separator to declare the action itself.

```
    LaunchRocket(req: LaunchRocketRequest): Rocket;
}

interface Rocket {
  id: string;
  // ...
}

interface LaunchRocketRequest {
  id: string;
}
```

> Custom methods follow similar naming conventions to standard methods (<Verb><Noun>).

Now that we've seen what a custom method looks like and gone through the bigger picture of why we need these in the first place, let's get into those details of how custom methods work.

9.3   *Implementation*

In most ways, custom methods look just like standard methods. There are a few differences, one being the format of the HTTP request. While standard methods rely on a combination of the request path and the HTTP method to indicate the behavior of the method (e.g., PATCH on a resource always indicates an update standard method), custom methods can't rely on that same mechanism; the HTTP verbs are quite limited. Instead, custom methods have their own special format that puts the relevant information in the path of the request. Let's go through this format piece by piece, relying on the example shown in figure 9.2.

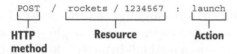

```
POST  /  rockets / 1234567  :  launch
```

HTTP   **Resource**   **Action**   Figure 9.2   HTTP request components for
method   a custom rocket launching method

First, the HTTP method for custom methods is almost always POST. It might make sense to have a custom method use the GET HTTP method, but it's far more likely that a singleton sub-resource (see chapter 12) will be a better fit. It also might make sense to rely on a DELETE method, but those examples are relatively rare.

While the resource path is identical to standard methods, there is one difference with the action at the very end of the path. To avoid any confusion about where the resource (or collection) stops and the custom action begins, it's critical that we don't reuse the forward slash character as a separator between these two key components (e.g., POST /rockets/1234567/launch). Instead, we can use the colon character (":") to indicate that the resource has ended and a custom action has begun. This might look a bit strange, but it's important to avoid any ambiguity, especially because the path is technically valid if we were to use a forward slash.

Finally, as shown in listing 9.3, the RPC name should follow the same naming convention of a verb followed by a noun, such as LaunchRocket or ArchiveDocument, just like any other standard methods. This is particularly important, especially the guidelines of avoiding using prepositions such as "with" or "for" (e.g., avoid custom methods like `CreateRocketForMars`), as these custom methods should be just as well formed as standard methods. In other words, custom methods are not a mechanism for parameterization of standard methods.

9.3.1 Side effects

Perhaps the largest difference between custom methods and standard methods is the acceptance of side effects. As we learned in chapter 7, the goal of standard methods is to be a limited mechanism to access and manipulate resource data. And one of the key principles of a standard method is that it does exactly what it says it does, without triggering other extra actions in the background that aren't core to what exactly the method is intended to do. In other words, if a method says it creates a resource, it should create that resource, but it also must *not* do anything else.

Custom methods have no such limitations. On the contrary: custom methods are exactly the right place to have actions with side effects. The reason for this is pretty simple: we have a set of expectations with standard methods about what they can and cannot do. Custom methods, by their very nature, are free of those limitations—all bets are off, so to speak. So side effects, such as sending emails, triggering background operations, updating multiple resources, and anything else you can imagine, are all on the menu.

For example, an email API will obviously need a mechanism for sending an email; however, relying on `CreateEmail` to both store the email in the system *and* send the email over SMTP is not an acceptable answer. Instead, `CreateEmail` might be used to create an email in a draft state, and then a custom `SendEmail` method could be used to do the work of talking to remote servers over SMTP and, only after the email has been sent successfully, transitioning the email into a sent state. Using this flow, shown in figure 9.3, means that the standard methods (in this case, the `CreateEmail` method) remains pure and simple, with one and only one job: save a record in a database somewhere. Then to do fancier, more complicated things (such as talking to remote SMTP servers), we rely on a custom method, which is free to perform whatever actions necessary to accomplish the goal of the method.

So far, we've hinted that custom methods can apply to both resources and collections just like standard methods, but this merits further exploration. Let's look at when it makes sense to use a resource-targeted custom method (e.g., the `SendEmail` example) versus a collection-targeted custom method.

9.3.2 Resources vs. collections

In our list of standard methods, some operate on a single resource (e.g., updating a resource) and others operate on a parent collection (e.g., listing resources), summarized in table 9.1. However, since custom methods are by definition customized to the circumstances, this may present a bit of a quandary when it comes to determining whether a custom method should operate on a single resource or a parent collection.

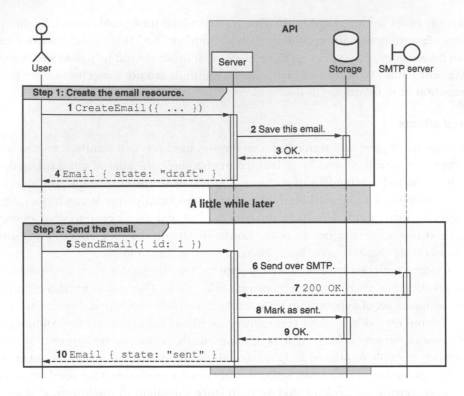

Figure 9.3   Sequence diagram demonstrating sending an email using custom methods

Table 9.1   Different aspects when importing and exporting data

Method	Target	HTTP equivalent
CreateEmail	Parent collection	POST /users/1/emails
ListEmails	Parent collection	GET /users/1/emails
GetEmail	Resource	GET /users/1/emails/2
UpdateEmail	Resource	PATCH /users/1/emails/2
DeleteEmail	Resource	DELETE /users/1/emails/2

For example, imagine we need to export all of the emails belonging to a single user (see chapter 23 for more on this pattern) or perform a single standard operation on a set of items (e.g., delete a bunch of emails with a single API call). Should these operations target the resource itself (e.g., POST /users/1:exportEmails) or the collection of resources (e.g., POST /users/1/emails:export). While technically there is no difference between these two, it's almost always a better choice to operate on a collection when there are multiple resources from that same collection involved, leaving the resource-targeted custom methods for operations involving just that single resource.

What about something like exporting all user information, including the set of emails? In this case, the focus of the custom method has shifted back to the parent resource and away from the collection of emails (they're still involved, just not the primary focus). As a result, this custom export method of an entire user's information would be better represented as POST /users/1:export.

Finally, what about a scenario where you're operating on a set of resources across multiple different parents? For example, perhaps we need to archive a set of emails that belong to a bunch of different users (e.g., users/1/emails/2 and users/2/emails/4). In this scenario, the same format would apply, with the caveat being that the parent identifier would be left as a wildcard. In other words, this operation as an HTTP request would look something like POST /users/-/emails:archive, relying on the hyphen character to indicate a wildcard and the body of the request to indicate which email IDs should be archived.

9.3.3 *Stateless custom methods*

So far, all of the custom methods in the examples have been attached to a specific target, either a resource itself or a collection and the parent resource. However, since custom methods technically can do whatever they want, there's a possibility that we haven't had to consider yet: what if the custom method doesn't have any state to handle and doesn't need to be attached to a resource or a collection?

This type of method, called a *stateless method*, is relatively common and can even become a critical piece of functionality as more and more restrictions on data storage enter the picture. For example, the different data privacy regulations, such as the General Data Protection Regulation (GDPR), impose some pretty specific rules about where data must live and how it must be stored. Requirements like these mean that having a stateless method that processes data on the fly and returns a result—notably without storing any of the data that was provided—is a valuable tool to add to the collection. And custom methods are an ideal way of handling requirements like these.

> **Listing 9.4 Stateless custom method to translate text**

```
abstract class TranslationApi {
  @post("/text:translate")
  TranslateText(req: TranslateTextRequest): TranslateTextResponse;
}

interface TranslateTextRequest {
  sourceLanguageCode: string;
  targetLanguageCode: string;
  text: string;
}

interface TranslateTextResponse {
  text: string;
}
```

In this case, "text" is sort of like a singleton sub-resource that has a stateless custom method called "translate" attached.

The request to translate text has no stored data whatsoever.

Similarly, the result has just the translated text and stores nothing.

Purely stateless methods are relatively rare. After all, many APIs will need to at least know the billing details to use to charge for the API request. As a result, it's quite common to have some parent resource that acts as a permission or billing container (e.g., a project, billing account, or organization) as the resource that's targeted with the custom method, attaching the otherwise stateless method to that containing resource. For example, translating text might not be something to give away for free, so an API might require a user to create a project resource that keeps track of billing details for all this translation going on.

Listing 9.5   Stateful custom method with a parent as an anchor

**In this case, we attach the custom method
to a parent project resource.**

```
abstract class TranslationApi {
   @post("/{parent=projects/*}/text:translate")
   TranslateText(req: TranslateTextRequest): TranslateTextResponse;
}

interface TranslateTextRequest {
   parent: string;
   sourceLanguageCode: string;
   targetLanguageCode: string;
   text: string;
}

interface TranslateTextResponse {
   text: string;
}
```

Most importantly, while stateless custom methods might seem like the best idea for the current moment, it's important to anticipate the future and any future functionality you might expect to introduce. For example, right now there might be one and only one way to translate some text. But as more machine learning technology comes out, perhaps in the future there will be a variety of different machine learning models capable of different forms of translation. This is particularly common in specific industries like medicine where translating text uses quite a lot of different terminology and syntax compared to translating text in casual conversation. Further, it's possible that API users want to deploy their own custom machine learning models or custom glossaries for translation. And none of these scenarios are well supported by our purely stateless custom method.

In this case, it might actually make more sense to provide users the ability to create translation ML models as resources and then attach the custom method to that specific resource. By doing that, the method itself is still somewhat stateless in that no data provided by the custom method results in any stored data.

Listing 9.6 Stateless custom method attached to a TranslationModel resource

TranslationModel resources have all the standard methods of normal resources.

```
abstract class TranslationApi {
    @post("/translationModels")
    CreateTranslationModel(req: CreateTranslationModelRequest):
        TranslationModel;

    // ...

    @post("/{id=translationModels/*}/text:translate")
    TranslateText(req: TranslateTextRequest): TranslateTextResponse;
}

interface TranslateTextRequest {
    id: string;
    sourceLanguageCode: string;
    targetLanguageCode: string;
    text: string;
}

interface TranslateTextResponse {
    text: string;
}
```

The other standard methods for managing TranslationModel resources would go here.

The TranslateText method targets a specific TranslationModel resource.

Now that we've seen how this works, let's look at how we might put it all together into a final API definition.

9.3.4 Final API definition

For the final example, we'll rely on the example email sending API. In this case, we have several standard methods for managing Email resources, as well as quite a few custom methods to handle things like state changes (e.g., archiving an email), sending emails, exporting an entire collection of a user's emails, and a stateless custom method that's capable of determining whether an email address is valid.

Listing 9.7 Final API definition

```
abstract class EmailApi {
    static version = "v1";
    static title = "Email API";

    // ...

    @post("/{id=users/*emails/*}:send")
    SendEmail(req: SendEmailRequest): Email;

    @post("/{id=users/*/emails/*}:unsend")
    UnsendEmail(req: UnsendEmailRequest): Email;

    @post("/{id=users/*/emails/*}:undelete")
    UndeleteEmail(req: UndeleteEmailRequest): Email;
```

All the normal standard methods (e.g., CreateEmail, DeleteEmail, etc.) would go here.

The custom methods to send an email message would transition the email to a sending state, delay for a few seconds, connect to the SMTP service, and return the result.

The unsend method would allow a send operation to abort during the delay introduced by the send method.

The undelete method would update the Email.deleted property, performing the inverse of the standard delete method (see chapter 25 for more information on soft deletion).

```
@post("/{parent=users/*}/emails:export")
ExportEmails(req: ExportEmailsRequest): ExportEmailsResponse;

@post("/emailAddress:validate")
ValidateEmailAddress(req: ValidateEmailAddressRequest):
    ValidateEmailAddressResponse;
}
interface Email {
    id: string;
    subject: string;
    content: string;
    state: string;
    deleted: boolean;
    // ...
}
```

This stateless email address validation method is clearly free (as it's not tied to any parent).

The export method would take all email data and push it to a remote storage location (see chapter 23 for more information on importing and exporting).

9.4   *Trade-offs*

In general, custom methods are a basic piece of functionality that help round out those provided by the standard methods and the resources for any API. However, as discussed in section 9.1.1, the very existence of these custom methods tends to present a contradiction with REST and the principles underpinning RESTful API design.

As we explored in detail earlier, it isn't necessary to do so again, but it is worth a reminder that anything you can do with a custom method should be possible with standard methods exclusively given a proper set of resources. In other words, custom methods are primarily a middle ground to ensure that the simplest and most familiar resource hierarchy also allows for nonstandard interactions.

It's also important to keep in mind that custom methods are quite often misused or overused as a crutch to justify a suboptimal resource layout. It's pretty common to see poorly designed APIs using custom methods for everything because the resources chosen and the relationships between those resources are simply wrong for the purpose of the API. An API that finds itself using custom methods for common actions that almost certainly should be handled by standard methods is generally a bad sign. And, unfortunately, custom methods can be used to hide this poor design for longer than most of us would hope, thereby preventing an actual improvement to the API. As a result, it's critical to be entirely certain that any new custom method is not acting as duct tape to avoid admitting that the resource layout is wrong.

9.5   *Exercises*

1 What if creating a resource requires some sort of side effect? Should this be a custom method instead? Why or why not?

2 When should custom methods target a collection? What about a parent resource?

3 Why is it dangerous to rely exclusively on stateless custom methods?

Summary

- Custom methods should almost always use the HTTP POST method and never use the PATCH method. They might use the GET method if the custom method is idempotent and safe.
- Custom methods use a colon (:) character to separate the resource target from the action being performed (e.g., /missiles/1234:launch).
- While side effects are forbidden for standard methods, they are permitted for custom methods. They should be used sparingly and documented thoroughly to avoid confusion for users.
- In general, custom methods should target a collection when multiple resources from a single collection are involved.
- Sometimes, particularly for computational work, APIs might choose to rely on stateless custom methods to perform the bulk of the work. This strategy should be used cautiously as it's easy for statefulness to eventually become important and can be difficult to introduce later on.

Long-running operations

10

This chapter covers

- How to use long-running operations for non-immediate API calls
- Storing metadata about operational progress
- Where operations should live in the resource hierarchy
- Finding operation status (including error results) via polling and blocking
- Interacting with running operations (e.g., pausing, resuming, and canceling)

In most cases, incoming requests can be processed quickly, generating a response within a few hundred milliseconds after the request is received. In the cases where responses take significantly longer, the default behavior of using the same API structure and asking users to "just wait longer" is not a very elegant option. In this chapter, we'll explore how to use long-running operations as a way of allowing API methods to behave in an asynchronous manner and ensuring that the slower API methods (including standard methods we saw in chapter 7) can provide quick and consistent feedback while executing the actual work in the background.

10.1 *Motivation*

So far, all of the API methods we've explored have been immediate and synchronous. The service receives a request, does some work right away, and sends back a response. And this particular manner of behavior is actually hardcoded into the API design as the return type is the result, not some promise to return a result later on down the line.

This has worked so far because most of the behavior in question was relatively simple, such as looking up a database row and returning the result. But what happens when the work becomes more involved, more complicated, and more resource intensive? This might be something relatively minor (such as connecting to an outside service) or it might involve some serious heavy lifting (such as processing many gigabytes or terabytes worth of data). Whether it's a minor or a major amount of work, one thing is clear: relying on the same API design for both consistently quick behavior and potentially very slow behavior is unlikely to work very well.

If we change nothing about the API and the method just takes longer, then we end up in a pretty scary situation. Generally, when we write code that sends requests to an API we have a familiar "write, compile, test" development cycle. If API requests take a long time, then we might think something's wrong with our code, kill the process, add some print statements (or fire up a debugger), and run the code again (see listing 10.1). If we see that it's definitely hanging on the API call, we might go through the cycle again, this time tweaking some parameters to make sure that we're not doing something silly. Only after it continues hanging on the API call do we notice the one sentence in the documentation saying that the request might take a while and that we should just wait on it to return.

> **Listing 10.1 Adding print statements to monitor progress through code**

```
function main() {
  let client = ChatRoomApiClient();
  let chatRoomName = generateChatRoomName();
  console.log(`Generated name ${chatRoomName}`);
  let chatRoom = client.CreateChatRoom({
    name: chatRoomName
  });
  console.log(`Created ChatRoom ${chatRoom.id}`);
}

main();
```

We add some console.log() statements to ensure that the problem is the CreateChatRoom method taking a long time.

Perhaps creating ChatRoom resources takes a while for some reason.

At this point we might feel a bit more confident of where the problem lies (after all, now we're pretty sure it's not in our code), but how long should we expect to wait on a response? How long is long enough? How do we know when it's too long and worth looking into the problem in more detail? How can we see the progress of this work? And what about if we want to cancel the work being done? Our current strategy of killing our running process locally does nothing to inform the server that all the work it's now doing is just going to go to waste. It'd be pretty useful to have a way of letting the API know when it should just stop doing all that work because we're no longer interested in the results.

Unfortunately, the API designs we've looked at so far are simply not up to the task of what we need. And expecting existing patterns to handle these long-running API calls is a bit unreasonable. This leads to the obvious question: what do we do? The goal of this design pattern is to answer this question.

10.2   Overview

This problem is not unique to web APIs. As a matter of fact, it's much more common with work being executed locally in a program. We want to do something that might take a while, but, if possible, we also want our program to continue doing other work while it's waiting on that slow function. This is actually such a common problem that many modern programming languages have created constructs to handle this asynchronous behavior and make it easy to manage in our programs. They vary in name from one language to another (Python calls them Futures, JavaScript calls them Promises), but the goal is simple: start some work but don't necessarily block on it. Instead, return an object that represents a placeholder for it. Then, perform the work and allow the placeholder to eventually either resolve (succeed with a result) or reject (throw an error). To handle these different scenarios, users can either register callbacks on the placeholder that will handle the result asynchronously or wait on the result to be returned, blocking code execution until resolution or rejection of that placeholder (effectively making the asynchronous work synchronous).

Listing 10.2   Awaiting and attaching callbacks to promises

```
async function factor(value: number): Promise<number[]> {
  // ...
}

async function waitOnPromise() {
  let factors = await factor(...);          ◁─┐  Here we can await the result.
                                              │  This will either return a result
  let promise = factor(...);                  │  or raise an error.
  let otherFactors = await promise;         ◁─┘
}

function promiseCallback() {
  let promiseForFactors = factor(...);      ◁──  Here we can attach
  promiseForFactors.then( (factors: number[]) => {   callbacks to the promise,
    // ...                                            handling both the result
  }).catch( (err) => {                                being resolved and an error
    // ...                                            from a rejection.
  });
}
```

The goal of this pattern is to design an equivalent of Promises or Futures for web APIs, which we'll call *long-running operations* or LROs. These API promises are primarily focused on providing a tool to track work the API does in the background and should support similar interaction patterns such as waiting (blocking) on the results, checking on the status, or being notified asynchronously of the results. In many cases, these LROs also provide the ability to pause, resume, or cancel the ongoing operation, but, as we'll see, that will depend on the circumstances. An example of an LRO and how it flows through the system is shown in figure 10.1.

While LROs will have quite a few similarities to promises, there will also be many big differences. First, since LROs are responsible for tracking the work done by

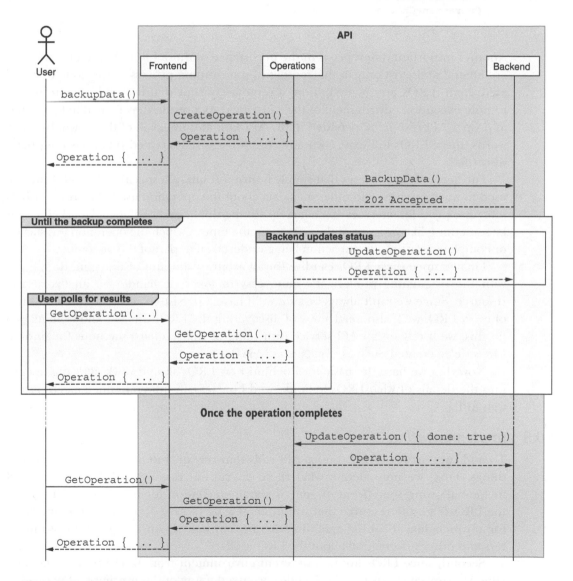

Figure 10.1 Life cycle of an LRO to backup data

another web API method, LROs are simply a new return type for these various methods. Unlike promises in programming languages, which can be explicitly created to execute arbitrary code in the background, there is rarely any reason to explicitly create an LRO.

Listing 10.3   A standard create method that returns an LRO

```
abstract class ChatRoomApi {
  @post("/chatRooms")
  CreateChatRoom(req: CreateChatRoomRequest):
    Operation<ChatRoom, CreateChatRoomMetadata>;    ◁——
}
```

Rather than returning a ChatRoom resource directly, the standard create method returns an LRO that will eventually result in a ChatRoom resource.

Another important difference is in the persistence of these LROs. While promises are ephemeral and exist only in the context of the running process of the code that created them, LROs are, by definition, a remote concept that live and operate in the remote execution environment of the API server. As a result, they'll need to be treated as proper API resources, persisted in the API with identifiers all of their own. In other words, these LROs will exist even after the process that created them has long been discarded.

Further, unlike promises that simply return a result of a specific type, LROs will be used to track progress and other metadata about the operation itself. As a result, LROs must also provide some sort of schema for storing this operational metadata. This might be something like progress of the operation, the time at which the operation was started or completed, or the current action being undertaken as part of the operation.

Finally, since these LROs can live for an arbitrary amount of time and do not die with the originating process, it's quite easy to lose our handle on an `Operation` resource. Since we can't always be sure we'll have a persistent record of the identifier of every LRO, we'll also need a way of discovering the LROs the API knows about. To do this, we'll rely on an API service with some of the standard methods for finding LROs we've created, such as `ListOperations()`.

Now that we have the basic idea behind how LROs should work, let's dig deeper into the details of what LROs look like and how we can integrate the concept into a web API.

10.3   *Implementation*

To add support for asynchronous API calls that rely on LROs, we'll need to do two things. First, we must define what these `Operation` resources look like. This will include allowing some form of generic parameterization for both the result type of the LRO (e.g., the resource that will ultimately be returned) as well as the interface for any metadata about the operation that we may want to store (e.g., progress indicators and other information about the LRO itself).

Second, since LROs live in a different environment from where they are created (the API service versus the client code), we need a way of discovering and managing these LROs in the API. This means we'll need to define several API methods to interact with LROs, primarily a standard list method, standard get method, and potentially even custom methods for pausing, resuming, and canceling operations. Let's start by defining what an LRO looks like.

10.3.1 *What does an LRO look like?*

To understand what an LRO interface should look like, we need to consider what we want to do with this resource. First, since it is a resource, we need the ability to interact with it, leading to a required identifier field. Next, the main goal of these LROs is to ultimately return a result. This means that we clearly need a way of representing that result. However, we also have to consider the cases where an error occurs and the operation doesn't complete successfully. Additionally, we must consider the fact that there may be some operations that will simply not have a result and instead success is indicated simply by no error being present. To handle all of these cases, we can use an optional result field, which can either be an `OperationError` interface (with a code number, message text, and additional details) or a parameterized result type. And for this last piece we can rely on TypeScript's generics, accepting an input generic type of `ResultT`.

Additionally, we must consider some concept of the status of the LRO. In many languages, promises have three potential states: pending, resolved (successfully completed), or rejected (completed with an error result). While we may be able to infer the status of the LRO from the result field not being present, this may be error prone when the end result is simply empty. To help with this, the `Operation` resource should have a separate Boolean flag to indicate whether the LRO is complete. To avoid any indication that this field represents the success or failure of the operation (e.g., `complete` might indicate that the resource completed successfully), we'll simply call this Boolean flag `done`.

Finally, we must consider the fact that these LROs may need to provide metadata about the work being performed before a result is available. For example, perhaps we want to provide users with a progress indicator or an estimated time remaining value. Rather than simply exposing a schema-less value for this metadata, we can instead accept an interface as a generic parameter for this value, called `MetadataT`.

Listing 10.4 Definition of the Operation and OperationError interfaces

We rely on the done field to indicate whether an Operation is still doing work.

```
interface Operation<ResultT, MetadataT> {
  id: string;
  done: boolean;
  result?: ResultT | OperationError;
  metadata?: MetadataT;
}

interface OperationError {
  code: string;
  message: string;
  details?: any;
}
```

We use the ResultT and MetadataT generics to define the interface of the result type as well as for metadata stored about the LRO.

It's worth calling out the idea that there's no real requirement that the `ResultT` be an API resource. In some cases this might be an empty value, such as when some work has no real results to report other than the work has been done. It also might be some sort of ephemeral value, such as a `TranslationResult` interface that may have the results of a request to translate text from one language to another. Further, if there's no metadata ever worth storing on the LRO, this type can obviously be set to `null`, effectively eliminating the field entirely.

Now that we have this LRO type, we have to actually use it. To do this, we simply return it as the result of an API method. For example, as we saw in listing 10.3, we can make a standard create method asynchronous by returning a type of `Operation <ChatRoom, CreateChatRoomMetadata>` rather than just `ChatRoom` as we learned in chapter 7. Under the hood, however, we need to create and store this `Operation` resource, which leads to an interesting question about the location of LROs in the resource hierarchy.

10.3.2 *Resource hierarchy*

Since the LROs created by asynchronous methods must be persisted somewhere, it brings an important and obvious question: where exactly in the resource hierarchy should these LROs live? We have two obvious options to choose from. First, we could store the collection of operations underneath the specific resource on which the LRO is operating on. Alternatively, we could store operations as a top-level collection, separate and apart from the resources they might be involved with.

In cases where LROs are being used to make standard methods asynchronous (as seen in listing 10.3), this might make perfect sense. However, as tempting as this option might be, it presents quite a few problems. First, what if the operation isn't necessarily centered on a resource? What if, instead, the operation is something more ephemeral such as transcribing some audio into text? Second, if we split these collections across a variety of resources (e.g., `chatRooms/1/operations/2` versus `chatRooms/2/operations/3`), this prevents us from being able to easily query the entire list of operations in the system.

Because of all these things, it's a far better idea to use a centralized top-level collection of `Operation` resources (e.g., `/operations/1`). With this type of centralized resource layout, as we'll see in later sections, we have the ability to discover other LROs across the system in addition to simply addressing a single LRO at a time.

Now that we have an idea of where these LRO resources will live, let's look at how we actually go about using them in practice.

10.3.3 *Resolution*

So far, we've noted that API methods can quickly become asynchronous by simply changing the return type. This shift from an immediate result to an LRO that will eventually return a result is certainly a quick and easy way to handle these types of issues; however, we've really not said anything about how we deal with this `Operation` resource that's returned to us. In other words, once we get this LRO resource, what exactly are we supposed to do with it? How do we get the final result?

In most programming languages, promises can end with one of two states: rejected or resolved. This act of resolution, where a promise completes successfully and ends with the final value being returned, is arguably the most important part of a promise (or, in our case, an operation). So how do we go about getting this result? It turns out there are quite a few ways to do this, as we saw in listing 10.2. However, in order to adapt these styles of resolving a promise locally to the world of web APIs, we need to make a few adjustments.

In the following few sections, we'll look at the two different ways we can go about determining the end result of an LRO, starting with polling for a result.

POLLING

The most straightforward way to determine whether an LRO is still running or has completed is to simply ask the service about the LRO. In other words, we can continually request the LRO resource over and over until its done field is set to true. In fact, many client libraries that rely on something like LROs will perform this check under the hood, either with a standard wait time between requests or with some form of exponential back-off, adding more and more time between each request.

Listing 10.5 Polling for updates about an LRO until it's done

```
async function createChatRoomAndWait(): Promise<ChatRoom> {
  let operation: Operation<ChatRoom, CreateChatRoomMetadata>;
  operation = CreateChatRoom({
    resource: { title: "Cool Chat" }
  });

  while (!operation.done) {
    operation = GetOperation<ChatRoom,
        CreateChatRoomMetadata>({
      id: operation.id
    });
    await new Promise( (resolve) => {
      setTimeout(resolve, 1000)
    });
  }

  return operation.result as ChatRoom;
}
```

Instead of returning a ChatRoom, the CreateChatRoom method returns an Operation, which is a promise to eventually resolve to a ChatRoom (or an OperationError).

We continue the loop as long as the operation's done field is still false.

Inside each iteration, we request the operation information all over again.

We wait for some time to pass, allowing more work to happen on the API server.

Finally, we return the operation result.

In this case, all we need to exist is the method that returns the Operation resource in the response (in this case, CreateChatRoom) and then the parameterized GetOperation method to retrieve the status of the LRO.

Listing 10.6   Definition of the standard get method for LROs

```
abstract class ChatRoomApi {
  @post("/chatRooms")
  CreateChatRoom(req: CreateChatRoomRequest):
    Operation<ChatRoom, CreateChatRoomMetadata>;

  @get("/{id=operations/*}")
  GetOperation<ResultT, MetadataT>(req: GetOperationRequest):
    Operation<ResultT, MetadataT>;        ◁──
}

interface GetOperationRequest {
  id: string;
}
```

> The method is parameterized to ensure the correct return type. This method will be used for all operation types, not just the CreateChatRoom method.

The obvious downside of this type of behavior is that there will almost certainly be a long list of requests that simply result in us trying again, which might be considered wasted effort (network traffic and compute time on both the client and the API server). This is clearly a bit inconvenient, but it is the simplest to understand, ensures that we hear about the results in a timely manner (according to our own definition of "timely"), and leaves the onus of asking for the results on the client, who is best informed about the timeframe in which they become interested in the results.

With that, let's move onto the next option for finding out the result of an LRO: waiting.

WAITING

Polling for updates about an LRO puts the control in the hands of the client. In other words, the client decides how frequently to check on the operation and can decide to stop checking for any reason at all, such as no longer being interested in the result of the operation. One drawback of polling is that it's very unlikely that we'll know about the results of the operation immediately. We can always get closer and closer to finding out immediately by reducing the time we wait between requesting an update on the operation, but this results in more and more requests with no updates at all. In essence, polling has an intrinsic trade-off between the maximum delay before we have an update and the amount of wasted time and resources.

One way to get around this is to rely on a long-lived connection to the API service that closes only once the operation is complete. In other words, we make a request to the API service asking to keep the connection open and only respond when the operation has its done field set to true. This type of blocking request ensures that the moment that the API service knows an operation is complete, we'll be informed about the result of that operation. And even though it's possible that the implementation of this on the server side may actually rely on polling, polling inside the API server is much simpler than polling from a remote client to the API server.

The downside of this option is that now the API server is responsible for managing all of these connections and ensuring that responses are issued to the requests as operations complete (which could take quite some time). This can become quite complex, but the end result is a very simple interaction pattern for API *users*.

To make this work, we need to add a new custom method: wait. This method looks almost identical to the GetOperation parameterized method, but instead of returning the status right away, it will wait until the operation is resolved or rejected.

Listing 10.7   Definition of the custom wait method for LROs

```
abstract class ChatRoomApi {                    Here we use the HTTP GET method
  @get("/{id=operations/*}:wait")       <─┐    as this should be idempotent.
  WaitOperation<ResultT, MetadataT>(req: WaitOperationRequest):
    Operation<ResultT, MetadataT>;
}

interface WaitOperationRequest {
  id: string;
}
```

It's worth noting that since the input and return types are identical between Wait-Operation and GetOperation it might have been easier to add a simple flag on the GetOperation method to wait or not. While this is certainly a more efficient use of space, it means that a single Boolean flag can meaningfully change the underlying behavior of the API method, which is generally a very bad idea. Further, by using a separate method we make it simple to monitor and enforce service-level objectives like the expected response time. If we use a flag to indicate whether we should wait on the resolution, it will be quite difficult to disentangle API calls that are slow because they're being waited on from immediate GetOperation methods that are slow because of an infrastructural problem.

How does this work in client-side code? In short, the client can simply wait on the response of the API call. In other words, this method is effectively making any asynchronous API call act like a synchronous call. With the WaitOperation method, our createChatRoomAndWait() function becomes far simpler.

Listing 10.8   Client code using the WaitOperation custom method

```
function createChatRoomAndWait(): Promise<ChatRoom> {
  let operation: Operation<ChatRoom, CreateChatRoomMetadata>;
  operation = CreateChatRoom({              <─┐  We can obtain a promise to create
    resource: { title: "Cool Chat" }           a ChatRoom resource by using the
  });                                           standard create method.

  operation = WaitOperation({ id: operation.id });   <─┐  Instead of a loop, we
  return operation.result as ChatRoom;       <──┐        can simply wait on
}                                                         the result of the
            Assuming there were no errors,              operation.
        the result is available once the
    WaitOperation method returns a result.
```

While this certainly leads to straightforward, synchronous client-side code, waiting on responses is fraught with potential issues. If a connection is lost for one reason or another (e.g., perhaps the client is a mobile device that may lose its signal), we're back where we started with having to poll (a different type of polling that's driven by external circumstances rather than timing events).

Now that we've looked at how to retrieve the result of an LRO, let's look at the (hopefully) less common scenario where the result is not successful and we instead need to handle an error.

10.3.4 Error handling

In most web APIs, errors manifest themselves in the form of HTTP error codes and messages. For example, we might get a `404 Not Found` error indicating that a resource wasn't found, or a `403 Forbidden` error indicating we don't have access to a resource. This works well when the response is immediate and synchronous, but how do we handle this in the asynchronous world of LROs?

While it's certainly tempting to simply pass along the error response when an LRO has failed, this could present some serious problems. For instance, if the response to `GetOperation` yields the error of the underlying operation, how can we tell the difference between a `500 Internal Server Error` that was the result of the operation and the same error that is actually just the fault of the code that handles the `GetOperation` method? Clearly this means we'll need an alternative.

As we saw previously, the way we'll handle this involves allowing either a result (of the indicated `ResultT` type) or an `OperationError` type, which includes both a machine-readable code, a friendly description for human consumption, and an arbitrary structure for storing additional error details. This means that the `GetOperation` method should only throw an exception (by returning an HTTP error) if there was an actual error in retrieving the `Operation` resource. If the `Operation` resource is retrieved successfully, the error response is simply a part of the result of the LRO. It's then up to the client code to decide whether to throw a client-side exception or handle the error result another way. For example, we can adjust our `createChatRoomAndWait()` function to handle a possible error result.

Listing 10.9 Checking for an error or returning the result

```
function isOperationError(result: any):
    result is OperationError {            ◁─┐  First we define a type-checking
  const err = result as OperationError;      │  function to figure out whether
  return err.code !== undefined && err.message !== undefined;  the result is an error.
}

function createChatRoomAndWait(): Promise<ChatRoom> {
  let operation: Operation<ChatRoom, CreateChatRoomMetadata>;
  operation = CreateChatRoom( { resource: { title: "Cool Chat" } });
  operation = WaitOperation({ id: operation.id });
  if (isOperationError(operation.result)) {  ◁─┐  Next we can check the result and
    // ...                                       do different things depending on
  } else {                                       whether the operation succeeded.
```

```
        return operation.result as ChatRoom;
    }
}
```

Before we move on, it's worth stressing how important it is that the error code value is unique, specific, and intended for machine and not human consumption. When error codes are not provided (or have overlap, or are intended for humans rather than computers), we end up in the scary situation where API users may begin to rely on the message contents to figure out what's wrong. This isn't a problem by itself (after all, error messages are there to help users figure out what went wrong); however, whenever an API user feels the need to write any code that relies on the content of that error message, it has suddenly become part of the API. This means that when we change the error message (say, by fixing a typo), we can unintentionally cause errors in previously working code. As we'll learn in chapter 24, this should always be avoided at all costs, and the best way to do that is to have error codes that are far more useful in code than error messages themselves.

In the cases where users need not only to know the error type, but also some additional information about the error, the details field is the perfect place to put this structured, machine-readable information. While this additional information is not strictly prohibited from being in the error message, it's far more useful in the error details and is certainly required. In general, if the error message was missing, we should not lose any information that can't be looked up in the API documentation.

With that, let's dig into the next interesting, but optional, aspect of LROs: monitoring progress.

10.3.5 Monitoring progress

Up until now, we've looked at operations as either done or not done, but we haven't really looked much at the points in between those two states. So how can we keep an eye on the progress of an LRO? This is exactly where the metadata field of the Operation resource comes into play.

As we saw in listing 10.4, the Operation resource accepts two types for two fields. The first was the type of the result, the second was a MetadataT that was assigned to the metadata field. It's this special interface we can use to store information not about the result but about the LRO itself. This could be simple information such as the timestamp of when the work began or, in this case, progress about the work being done, estimated time left until completion, or number of bytes processed.

While progress often means "percent completed," there's no firm requirement that this is the case. In many scenarios a percentage might be useful, but an estimated completion time is even more useful, or perhaps a measurement of the progress in real terms, such as records processed. Further, there's no guarantee that we'll have a meaningful percentage value—and we all know how frustrating it can be for a percent complete to start going backward! Luckily, we can use any interface we want for the metadata field. Listing 10.10 shows an example analyzing the conversation history of a

ChatRoom resource for some linguistic statistics, using the number of messages analyzed and counted so far as progress indicators.

Listing 10.10   Definition of the AnalyzeMessages custom method with metadata type

```
abstract class ChatRoomApi {
  @post("/{parent=chatRooms/*}/messages:analyze")
  AnalyzeMessages(req: AnalyzeMessagesRequest):
    Operation<MessageAnalysis, AnalyzeMessagesMetadata>;
}

interface AnalyzeMessagesRequest {
  parent: string;
}

interface MessageAnalysis {
  chatRoom: string;
  messageCount: number;
  participantCount: number;
  userGradeLevels: map<string, number>;
}

interface AnalyzeMessagesMetadata {
  chatRoom: string;
  messagesProcessed: number;
  messagesCounted: number;
}
```

> The result of this method is not a resource, but an analysis interface showing grade levels of writing per user, among other things.

> The metadata interface uses messages processed and counted to determine progress.

How do we actually use this? In section 10.3.3, we saw how to use polling to continually check on an LRO in the hopes that it was completed. In this same manner, we can use the GetOperation method to retrieve progress information stored in the Analyze-MessagesMetadata interface.

Listing 10.11   Showing progress using the metadata interface

```
async function analyzeMessagesWithProgress(): Promise<MessageAnalysis> {
  let operation: Operation<MessageAnalysis, AnalyzeMessagesMetadata>;
  operation = AnalyzeMessages({ parent: 'chatRooms/1' });

  while (!operation.done) {
    operation = GetOperation<MessageAnalysis, AnalyzeMessagesMetadata>({
      id: operation.id
    });
    let metadata = result.metadata as
        AnalyzeMessagesMetadata;
    console.log(
      `Processed ${metadata.messagesProcessed} of ` +
      `${metadata.messagesCounted} messages counted...`);
    await new Promise( (resolve) => setTimeout(resolve, 1000));
  }

  return operation.result as MessageAnalysis;
}
```

> First we retrieve the metadata from the operation at its current state.

> Next we print a line to the console updating the progress of messages as they're processed and counted.

Now that we know how to check the progress of an operation, we can start exploring other ways we can interact with operations. For example, what if the progress of an operation is going far slower than we had anticipated? Perhaps we made a mistake? How can we cancel the operation?

10.3.6 *Canceling operations*

So far, all of our interactions with LROs have assumed that, once started, operations continue executing their work until they either resolve successfully or reject with an error. But what if we don't want to wait for the operation to complete?

There are a variety of reasons we might want to do this. Typos and "brain-o's" (a mental version of a typo) happen far more often than we might like to admit. Cases like these lead to us writing code that creates an LRO for the wrong data, with the wrong destination for the output, or sometimes even just the wrong method entirely! If all of these cases were locally running promises, we'd simply kill the process and stop the execution. However, since we're dealing with a remote execution environment, we'll need a way of requesting the equivalent of this. To make that happen, we can use a custom method: `CancelOperation`.

> **Listing 10.12 Definition of the custom cancel method**

```
abstract class ChatRoomApi {
  @post("/{id=operations/*}:cancel")
  CancelOperation<ResultT, MetadataT>(req: CancelOperationRequest):
    Operation<ResultT, MetadataT>;
}

interface CancelOperationRequest {
  id: string;
}
```

The custom method returns the fully canceled Operation resource after it's been aborted.

Just like the `GetOperation` method, the `CancelOperation` method will return the parameterized `Operation` resource, and this resource will have its done field set to true (recall that done was chosen specifically because it doesn't imply true completion or success of the operation). To ensure that the result is always considered done, this method should block until the operation is fully cancelled and only then return the result. There are cases where this might take a while (perhaps there are several other subsystems that need to be contacted); however, it's still reasonable to wait for a response, just like the `WaitOperation` method in section 10.3.3.

It's also important that, if possible, any intermediate work product or other output that came about as a result of the LRO's execution be removed. After all, the goal of canceling an LRO is to end with a system that looks as though the operation had never been initiated in the first place. In the cases where it's not possible to clean up after the cancellation of an operation, we should ensure that all information necessary for the user to do this cleanup on their own is present in the metadata field on the operation. For example, if the operation created several files in a storage system which, for whatever reason, cannot be erased before canceling the operation, the metadata must include references to this intermediate data so that the user can erase the files themselves.

Finally, while it would certainly be lovely if all the LRO types were able to be canceled, there should be no firm requirement that this be the case across the entire API. The reason for this is simply that operations tend to differ in their purpose, their complexity, and their innate ability to be canceled or not. Often it makes sense to cancel some operations and others simply don't follow that pattern. And we should never add support for canceling LROs that have no benefit to the user.

With that, let's look at a different type of interaction that's similar in nature to cancelation, just less permanent: pause and resume.

10.3.7 *Pausing and resuming operations*

Now that we've opened the door to interacting with operations in ways that meaningfully change their behavior (e.g., canceling their work), we can start looking at one other important aspect of LROs: the ability to pause ongoing work and then resume it later. While we can rely on a similar custom method to the `CancelOperation` method we just learned about, there's a bit more to think about when considering this scenario.

Most importantly, if an operation is paused, we certainly need a way to tell that it's been paused. Unfortunately, the `done` field on the `Operation` resource doesn't quite work here. A paused operation is not done, so we can't just repurpose that field for our uses. This leaves us with two choices: add a new field to the `Operation` interface (paused or something similar) or rely on metadata for the operation.

As nice and simple as it would be to add a new field to the `Operation` interface, this presents its own problem: there's no guarantee that every operation will be able to be paused and resumed. In some cases this might make sense, but in others these LROs are all-or-nothing affairs, with users obtaining no real benefits from attempting to pause an operation. For example, try pausing an API that launches a rocket after that rocket has lifted off. It just doesn't make sense!

In short, this leaves us with the less elegant but better solution: relying on metadata for this type of status. This means that there's an important rule: for an operation to be able to be paused and resumed, the metadata type (`MetadataT`) must have a Boolean field called "paused."

Listing 10.13   Adding a paused field to the metadata interface

```
interface AnalyzeMessagesMetadata {
  chatRoom: string;
  paused: boolean;          ◁──── In order to support pausing and resuming
  messagesProcessed: number;       an operation, the metadata interface must
  messagesCounted: number;         have a paused Boolean field.
}
```

The pause and resume methods (`PauseOperation` and `ResumeOperation`) are basically identical to the other operation-focused resources we learned about earlier. They accept the identifier of the Operation resource as well as the parameters for the types (ResultT and MetadataT) that will be returned on the operation. And just like the CancelOperation method, these methods should return only once the operation has been successfully paused or resumed.

> **Listing 10.14   Definition of the custom pause and resume methods**

The custom methods return the paused (or resumed) operation.

```
abstract class ChatRoomApi {
  @post("/{id=operations/*}:pause")
  PauseOperation<ResultT, MetadataT>(req: PauseOperationRequest):
    Operation<ResultT, MetadataT>;

  @post("/{id=operations/*}:resume")
  ResumeOperation<ResultT, MetadataT>(req: ResumeOperationRequest):
    Operation<ResultT, MetadataT>;
}

interface PauseOperationRequest {
  id: string;
}

interface ResumeOperationRequest {
  id: string;
}
```

The actual process of pausing or resuming the underlying work is left as an implementation detail for the API. As fun as it would be to explore all the different mechanisms to pause and resume work in a variety of different APIs, the most to be said here is simply that we should only support these methods in circumstances where it both makes sense and is possible. This means if we wanted to support pausing an API method that, for example, copies data from one place to another, we must store a pointer to the process executing the copying and ensure that we can kill that process, but also potentially clean up the mess that was made while copying the data. The rest of the details, though, are left to the actual API designer.

10.3.8   *Exploring operations*

One of the unique things about LROs is that the code that creates the API promise is separate from the environment that's executing the promise and doing all the work. This means we could find ourselves in quite a predicament if the code that initiated the work was, somehow, to crash before the promise completed. Unless we persist the operation ID such that we can resume our polling loop later, that pointer to the operation performing the work we requested will be lost with all the other state when the process dies in our local execution environment.

This scenario illustrates a pretty large oversight: we can retrieve the information about a single Operation resource given its identifier, but we have no way of discovering the ongoing work or inspecting the state and history of the API system. Luckily, this is an easy problem to remedy. To fill in this gap, all we need to do is define a standard list method for the collection of Operation resources in our API.

This method should behave like the other standard list methods, but it's critically important that we support at least some form of filtering. Otherwise, it could become difficult when trying to ask questions such as, "What `Operation` resources are currently still not done?" Further, the filtering must also support querying metadata on resources. Otherwise, we have no way to answer other questions like, "What operations are paused?"

Listing 10.15   Definition of the standard list method for LROs

```
abstract class ChatRoomApi {
  @get("/operations")
  ListOperations<ResultT, MetadataT>(req:
      ListOperationsRequest):                      ←——  This follows the standard
    ListOperationsResponse<ResultT, MetadataT>;          list method but allows
}                                                        parameterization.

interface ListOperationsRequest {
  filter: string;        Later we'll look at how
                    ←——| to apply pagination.
}

interface ListOperationsResponse<ResultT, MetadataT> {
  results: Operation<ResultT, MetadataT>[];
}
```

This simple API method allows us to answer all the questions we might have about operations, specifically in the case where we don't happen to have the identifiers ahead of time. Note that the operation does accept parameters for the types of the result and metadata types, but this shouldn't prohibit the ability to ask for all operations, regardless of the types involved. We might do this using the TypeScript any keyword; however, it will be up to the caller to inspect the result to determine the specific type (in most cases, the identifier of the result will include the resource type).

As you can imagine, filtering through all these resources is quite powerful, but once these operations are done, we have to consider how long to keep these records around. In the next section, we'll explore the persistence criteria for these LRO records.

10.3.9   *Persistence*

While it's true that these LROs are resources (`Operation` resources, to be specific), they are a bit different from the resources we've defined ourselves. First, they aren't explicitly created but instead come into existence by virtue of other behavior in the system (e.g., requesting an analysis of the data might lead to an `Operation` resource being created to track the work being done). This implicit creation is fundamentally different from our typical way of bringing resources into existence, usually with a standard create method.

More importantly, though, these resources go from a place of being critically important to old news very quickly. For example, any LRO that is the result of a standard method (e.g., CreateChatRoom) is very important when it's processing but becomes practically useless once it's finished. The reason for this is that the result itself is the permanent recorded output of the operation, so the process that tracked the creation of that resource isn't particularly valuable after that point.

This means we have to address a confusing issue: do we treat LROs like any other resource and persist them forever? Or do they have a slightly different persistence policy than other, more traditional resources? If they do have a different policy for persistence, what is the right policy?

It turns out there are quite a few different options, each with their own benefits and drawbacks. The easiest to manage and quickest to implement is to treat Operation resources like any other and keep them forever. In general, most APIs should rely on this method unless it would place undue burden on the system (typically when you have many millions of Operation resources being created on a daily basis).

If the interaction patterns of an API make this perpetual storage method particularly wasteful, then the next best option is to rely on a rolling window, with Operation resources being purged based on their completion timestamp (not their creation timestamp), defined in an expireTime field set on the Operation resource. In short, if a resource has been around longer than, say, 30 days, it should be deleted permanently.

Listing 10.16   Adding an expiration field to the Operation interface

```
interface Operation<ResultT, MetadataT> {
  id: string;
  done: boolean;
  expireTime: Date;                          ◀—— We can use an expiration
  result?: ResultT | OperationError;              time to show when the
  metadata?: MetadataT;                           resource will be deleted
}                                                  from the system.
```

There are many more complex and feature-rich options (such as deleting operations when the resources they're tied to are deleted, or archiving operations after a certain amount of time and then deleting them after they've been archived for another window of time), but these should be avoided. Ultimately, they cause more difficulty due to confusion and complicated purging algorithms. Instead, relying on a simple expiration time is easy for everyone to follow and unambiguous about the end results.

The most important thing to remember is that expiration times of resources should not depend on the underlying result types of the operation. In other words, an operation that represented work to create a resource should expire after the same amount of time as an operation that represented work to analyze data. If we use different expiration times for different types of operations, it can lead to more confusion, with results disappearing in what appears to be an unpredictable manner.

10.3.10 *Final API definition*

Putting everything together, listing 10.17 shows the full API definition for all of these various methods and interfaces related to LROs.

Listing 10.17   Final API definition

```
abstract class ChatRoomApi {
  @post("/{parent=chatRooms/*}/messages:analyze")
  AnalyzeMessages(req: AnalyzeMessagesRequest):
    Operation<MessageAnalysis, AnalyzeMessagesMetadata>;

  @get("/{id=operations/*}")
  GetOperation<ResultT, MetadataT>(req: GetOperationRequest):
    Operation<ResultT, MetadataT>;

  @get("/operations")
  ListOperations<ResultT, MetadataT>(req: ListOperationsRequest):
    ListOperationsResponse<ResultT, MetadataT>;

  @get("/{id=operations/*}:wait")
  WaitOperation<ResultT, MetadataT>(req: WaitOperationRequest):
    Operation<ResultT, MetadataT>;

  @post("/{id=operations/*}:cancel")
  CancelOperation<ResultT, MetadataT>(req: CancelOperationRequest):
    Operation<ResultT, MetadataT>;

  @post("/{id=operations/*}:pause")
  PauseOperation<ResultT, MetadataT>(req: PauseOperationRequest):
    Operation<ResultT, MetadataT>;

  @post("/{id=operations/*}:resume")
  ResumeOperation<ResultT, MetadataT>(req: ResumeOperationRequest):
    Operation<ResultT, MetadataT>;
}

interface Operation<ResultT, MetadataT> {
  id: string;
  done: boolean;
  expireTime: Date;
  result?: ResultT | OperationError;
  metadata?: MetadataT;
}

interface OperationError {
  code: string;
  message: string;
  details?: any;
}

interface GetOperationRequest {
  id: string;
}
```

```
interface ListOperationsRequest {
  filter: string;
}

interface ListOperationsResponse<ResultT, MetadataT> {
  results: Operation<ResultT, MetadataT>[];
}

interface WaitOperationRequest {
  id: string;
}

interface CancelOperationRequest {
  id: string;
}

interface PauseOperationRequest {
  id: string;
}

interface ResumeOperationRequest {
  id: string;
}

interface AnalyzeMessagesRequest {
  parent: string;
}

interface MessageAnalysis {
  chatRoom: string;
  messageCount: number;
  participantCount: number;
  userGradeLevels: map<string, number>;
}

interface AnalyzeMessagesMetadata {
  chatRoom: string;
  paused: boolean;
  messagesProcessed: number;
  messagesCounted: number;
}
```

10.4 Trade-offs

Clearly there are many ways to handle API calls that might take a while. For example, one of the simplest also happens to be the easiest to manage for clients: just make the request take as long as it needs. The trade-off with these more simple options is that they don't lend themselves very well to distributed architecture (e.g., one microservice to initiate the work, another to monitor its progress).

Another trade-off is that it can become a bit more complicated to actually monitor the progress of an API call that hangs until completion. While the API can push data over time, if the connection is broken for any reason (perhaps a process crashes, a network connection is interrupted, etc.), we lose our ability to resume monitoring that progress. And further, if we decide to implement something to resume monitoring progress after a network failure like that, there's a good chance that what we build will start to resemble the concept of LROs.

LROs can also be a bit tricky to understand at first. They are complicated, generic, parameterized resources that aren't explicitly created but instead come into existence by virtue of other work being requested. This certainly breaks the mold of resource creation that we've learned about so far. Further, there is often confusion when it comes to the idea of "rerunnable jobs" and LROs, which we'll discuss in more detail in chapter 11.

In short, while this design pattern can be difficult to grasp at first, the concept of API promises can become easily relatable to API users over time. And the pattern itself imposes almost no practical limitations—after all, there's nothing stopping us from keeping a synchronous version of the various API methods if that's what users need and expect.

10.5 *Exercises*

1 Why should operation resources be kept as top-level resources rather than nested under the resources they operate on?
2 Why does it make sense to have LROs expire?
3 If a user is waiting on an operation to resolve and the operation is aborted via the custom cancel method, what should the result be?
4 When tracking progress of an LRO, does it make sense to use a single field to store the percentage complete? Why or why not?

Summary

- LROs are promises or futures for web APIs that act as a tool for tracking work being done in the background by an API service.
- LROs are parameterized interfaces, returning a specific result type (e.g., the resource resulting from the operation) and a metadata type for storing progress information about the operation itself.
- LROs resolve after a certain amount of time to a result or an error and users discover this either by polling for status updates periodically or being notified of a result while waiting.
- LROs may be paused, resumed, or canceled at the discretion of the API and rely on custom methods to do so.
- LROs should be persisted to storage but should generally expire after some standard period of time, such as 30 days.

Rerunnable jobs

This chapter covers

- What rerunnable jobs are
- How rerunnable jobs differ from long-running operations
- How to represent rerunnable jobs as resources
- The benefits of supporting rerunnable jobs over custom methods returning LROs
- How to represent job results with job execution resources

There are many cases where an API needs to expose some customizable functionality that runs repeatedly; however, we don't always want to be required to provide all the details for that functionality each time it needs to be run. Further, we may want the ability to execute this chunk of configurable work on a schedule that is owned and maintained by the API server rather than invoked by the client. In this pattern, we explore a standard for defining specific units of work that are configurable and rerunnable, potentially by users with different levels of access in the API. We also provide a pattern for storing the output of each of these executions.

11.1 *Motivation*

As we learned in chapter 10, sometimes we'll come across methods in an API that cannot, or should not, return immediately. Having the ability to handle asynchronous execution is clearly very valuable; however, it still requires that a client trigger the invocation somewhere by calling the API method. This works fine for methods that are only ever intended to run on demand, but there are three scenarios worth considering that aren't quite solved by simply having a method that returns an LRO.

First, with a typical custom method that runs asynchronously, each invocation requires the caller to provide all the relevant configuration necessary for the method. This might be simple and straightforward when the method doesn't require much configuration, but as the number of configuration parameters increases over time there will be quite a lot of information provided at each invocation. This makes source control all the more important, because chasing down a mistake in the configuration parameters that is stored somewhere on Jim's laptop can raise a variety of challenges. Having the ability to store these configuration parameters in the API itself might be a very useful bit of functionality.

Second, with an on-demand model of invoking a method, we conflate two sets of permissions: the ability to run the method and the ability to choose the parameters for the invocation of that method. Often this is not a big deal, but, again, as the complexity of configuration parameters grows more and more over time, we may want to split the responsibilities up into two groups: those that can configure how the method should be called and those that can call the method. This becomes particularly important when API users begin to distinguish between developers and operations as distinct teams with distinct responsibilities and permissions. As you might guess, it's tough to enforce permissions that say things like "User A can only call this method with these exact configuration parameters."

Finally, while running methods on demand has gotten us quite a long way, there is a good chance that eventually we'll want to be able to automatically invoke methods on some sort of recurring schedule. And even though it's certainly possible to set up a client device to make these various API calls on a specific schedule (e.g., with a server that runs a script based on definitions in `crontab`), that introduces a new, potentially faulty subsystem responsible for the success of this work. Instead, it'd be much simpler if we could configure the scheduling in the API itself so that the service can invoke the method for us without external participation.

We should probably define a standard for configurable jobs that can store the various configuration parameters and be rerun as needed (potentially on a schedule).

11.2 *Overview*

To address these three scenarios, we can rely on a simple but powerful concept: a *job*. A job is a special type of resource that breaks the on-demand version of an API method into two pieces. When we call a typical API method, we provide the configuration for the work to be done and the method executes the work using that configuration right then and there. With a job, these become two distinct bits of functionality. First, we create a job with the configuration for the work that should be done. Then, later, we can perform the actual work by calling a custom method on the `Job` resource, called "run." An example sequence of API calls outlining how we might use jobs is shown in figure 11.1.

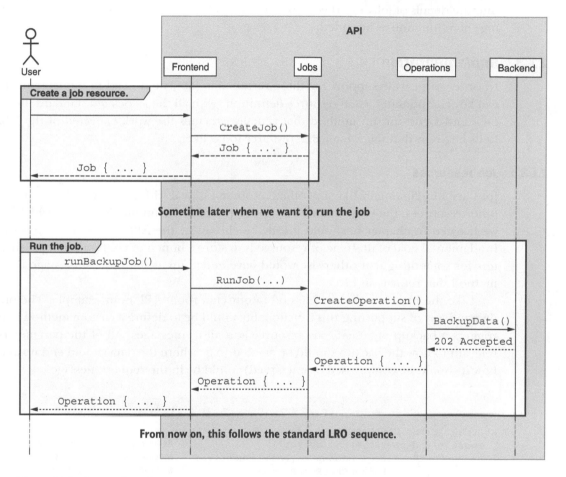

Figure 11.1 Interaction with a `Job` resource

By splitting the work into two separate components, we lay the groundwork for solving all three of the use cases described in section 11.1. First, there's no need to worry as the number of configuration parameters grows because we only need to manage them once: when we create the job resource. From there on out, we call the run method without any parameters. Second, since these are two distinct API methods, we can control who has access to which ones. It's quite simple to say that a specific user may have access to execute a preconfigured job but is not allowed to create or modify jobs. Finally, this provides a simple way to handle scheduling as part of the API in the future. Rather than a complicated scheduling system that accepts lots of parameters, we can simply request that a single API method is called with no parameters at all on a specific schedule.

It's much easier to describe what we want out of jobs and much more complicated to get into the details of how these magical jobs work. In the next section, we'll dive into the details of jobs and the various standard and custom methods involved in making them function as intended.

11.3   Implementation

In order to provide support for these rerunnable jobs, we'll need to implement the two key components: a Job resource definition (with all the associated standard methods) and a custom run method that actually executes the work expected of the job. Let's begin by defining what a Job resource looks like.

11.3.1   Job resources

Jobs are fundamentally like any other resource we deal with in an API. And just like other resources, the only field that's truly required is the unique identifier, which, as we learned in chapter 6, should ideally be chosen by the API service. However, the fundamental goal of this type of resource is to store a bunch of configuration parameters for something that otherwise would have ended up as the request message for a method that returns an LRO.

Take the idea of a backup method in our chat room API as an example. The on-demand way of supporting this functionality would be to define a custom method that triggers a backup of a ChatRoom resource and all its messages. All of the parameters relevant to how the backup should be created (e.g., where the data should end up and how it should be compressed or encrypted) would be in the request message.

Listing 11.1   On-demand custom backup method

```
abstract class ChatRoomApi {
  @post("/{id=chatRooms/*}:backup")
  BackupChatRoom(req: BackupChatRoomRequest):
    ➥ Operation<BackupChatRoomResponse,
              BackupChatRoomMetadata>;
}

interface BackupChatRoomRequest {
  id: string;
  destination: string;
  compressionFormat: string;
  encryptionKey: string;
}
```

As an on-demand asynchronous method, we return an LRO with a standard response interface result type.

This identifier refers to the ChatRoom resource being backed up.

These represent the different configuration parameters for a backup operation.

```
interface BackupChatRoomResponse {
  destination: string;
}

interface BackupChatRoomMetadata {
  messagesCounted: number;
  messagesProcessed: number;
  bytesWritten: number;
}
```

> The response simply points to where the backed-up data lives in an external storage system.

As we will learn in chapter 23, this method would certainly work and respond with the resulting backup location. However, as we discussed in section 11.1, this can present a variety of problems. Perhaps we want administrators to be able to trigger a backup operation, but we don't want them to choose the encryption key or configure the details of the operation in any significant way outside of the timing. Alternatively, perhaps we want to have a scheduling service responsible for triggering the backup, but we want to be able to configure the recurring behavior separately, meaning the scheduling service should only ever trigger the backup and leave all configuration aspects to someone else.

We can turn this on-demand API method into a rerunnable job resource quite easily: simply move whatever would have been provided in the request message and treat those fields as configurable fields on a `BackupChatRoomJob` resource instead.

Listing 11.2 A Job resource for backing up chat data

```
interface BackupChatRoomJob {
  id: string;
  chatRoom: string;
  destination: string;
  compressionFormat: string;
}
```

> Note that this new resource has an identifier, and we rename the request's identifier field to chatRoom, acting as a reference to the resource that will be backed up.

> All the other fields from the request message should also live in the BackupChatRoomJob resource.

Since we're now dealing with a resource rather than an on-demand API method that returns an LRO, we need to support the typical collection of standard methods. We'll cover these in detail in the final API definition (see section 11.3.4), but table 11.1 summarizes the standard methods we should implement and the rationale for doing so.

Table 11.1 Standard methods and the rationale for each

Standard method	Rationale
GetBackupChatRoomJob	View configuration details about a backup job.
CreateBackupChatRoomJob	Create a new rerunnable backup job.
UpdateBackupChatRoomJob	Update an existing rerunnable backup job.
DeleteBackupChatRoomJob	Remove an existing rerunnable backup job.
ListBackupChatRoomJobs	See the list of available rerunnable backup jobs.

As we saw in chapter 7, there are scenarios where certain methods might be omitted from an API service. In this case, there's the possibility that these `BackupChatRoomJob` resources can be considered immutable. In other words, it's not unusual for these resources to be created and then never modified. Instead, users might delete an existing resource and create a new one to avoid any potential issues with concurrency (for example, if the job is running while we're updating it). In cases like these, it's certainly acceptable to omit the standard update method.

Additionally, while the on-demand method returned a long-running operation (as it had potentially a large amount of work to perform), these standard methods should be instantaneous and synchronous. This is because we've taken out the actual work from these methods and left them to focus exclusively on the configuration. In the next section, we'll look at how to actually trigger the job resource itself to do the work we're configuring with these standard methods.

11.3.2 *The custom run method*

Assuming we've created and preconfigured a `Job` resource, the next piece of the puzzle is to actually execute the job so that the work that we've configured is performed. To do this, each `Job` resource should have a custom run method responsible for doing the underlying work. This run method should not accept any other parameters (after all, we want to ensure all relevant configuration is persisted as part of the `Job` resource) and should return an LRO, as seen in chapter 10, that ultimately resolves to something like the response message of our on-demand custom method.

Listing 11.3   Custom run method for rerunnable backup jobs

```
abstract class ChatRoomApi {                      The custom run method follows the
  @post("/{id=backupChatRoomJobs/*}:run")   ◀──   standards discussed in chapter 9.
  RunBackupChatRoomJob(req: RunBackupChatRoomJobRequest):
    Operation<RunBackupChatRoomJobResponse,
          RunBackupChatRoomJobMetadata>;   ◀──   Since there's quite a bit of work to
}                                                 do, we can return an LRO right away.

interface RunBackupChatRoomJobRequest {
  id: string;                              ◀──   It's critical that no extra configuration
}                                                 is passed in at runtime.

interface RunBackupChatRoomJobResponse {  ◀──
  destination: string;
}                                                These are renamed but use the
                                                 same fields as the on-demand
interface RunBackupChatRoomJobMetadata {  ◀──    custom method.
  messagesCounted: number;
  messagesProcessed: number;
  bytesWritten: number;
}
```

As you can see, while most of the fields remain the same, several of the message names are slightly altered to fit with this new structure. For example, rather than a `Backup-ChatRoomResponse` message, we'd have a `RunBackupChatRoomJobResponse`. It's also critically important to point out that the `RunBackupChatRoomJobRequest` accepts only a single input: the identifier of the `Job` resource to run. Any other information relevant to the execution of the job itself should be stored on the resource, never provided at execution time.

It's also important to note that while this example has a clear output in the form of a response that states the destination of the backup data (perhaps `s3://backup-2020-01-01.bz2`), many other rerunnable jobs might not follow this same pattern. Some might perform their work by modifying other preexisting resources (e.g., a `BatchArchiveChatRoomsJob`) or creating new resources (e.g., an `ImportChatRooms-Job` which we'll see in chapter 23). Others still may have output that is completely ephemeral, producing analysis of some sort that wasn't designed to be stored permanently. Unfortunately, these cases may present a problem for an important reason: retention of LRO resources is not set in stone (see section 13.3.10). So what can we do?

11.3.3 *Job execution resources*

In some cases, the results of a rerunnable job won't have any persistent effect on the API. This means that calling the job's custom run method doesn't write any actual data to the API except for creating the LRO resource; no updates to existing resources, no creation of new resources, no written data to external data storage systems, nothing!

While there's nothing inherently wrong with this, it leads us to an important dependency. Suddenly, the persistent nature of the work being done by this job is at the mercy of whatever the API's policy on persistence for LROs happens to be. And, as we noted in section 13.3.10, this policy is pretty broad. While it encourages eternal persistence and never deleting any records, there's nothing stopping APIs from having `Operation` resources expire and disappear after a certain period of time.

Since we may want to have a durability policy of the output from these jobs that could be different from the durability policy of all the LROs in the system, we're left with two choices. The first is to change the policy of how long we keep LRO resources around to fit with the expectations we have with this specific type of job. The second is to have different operations expire in different amounts of time (e.g., most operations expire in 30 days, but operations for a specific type of job last forever). While the first is reasonable, though potentially excessive, the second leads to inconsistency and unpredictability, ultimately meaning our API will be more confusing and less usable. So what else can we do?

A third option is to rely on a subcollection of resources that acts a bit like `Operation` resources, called *executions*. Each `Execution` resource will represent the output of the custom run method that can be invoked on these different job resources, and unlike the LROs, they can have their own (usually perpetual) persistence policy.

For example, let's consider an analysis method that looks at a chat room and comes up with ratings for sentence complexity, overall sentiment of the messages, and a rating for whether there is abusive language present in the chat. Since we want to run this on a recurring basis, we want this functionality available as a rerunnable job instance, but obviously the results of this analysis job are not existing resources or external data sources. Instead, we'll have to define an `Execution` resource to represent the output of a single run of the analysis job.

Listing 11.4   An example Execution resource for analyzing chat data

```
interface AnalyzeChatRoomJobExecution {
  id: string;                              ←——  Since this is a proper
  job: AnalyzeChatRoomJob;         ←           resource, it requires its
  sentenceComplexity: number;   ←             own unique identifier.
  sentiment: number;
  abuseScore: number;                      To ensure we know what configuration went
}                                          into producing this execution, we store a
                                           snapshot of the AnalyzeChatRoomJob
        All the resulting analysis information    resource.
          is stored in the Execution resource.
```

Now, a call to the custom run method would still create an `Operation` resource to track the work of the job being performed, but when once complete, rather than returning an ephemeral output interface for immediate consumption (e.g., something with the `sentiment` field), the API would create an `AnalyzeChatRoomJobExecution` resource and the LRO would return a reference to that resource. This is a bit like the way an asynchronous standard create method would ultimately return the resource that was created when the LRO resolves.

Listing 11.5   Definition of the custom run method with Execution resources.

```
abstract class ChatRoomApi {              A standard create method
  @post("/analyzeChatRoomJobs")     ←——  for the analysis jobs
  CreateAnalyzeChatRoomJob(req: CreateAnalyzeChatRoomJob):        Notice we return
    AnalyzeChatRoomJob;                                           an Operation
                                                                  resource with an
                                                                  Execution resource
  @post("/{id=analyzeChatRoomJobs/*}:run")               ←——     result type.
  RunAnalyzeChatRoomJob(req: RunAnalyzeChatRoomJobRequest):
    Operation<AnalyzeChatRoomJobExecution, RunAnalyzeChatRoomJobMetadata>;
}
```

As you can see, the custom run method is almost identical to our previous backup example, but the result is an `Execution` resource instead of the ephemeral response interface. To see this more clearly, figure 11.2 shows the process of running the job and what should be happening under the hood in the API.

Finally, since these executions are true resources, we have to implement a few of the standard methods in order to make them useful. In this case, these resources are immutable, so we don't need to implement the standard update method; however, they are also created by internal processes only (never by end users). As a result, we

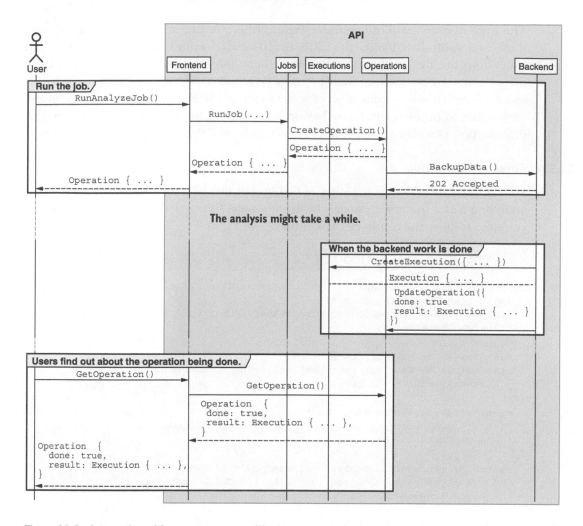

Figure 11.2 Interaction with a Job resource with Execution results

also shouldn't implement the standard create method. Table 11.2 shows a summary of the standard methods we need for executions as well as the rationale behind them.

Table 11.2 Summary of standard methods and rationale for each

Standard method	Rationale
GetAnalyzeChatRoomJobExecution	View details of a specific execution.
ListAnalyzeChatRoomJobExecutions	List the executions that have occurred.
DeleteAnalyzeChatRoomJobExecution	(Optional) Delete a specific execution.

The final question is about resource layout: where in the resource hierarchy should these executions live? Unlike the LROs that deal with resources from all over the API, executions are designed and scoped to a single job type. Further, since one of the most common questions we want to ask is "What executions have happened for this specific job?", it makes quite a bit of sense to scope the executions inside the context of that job. In other words, the behavior we're looking for out of executions indicates that the best place for these resources is as children of the job resources themselves.

11.3.4 *Final API definition*

For the final API definition, listing 11.6 shows all the API methods and interfaces for analyzing a chat room's messages. In this instance, the output relies on an execution resource to store the results permanently.

Listing 11.6   Final API definition

```
abstract class ChatRoomApi {
  @post("/analyzeChatRoomJobs")
  CreateAnalyzeChatRoomJob(req: CreateAnalyzeChatRoomJobRequest):
    AnalyzeChatRoomJob;

  @get("/analyzeChatRoomJobs")
  ListAnalyzeChatRoomJobs(req: ListAnalyzeChatRoomJobsRequest):
    ListAnalyzeChatRoomJobsResponse;

  @get("/{id=analyzeChatRoomJobs/*}")
  GetAnalyzeChatRoomJob(req: GetAnalyzeChatRoomJobRequest):
    AnalyzeChatRoomJob;

  @patch("/{resource.id=analyzeChatRoomJobs/*}")
  UpdateAnalyzeChatRoomJob(req: UpdateAnalyzeChatRoomJobRequest):
    AnalyzeChatRoomJob;

  @post("/{id=analyzeChatRoomJobs/*}:run")
  RunAnalyzeChatRoomJob(req: RunAnalyzeChatRoomJobRequest):
    Operation<AnalyzeChatRoomJobExecution, RunAnalyzeChatRoomJobMetadata>;

  @get("/{parent=analyzeChatRoomJobs/*}/executions")
  ListAnalyzeChatRoomJobExecutions(req
    ListAnalyzeChatRoomJobExecutionsRequest):
    ListAnalyzeChatRoomJobExecutionsResponse;

  @get("/{id=analyzeChatRoomJobs/*/executions/*}")
  GetAnalyzeChatRoomExecution(req: GetAnalyzeChatRoomExecutionRequest):
    AnalyzeChatRoomExecution;
}

interface AnalyzeChatRoomJob {
  id: string;
  chatRoom: string;
```

```
    destination: string;
    compressionFormat: string;
}

interface AnalyzeChatRoomJobExecution {
    id: string;
    job: AnalyzeChatRoomJob;
    sentenceComplexity: number;
    sentiment: number;
    abuseScore: number;
}

interface CreateAnalyzeChatRoomJobRequest {
    resource: AnalyzeChatRoomJob;
}

interface ListAnalyzeChatRoomJobsRequest {
    filter: string;
}

interface ListAnalyzeChatRoomJobsResponse {
    results: AnalyzeChatRoomJob[];
}

interface GetAnalyzeChatRoomJobRequest {
    id: string;
}

interface UpdateAnalyzeChatRoomJobRequest {
    resource: AnalyzeChatRoomJob;
    fieldMask: string;
}

interface RunAnalyzeChatRoomJobRequest {
    id: string;
}

interface RunAnalyzeChatRoomJobMetadata {
    messagesProcessed: number;
    messagesCounted: number;
}

interface ListAnalyzeChatRoomJobExecutionsRequest {
    parent: string;
    filter: string;
}

interface ListAnalyzeChatRoomJobExecutionsResponse {
    results: AnalyzeChatRoomJobExecution[];
}

interface GetAnalyzeChatRoomJobRequest {
    id: string;
}
```

11.4 Trade-offs

As we've seen, rerunnable jobs are a very useful concept to rely on, but they are one solution of many for the problem set. For instance, if we were concerned about permissions to configure versus execute a custom method, we could implement a more advanced permission system that inspected the request and verified that a given user could not only call a specific API method but could call that method with a specific set or range of parameters. This is certainly much more work for everyone involved, but it's a more granular option than splitting the method into two pieces (configure and run).

When it comes to execution resources, we certainly have an alternative option to simply keep `Operation` resources around forever as the reference of the output. The only downside to this is the requirement to filter through the list of `Operation` resources to retrieve those related to the `Job` resource of interest, but it is definitely an alternative.

11.5 Exercises

1 How do rerunnable jobs make it possible to differentiate between permissions to perform an action and permission to configure that action?
2 If running a job leads to a new resource being created, should the result be an execution or the newly created resource?
3 Why is it that execution resources should never be explicitly created?

Summary

- Rerunnable jobs are a great way to isolate users capable of configuring a task from those capable of executing the same task.
- Jobs are resources that are first created and configured. Later, these jobs may be executed using a custom run method.
- When the job doesn't operate on or create an existing resource, the result of a `Job` resource being run is typically an `Execution` resource.
- Execution resources are like read-only resources that may be listed and retrieved but not updated or created explicitly.

Part 4

Resource relationships

In any API we design, different components need to relate to one another in different ways. In the next few chapters, we'll examine a variety of ways in which resources can associate and how to design the right API methods to allow users to manage those relationships between resources.

First, in chapter 12, we'll look at a special type of resource called a singleton sub-resource and how we can rely on this concept to store isolated data with unique access patterns. In chapter 13, we'll explore how resources can reference one another, as well as how to maintain integrity with these references. In chapters 14 and 15, we'll look closely at two different ways of managing many-to-many relationships between resources (using association resources or custom add and remove methods). Finally, in chapter 16, we'll look at polymorphic resources that provide a unique ability for resources to take on multiple roles depending on specific parameters.

Singleton sub-resources

This chapter covers

- What singleton sub-resources are
- Why and when we should split data off into a singleton sub-resource
- How standard methods interact with sub-resources
- Where singleton sub-resources live in the resource hierarchy

In this pattern, we'll explore a way of structuring related but independent data by moving it from a set of properties on a resource to a singleton child of that resource. This pattern handles scenarios where a specific collection of data might change independently of the parent, have different security requirements, or simply might be too large to store directly as part of the resource.

12.1 Motivation

When building APIs, we sometimes have situations where there are components of resources that obviously belong as properties on the resource, but for one reason or another the component wouldn't be practical as a regular property. In other words, according to API design best practices the component is definitely best suited to be a property, but it would be impractical to follow those best practices in this case and would end up making a worse experience for those using the API. For example, if there was a resource that represented a shared document, it might also need to store the access control list (ACL) that determines who has access to the document and in what capacity. As you might imagine, this list of ACLs could become immensely large (hundreds or even thousands of access rules), and retrieving the entire ACL every time we browse through the list of documents (e.g., using a `ListDocuments` method) would often be a waste of bandwidth and compute resources. Further, in most scenarios the details of the ACL aren't even what we're interested in. We care about the ACL only in very specific scenarios.

The obvious answer is to separate components like this, but this leads us to two inevitable questions. First, how do we decide whether something merits being split apart somehow? Second, once we've decided that something should be separated from the main resource, how do we implement this separation?

Let's start by focusing on the first question and explore some possible reasons we might want to move components away from their parent resources into separate sub-resources. After that, we can dig into how to implement this separation using the singleton sub-resource pattern.

12.1.1 Why should we use a singleton sub-resource?

There are many potential reasons to separate a component from the resource that would normally own the component. Some of these reasons are obvious (e.g., the component is several times larger than the resource itself), but others are a bit more subtle. Let's explore a few common reasons for separating components from their parent resources.

SIZE OR COMPLEXITY

Often a single component can become particularly large when measured in comparison to the resource itself. If a component will potentially become larger than all other pieces of a resource combined, it may make sense to separate that component from the resource. For example, if you have an API that stores large binary objects (like Amazon's S3), it would be unusual to store the binary data itself alongside the metadata about the object. In this case, you'd separate the two: `GetObject` or `GetObject-Metadata` might return metadata about the object that is stored in a database but explicitly *not* include the binary data itself. This would instead be retrieved separately with an entirely different RPC, such as `GetObjectData`.

SECURITY

Often there are pieces of a resource that have very different access restrictions from the resource they nominally belong to. In cases like these, it may actually end up being a strict requirement that this information be kept entirely separate from the resource to which it would otherwise belong. For example, you might have an API that represents employee data in a company, but the compensation information attached to each employee is likely to be much more highly restricted than more common things such as the employee's nickname, hometown, and telephone number. As a result, it would probably make the most sense to separate that information, either as a completely separate resource or using the singleton sub-resource pattern described here.

VOLATILITY

In addition to size and security concerns, there are often scenarios where specific components of a resource have unusual access patterns. In particular, if there is a component that is updated much more frequently than the other components on a resource, keeping these together could lead to a significant amount of write contention, which could ultimately lead to write conflicts or, in extreme cases, data loss. For example, let's imagine a ride-sharing API where there is a `Driver` resource. When the driver's car is moving, we'll want to update the resource's location information as frequently as possible to show the latest location and the driver's movement. On the other hand, more general metadata, such as the license plate, might not change very frequently, maybe not at all. As a result, it would make sense to separate the frequently changing location information from the other metadata so that updates can be done independently.

Obviously this is not an exhaustive list, as there are many reasons for separating components from resources, but these categories are some of the most frequently seen scenarios. Now that we have an understanding of some general reasons we might split things apart, let's look in more detail at how we might model this separation in an API using the singleton sub-resource pattern.

12.2 Overview

Since our goal is to move a component of a resource from a simple property to some sort of separate entity, one tactic we could employ is to design an interface such that the component in question is a hybrid of sorts between a full-fledged resource and a simple attribute on a resource. In essence, we can create something that has some characteristics and behaviors of a full resource and others of a simple resource property.

To accomplish this, we need to define a concept of a singleton sub-resource, which has some unique properties and interaction methods (figure 12.1). This singleton sub-resource will act as a hybrid of sorts between a simple property and a complete resource, which means we'll impose some limitations on what we've come to expect from resources and add some abilities to enhance what we expect from resource properties.

Now that we understand the high-level idea of how this pattern works, let's look at some more specifics about how these singleton sub-resources should behave.

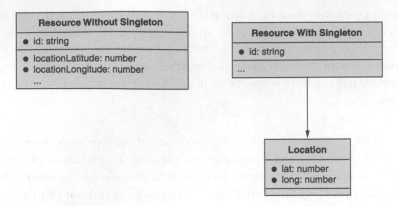

Figure 12.1   Resource moving the location property to a Location singleton sub-resource

12.3   *Implementation*

Once we've decided that something should be split from a simple resource property into a separate singleton sub-resource, we need to figure out exactly what the interface for interacting with these sub-resources looks like. As you can see in table 12.1, if we think of interacting with a singleton sub-resource by looking at the set of standard methods we learned about earlier, it's clear that certain methods take on the behavior of a regular resource and others take on that of a simple resource property.

Table 12.1   Summary behavior of singleton sub-resources

Standard method	Acts like a . . .
Get<Singleton>	Separate resource
Update<Singleton>	Separate resource
Create<Singleton>	Property
Delete<Singleton>	Property
List<Singletons>	n/a

12.3.1   *Standard methods*

GET AND UPDATE

As we can see in table 12.1, both retrieval (get) and modification (update) standard methods act just like they would on any other resource. This means that singleton sub-resources are uniquely addressable with an identifier as regular resources are and can be modified in the traditional way using a partial replacement of properties (e.g., via the PATCH HTTP verb). For complete clarity, the following sequence diagram (see figure 12.2) shows how we might retrieve and modify a singleton sub-resource.

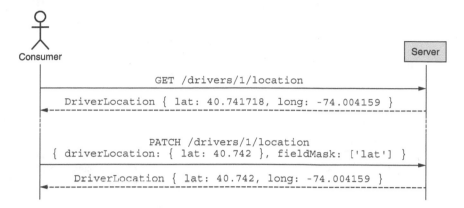

Figure 12.2 Summary of interaction with singleton sub-resource

Ultimately, this means that the get and update methods we'd define for a singleton sub-resource would be identical to those of a regular resource. It's important to remember that addressing the singleton sub-resource is done by a unique identifier rather than using the identifier of the parent resource. In other words, `GetDriver-Location` accepts a unique identifier (e.g., `drivers/1/location`) like any other retrieval method and *not* a parent identifier as we've seen in list methods.

CREATE

Continuing with table 12.1, we can see that the create method acts more like a property. This means that singleton sub-resources simply exist by virtue of their parent existing. In other words, just as there's no need to explicitly create properties on a resource (e.g., a `Driver.licensePlate` property), there's also no need to explicitly create a `DriverLocation` resource. Instead, it must come into existence exactly when the parent resource does.

This also means that there must be no explicit initialization required in order to interact with the singleton sub-resource. This isn't to say that there will never be a need to update properties of the sub-resource after the parent has been created; it is saying that there should not be a specific initialization method that needs to be executed in order to begin updating the sub-resource itself. A sample interaction with a parent resource creating a singleton sub-resource is shown in figure 12.3.

This leads to an obvious question: how can we initialize the data stored in a singleton sub-resource exactly when we create the parent resource? In other words, is there a way to create a `Driver` resource and initialize the `DriverLocation` information exactly when the `Driver` resource is created? The simple answer is no.

The entire point of separating something into a sub-resource is to isolate it in some way from the parent resource. This could be in response to any of the topics discussed in section 12.1 (e.g., volatility), but the consequences of this separation are that the sub-resource is kept generally apart from the parent. While the creation of the parent

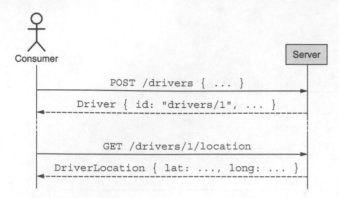

Figure 12.3 Creating a parent resource causes a singleton sub-resource to be created.

implies the existence of the sub-resource, any changes to the information stored in the sub-resource would need to be done separately as the two are ultimately completely separate resources. In other words, creating a `Driver` *and* setting the information in the `DriverLocation` sub-resource isn't any more possible in a single `CreateDriver` method than creating two individual `Driver` resources through a single `CreateDriver` call. This means that it's important to choose reasonable defaults for singleton sub-resources so that they might be useful even when implicitly initialized.

DELETE

Just as creating a parent resource causes a singleton sub-resource to be created, deleting that parent resource must also delete the singleton sub-resource. In other words, sort of like how relational databases allow cascading deletes based on foreign key constraints, deletes of parent resources cascade downward to any singleton sub-resources attached. In essence, this means that when it comes to deleting, singleton sub-resources act more like properties than separate resources. To demonstrate this, a sample interaction of a cascading delete is shown in figure. 12.4.

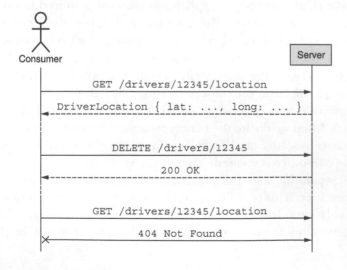

Figure 12.4 The singleton sub-resource is deleted along with the parent resource.

WARNING If a cascading deletion would be surprising or not fit with the expectations of a typical consumer, this is often a good sign that the singleton sub-resource pattern isn't a great fit for the use case.

This covers the standard deletion operation, but it also leads to some important questions about nonstandard deletion, such as, "What do we do when deleting the parent is not instantaneous and uses an LRO (see chapter 10) or relies on the soft-deletion pattern (section 6.1)?" Since deleting causes the sub-resource to act primarily like a property and not like a separate resource, we can transfer that over with the nonstandard behavior. This means that a parent resource that has been flagged for deletion would still exist until the parent deletion stops existing. Likewise, if deleting a parent resource might take a while and therefore relies on an LRO to track the progress of that deletion, the sub-resource must only be deleted once the operation to delete the parent resource completes.

12.3.2 Resetting

In some cases there may be a need to revert the singleton sub-resource itself to a set of reasonable default values, in particular the ones that were set when the parent resource was first created. In that case, the API should support a reset method that would atomically set those values to their original defaults as though the singleton sub-resource had just come into existence as the parent was created. A sample interaction of resetting the sub-resource is shown in figure 12.5.

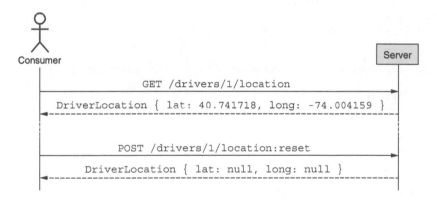

Figure 12.5 Resetting the singleton sub-resource, if implemented, must restore reasonable default values.

12.3.3 Hierarchy

Now that we understand how to interact with singleton sub-resources, it's important that we clarify a few important details about the hierarchical relationship between these singletons and their parents.

REQUIRED PARENTS

As the name implies, sub-resources should be subordinate to some parent resource. This means that a singleton sub-resource should always have a parent resource and should not be attached at the root level of the hierarchy of an API. The reason for this is that global singletons are functionally equivalent to a global shared lock, with a single instance of a resource shared across all of the potential consumers of the API. As you might imagine, sharing global state across all the potential consumers of an API introduces significant write contention, focusing all write traffic toward a single resource.

FULL-RESOURCE PARENTS

Another common edge case to consider is whether singleton sub-resources can have singleton sub-resources of their own. In short, if a singleton sub-resource acts as a parent to other singletons, these should instead be made siblings of the parent itself. Put simply, there really isn't any value added in having one singleton act as a parent to another.

12.3.4 *Final API definition*

Taking all of the details from this implementation, we can define the API for our example service where we have `Driver` resources that have `DriverLocation` singleton sub-resources. This final API definition is shown in listing 12.1.

Listing 12.1 Final API definition using the singleton sub-resource pattern

```
abstract class RideSharingApi {
  static version = "v1";
  static title = "Ride Sharing API";

  @get("/drivers")
  ListDrivers(req: ListDriversRequest): ListDriversResponse;

  @post("/drivers")
  CreateDriver(req: CreateDriverRequest): Driver;

  @get("/{id=drivers/*}")
  GetDriver(req: GetDriverRequest): Driver;

  @patch("/{resource.id=drivers/*}")
  UpdateDriver(req: UpdateDriverRequest): Driver;

  @delete("/{id=drivers/*}")
  DeleteDriver(req: DeleteDriverRequest): void;

  @get("/{id=drivers/*/location}")
  GetDriverLocation(req: GetDriverLocationRequest): DriverLocation;

  @patch("/{resource.id=drivers/*/location}")
  UpdateDriverLocation(req: UpdateDriverLocationRequest): DriverLocation;
}
```

```
interface Driver {
  id: string;
  name: string;
  licensePlate: string;
}
```

Note that the driver's location is not set as a location property. It's separated into a singleton sub-resource.

```
interface DriverLocation {
  id: string;
  lat: number;
  long: number;
  updateTime: Date;
}
```

Remember that the unique identifier of the DriverLocation resource is dependent entirely on that of the Driver resource. In other words, a Driver called drivers/1 would have a DriverLocation called drivers/1/location.

```
interface GetDriverRequest {
  id: string:
}

interface UpdateDriverRequest {
  resource: Driver;
  fieldMask: FieldMask;
}

interface ListDriversRequest {
  maxPageSize: number;
  pageToken: string;
}

interface ListDriversResponse {
  results: Driver[];
  nextPageToken: string;
}

interface CreateDriver {
  driver: Driver;
}

interface DeleteDriverRequest {
  id: string;
}

interface GetDriverLocationRequest {
  id: string;
}

interface UpdateDriverLocationRequest {
  resource: DriverLocation;
  fieldMask: FieldMask;
}
```

12.4   Trade-offs

As we learned when implementing this pattern, there are a few trade-offs that come with using this design, specifically things we lose. Let's dig into these a bit more deeply, starting with atomicity on a parent and sub-resource.

12.4.1 *Atomicity*

When using the singleton sub-resource pattern, we saw that the sub-resource had some characteristics of a property and others of a resource, specifically that creating acted like a property (we never create a singleton sub-resource; it just exists) and others acted more like an actual resource (we update a resource directly rather than by addressing its parent). One side effect of this is that there is no longer a way for us to interact with both the resource and the sub-resource together. In other words, we don't have a way to atomically interact with both the parent resource and the sub-resource at the same time.

Though this is certainly a limitation (after all, when `DriverLocation` information was a property on a `Driver` resource we could atomically create a `Driver` resource with a specific location), this limitation is by design. Our main goal in separating the sub-resource from the parent resource is to isolate this specific set of information, maybe because it's large or maybe because it has very specific security requirements. In other words, this trade-off is meant more as a feature, even though it might mean that certain common actions that were easy to do before are no longer possible.

12.4.2 *Exactly one sub-resource*

Another important trade-off of relying on the singleton sub-resource pattern is that there can only ever be one of the sub-resources. This means that, unlike a traditional subcollection that can contain many sub-resources of the same type, once we've adopted this pattern there can only ever be one instance of this specific sub-resource.

12.5 *Exercises*

1. How big does attribute data need to get before it makes sense to split it off into a separate singleton sub-resource? What considerations go into making your decision?
2. Why do singleton sub-resources only support two of the standard methods (get and update)?
3. Why do singleton sub-resources support a custom reset method rather than repurposing the standard delete method to accomplish the same goal?
4. Why can't singleton sub-resources be children of other singleton sub-resources in the resource hierarchy?

Summary

- Singleton sub-resources are hybrids between properties and resources, storing data that is inherent to a resource but in a separate isolated location.
- Data might be separated from a resource into a singleton sub-resource for a variety of reasons, such as size, complexity, separate security requirements, or differing access patterns and the resulting volatility.

- Singleton sub-resources support the standard get and update methods, but they should never be created or deleted and therefore should not support the standard create or delete methods.
- Singleton sub-resources should generally also support a custom reset method, which restores the resource's attributes to their default states.
- Singleton sub-resources should be attached to a parent resource, and that resource should not, itself, be another singleton sub-resource.

should ... be used in fields and list methods to ... compute what ... ... resource's ...

... Similarly, resources should generally only rely on reference ... what ... the resource's version of the referenced ...

... ... should be limited to a narrow ... ... their single sub-resource.

Cross references

13

In any API with multiple resource types, it's likely that there will be a need for resources to point at one another. Though this manner of referencing resources may appear trivial, many of the behavioral details are left open for interpretation, which means there is the opportunity for inconsistency. This pattern aims to clarify how these references should be defined and, more importantly, how they should behave.

13.1 Motivation

Resources rarely live in a vacuum. As a result, there must be a way for resources to reference one another. These references range from the local (e.g., other resources in the same API) to the global (e.g., resources that live elsewhere on the wider internet) and may fall in between as well (e.g., resources in a different API offered by the same provider) (figure 13.1).

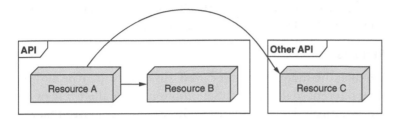

Figure 13.1 Resources can point at others in the same API or in external APIs.

While it might seem obvious to simply refer to these resources by a unique identifier, the behavioral aspects are largely left to the implementer to determine. As a result, we'll need to define a set of guidelines for referring to resources and the patterns of behavior underpinning those references. For example, should you be allowed to delete something that is being pointed at or should this be prohibited? If that's allowed, should there be any postprocessing on the value (such as resetting it to the zero value) given that the resource it pointed to has gone away? Or should the invalid pointer be left alone?

In short, while the general idea behind referencing resources is quite simple, the details can be fairly complicated.

13.2 *Overview*

As you might expect, the cross-reference pattern relies on a reference property on one resource that points to another, using the field name to imply the resource type. This reference is represented using a unique identifier represented as a string value (see chapter 6) as it can then reference resources in the same API, different APIs by the same provider, or entirely separate resources living elsewhere on the internet as a standard URI.

Additionally, this reference is completely decoupled from the resource it points to. This allows for maximum flexibility when manipulating resources, prevents circular references from locking resources into existence, and scales in cases where a single resource is referenced by many thousands of others. However, this also means that consumers must expect that pointers may be out of date and potentially invalid in cases where the underlying resource being referred to has been moved or deleted.

13.3   *Implementation*

There are several important aspects to this pattern. In this section, we'll explore in much more detail the various questions that must be answered regarding how one resource should reference another. Let's start by looking at an example reference and how we should name the field to refer to another resource.

13.3.1   *Reference field name*

While it's possible that the unique identifier used can convey the type and purpose of the resource being referenced, it's a much safer option to use the name of the field to convey both of these aspects. For example, if we have a Book resource that refers to an Author resource, we should name the field storing the reference as authorId to convey that it's the unique identifier of an Author resource.

Listing 13.1   Definition of `Author` and `Book` resources

```
interface Book {
  id: string;
  authorId: string;          ◁  We store a reference to the Author
  title: string;                resource using a string field holding
  // ...                        a unique identifier of an author.
}                          ◁  We'll leave out extra
                              fields for brevity.
interface Author {         The unique identifier of the Author
  id: string;        ◁    resource. This is the value that
  name: string;            appears in the authorId field.
}
```

Most times the resource we'll refer to will be a static type, meaning that we might point to different Author resources, but the type of the resource in question will always be an author. In some cases, however, the type of the resource we're pointing to can vary from case to case, which we'll call *dynamic resource type* references.

   For example, we may want to store a change history of authors and books. This means we'll need the ability to point to not just many different resources, but many different resource types. To do this, we should rely on an additional type field that specifies the type of the target resource in question.

Listing 13.2   Example `ChangeLogEntry` resource with dynamic resource types

```
interface ChangeLogEntry {      The unique identifier of the target
  id: string;                   resource (e.g., the author ID)
  targetId: string;       ◁
  targetType: string;     ◁    The type of the target resource
  // ...        ◁               (e.g., api.mycompany.com/Author)
}                          Here we'd store more details about this
                           particular change to the target resource.
```

Now that we've seen how to define a reference field, let's look more deeply at an important aspect of behavior called *data integrity*.

13.3.2 Data integrity

Since we're using simple string values to point from one resource to another, we have to worry about the freedom provided by this data type: there's no type-level validation. For example, imagine the following order of events with some book and author resources.

Listing 13.3 Deleting an author referred to by a book

```
let author = CreateAuthor({ name: "Michelle Obama" });
let book = CreateBook({           ◁──┐   Here we create an author
  title: "Becoming",                  │   and then a book referring
  authorId: author.id                 │   to that author.
});
DeleteAuthor({ id: author.id });   ◁──┐   After that, we delete the
                                       │   Author resource from our API.
```

At this point, we have what's called a *dangling pointer* (sometimes known as an *orphaned record*), where the book resource is pointing to an author that no longer exists. What should happen in this scenario? There are a few options:

1 We can prohibit the deletion of the author and throw an error.
2 We can allow the deletion of the author but set the authorId field to a zero value
3 We can allow the deletion of the author and deal with the bad pointer at runtime.

If we choose to prohibit the deletion of the author (or, for that matter, any author who still has books registered in the system), we run the risk of serious inconvenience to API consumers who may need to delete hundreds or thousands of books just to delete a single author. Further, if we had two resources that pointed at one another, we would never be able to delete either of them. For example, consider if each Author resource had an additional field for their favorite book and (being selfish) an author had their own book as a favorite, shown in figure 13.2. In this scenario, we could never delete the book because the author has it listed as a favorite. We could also never delete the author because there are still books that point to that author.

Figure 13.2 It's possible to have circular references between two resources.

If we choose to allow the deletion by resetting the author pointer to a zero value, we avoid this circular reference problem; however, we may have to update a potentially large number of resources due to a single call. For example, imagine one particularly prolific author who has written hundreds or even thousands of books. In that case, deleting a single author resource would actually involve updating many thousands of records. This not only might take a while, but it may be the case that this isn't something the system can do in an atomic manner. And if it can't be done atomically, then we run the risk of leaving dangling pointers around when the whole point is to avoid any invalid references.

These issues leave us with the third option: simply ask API consumers to expect that reference fields might be invalid or point to resources that may have been deleted. While this might be inconvenient, it provides the most consistent behavior to consumers with clear and simple expectations: references should be checked. It also doesn't violate any of the constraints imposed by standard methods, such as deletes being atomic and containing no side effects.

Now that we've explored how references should behave in the face of changes to the underlying data, let's look at a commonly raised concern about references versus cached values.

13.3.3 *Value vs. reference*

So far we've operated on the assumption that string identifier references should be used to refer to other resources in an API, but that's clearly not the only option. On the contrary, when considering how we can refer to things in other places of the API, one of the first questions is whether to store a simple pointer to the other resource or a cached copy of the resource itself. In many programming languages, this is the difference between *pass by reference* or *pass by value*, where the former passes around a pointer to something in memory and the latter passes a copy of the data in question.

The distinguishing factor here is that by relying on references, we can always be sure that the data we have on hand is fresh and up-to-date. On the other hand, whenever copies enter the picture we have to concern ourselves with whether the data we have on hand has changed since we last retrieved it. On the flip side, storing a reference to the resource only means that anyone using the API must make a second request to retrieve the data at that location. When we compare this to having a copy of the data right in front of us, the convenience alone seems tempting. For example, in order to retrieve the name of a given author of a book, we'll need to do two separate API calls.

Listing 13.4   Retrieving a book author's name with two API calls

```
let book = GetBook({          Here we retrieve a book by a
  "id: "books/1234"           (random) unique identifier.
});
let authorName = GetAuthor({ id: book.authorId }).name;        To see the name of
                                                               the author, we need
                                                               a separate API call.
```

These two calls, while simple, are still double the number we'd need in the alternative design where we return the full `Author` resource in the response when retrieving a book.

Listing 13.5 Redefining the `Book` and `Author` resources to use values

```
interface Book {
  id: string;
  title: string;
  author: Author;        ◁─┐  Here we have the entire Author
}                            │  resource value stored rather
                             │  than a reference to the author.
interface Author {
  id: string;
  name: string;
}
```

While we now have immediate access to the book's author information without a second API call, we have to make a decision about how to populate that data on the server side. We could either retrieve the author information alongside the book information from our database at the time of each GetBook request (e.g., use a SQL JOIN statement), or we could store a cached copy of the author information within the book resource. The former will put more load on the database but will guarantee that all information is fresh when requested while the latter will avoid that problem but introduce a data consistency problem where we now have to come up with a strategy of how to keep this cache of author information fresh and up-to-date.

Further, we now need to deal with the fact that the size of the GetBook response will grow every time the Author resource grows. If we follow this strategy with other aspects of a book (e.g., if we start storing the information about the publisher of a given book), then the size can continue to grow even further, potentially getting out of hand.

Finally, this type of schema can cause confusion when consumers are expected to make modifications to the Book resource. Can they update the author's name by updating the Book resource itself? How do they go about updating the author?

Listing 13.6 Example code snippet with annotation

```
let author = CreateAuthor({ name: "Michelle Robinson" });
let book = CreateBook({     ◁─┐  Creating a book requires some unusual syntax
  title: "Becoming",          │  where we set the author's ID field only and allow
  author: { id: author.id }   │  the rest to be populated automatically.
});
UpdateBook({                ◁─┐  Is this valid? Can we update
  id: book.id,                │  the name of the author by
  author: { name: "Michelle Obama" }  │  updating the book?
});
```

As a result of all these potential issues and thorny questions, it's usually best to use references alone and then rely on something like GraphQL to stitch these various references together. This allows API consumers to run a single query and fetch all (and exactly all) the information they want about a given resource and those referenced by that resource, avoiding the bloat and removing the need to cache any information.

13.3.4 *Final API definition*

We can see the final set of interfaces that illustrate how to properly reference resources from one resource to another.

Listing 13.7   Final API definition

```
interface Book {
  id: string;
  authorId: string;
  title: string;
}

interface Author {
  id: string;
  name: string;
}

interface ChangeLogEntry {
  id: string;
  targetId: string;
  targetType: string;
  description: string;
}
```

13.4   *Trade-offs*

As noted previously, the main trade-off we suffer by relying on references is the requirement that we either make multiple API calls to get related information or use something like GraphQL to retrieve all the information we're interested in.

13.5   *Exercises*

1 When does it make sense to store a copy of a foreign resource's data rather than a reference?
2 Why is it untenable to maintain referential integrity in an API system?
3 An API claims to ensure references will stay up-to-date across an API. Later, as the system grows, they decide to drop this rule. Why is this a dangerous thing to do?

Summary

- Fields storing a reference should generally be string fields (i.e., whatever the type of the identifier is) and should end with a suffix of "ID" (e.g., `authorId`). Fields holding a copy of foreign resource data should, obviously, omit this suffix.
- References should generally not expect to be maintained over the lifetime of the resource. If other resources are deleted, references may become invalid.
- Resource data may be stored in-line in the referencing resource. This resource data may become stale as the data being referenced changes over time.

Association resources

14

This chapter covers

- How to handle many-to-many relationships with association resources
- What name to choose for association resources
- How to support standard methods for association resources
- Strategies for handling referential integrity

In this chapter, we'll explore a pattern for modeling many-to-many relationships between two resources using a separate association resource to represent the connection between the two. This pattern allows consumers to explicitly address an individual relationship between two resources as well as storing and managing extra metadata about that relationship.

14.1 Motivation

Most of the time, the relationships we'll define between resources in an API will be simple and obvious because they tend to be unidirectional in nature, acting as pointers or references going from one resource to another (e.g., database 1 belongs to project 1), as shown in figure 14.1. When one resource type refers to

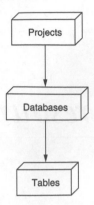

Figure 14.1   Unidirectional, or hierarchical, relationships between resources

another in this way, we say they have a *one-to-many* relationship. While these types of relationships are typically easy to manage when designing an API (often just a property referencing the other resource), there are other times the relationships needed are more complicated and, as a result, are more difficult to express in an easy-to-use API.

One of the most common types of these more complicated relationships is a *many-to-many* relationship, where resource types are associated with one another rather than one merely pointing to another. For example, let's imagine a scenario where we need to track people (users) and the various groups they belong to (groups). These users may be members of lots of different groups and, obviously, groups are made up of many different users as members. Additionally, there may be some specific information about the relationship itself we want to keep track of. For example, maybe we want to store the exact time a user joined a group or the specific role they might hold in the group.

While these many-to-many relationships have a standard canonical representation in most relational databases (relying on a *join table* or *link table*, which contain rows responsible for keeping track of the associations between instances of the two types), it's not always clear how we expose this concept in an API. The goal of this pattern is to outline a specific way in which we can expose the rows in these *join tables* as separate resources that represent the association between two resources in an API.

14.2   *Overview*

As mentioned, the most common way of storing many-to-many relationships, particularly in relational databases, is by using a *join table* with rows representing the relationship between two resources. For example, we might have a table of User resources, another of Group resources, and then a table mapping these two resources together (e.g., UserGroup resources), as shown figure 14.2. As a result, one obvious way to present these resources and their relationship via an API is simply to expose all tables as resources. In this scenario, the database schema actually lines up one-to-one with the

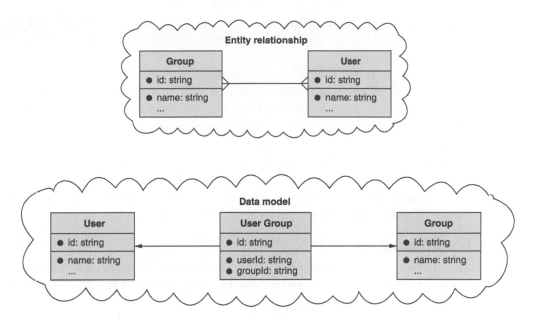

Figure 14.2 Using a join table to store many-to-many relationships

API surface, so we would define an API consisting of three resources: User, Group, and UserGroup (the mapping or association resource).

This leads to the obvious question: how does this work? At a high level, we can rely on the association resource to do most of the heavy lifting. Since the relationship is represented by an actual resource, it is created and deleted like any other. In this example, creating a UserGroup resource represents someone joining a group and deleting one represents someone leaving a group. Additionally, we can always view a specific association by retrieving it using its identifier (e.g., GetUserGroup), and we can list all associations by retrieving the collection based on its parent (e.g., ListUser-Groups). To see only specific associations (e.g., those belonging to a single group or a single user), we can apply a filter when listing.

Finally, the most powerful aspect of using an association resource is the ability to store metadata about the relationship itself. For example, rather than simply storing that a user has joined a specific group, we can store extra information such as when they joined or what role they might have (e.g., administrator). This is the primary reason retrieving a UserGroup resource makes sense: we might want to know more detail about the relationship itself.

14.2.1 Association alias methods

Sometimes the association resource has a sense of ownership by one or both of the associated resources. In other words, it seems natural to see a group as containing a list of users. Likewise, it seems natural to see a user as being a member of many different groups. Further, in both of these cases, it's natural to want to ask both of those questions of our API, for example, "What groups is this user a member of?" and "What users are in this group?"

While we've noted that we can simply make a request to list associations with an appropriate filter, often in resource-oriented APIs, consumers want the ability to think of relationships in a more direct fashion and, as a result, it sometimes makes sense to provide convenient aliases for these types of common questions. To express this natural alignment of the association resources, we can optionally alias a subcollection underneath each of the resources being associated so that we can ask these questions using a single unfiltered request. We'll explore this in more detail later, but for now it should suffice to say that the strategy here is to rely on aliases to provide the convenience of asking common questions about many-to-many relationships.

14.3   Implementation

Now that we understand the high-level strategy for this pattern, let's look more closely at the details of how it works and how we can implement it. Let's start at the beginning by looking at naming.

14.3.1   Naming the association resource

Before we can do anything else, we first have to choose a name for the association resource. In some cases this may be obvious based on the context of the application itself. For example, in an API for a school that allows students to enroll in courses, the association resource might be called `CourseRegistration` or `CourseEnrollment`.

Other times, the name might be harder to find. For example, in that same API, storing the association between the list of teachers (and assistants, lab assistants, etc.) isn't technically an enrollment or a registration, so we're stuck looking for an alternative. A common choice for handling this is to use something like Membership or Association with some modifiers to clarify at least one of the two resources being joined (e.g., `CourseMembership`). In some cases, like with users joining groups or clubs, we might just call the association `Membership` with no extra modifier, but this should always make sense in context.

Once we have a name for the resource, we can start looking at how we implement the various ways to interact with it.

14.3.2   Standard method behavior

For each association resource, we'll need to implement at least some of the standard methods. As we can see in table 14.1, we'll certainly need the create and delete standard methods, and in the common scenario where the association resource holds metadata (i.e., when we care about extra information about the relationship), we'll need get and update standard methods. Finally, we'll need the list method to browse through the various memberships. All of these methods should conform exactly to the standard methods, which should be easy given that memberships are represented like any other resource.

Table 14.1 Summary of standard methods on an association resource

Standard method	Behavior	Required?
Create	Joins the two resources	Yes
Get	Shows metadata about the relationship	Only if there's metadata
List	Lists the associations between the resources	Yes
Update	Updates metadata about the relationship	Only if there's metadata
Delete	Removes the association between the resources	Yes

Before we continue, it's important to take note of one extra requirement that might not be present in other resources' standard method implementations: uniqueness constraints.

14.3.3 *Uniqueness*

Unlike most resources, association resources tend to have a very important uniqueness constraint that we must apply: there should be only one association resource that represents the two resources being associated. In other words, we usually want to be certain that a user is only a member of a group once. To enforce this, there is a new validation requirement on the API when creating an association resource.

Typically, we only return a resource conflict error (HTTP code `409 Conflict`) when the resource in question is created with an identifier that already exists. In this case, however, an association resource is only fundamentally distinct from another if the two resources being associated are different. Put simply, the example in listing 14.1, where we try to add a user to the same group twice, should fail as it's creating a conflicting resource.

Listing 14.1 Associating the same data causing a conflict error

```
let membershipData = { userId: "Jimmy", groupId: "2" };      First we add Jimmy
let membership1 = CreateMembership(membershipData);    ◁──   to group 2. This
let membership2 = CreateMembership(membershipData);    ◁─┐   should succeed.

              Jimmy is already a member of group 2, so this  │
              request should fail with a 409 Conflict HTTP error.  │
```

Next, let's look at how updating association resources might be slightly different than we've seen in the past.

14.3.4 *Read-only fields*

While the metadata about a relationship might change from time to time, the resources being associated should not change in the lifetime of the resource. In other words, when we have a resource that represents a user joining a group, we should not be able to change this to make this same resource represent a different user joining the group (or the same user joining a different group). Instead, in that scenario we should simply delete the old association resource and create a separate one to represent the new user-group association.

This leads to the question of whether it should result in an error or a silent failure when a consumer tries to make this type of change. In this case, the two cross-referencing fields (the user and group fields) should be considered output only and therefore ignored whenever specified during an update request.

Listing 14.2   Ignoring read-only fields at update time

```
let membership1 = CreateMembership({        ◁──┐   Here, we add Jimmy to group 2
  userId: "Jimmy",                              │   in an administrative role.
  groupId: "2",
  role: "admin" });

UpdateMembership({        ◁──┐   When we try to change the user to Sally and the
  id: membership1.id,         │   role to be a regular user, only the role is updated.
  userId: "Sally",            │   This request just makes Jimmy a regular user of
  role: "user"                │   group 2 and does nothing at all for Sally.
};
```

Now that we've looked at the standard methods and how they should behave with an association resource, let's look at some of the optional convenience methods we might implement to cover common consumer scenarios.

14.3.5 *Association alias methods*

As we discussed earlier, one of the most common questions we might want to ask is which resources are associated with which other resources. For example, we want to quickly ask, "What groups is Jimmy a member of?" or "What members are in group 2?" While this is perfectly possible using a specific filter applied on the `ListMemberships-Request`, we can simplify these common queries by providing alias methods that answer these two specific questions.

Listing 14.3   Listing associations using a filter

```
                                                          Here we construct a
                                                          ListMembershipsRequest
memberships = ListMemberships({ filter: "groupId: 2" });  ◁──  that only returns those
usersInGroup2 = memberships.map(            ◁──┐              for group 2.
  (membership) => membership.user );            │
                                                │     To get the users who are members of
                                                │     group 2, we simply grab the user field
memberships = ListMemberships({        ◁──┐     │     from each membership.
  filter: "userId: Jimmy" });              │
jimmysGroups = memberships.map(            │    Here we construct a
  (membership) => membership.groupId );    │    ListMembershipsRequest that only
                                                returns those with Jimmy as the user.
 To see the groups Jimmy is a member
 of, we simply grab the group field
 from each membership.
```

While this certainly works, it might make sense to make methods that focus specifically on these use cases. We can do this by creating alias methods that have an implied (and required) filter parameter for the query we want to do. In the example of User and Group resources joined by a Membership association resource, we might have two aliases, shown in table 14.2.

Table 14.2 Aliases for common queries of association resources

Question	List with filter	Custom method

What groups is Jimmy in?	`ListMemberships({`
	`    filter: "userId: Jimmy"`
	`})`
		`ListUserGroups({`
		`    userId: "Jimmy"`
		`})`

What users are in group 2?	`ListMemberships( {`
	`    filter: "groupId: 2"`
	`})`
		`ListGroupUsers({`
		`    groupId: 2`
		`})`

The naming might be a bit confusing, so try to remember that the first (singular) portion of the name is the owning resource and the second (plural) portion is what's being listed. So when listing UserGroups we're looking at the groups for a given user, and when listing GroupUsers, we're looking at the users for a given group.

14.3.6 *Referential integrity*

As we saw in chapter 13, referential integrity in an API refers to the fact that when we refer to another resource, we need to consider whether that reference is valid. For example, what happens if we delete a resource that is still being pointed to by other resources? More specifically, if we have an association resource that ties two resources together, how do we handle requests that would delete one of the resources being associated?

In scenarios like this, we have a few different options, provided and standardized by most modern relational databases and summarized in table 14.3.

Table 14.3 Summary of referential integrity behavior

Option	Behavior
Cascade	Delete all other resources that point to the deleted resource.
Restrict	Prevent deleting any resources that are still pointed to by others.
Set null	Any pointers to the resource being deleted are set to null.
Do nothing	Deleting resources does nothing to the pointers and leaves them as invalid.

While there are many reasons to choose each of these options, in the case of dealing with association resources the API should generally choose to either restrict deletion while other resources still point to the resource or simply do nothing and allow the association resource's reference to become invalid. If we instead choose to cascade or set the pointer to null, there is a possibility that we could trigger a stampede of writes to set values to null (e.g., there are 10 billion resources that point to the resource being deleted) or an avalanche of deletions (e.g., if one deletion triggers another, which triggers another, and onward). In short, this means that if we were to try deleting a resource that had an association resource referring to it, we should either return a precondition failed error (HTTP code 412) or simply delete the resource and leave the association resource as a dangling pointer to be dealt with later by the consumer.

14.3.7 *Final API definition*

Finally it's time to look at a complete example of defining an API for an association resource of User, Group, and Membership resources.

> **Listing 14.4   Final API definition using association resources**

```
abstract class GroupApi {
  static version = "v1";
  static title = "Group API";

  // ... Other methods left out for brevity.

  @post("/memberships")
  CreateMembership(req: CreateMembershipRequest): Membership;

  @get("/{id=memberships/*}")
  GetMembership(req: GetMembershipRequest): Membership;

  @patch("/{resource.id=memberships/*}")
  UpdateMembership(req: UpdateMembershipRequest): Membership;

  @delete("/{id=memberships/*}")
  DeleteMembership(req: DeleteMembershipRequest): void;

  @get("/memberships")
  ListMemberships(req: ListMembershipsRequest): ListMembershipsResponse;

  @get("/{groupId=groups/*}/users")
  ListGroupUsers(req: ListGroupUsersRequest): ListGroupUsersResponse;

  @get("/{userId=users/*}/groups")
  ListUserGroups(req: ListUserGroupsRequest): ListUserGroupsResponse;
}

interface Group {
  id: string;
  userCount: number;
  // ...
}

interface User {
  id: string;
  emailAddress: string;
  // ...
}
```

Optional aliasing for listing users in a group ⟶ (points to `@get("/{groupId=groups/*}/users")`)

Optional aliasing for listing the groups a user is a member of ⟶ (points to `@get("/{userId=users/*}/groups")`)

Note that we do not in-line the list of users here. To view members of a group, we simply list memberships with a filter for a single group or rely on an aliased subcollection (ListGroupUsers). ⟵ (points to `interface Group`)

Note that we do not in-line the groups here. To view the groups a user is a member of, we simply list memberships with a filter for a single user or rely on an aliased subcollection (ListUserGroups). ⟵ (points to `interface User`)

```
interface Membership {
  id: string;
  groupId: string;
  userId: string;
  role: string;
  expireTime: DateTime;
}
```

Note that we choose the name "Membership" here for the association resource of users to groups.

Here we store references to the user and the group being associated, not an entire copy of the resources.

The rest of the fields are extra metadata about the association.

```
interface ListMembershipsRequest {
  parent: string;
  maxPageSize: number;
  pageToken: string;
}

interface ListMembershipsResponse {
  results: Membership[];
  nextPageToken: string;
}

interface CreateMembershipRequest {
  resource: Membership;
}
```

Note that there is no parent here as Membership resources are top-level resources.

```
interface GetMembershipRequest {
  id: string;
}

interface UpdateMembershipRequest {
  resource: Membership;
  fieldMask: FieldMask;
}

interface DeleteMembershipRequest {
  id: string;
}

// Optional from here on.

interface ListUserGroupsRequest {
  userId: string;
  maxPageSize: number;
  pageToken: string;
}

interface ListUserGroupsResponse {
  results: Group[];
  nextPageToken: string;
}

interface ListGroupUsersRequest {
  groupId: string;
  maxPageSize: number;
  pageToken: string;
}
```

```
interface ListGroupUsersResponse {
  results: User[];
  nextPageToken: string;
}
```

Now that we've seen how each of these three options works, let's pause to look at some of the things we lose out on when using this pattern.

14.4   Trade-offs

When using an association resource to represent a many-to-many relationship, you get the most freedom to design all the details about how that relationship works, but it comes with a few drawbacks.

14.4.1   Complexity

In exchange for an extreme level of flexibility, we pay the price of a slightly more complicated interface that at times may not feel intuitive. For example, when we want a user to join a group, we use a standard create method to make a new membership rather than calling a `JoinGroup` method.

Additionally, we have an extra association resource to consider, which means a larger API surface as the API now has both one extra resource per association and up to seven additional methods to consider (five for the standard methods and two optional alias methods). Often these methods are easy to learn and understand and as a result are worth the additional cognitive load; however, it's worth pointing out that there are simply more things to learn.

14.4.2   Separation of associations

When using an association resource, even though we can provide alias methods to make it easier to ask questions about resource relationships, we still treat the association between the two resources as separate from the information about each resource. For example, the description of a group and the list of members of a group are both considered information about the group; however, we retrieve these in two very different ways. Getting the group description would be using a `GetGroup()` method, whereas finding all the members of the group might use the `ListGroup-Users()` alias method.

As we learned, there is a good reason for this (the list of users could get very large), but it does mean that there's a separation of these two things despite both being closely related to the nature of the group in question.

14.5   Exercises

1 Design an API for associating users with chat rooms that they may have joined and that also stores a role and the time when they join.

2 In a chat application, users might leave and join the same room multiple times. How would you model the API such that you maintain that history while

ensuring that a user can't have multiple presences in the same chat room at the same time?

Summary

- Many-to-many relationships are when two resources each have many of the other. For example, a user might be a member of many groups, and a group has many users as members.
- We can use association resources as a way to model many-to-many relationships between resources in an API.
- Association resources are the most flexible way of representing a relationship between two resources.
- We can use these association resources to store additional metadata about the relationship between the two resources.

Add and remove
custom methods

15

This chapter covers

- How to manage many-to-many relationships implicitly
- The benefits and drawbacks of implicit rather than explicit association
- How to use custom methods to associate resources together
- Handling issues with data integrity of associated resources

In this chapter, we'll explore an alternative pattern for modeling many-to-many relationships that relies on custom add and remove methods to associate (and disassociate) two resources. This pattern allows consumers to manage many-to-many relationships without introducing a third association resource as a necessary requirement.

15.1 Motivation

As we learned in chapter 14, sometimes we have a need to keep track of the relationships between resources, and sometimes those relationships can be complicated. In particular, we often have to handle situations where two resources can both have many of one another, known as a many-to-many relationship.

While the association resource pattern offers a very flexible and useful way to model this type of relationship, it seems worth asking whether there could be a simpler way to do this if we can live with some limitations. In other words, given some restrictions, can we make the API simpler and more intuitive? And if so, what are the specific limitations? This pattern explores a simpler alternative to the association resource pattern.

15.2 Overview

As you might guess, there certainly are simpler ways of representing and manipulating many-to-many relationships in an API, but they come with several restrictions. In this particular pattern, we'll look at a way of hiding the individual resources that represent these relationships and use custom methods to create and delete associations. Let's start by first summarizing the methods and then exploring the specific limitations that come up when relying on this design pattern.

At the most basic level, we simplify the API by completely hiding the association resource from consumers and instead manage the relationship using add and remove custom methods. These methods act as shortcuts to create and delete associations between the two resources in question and hide all of the details about that relationship, except for the fact that it exists (or doesn't exist). In the classic example of users who can be members of multiple groups (and groups that obviously contain multiple users), this means we could simply use these methods to represent users joining (add) or leaving (remove) a given group.

To adopt this pattern, let's look at a few of the limitations we'll need to take into consideration. First, since we only ever store the simple fact that two resources are associated, we won't be able to store any metadata about the relationship itself. This means, for example, that if we use this pattern for managing users as members of groups, we can't store details about the membership such as the date a user joined a group or any specific role a user might play in a given group.

Next, since we're going to use custom methods to add and remove the association between the resources, we have to consider one of the resources the *managing resource*— sort of like one being the parent of the other. More concretely, we'll have to choose whether we add users to groups or add groups to users. If the former, then the user resources are the ones being passed around and group resources are managing the relationship. If the latter, then users are managing the relationship while groups are passed around. Thinking in terms of actual code (in this case, in object-oriented programming style), the managing resource is the one that would have the add and remove methods attached to it.

Listing 15.1 Code snippets for two alternatives when choosing a managing resource

```
group.addUser(userId);
user.addGroup(groupId);
```

When a user manages the relationship,
we add groups to a given user.

When a group manages
the relationship, we add
users to a given group.

Sometimes the choice of a managing resource will be obvious, but other times it might be more subtle and both options make sense. In some cases, neither will seem intuitive as the managing resource, but at the end of the day using this pattern requires that we choose a single managing resource. Assuming we can live with both of these limitations, let's look at the specifics of how this particular pattern must work.

15.3 *Implementation*

Once we've identified the managing resource, we can define add and remove custom methods. The full name of the method should follow the form of Add<Managing-Resource><Associated-Resource> (and likewise for remove). For example, if we have users who can be added and removed from groups, the user would be the associated resource and the group managing the resource. This means the method names would be AddGroupUser and RemoveGroupUser.

These methods should accept a request that contains both a parent resource (in this case, the managing resource) and the identifier of the resource being added or removed. Notice that we use the identifier only and not the full resource. This is because the other information would be extraneous and potentially misleading if consumers were led to believe that they had the ability to associate two resources and update one of them at the same time. A summary of the add and remove methods and their HTTP equivalents are shown in table 15.1.

Table 15.1 Add and remove method summary

Action	Method	HTTP equivalent

Add user 1 to group 1.	`AddGroupUser({`
	`    parent: "groups/1",`
	`    userId: "users/1"`
	`});`
		`POST /groups/1/users:add`
		
		`{ userId: "users/1" }`

Remove user 1 from group 1.	`RemoveGroupUser({`
	`    parent: "groups/1",`
	`    userId: "users/1"`
	`});`
		`POST /groups/1/users:remove`
		
		`{ userId: "users/1" }`

15.3.1 *Listing associated resources*

To list the various associations we will rely on customized list standard methods that look just like the alias methods we discussed in the association resource method. These methods simply list the various associated resources, providing pagination and filtering over the results. Since we have two ways to look at the relationship (for example, we might want to see which users are members of a given group as well as which groups a given user is a member of), we'll need two different methods for each of the scenarios.

These methods follow a similar naming convention to the add and remove methods, with both resources in the name of the method. Using our users and groups example, we provide two different methods to list the various users and groups given a specific condition: ListGroupUsers provides the list of users belonging to a given group and ListUserGroups provides the list of groups that a given user is a member of. Just like other custom methods, these follow a similar HTTP mapping naming convention but rely on an implicit subcollection, summarized in table 15.2.

Table 15.2 List method summary

Action	Method	HTTP equivalent
What users are in group 1?	ListGroupUsers({ parent: "groups/1" })	GET /groups/1/users
What groups is user 1 a member of?	ListUserGroups({ parent: "users/1" });	GET /users/1/groups

15.3.2 *Data integrity*

One common question arises when we run into issues of duplicate data. For example, what if we try to add the same user to a group twice? On the other hand, what if we attempt to remove a user from a group they aren't currently a member of?

As we saw in chapter 7, the behavior in these cases is going to be very similar to deleting a resource that doesn't exist and creating a duplicate (and therefore conflicting) resource. This means that if we attempt to add a user twice to the same group, our API should respond with a conflict error (e.g., 409 Conflict) and if we attempt to remove a user from a group that doesn't exist, we should return an error expressing a failed assumption (e.g., 412 Precondition Failed) to signal that we're not able to execute the requested operation.

This means that if all a consumer cares about is making sure a user is (or isn't) a member of a given group, they can simply treat these error conditions as their work having already been done. In other words, if we just want to be sure that Jimmy is a member of group 2, a successful result or a conflict error are both valid results as both signify that Jimmy is currently a member of the group as we intended. The difference in response code simply conveys whether we were the ones responsible for the addition to the group, but either conveys that the user is now a member of the group.

15.3.3   *Final API definition*

A full example of this pattern implemented, using the same users and groups example, is shown in listing 15.2. As you can see, this is much shorter and simpler than relying on an association resource; however, we lack the ability to store metadata about the relationship of users belonging to groups.

Listing 15.2   Final API definition using the add/remove pattern

```
abstract class GroupApi {
  static version = "v1";
  static title = "Group API";

  @get("{id=users/*}")
  GetUser(req: GetUserRequest): User;

  // ...

  @get("{id=groups/*}")
  GetGroup(req: GetGroupRequest): Group;

  // ...

  @post("{parent=groups/*}/users:add")
  AddGroupUser(req: AddGroupUserRequest): void;

  @post("{parent=group/*}/users:remove")
  RemoveGroupUser(req: RemoveGroupUserRequest): void;

  @get("{parent=groups/*}/users")
  ListGroupUsers(req: ListGroupUsersRequest):
    ListGroupUsersResponse;

  @get("{parent=users/*}/groups")
  ListUserGroups(req: ListUserGroupsRequest):
    ListUserGroupsResponse;
}

interface Group {
  id: string;
  userCount: number;

  // ...

}

interface User {
  id: string;
  emailAddress: string;
}

interface ListUserGroupsRequest {
  parent: string;
  maxPageSize?: number;
```

For brevity we're going to omit all of the other standard methods for the User and Group resources.

We use AddGroupUser and RemoveGroupUser to manipulate which users are associated with which groups.

To see which users are in a given group, we use an implicit subcollection mapping to a ListGroupUsers method.

To see which groups a user is a member of, we use the same idea and create a ListUserGroups method.

Note that we do not in-line the users here since the list could be very long. To see the list of users we instead use ListGroupUsers.

```
    pageToken?: string;
    filter?: string;
}

interface ListUserGroupsResponse {
    results: Group[];
    nextPageToken: string;
}

interface ListGroupUsersRequest {
    parent: string;
    maxPageSize?: number;
    pageToken?: string;
    filter?: string
}

interface ListGroupUsersResponse {
    results: User[];
    nextPageToken: string;
}

interface AddGroupUserRequest {
    parent: string;
    userId: string;
}

interface RemoveGroupUserRequest {
    parent: string;
    userId: string;
}
```

15.4 Trade-offs

As we noted at the start of this chapter, the primary goal of this pattern is to provide the ability to manage many-to-many relationships without taking on the complexity of a full-blown association resource. In exchange for this simplification, we make a few trade-offs in the form of functional limitations.

15.4.1 Nonreciprocal relationship

Unlike an association resource, using add and remove custom methods requires that we choose one of the resources to be the managing resource and another to be the managed resource. In other words, we need to decide which resource is the one being added (and removed) to (and from) the other. In many cases this nonreciprocity is convenient and obvious, but other times this can seem counterintuitive.

15.4.2 Relationship metadata

By using custom add and remove methods rather than an association resource, we give up the ability to store metadata about the relationship itself. This means that we won't be able to store any information other than the existence (or lack of existence) of a relationship. In other words, we can't keep track of when the relationship was created or anything specific to the relationship and instead will have to put that elsewhere.

15.5 *Exercises*

1 When would you opt to use custom add and remove methods rather than an association resource to model a many-to-many relationship between two resources?

2 When associating `Recipe` resources with `Ingredient` resources, which is the managing resource and which the associated resource?

3 What would the method be called to list the `Ingredient` resources that make up a specific recipe?

4 When a duplicate resource is added using the custom add method, what should the result be?

Summary

- For scenarios where association resources are too heavyweight (e.g., there's no need for any extra relationship-oriented metadata), using add and remove custom methods can be a simpler way to manage many-to-many relationships.

- Add and remove custom methods allow an associated resource (i.e., the subordinate) to be added or removed in some association to a managing resource.

- Listing associated resources can be performed using standard list methods on the meta-resources.

Polymorphism *16*

This chapter covers

- What polymorphism is
- The benefits of polymorphism and when to use it in an API
- How best to structure polymorphic resources
- Why polymorphic methods should be avoided in resource-oriented APIs

When building software systems, polymorphism provides the ability for objects to take many different forms, typically relying on explicit object inheritance. In this pattern, we'll explore how to translate this powerful tool from the world of object-oriented programming to that of resource-oriented API design. We'll also investigate a few guidelines for when to rely on polymorphic resources over completely independent resources.

16.1 Motivation

In object-oriented programming (OOP), polymorphism is the idea of using single common interfaces across different concrete types, minimizing the implementation details we need to understand in order to interact with a specific type. In other words, if we have `class Triangle` and `class Square`, they might both implement a common `countSides()` method and specify this by extending a shared `interface Shape`.

Listing 16.1   Example of polymorphism in TypeScript

```typescript
interface Shape {
  countSides(): number;        ◁—| The interface declares a single
}                                  function that must be implemented.

class Triangle implements Shape {   ◁—
  countSides() { return 3; }             Two different classes implement
}                                        the interface and therefore
                                         implement the method declared.
class Square implements Shape {   ◁—
  countSides() { return 4; }
}
```

Since we have this common interface, we can write code that deals only with `Shape` interfaces, which means that we wouldn't have to care whether the specific shape is a `Triangle` or a `Square` (or something else) so long as it implements the requirements specified by the `Shape` interface.

Listing 16.2   Polymorphic method to count sides on any shape

```typescript
function countSides(shape: Shape): number {   ◁—  We don't have to specify a Triangle
  return shape.countSides();                        or a Square as input. We can just
}                                                    require that the class implement
                                                     the Shape interface.
```

This idea is very powerful in OOP, leading to much cleaner and more modular code, so it only makes sense that we might desire this same ability in a web API. The problem arises when we try to figure out how to accurately translate this concept from a world of object-oriented programming languages to a world of JSON and HTTP. After all, what is the equivalent of the `countSides()` method in a resource-oriented web API? What is the right resource to represent what we want? The goal of this pattern is to illustrate a safe, flexible, and sustainable way to bring one of the most powerful features of object-oriented programming into the world of resource-oriented APIs.

16.2   Overview

In this pattern, we'll explore the concept of polymorphic resources. These are resources that take the form of the generic interface (e.g., `Shape`) with an explicit field specifying the more detailed type of the resource (e.g., triangle or square). While there are many benefits of relying on this strategy, the most important one is that we won't have to duplicate standard methods for each specific implementation. In other words, rather than `ListTriangles` and `ListSquares`, we can use a single `ListShapes` method.

While this strategy simplifies the polymorphic behavior (e.g., methods that interact with the generic resource rather than the specific implementation), it says nothing about the data storage aspects of polymorphism. In other words, while a square has a side length, a triangle has a base and a height, meaning that to truly represent the details of these different shapes, we actually need to store different fields on the resource. To address this, we'll ultimately have to employ some server-side validation, such that our generic interface is a superset of the fields necessary and therefore capable of storing fields corresponding to all the various subtypes. In other words, the Shape resource might have a way to store both a radius (for circles), base and height (for triangles), and length (for squares) and to validate these values depending on the type specification.

As always, however, the details are where things get complicated. For example, what should we do if an API request includes fields that apply to the wrong type of resource (e.g., a radius definition for a Shape with type square)? Should that be an error, or should it be ignored? In the next section, we'll explore how all of this works in much more detail.

16.3 Implementation

Polymorphism is obviously a very powerful tool in many programming languages, so it stands to reason that polymorphic resources are similarly quite valuable for web APIs. To get the most out of this concept, we'll need to understand how these resources work, on both a behavioral level and a structural level. But before we do that, we need to understand when it makes sense to rely on polymorphism in the first place.

16.3.1 Deciding when to use polymorphic resources

Often when designing an API we'll find commonality between two proposed resources that makes us think twice about these being two separate resources. For example, in a chat API, we might consider a TextMessage resource as well as PhotoMessage, VideoMessage, or AudioMessage resources. Each of these has something in common (e.g., they all represent a message being sent over the chat API), but they all have something slightly different from one another (in this case, that's the content of the message).

If we were to run into this same scenario when programming locally, we might consider a Message interface and several other classes that implement that interface, with the goal being to write code that deals only with values of the generic Message interface type rather than specific implementations of that interface. But does this same logic carry over to a web API? Put differently, should we use the same argument of generality to determine whether or not to use a single Message resource rather than several independent resources for each message type?

While the intuition is likely correct, the logic doesn't exactly translate. To be more specific, our concern when working in a local programming language is about generality and writing functions that support things like future expansion and code reuse. In our web API, our concern should be more about how we intend the various standard methods to work and whether those standard methods operate identically on all of these resources or have some behavioral differences for the different types.

For example, a great indicator that something should rely on a polymorphic resource (e.g., Message) rather than independent resources (e.g., VideoMessage) is to consider whether it makes sense to list all the different types together. In other words, do we want to call a single method and retrieve all of the resource types in a single response, or do we only ever need to list resources by their distinct subtypes? In the case of the chat API, the answer is pretty obvious: we almost certainly want to list all messages in a ChatRoom resource, regardless of their type. Otherwise, we'd have a pretty tough time retrieving a proper list of messages, requiring us to make several API calls (and then interleaving the results by their creation time) in order to display the chat content appropriately.

Consider a different scenario where an API might have ChatRoom resources as well as broadcast groups, where a central authority can send out unidirectional updates to all users. While this "broadcast" concept is similar in nature to a ChatRoom resource in that they both contain messages, the way we interact with them differs enormously. The membership is indeterminate, they can only be created by administrators of the API, the messages are only ever sent in one direction, the list goes on. As a result, even though this concept could potentially be squeezed into a polymorphic ChatRoom resource (with a special type for broadcast), it's far more likely that the access patterns will be easier to manage if we were to create a separate Broadcast resource that, while similar to a ChatRoom, is fundamentally different and treated independently.

Now that we have some indication about how to decide between independent resources and polymorphic resources, let's explore how to structure these special resources.

16.3.2 *Polymorphic structure*

Polymorphic resources have one important distinguishing field: a type. Since the polymorphic resource itself is akin to the generic interface in our programming language, we need an explicit way of communicating that the instance of this generic interface is a specific subtype. For example, with our Message interface, we need a way of specifying whether the message is a video message, audio message, and so on. But what should this type field look like?

DEFINING THE TYPE FIELD

While it might be tempting to rely on an enumeration, recall from chapter 5 that enumerations tend to come with many issues and have a very specific set of criteria for their use. Instead, we can use a simple string field with some validation about the values that can be stored in this string field.

Listing 16.3   Example of polymorphic resource with type field

```
interface Message {
  id: string;
  sender: string;
  type: 'text' | 'photo' | 'audio' | 'video';    ◁⎯⎯  The type field is just
  // ...                                                 a simple string storing
}                                                        the allowed subtypes.
```

Since this field is a simple string, we can now use it like we would any other. For example, if we wanted to list all the messages but only the photos, we can make a `List-Messages()` call with a filter applied to the `type` field, as we'll see in chapter 22. This also means that creating a new `Message` resource can take any of the relevant forms, with the proper values passed into a `CreateMessage()` call.

Despite this being just like any other field, we do have an important question to address: should this field be permanent or can it be changed on an existing resource? In other words, can we morph a resource from one type (e.g., a video message) to another type (e.g., a text message)? While there's technically nothing directly on the resource preventing this from working as expected, it's generally discouraged. The reason is that as APIs get more complex and there are more relationships between different resources, changing the type of a polymorphic resource might end up breaking an assumption made by an existing resource that happens to reference the polymorphic one. When we go around changing types and breaking assumptions like that, it often leads to confusing situations for users and bugs in the API itself. As a result, this should be avoided if at all possible.

This idea of polymorphic resource data leads us to the next problem: how exactly do we store the content of the message? After all, for each different message type there's vastly different content being stored.

DATA STRUCTURE

The primary benefit of a polymorphic resource is that, by definition, it's able to take on many different forms. And while this is often rooted in the behavior of the resource (e.g., different things happen when we call the same API method on different types of a polymorphic resource), it's very rare that these resources will have the exact same structure. On the contrary, it's almost a guarantee that different types will need to store different information.

In the example of shapes, we need to store a radius for circles but a length for squares. For our `Message` resource in a chat, text messages can just store the text content; however, photo messages need to store an image of some sort, which is obviously quite different. So how do we go about this?

The simplest method for handling this (and just so happens to be the method preferred with stricter interface definition languages) is to have the resource act as a superset of all the fields for each individual type. In other words, a `Message` resource might have a field for storing text content, another for storing photo content, another for video content, and so on.

Listing 16.4 **Storing data with a different field for each attribute**

```
interface Message {
  id: string;
  sender: string;
  type: 'text' | 'photo' | 'audio' | 'video';      The resource acts a
  text?: string;                               ◁─┐ superset by defining all
  photoUri?: string;                                fields that are relevant.
```

```
  videoUri?: string;
  audioUri?: string;
}
```

Sometimes this type of superset arrangement is a requirement, but in many interface definition languages (such as the TypeScript one we're using throughout this book), we can actually reuse a single field to represent each of these fields. In other words, rather than having a field for `text`, `videoUri`, and so on, we can have a single field for content, which takes on a different meaning depending on the `type` field.

Listing 16.5   Single fields storing data for multiple fields

```
interface Message {
  id: string;
  sender: string;
  type: 'text' | 'photo' | 'audio' | 'video';
  content: string;                          ◁──
}
```

This field now represents the text content or media URIs, but depends on the type of the Message resource.

In this example so far, each of the different content types is represented as a simple string, but what if there's more to this? For example, what if we needed to keep track of the media content type (e.g., the encoding format for a video) as well as the location of the video file? In this case, we might define a separate interface for the media content, while still using a simple string value for the text-based content.

Listing 16.6   Fields with different types depending on the message type

```
interface Message {
  id: string;
  sender: string;
  type: 'text' | 'photo' | 'audio' | 'video';
  content: string | Media;        ◁──
}
```

In this case, the content can take on multiple different types.

```
interface Media {              ◁──
  contentUri: string;
  contentType: string;
}
```

We might define Media as a reference to a URI holding the actual content as well as a content type, such as video/mp4.

In all of these examples, the general guideline is that we should attempt to abstract only to the point where the structure continues to make practical sense. In the case of messages, we have no issue abstracting between text and a generic idea of media, and it still makes perfect sense to check the type of the resource and then interpret the `content` field appropriately.

However, in the case of a `Shape` resource with different types, despite the fact that most fields will all be number types, the names of the fields are actually quite important. As a result, we might have a `dimension` field that holds the various dimensions, but have a variety of types to store the different dimension information for each shape.

Listing 16.7   Storing different field names for different shapes

```
interface Shape {
  id: string;
  type: 'square' | 'circle' | 'triangle';
  dimension: SquareDimension | CircleDimension |
    ➥ TriangleDimension;          ◁──┐  A dimension field stores the
}                                     │  various ways of defining
                                      │  different shapes.
interface SquareDimension {
  length: number;              ◁──┐
}
                                  Each shape's
interface CircleDimension {       dimension has a
  radius: number;          ◁──    different numbers
}                                 of fields, each with
                                  different names.
interface TriangleDimension {
  base: number;              ◁──┘
  height: number;
}
```

Now that we've covered the structure, it might make sense to take a moment to consider how we might interact with that structure. More importantly, what should happen when we attempt to bend the rules, so to speak?

DATA VALIDATION

As we've seen in the last topic, different types of a polymorphic resource might store different information. Further, while sometimes it's possible to use the exact same field and interpret it differently depending on the type, other times we need to specify different fields with different types for the divergent information that needs to be stored. Both of these scenarios lead to more complications when invalid data is provided when creating or updating a polymorphic resource.

Put another way, just as fields might be interpreted differently depending on the type field of the resource, this also means that validation rules will need to be applied differently. For example, if we rely on a simple Message resource with a content: string field, this field might store arbitrary textual content if the type is text, but it should be a URI if the type is a media type, such as a photo. As a result, if someone specifies that a message is to be treated as a photo message, it's critical that we return an error if the content field isn't a valid URI.

Other structures are more subtle in their requirements. For example, with our example of the various shapes available, each interface for the dimension field has a different set of field names (despite all having the same type). What happens if we provide additional fields such that the requirements are met but the data doesn't quite make sense? In other words, what if we create a Shape resource by calling CreateShape({ type: 'square', dimension: { radius: 10, length: 10 } })? Obviously a square doesn't have radius, so this extra information is completely useless.

While it might be tempting to throw an error as we might with an incorrectly formatted URI, in this case, the better choice is to validate that the inputs we do need are provided as expected and simply discard anything else, as we would do with unknown fields when creating or updating any other resource.

Now that we have an idea of how to deal with data on a polymorphic resource, let's explore the behavioral differences of these special resources.

16.3.3 *Polymorphic behavior*

So far, our discussion has been entirely about the structure and design of polymorphic resources, but we've said very little about how we might interact with these resources. As we saw in section 16.1, part of the benefit of polymorphism, either in a programming language or a web API, is that we can operate on a generic interface rather than a specific implementation, but the results of the operation will be different depending on that specific implementation. Taking our example of a `countSides()` function from section 16.1, we could translate this to a web API quite easily.

Listing 16.8   API methods to count sides of different shapes

```
abstract class ShapeApi {
  @post("/{id=shapes/*}:countSides")
  CountShapeSides(req: CountShapeSidesRequest): CountShapeSidesResponse;
}

interface CountShapeSidesRequest {
  id: string;
}

interface CountShapeSidesResponse {
  sides: number;
}
```

In this example, you can imagine the responses: a square would return { `sides: 4` }, whereas a triangle would return { `sides: 3` }, and so on for the other shape types. In short, thanks to our choice of resource as the generic interface (e.g., `Shape` or `Message`), the methods we define will operate as always on the resource, and any deviations in behavior can be blamed on the typical ones we've come to expect from resources with differing values for a variety of fields. In short, our earlier design choices have led to a very convenient result not much different from any other standard or custom method on a resource.

But this does raise an important question that really should be addressed: what about the case where we have separate resources and want a single API method to be able to operate on a variety of resource types? In the next section, we'll explore this in detail and explain why it's generally a bad idea.

16.3.4 *Why not polymorphic methods?*

So far, we've talked almost exclusively about a single resource that can take on many forms. This has led to a great deal of simplicity with API methods in that they behave exactly like they would for any other resource; however, there's an entirely different type of polymorphism that we haven't even mentioned: polymorphic methods.

For the purposes of this section, we'll define a polymorphic method as an API method that is able to operate on multiple different resource types. To see a contrived example, let's picture a generic `DeleteResource()` method in an API, which is capable of deleting any resource in the API regardless of the resource type. Take special note of the HTTP URL mapping to `"*/*"` rather than a specific collection like `"chatRooms/*"`.

Listing 16.9 Polymorphic method supports behavior on different resource types

```
abstract class GenericApi {                  This URL mapping would correspond
  @delete("/{id=*/*}")          ◄┐           to resources of any type.
  DeleteResource(req: DeleteResourceReqeuest): void;
}


interface DeleteResourceRequest {
  id: string;          ◄┐   This field can represent an
}                           identifier for any resource type.
```

It's a common knee-jerk reaction upon seeing this example to think, "Wait. This is so much simpler. Why don't we just do this instead of having all of these separate standard delete methods for each resource?" The interesting bit is that on a technical level this would actually work since the method here is capable of handling deletion for basically any resource. In other words, since the identifier provided in the `Delete-ResourceRequest` interface is an arbitrary string, we can pass in any valid resource identifier, referring to any of the possible resource types, and the resource will be deleted. In a way, this is sort of like defining a function with a method signature in TypeScript, looking something like `function deleteResource(resource: any): void`. However, methods like this tend to cause more harm than good.

It's important to remember that just because two API methods have the same name, goal, request format, or method signature doesn't mean they're identical. And when we pretend that the two methods are identical and combine them, as we have here, we're likely to run into trouble in the future.

In this case of a polymorphic standard delete method, we can clearly delete any resource, but it's not guaranteed that all resources should be deleted in exactly the same way. For example, maybe we want to support soft deletion (chapter 25) or validation requests (chapter 27) on specific resources but not all resources. And this goes beyond this single example and extends to any method that might operate on multiple resource types.

The implication with any method capable of operating on many different types of resources (or all resources) is that these resource types behave so similarly to one another that they deserve a single shared API method to interact with them. However, somehow, at the same time, their representations are so critically different that they deserve to be entirely separate resource types.

The other important implication is that the resources in question will, always and forever, remain sufficiently similar in their behavior, and any changes in the desired behavior of the polymorphic method will apply to all the resources. In other words, the behavior of the method will always change for all resource types rather than on a case-by-case basis.

In both of these cases we're making quite large leaps. In the first, we're saying that resources are identical in behavior and merit a single API method, but also are completely different in representation, meriting independent resource definitions. In the second, we're assuming that this identical behavior is a permanent fixture such that all resources will change their behavior uniformly across the entire API.

While it's certainly possible that there is a scenario that makes these implications reasonable, it's far more likely that either now or in the future one of them will unravel. And since we don't have a crystal ball to help predict the future of an API, it's far safer to assume that things will change and will do so in their own unique ways, not as a uniform group. Based on this, it's almost never a good idea to support polymorphic API methods.

Unfortunately, this does mean more typing. On the other hand, the API remains flexible and adaptable rather than brittle and clunky.

16.3.5 *Final API definition*

In the following example we can see how we might rely on resource-oriented polymorphism for the Message resource, leading to a simplified set of API methods with the benefits of polymorphism on the resource layout.

Listing 16.10   Final API definition

```
abstract class ChatRoomApi {
  @post("/{parent=chatRooms/*}/messages")
  CreateMessage(req: CreateMessageRequest): Message;
}

interface CreateMessageRequest {
  parent: string;
  resource: Message;
}

interface Message {
  id: string;
  sender: string;
  type: 'text' | 'image' | 'audio' | 'video';
  content: string | Media
}
```

```
interface Media {
  uri: string;
  contentType: string;
}
```

16.4 Trade-offs

Polymorphism in APIs is a very powerful tool, but it can also be complicated. While many times it might be a perfect fit (e.g., the example of multiple types of Message resources), there may be others where resources might seem similar but still have some fundamental differences. A good rule of thumb is to consider whether the resources are all truly special types of the generic resource type (just like PhotoMessage is certainly a specific type of Message). The reason is that relying on this pattern does lock the resources into a specific representation that is hard (if not impossible) to disentangle in the future in a nonbreaking manner.

Above all else, polymorphism in web APIs should ideally be focused on polymorphic resources and not polymorphic methods, for the reasons discussed earlier. While there are possibly some cases where a polymorphic method might be useful, think very carefully about how likely it is that the resources' behaviors will begin to deviate over time. This is because these types of methods might come with convenience and less typing now, but the price for this is a pair of handcuffs that limit the future flexibility of the API.

16.5 Exercises

1 Imagine you're creating an API that relies on URL bookmarks for a web browser that can be arranged into collections or folders. Does it make sense to put these two concepts (a folder and a bookmark) into a single polymorphic resource? Why or why not?

2 Why should we rely on a string field for storing polymorphic resource types instead of something like an enumeration?

3 Why should additional data be ignored (e.g., providing a radius for a Shape resource of type square) rather than rejected with an error?

4 Why should we avoid polymorphic methods? Why is it a bad idea to have a polymorphic set of standard methods (e.g., UpdateResource())?

Summary

- Polymorphism in APIs allows resources to take on varying types to avoid duplicating shared functionality.
- Generally, it makes sense to rely on polymorphism when users can reasonably expect to list resources of multiple types together (e.g., listing messages in a chat room where each message might be of a different type).

- The type information for a polymorphic resource should be a string field, but the possible choices for this field should be changed (added to or removed from) carefully to avoid breaking existing client code.

- Rather than throwing errors for invalid input data, validation should instead check whether the required data is present and ignore any irrelevant data.

- Polymorphic methods should generally be avoided as they prohibit future deviation in behavior over time.

Part 5

Collective operations

Thus far, most of the API design patterns we've looked at have focused on one or two resources at a time. In this section, we expand beyond this narrow focus and look at design patterns aimed at dealing with larger collections of resources.

In chapters 17 and 23, we'll explore how to copy, move, import, and export resources across collections, and all of the headaches that come with this functionality. In chapter 18, we'll learn how to apply the set of standard methods to handle chunks of resources by operating on batches rather than one resource at a time. And while we can apply this idea to the standard delete method, we'll take things a step further in chapter 19 by looking at how to delete many resources at once by applying a filter across a collection (which we'll learn more about in chapter 22) rather than by knowing each resource's unique identifier.

In chapter 20, we'll explore how to load data points for aggregate use rather than individual addressability as we've seen thus far with resources. In chapter 21, we'll look at how to handle large numbers of resources in a manageable way by using pagination.

Copy and move

This chapter covers

- How to use the copy and move custom methods for rearranging resources in an API
- Choosing the right identifier (or identifier policy) for copy and move operations
- How to handle child and other resources when copying or moving parent resources
- Dealing with external data references for copied or moved resources
- What level of atomicity should be expected from these new custom methods

While very few resources are considered immutable, there are often certain attributes of a resource that we can safely assume won't change out from under us. In particular, a resource's unique identifier is one of these attributes. But what if we want to rename a resource? How can we do so safely? Further, what if we want to move a resource from belonging to one parent resource to another? Or duplicate a resource? We'll explore a safe and stable method for these operations, covering both copying (duplication) and moving (changing a unique identifier or changing a parent) of resources in an API.

17.1   *Motivation*

In an ideal world, our hierarchical relationships between resources are perfectly designed and forever immutable. More importantly, in this magical world, users of an API never make mistakes or create resources in the wrong location. And they certainly never realize far too late that they've made a mistake. In this world, there should never be a need to rename or relocate a resource in an API because we, as API designers, and our customers, as API consumers, never make any mistakes in our resource layout and hierarchy.

This is the world we explored in chapter 6 and discussed in detail in section 6.3.6. Unfortunately, this world is not the one we currently exist in, and therefore we have to consider the possibility that there will come a time where a user of an API needs the ability to move a resource to another parent in the hierarchy or change the ID of a resource.

To make things more complicated, there may be scenarios where users need to duplicate resources, potentially to other locations in the hierarchy. And while both of these scenarios seem quite straightforward at a quick glance, like most topics in API design they lead us down a rabbit hole full of questions that need to be answered. The goal of this pattern is to ensure that API consumers can rename and copy resources throughout the resource hierarchy in a safe, stable, and (mostly) simple manner.

17.2   *Overview*

Since we cannot use the standard update method in order to move or copy a resource, we're left with the obvious next best choice: custom methods. Luckily, the high-level idea of how these copy-and-move custom methods might work is straightforward. As with most API design issues, the devil is in the details, such as in copying a `ChatRoom` resource as well as moving `Message` resources between different `ChatRoom` parent resources.

Listing 17.1   **Move-and-copy examples using custom methods**

For both custom methods, we use the POST HTTP verb and target the specific resource we want to copy or move.

```
abstract class ChatRoomApi {
  @post("/{id=chatRooms/*/messages/*}:move")
  MoveMessage(req: MoveMessageRequest): Message;

  @post("/{id=chatRooms/*}:copy")
  CopyChatRoom(req: CopyChatRoomRequest): ChatRoom;
}
```

For both custom methods, the response is always the newly moved or copied resource.

Not shown here are quite a few important and subtle questions. First, when you copy or move a resource, do you choose a unique identifier or does the service do so as though the new resource is being created? Is there a difference when working across parents (where you might want the same identifier as before, just belonging to a different parent) versus within the same parent (where you, presumably, just want the ability to change the identifier)?

Next, when you copy a ChatRoom resource, do all of the Message resources belonging to that ChatRoom get copied as well? What if there are large attachments? Does that extra data get copied? And the questions don't end there. We still need to figure out how to ensure that resources being moved (or copied) are not currently being interacted with by other users, what to do about the old identifiers, as well as any inherited metadata such as access control policies.

In short, while this pattern relies on nothing more than a specific custom method, we're quite far from simply defining the method and calling it done. In the next section, we'll dig into all of these questions in order to land on an API surface that ensures safe and stable resource copying (and moving).

17.3   Implementation

As we saw in section 17.2, we can rely on custom methods to both copy and move resources around the hierarchy of an API. What we haven't looked at are some of the important nuances about these custom methods and how they should actually work. Let's start with the obvious: how should we determine the identifier of the newly moved or copied resource?

17.3.1   Identifiers

As we learned in chapter 6, it's generally best to allow the API service itself to choose a unique identifier for a resource. This means that when we create new resources we might specify the parent resource identifier, but the newly created resource would end up with an identifier that is completely out of our control. And this is for a good reason: when we choose how to identify our own resources, we tend to do so pretty poorly. The same scenario shows up when it comes to copying and moving resources. In a sense, both of these are sort of like creating a new resource that looks exactly like an existing one and then (in the case of a move) deleting the original resource.

But even if the newly created resource has an identifier chosen by the API service, what should that be? It turns out that the most convenient option depends on our intent. If we're trying to rename a resource such that it has a new identifier but exists in the same position in the resource hierarchy, then it might be quite important for us to choose the new identifier. This is especially so if the API permits user-specified identifiers, since we're likely to be renaming a resource from some meaningful name to another meaningful name (for example, something like databases/database-prod to databases/database-prod-old). On the other hand, if we're trying to move something from one position in the hierarchy to another, then it might actually be a better scenario if the new resource has the same identifier but belongs to a new parent (e.g., moving from an existing identifier of chatRooms/1234/messages/abcd to chatRooms/5678/messages/abcd, note the commonality of messages/abcd). Since the scenarios differ quite a bit, let's look at each one individually.

COPYING

Choosing an identifier for a duplicate resource turns out to be pretty straightforward. Whether or not you're copying the resource into the same or a different parent, the copy method should act identically to the standard create method. This means that if your API has opted for user-specified identifiers, the copy method should also permit the user to specify the destination identifier for the newly created resource. If it supports only service-generated identifiers, it should not make an exception and permit user-specified identifiers just for resource duplication. (If it did, this would be a loophole through which anyone could choose their own identifiers by simply creating the resource and then copying the resource to the actual intended destination.)

The result of this is that the request to copy a resource will accept both a destination parent (if the resource type has a parent), and, if user-specified identifiers are permitted, a destination ID as well.

Listing 17.2   Copy request interfaces

We always need to know the ID of the resource to be copied.

```
interface CopyChatRoomRequest {
  id: string;
  destinationId: string;
}

interface CopyMessageRequest {
  id: string;
  destinationParent: string;
  destinationId: string;
}
```

This field is optional. It should only be present if the API supports user-specified identifiers.

When the resource has a parent in the hierarchy, we should specify where the newly copied resource should end up.

This can lead to a few surprising results. For example, if the API doesn't support user-chosen identifiers, the request to copy any top-level resources takes only a single parameter: the ID of the resource to be copied. In another case, it's possible that we might want to copy a resource into the same parent. In this case, the destinationParent field would be identical to the parent of the resource pointed to in the id field.

Additionally, even in cases where the API supports user-chosen identifiers, we might want to rely on an auto-generated ID when duplicating a resource. To do this, we would simply leave the destinationId field blank and allow that to be the way we express to the service, "I'd like you to choose the destination identifier for me."

Finally, when user-specified identifiers are supported, it's possible that the destination ID inside the destination parent might already be taken. In this case, it might be tempting to revert to a server-generated identifier in order to ensure that the resource is successfully duplicated. This should be avoided, however, as it breaks the user's assumptions about the destination of the new resource. Instead, the service should return the equivalent of a 409 Conflict HTTP error and abort the duplication operation.

MOVING

When it comes to moving resources, we actually have two subtly different scenarios. On the one hand, users may be most concerned about relocating a resource to another parent in the resource hierarchy, such as moving a `Message` resource from one `Chat-Room` to another. On the other hand, users may want to rename a resource, where the resource is technically moved to the same parent with a different destination ID. It's also possible that we might want to do both at the same time (relocate and rename). To further complicate things, we must remember that renaming resources is only something that makes sense if the API supports user-chosen identifiers.

To handle these scenarios, it might be tempting to use two separate fields again, as in listing 17.2, where you have a destination parent as well as a destination identifier. In this case though, we always know the final identifier no matter what (compared to the copy method where we might rely on a server-generated identifier). The ID is either the same as the original resource except for a different parent or a completely new one of our choosing. As a result, we can use a single `destinationId` field and enforce some constraints on the value for that field depending on whether user-chosen identifiers are supported. If they are, then any complete identifier is acceptable. If not, then the only valid *new* identifiers are those that exclusively change the parent portion of the ID and keep the rest the same.

All of this leads us to a move request structure that accepts only two fields: the identifier of the resource being moved and the intended destination of the resource after the relocation is complete.

Listing 17.3 Move request interfaces

We always need to know the ID of the resource to be copied.

```
interface MoveChatRoomRequest {
  id: string;
  destinationId: string;
}
```

Since ChatRoom resources have no hierarchical parents, this method only makes sense if user-specified identifiers are supported by the API.

```
interface MoveMessageRequest {
  id: string;
  destinationId: string;
}
```

Since Message resources have parents, we can move the resource to different parents by changing the destination ID.

As you can see, for top-level resources (those with no parents) the entire move method only makes sense if the API supports user-specified identifiers. This stands in stark contrast to the copy method, which still makes sense in this case. The issue is primarily that moving accomplishes two goals: relocating a resource to a different parent and renaming a resource. The latter only makes sense given support for user-specified identifiers. The former only makes sense if the resource has a parent. In cases where neither of these apply, the move method becomes entirely irrelevant and should not be implemented at all.

Now that we have an idea of the shape and structure of requests to copy and move resources around, let's keep moving forward and look at how we handle even more complicated scenarios.

17.3.2 *Child resources*

So far, we've worked with the condition that each resource we intend to move or copy is fully self-contained. In essence, our big assumption was that the resource itself has no additional information that needs to be copied outside of a single record. This assumption certainly made our work a bit easier, but unfortunately it's not necessarily a safe assumption. Instead, we have to assume that there will be additional data associated with resources that need to be moved or copied as well. How do we handle this? Should we even bother with this extra data?

The short answer is yes. Put simply, the external data and associated resources (e.g., child resources) are rarely there without purpose. As a result, copying or moving a resource without including this associated data is likely to lead to a surprising result: a new destination resource that doesn't behave the same as the source resource. And since one of the key goals of a good API is predictability, it becomes exceptionally important to ensure that the newly copied or moved resource is identical to the source resource in as many ways as possible. How do we make this happen?

First, whether copied or moved, all child resources must be included. For example, this means that if we copied or moved a `ChatRoom` resource, all the `Message` child resources must also be copied or moved with the new parent ID. Obviously this is far more work than updating a single row. Further, the number of updates is dependent on the number of child resources, meaning that, as you'd expect, copying a resource with few child resources will take far less time than a similar resource with a large number of child resources. Table 17.1 shows an example of the identifiers of resources before and after a move or copy operation.

Table 17.1   New and old identifiers after moving (or copying) a `ChatRoom` resource

Resource type	Original identifier	New identifier
ChatRoom	chatRooms/old	chatRooms/new
Message	chatRooms/old/messages/2	chatRooms/new/messages/2
Message	chatRooms/old/messages/3	chatRooms/new/messages/3
Message	chatRooms/old/messages/4	chatRooms/new/messages/4

While our issues with copying are complete here, this is unfortunately not the case when resources have been moved. Instead, after we've finished updating all of the IDs, we've actually created an entirely new problem: anywhere else that previously pointed at these resources now has a dead link, despite the resource still existing! In the next section, we'll explore how to handle these references, both internal and external.

17.3.3 *Related resources*

While we've decided that all child resources must be copied or moved along with the target resource, we've said nothing so far about related resources. For example, let's imagine that our chat API supports reporting or flagging messages that might be inappropriate with a `MessageReviewReport` resource. This resource is sort of like a support case of a message that has been flagged as inappropriate and should be reviewed by the support team. This resource is not necessarily a child of a `Message` resource (or even a `ChatRoom` resource), but it does reference the `Message` resource that it is targeting.

Listing 17.4   A MessageReviewReport resource that references a Message resource

```
interface MessageReviewReport {
  id: string;
  messageId: string;       ←——┐   This field contains the ID of a Message
  reason: string;             │   resource, acting as a reference.
}
```

The existence of this resource (and the fact that it's a `messageId` field is a reference to a `Message` resource) leads to a couple of obvious questions. First, when you duplicate a `Message`, should it also duplicate all `MessageReviewReport` resources that reference the original message? And second, if a `Message` resource is moved, should all `MessageReviewReport` resources that reference the newly moved resource be updated as well? These questions get even more complicated when we remember that copying and moving `Message` resources may not be due specifically to an end-user request targeted at the `Message` resource but instead could be the cascading result of a request targeted at the parent `ChatRoom` resource!

It should come as no surprise that there is no single right answer to what's best to do in all of these scenarios, but let's start with the easy ones, such as how related resources should respond to resources being moved.

REFERENTIAL INTEGRITY

In many relational database systems, there is a way to configure the system such that when certain database rows change, those changes can cascade and update rows elsewhere in the database. This is a very valuable, though resource intensive, feature that ensures you never have the database equivalent of a segmentation fault by trying to de-reference a newly invalid pointer. When it comes to moving resources inside an API, we ideally want to strive for the same result.

Unfortunately, this is simply one of those very difficult things that comes along with needing a move custom method. Not only do we need to keep track of all the resources that refer to the target being moved, we also need to keep track of the child resources being moved along with the parent and ensure that any other resources referencing those children are updated as well. As you can imagine, this is extraordinarily complex and one of the many reasons renaming or relocating resources is discouraged!

For example, following this guideline means that if we were to move a `Message` resource that had a `MessageReviewReport` referring to it, we would also need to update that `MessageReviewReport` as well. Further, if we moved the `ChatRoom` resource that was the parent to this `Message` with a `MessageReviewReport`, we would have to do the same thing because the `Message` would be moved by virtue of being a child resource of the `ChatRoom`.

Now let's take a brief look at how we should handle related resources when it comes to the copy custom method.

RELATED RESOURCE DUPLICATION

While moving resources certainly creates quite a headache for related resources, is the same thing true of copying resources? It turns out that it also creates a headache, but it's a headache of a different type entirely. Instead of having a hard technical problem to handle, we have a hard design decision. The reason for this is pretty simple: whether or not to copy a related resource along with a target resource depends quite a bit on the circumstances.

For example, a `MessageReviewReport` resource is certainly important to have around, but if we duplicate a `Message` resource we wouldn't want to duplicate the report exactly as it is. Instead, perhaps it makes more sense to allow a `Message-ReviewReport` to reference more than one `Message` resource, and rather than duplicating the report we can simply add the newly copied `Message` resource to the list of those being referenced.

Other resources should simply never be duplicated. For example, when we copy a `ChatRoom` resource we should never copy the `User` resources that are listed as members in that resource. Ultimately, the point is that some resources will make sense to copy alongside the target while others simply won't. It's a far less complicated technical problem and instead will depend quite a lot on the intended behavior for the API.

Now that we've covered the details on maintaining referential integrity in the face of these new custom methods, let's explore how things look when we expand that to encompass references outside our control.

EXTERNAL REFERENCES

While most references to resources in an API will live inside other resources in that same API, this isn't always the case. There are many scenarios where resources will be referenced from all over the internet, in particular anything related to storing files or other unstructured data. This presents a pretty obvious problem given that this entire chapter is about moving resources and breaking those external references from all over. For example, let's imagine that we have a storage system that keeps track of files. These `File` resources are clearly able to be shared all over the internet, which means we'll have lots of references to these resources all over the place! What can we do?

```
abstract class FileApi {
  @post("/files")
  CreateFile(req: CreateFileRequest): File;

  @get("/{id=files/*}")                    ◁─┐   These URIs might be used to
  GetFile(req: GetFileRequest): File;            reference a given File resource
}                                                from outside the API.

interface File {
  id: string;
  content: Uint8Array;
}
```

It's important to remember that the internet is not exactly a perfect representation of referential integrity. Most of us encounter HTTP 404 Not Found errors all the time, so it's not quite fair to take the referential integrity requirements internal to an API and expand them to the entire internet. Very rarely when we provide a web resource to the world do we actually intend to sign a lifelong contract to continue providing that same resource with those exact same bytes and exact same name for the rest of eternity. Instead, we often provide the resource until it no longer makes sense. The point is that resources provided to the open internet are often best effort and rarely come with a lifetime guarantee.

In this case, our example File resource is probably best categorized under this same set of guidelines: it'll be present until it happens to be moved. This could be tomorrow due to an urgent request from the US Department of Justice, or it could be next year because the cost of storing the file didn't make sense anymore. The point is that we should acknowledge up front that external referential integrity is not a critical goal for an API and focus on the more important issues at hand.

17.3.4 *External data*

So far, all the resources we've copied or moved have been the kind you'd store in a relational database or *control plane* data. What about scenarios where we want to copy or move a resource that happens to point to a raw chunk of bytes, such as in our File resource in listing 17.5? Should we also copy those bytes in our underlying storage?

This is actually a well-studied problem in computer science and shows up in many programming languages as the question of *copy by value* versus *copy by reference* of variables. When a variable is copied by value, all of the underlying data is duplicated and the newly copied variable is entirely separate from the old variable. When a variable is copied by reference, the underlying data remains in the same place and a new variable is created that happens to point to the original data. In this case, changing the data of one variable will also cause the data of the other variable to be updated.

Listing 17.6   Pseudo-code for copying by reference vs. by value

```
let original = [1, 2, 3];
let copy_by_reference = copyByReference(original);     ◁──┐   First we copy the original
let copy_by_value = copyByValue(original);                │   list twice, once by value
                                                          │   and once by reference.
copy_by_reference[1] = 'ref';    ◁──┐  Then we update each
copy_by_value[1] = 'val';           │  of the copies (results
                                    │  shown in figure 17.1).
```

Listing 17.6 shows an example of some pseudo-code that performs two copies (one by value, another by reference) and then updates the resulting data. The final values are then shown in figure 17.1. As you can see, despite having three variables, there are only two lists, and the changes to the copy_by_reference variable are also visible in the original list.

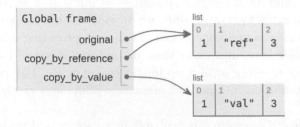

Figure 17.1   Visualization of copying by reference vs. by value

When moving resources that point to this type of external data, the answer is simple: leave the underlying data alone. This means that while we might relocate the resource record itself, the data should remain untouched. For example, renaming a File resource should change the home of that resource, but the underlying bytes should not be moved anywhere else.

When copying resources, the answer is clear but happens to be a bit more complicated. In general, the best solution for this type of external data is to begin by copying by reference only. After that, if the data ever happens to change, we should copy all of the underlying data and apply the changes because it can be wasteful to copy a whole bunch of bytes when we might be able to get away with copying by reference. However, we certainly cannot have changes on the duplicate resource showing up as changes on the original resource, so we must make the full copy once changes are about to be made.

This strategy, called *copy on write*, is quite common for storage systems, and many of them will do the heavy lifting for you under the hood. In other words, you might be able to get away with calling a storage system's copy() function and it will properly handle all the semantics to do a true copy by value only when the data is later altered.

17.3.5 Inherited metadata

In many APIs, there is some set of policy or metadata that is inherited by a child resource to a parent resource. For example, let's imagine a world where we want to control the length of messages in different chat rooms. This length limit might vary from one room to another, so it would be an attribute set on the ChatRoom resource that ultimately applies to the Message child resources.

Listing 17.7   ChatRoom resources with conditions inherited by children

```
interface ChatRoom {
  id: string;
  // ...
  messageLengthLimit: number;    ←┘
}
```
> This setting is inherited by child Message resources to limit the length of the message content.

This is all well and good but gets more confusing when Message resources are being copied from one ChatRoom resource to another. The most common potential problem is when these different inherited restrictions happen to conflict, such as a Message that happens to meet the length requirements of its current ChatRoom resource being copied into another ChatRoom with more stringent requirements, not met by the resource as it exists currently. In other words, what happens if we want to copy a Message resource that has 140 characters into a ChatRoom that only allows messages of 100 characters?

One option is to simply permit the resource to break the rules, so to speak, and exist inside the ChatRoom resource despite being beyond the length limits. While this technically works, it introduces further complications as the standard update methods on this resource may begin to fail until the resource has been modified to conform to the rules of the parent. Often, this can make the destination resource effectively immutable, causing confusion and frustration for those interested in changing other aspects of the resource without modifying the content length.

Another option is to truncate or otherwise modify the incoming resource so that it adheres to the rules of the destination parent. While this is technically acceptable as well, it can be surprising to users who were not aware of the destination resource's requirements. In particular, in these cases where you are permanently destroying data, this type of "force it to fit" solution breaks the best practices for good APIs by being unpredictable. The irreversible nature of this type of solution is yet another reason why it should be avoided.

A better option is to simply reject the incoming resource and abort the copy or move operation due to the violation of these rules. This ensures that users have the ability to decide what to do to make the operation succeed, whether that is altering the length requirement stored in the ChatRoom resource or truncating or removing any offending Message resources before attempting to copy or move the data.

This also applies to cases where copying is triggered by virtue of the resource being a child or related resource to the actual target. In these scenarios, a failure of any sort of validation check or problem due to any inherited metadata from the new destination parent should cause the entire operation to fail, with a clear reason for all of the failures standing in the way of the operation. The user then has the ability to inspect the results and decide whether to abandon the task at hand or retry the operation after fixing the issues reported.

17.3.6 *Atomicity*

As we've seen throughout this chapter, the key takeaway of both the copy and move methods should be that they can be far more complex and resource intensive than they look. While in some cases they can be pretty innocuous (e.g., copying a resource with no related or child resources) others can involve copying and updating hundreds or thousands of other resources in the API. This presents a pretty big problem because it's rare that these copy or move operations happen when no one else is using the API and modifying the underlying resources. How do we ensure that these operations complete successfully in the face of a volatile data set? Further, it's important that if an error is encountered along the way we are able to undo the work we've done. In short, we want to make sure that both our move and copy operations occur in the context of a transaction.

Interestingly, when it comes to the data storage layer, the copy and move operations tend to work in pretty different ways. In the case of the copy operation, we'll make mostly queries to read data and then create new entries in the storage system based on those entries. In the case of the move operation, on the other hand, we'll mostly update existing entries in the storage system, modify identifiers in place in order to move resources from one place to another, and update the existing resources that might reference the newly modified resources. While the ideal solution to both is the same, the problems encountered are slightly different, and, as a result, it makes more sense for us to address these two separately.

COPYING

In the case of copying a resource (and its children and related resources), our focus when it comes to atomicity is about data consistency. In other words, we want to make sure that the data we end up with in our new destination is exactly the same data that existed at the time we initiated the copy operation, often referred to as a *snapshot* of the data. If your API is built on top of a storage system that supports point-in-time snapshots or transactions like this, then this problem is a lot more straightforward. You can simply specify the snapshot timestamp or revision identifier when reading the source data before copying it to the new location or perform the entire operation inside a single database transaction. Then, if anything happens to change in the meantime, that's completely acceptable.

If you don't have that luxury, there are two other options. First, you can simply acknowledge that this is not possible and that any data copied will be more of a smear of data across a stretch of time rather than a consistent snapshot from a single point in time. This is certainly inconvenient and can be potentially confusing, especially with extremely volatile data sets; however, it may be the only option available given the technology constraints and up-time requirements.

Next, we can lock the data for writing at either the API level (by disabling all API calls that modify data) or at the database level (preventing all updates to the data). While not always feasible, this method is sort of the "sledgehammer" option for ensuring consistency during these operations, as it will ensure that the data is exactly as it appeared at the time of the copy operation, specifically because the data was locked down and prohibited from all changes for the duration of the operation.

In general, this option is certainly not recommended as it basically provides an easy way to attack your API service: simply send lots and lots of copy operations. As a result, if your storage system doesn't support point-in-time snapshots or transactional semantics, this is yet another reason to discourage supporting copying resources around the API.

MOVING

Unlike copying data, moving data depends a lot more on updating resources, and therefore we have slightly different concerns. At first glance, it might seem like we really don't have any major problems, but it turns out that data consistency is still an issue. To see why, let's imagine that we have a `MessageReviewReport` that points at the `Message` we just moved. In this case, we need to update the `MessageReviewReport` to point to the `Message` resource's new location. But what if someone updated the `MessageReviewReport` to point to a *different* message in the meantime? In general, we need to be sure that related resources haven't been changed since we last evaluated whether they needed to be updated to point to the newly moved resource.

To do this, we have similar options to our copying operation. First, the best choice is to use a consistent snapshot or database transaction to ensure that the work being done happens on a consistent view of the data. If that's not possible, then we can lock the database or the API for writes to ensure that the data is consistent for the duration of the move operation. As we noted before, this is generally a dangerous tactic, but it may be a necessary evil.

Finally, we can simply ignore the problem and hope for the best. Unlike a copy operation, ignoring the problem with a move results in a far worse outcome than a simple smear of data over time. If we don't attempt to get a consistent view of the data during a move we actually run the risk of undoing changes that were previously committed by other updates. For example, if a `MessageReviewReport` is marked as needing to be updated due to a move and someone modifies the target of that resource in the meantime, it's very possible the move operation will overwrite that update as though it had never been received in the first place. While this might not be catastrophic to all APIs, it's certainly bad practice and should be avoided if at all possible.

17.3.7 *Final API definition*

As we've seen, the API definition itself is not nearly as complex as the behavior of that API, particularly when it comes to handling inherited metadata, child resources, related resources, and other aspects related to referential integrity. However, to summarize everything we've explored so far, listing 17.8 shows a final API definition that supports copying `ChatRoom` resources (with supporting user-specified identifiers) and moving `Message` resources between parents.

> **Listing 17.8   Final API definition**

```
abstract class ChatRoomApi {
  @post("/{id=chatRooms/*}:copy")
  CopyChatRoom(req: CopyChatRoomRequest): ChatRoom;

  @post("/{id=chatRooms/*/messages/*}:move")
  MoveMessage(req: MoveMessageRequest): Message;
}

interface ChatRoom {
  id: string;
  title: string;
  // ...
}

interface Message {
  id: string;
  content: string;
  // ...
}

interface CopyChatRoomRequest {
  id: string;
  destinationParent: string;
}

interface MoveMessage {
  id: string;
  destinationId: string;
}
```

17.4 *Trade-offs*

Hopefully after seeing how complicated it is to support move and copy operations, your first thought is that these two should be avoided whenever possible. While these operations seem simple at first, it turns out that the behavioral requirements and restrictions can be exceptionally difficult to implement correctly. To make things worse, the consequences can be pretty dire, resulting in lost or corrupted data.

That said, copy and move are not equally complex and do not have equal standing in an API. In many cases, copying resources can actually be a critical piece of functionality. Moving resources, on the other hand, often only becomes necessary as the result of a mistake or poor resource layout. As a result, while even the best laid out APIs might find a great deal of value in supporting the copy method, it's best to reevaluate the resource layout before deciding to implement the move method. Often, it turns out that a need to move resources across parents (or rename resources) is caused by poorly chosen resource identifiers or by relying on a parent–child relationship in what should have been a referential relationship.

Finally, it's important to note that while the complexity spelled out in this chapter for the behavior of the move and copy operations might be onerous and challenging to implement, cutting corners here is far more likely to lead to nasty consequences down the road.

17.5 Exercises

1 When copying a resource, should all child resources be copied as well? What about resources that reference the resource being duplicated?

2 How can we maintain referential integrity beyond the borders of our API? Should we make that guarantee?

3 When copying or moving data, how can we be sure that the resulting data is a true copy as intended and not a smear of data as it's being modified by others using the API?

4 Imagine we're moving a resource from one parent to another, but the parents have different security and access control policies. Which policy should apply to the moved resource, the old or the new?

Summary

- As much as we'd love to require permanence of resources, it's very likely that users will need to duplicate or relocate resources in an API.
- Rather than relying on standard methods (update and create) to relocate or duplicate resources, we should use custom move and copy methods instead.
- Copy and move operations should also include the same operation on child resources; however, this behavior should be considered on a case-by-case basis and references to moved resources should be kept up-to-date.
- When resources address external data, API methods should clarify whether a copied resource is copy by reference or copy by value (or copy on write).
- Copy and move custom methods should be as atomic as reasonably possible given the limitations of the underlying storage system.

Batch operations

18

This chapter covers

- Batch operations and their differences from executing a series of standard methods
- Why batch operations should be atomic
- How batch request methods can hoist common fields to avoid repetition
- An exploration of each batch standard method (get, delete, create, and update)

This pattern provides guidelines by which users of an API can manipulate multiple resources in bulk without making separate API calls. These so-called *batch operations* behave similarly to the standard methods (discussed in chapter 7), but they avoid the necessity of multiple back-and-forth interactions of multiple API calls. The end result is a set of methods that permit retrieving, updating, or deleting a collection of resources with a single API call rather than one per resource.

18.1 *Motivation*

So far, most of the design patterns and guidelines we've explored have been focused on interacting with individual resources. In fact, we've taken this even further in chapter 8 by exploring how to operate even more narrowly, focusing on addressing individual fields on a single resource. While this has proven quite useful thus far, it leaves a gap on the other end of the spectrum. What if we want to operate more broadly, across multiple resources simultaneously?

In a typical database system, the way we address this is by using transactions. This means that if we want to operate on multiple different rows in a database at the same time, we simply begin a transaction, operate as normal (but within the context of the transaction), and commit the transaction. Depending on the locking functionality of the database and the level of volatility of the underlying data, the transaction may succeed or fail, but the key takeaway here is this atomicity. The operations contained inside the transaction will either all fail or all succeed; there will be no partial success scenario where some operations execute successfully while others don't.

Unfortunately (or not, depending on who you're talking to), most web APIs don't provide this generic transactional functionality—unless the API is for a transactional storage service. The reason for this is quite simple: it's exceptionally complex to provide this ability. However, this doesn't take away the need for transaction-like semantics in a web API. One common scenario is when an API user wants to update two separate resources but really needs these two independent API requests to either both succeed or both fail. For example, perhaps we have a ChatRoom logging configuration resource that can be enabled or disabled. We don't want to enable it before it's being used, but we don't want to refer to it as the default logging configuration before it's enabled. This sort of catch-22 is one of the primary reasons that transactional semantics exist, because without them, our only other option is to try to perform these two independent operations (enable the config and assign it as the default) as close together as possible.

Obviously this is insufficient, but that leads us to the big question: what can we do? How do we get some semblance of atomicity or transactional semantics across multiple API requests without building an entire transaction system like most relational databases have?

18.2 *Overview*

As much fun as it might be to develop a fully-fledged generic transaction design pattern, that is certainly a bit excessive. So what can we do that gives us the most value for our time? In other words, what corners can we cut to reduce the amount of work needed while still providing support for operating on multiple resources atomically?

In this design pattern, we'll explore how to provide a limited version of these transactional semantics by specifying several custom methods, analogous to the standard methods we saw in chapter 7, that permit atomic operation on arbitrary groups of resources called *batches*. These methods will be named quite similarly to the standard methods (e.g., `BatchDeleteMessages`) but will vary in their implementation depending on the standard method being performed on the batch.

Listing 18.1   Example of a batch Delete method

```
abstract class ChatRoomApi {
  @post("/{parent=chatRooms/*}/messages:batchDelete")
  BatchDeleteMessages(req: BatchDeleteMessagesRequest): void;
}
```

As with most proposals like this, it leads to quite a few questions before we can get to work. For example, what HTTP method should we use for each of these methods? Should it always be POST as required for custom methods (see chapter 9)? Or should it match with the HTTP method for each of the standard methods (e.g., GET for Batch-GetMessages and DELETE for BatchDeleteMessages)? Or does it depend on the method?

    And how extreme do we get with our atomicity requirements? If I attempt to retrieve a batch of Message resources using `BatchGetMessages` and one of these resources has since been deleted, do I really have to fail the entire operation? Or is it acceptable to skip right past that and return those that did still exist at the time? What about operating on resources across multiple parent resources? In other words, should it be possible to delete Message resources from multiple ChatRooms?

    In this pattern, we'll explore how to define these batch methods, how they work, and all of these curious edge cases that we'll inevitably run into when building out this functionality in an API.

18.3   *Implementation*

As we just learned in section 18.2, we will rely on specially named custom methods to support these batch operations. These methods are simply batch versions of the standard methods, with one exception: there is no batch version of the standard list method. This leads to the following batch custom methods:

- BatchGet<Resources>()
- BatchCreate<Resources>()
- BatchUpdate<Resources>()
- BatchDelete<Resources>()

While we'll explore the details of each method individually in later sections, it's certainly worth going through some of the aspects that are common to each, starting with the most important: atomicity.

18.3.1   *Atomicity*

When we say a set of operations is *atomic* we mean that these operations are indivisible from one another. So far, all operations we've discussed have been themselves considered atomic. After all, you cannot have a standard create method fail partially. The resource is either created or it's not, but there's no middle ground. Unfortunately, the way we've designed the standard methods to be atomic individually simply doesn't provide the same guarantee collectively. The goal of these batch operations is to extend that same principle of atomicity to methods performed on multiple resources rather than just a single one.

Meeting this goal means that the action must be atomic even when it might be a bit inconvenient. For example, imagine that we're trying to retrieve a batch of `Message` resources using a `BatchGetMessages` method. If retrieving even one of these resources happens to result in an error, then the entire request must result in an error. This must be the case whether it's 1 in 5 resulting in an error or 1 in 10,000.

The reason for this is two-fold. First, in many cases (like updating batches of resources), atomicity is the entire point of the operation. We actively want to be sure that either all changes are applied or none of them. While this isn't *exactly* the scenario with batch retrieval (we might be okay to get back a `null` value for items that might not exist), it leads to the second reason. If we have to support partial success, the interface to managing the results can get pretty intricate and complex. Instead, by ensuring either complete success or a single error, the interface is always geared toward complete success and simply returns the list of resources involved in the batch.

As a result, all the batch methods that we'll explore in this pattern will always be completely atomic. The response messages will be designed such that they can only ever completely succeed or completely fail; there will never be a middle ground.

18.3.2 Operation on the collection

As we learned in section 9.3.2, when it comes to custom methods that interact with collections, we have two different options for the URL format for the method. We can either target the parent resource itself and have the custom method name include the resources it's interacting with, or we can leave the custom action section as a verb and operate on the collection itself. These two options are summarized in table 18.1.

Table 18.1 Options of targets and corresponding URLs for batch methods

Target	URL
Parent resource	`/chatRooms/*:batchUpdateMessages`
Collection	`/chatRooms/*/messages:batchUpdate`

What was pointed out in chapter 9 holds true today. Whenever we're dealing with a collection where we have multiple resources of the same type, it's almost always better to operate on the collection itself. This holds true for all of the batch methods we'll discuss in detail: they'll all target the collection and therefore have URLs ending in `:batch<Method>`.

18.3.3 *Ordering of results*

When we operate on an arbitrary group of resources, we'll need to send them in a request of sorts. In some cases this might just be a list of unique identifiers (e.g., when retrieving or deleting resources), but in others it will need to be the resources themselves (e.g., when creating or updating resources). In all of these cases though, it's going to become successively more important that the order of the resources be preserved.

The most obvious example of why it's important to preserve order is when we're creating a batch of new resources and not choosing the identifiers ourselves but allowing the service to do so. Since we have no prearranged way of identifying these newly created resources, the simplest way is to use their index in the repeated field of resources that were provided to the request. If we don't preserve the order, we'll have to do a deep comparison between the resources we provided and those returned from the batch creation to match up the items created with their server-assigned identifiers.

Listing 18.2   Example code to match request resources

```
let chatRoom1 = ChatRoom({ title: "Chat 1", description: "Chat 1" });
let chatRoom2 = ChatRoom({ title: "Chat 2", description: "Chat 2"});

let results = BatchCreateChatRooms({ resources: [chatRoom1, chatRoom2] });

chatRoom1 = results.resources[0];
chatRoom2 = results.resources[1];
```

In the case where we know the order, we can easily associate the results with the requested action.

```
for (let resource of results.resources) {
  if (deepCompare(chatRoom1, resource))
    chatRoom1 = resource;
  else if (deepCompare(chatRoom2, resource))
    chatRoom2 = resource;
  }
}
```

When we don't know the order, we have to do a full comparison of the resources for equality of each of their fields (except the ID field) to be sure we have the right resource.

As a result, it's an important requirement that when a batch method returns the resources involved in a batch they are returned in the same order in which they were provided.

18.3.4 *Common fields*

When it comes to batch operations, we have two primary strategies to choose from. The first, simpler option is to treat the batch version of a request as just a list of normal, single-resource requests. The second option is a bit more complicated but can reduce duplication by hoisting up the fields that are relevant to the request and simply repeat those.

```
interface GetMessageRequest {
  id: string;
}

interface BatchGetMessagesRequest {
  requests: GetMessageRequest[];      ◄─┐  Here we simply have a list
}                                          of GetMessageRequest
                                           interfaces.

interface BatchGetMessagesRequest {   ◄─┐  Here we hoist out the relevant
  ids: string[];                           field (id) and embed it as a list
}                                          of IDs for a batch.
```

It turns out that we'll need to rely on both strategies, depending on the method in question, because the simpler strategy (providing a list of requests) is a much better fit for cases where we need quite a bit of customization (e.g., if we need to create resources that might have different parents), while the strategy of hoisting fields out of the request is a much better fit for simpler actions such as retrieving or deleting resources, as no additional information is necessary.

Additionally, these strategies are not necessarily mutually exclusive. In some cases, we will actually hoist some values while still relying on the strategy of using a list of requests to communicate the important information. A good example of this is updating a batch of resources, where we will rely on a repeated list of update requests but also hoist the parent field and potentially the field mask to handle partial batch updates.

While this combination of strategies sounds great, it leads to an important question: what happens when a hoisted field is different from the field set on any of the individual requests? In other words, what if we have a hoisted parent field set to Chat-Room 1 and one of the to-be-created resources has its parent field set to ChatRoom 2? The short answer keeps with the philosophy of fast and nonpartial failure: the API should simply throw an error and reject the request. While it might be tempting to treat the resource's redefinition of the hoisted field as a more specific override, it's quite possible that there is a semantic mistake in the code here, and operating on groups of resources is certainly not the time to try to make inferences about user intentions. Instead, if a user intends to vary the hoisted field across multiple resources, they should leave the hoisted field blank or set it to a wild card value, which we'll discuss in the next section.

18.3.5 *Operating across parents*

One of the most common reasons for relying on a list of individual requests rather than hoisting fields upward into the batch request is to operate on multiple resources that might also belong to multiple different parents. For example, listing 18.4 shows one option to define an example BatchCreateMessages method, which supports creating resources across multiple different parents, but doing so in an unusual (and incorrect) way.

Listing 18.4   Incorrect way of supporting multi-parent creation in a batch method

```
interface Message {
  id: string;
  title: string;
  description: string;
}

interface CreateMessageRequest {
  parent: string;
  resource: Message;
}

interface BatchCreateMessageRequest {
  parents: string[];
  resources: Message[];
}
```

> We need a list of the parents to which these Message resources will belong.

> Here we've hoisted the Message resources from the CreateMessageRequest interface.

As you can see, it relies on a list of the resources to be created, but we also need to know the parent of each of these. And since that field doesn't exist on the resource itself, we now need a way of keeping track of each resource's parent. Here, we've done this by having a second list of parents. While this does technically work, it can be quite clumsy to work with due to the strict dependence on maintaining order in the two lists. How do we handle this cross-parent batch operation?

The simple answer is to rely on a wild card value for the parent and allow the parent itself to vary inside the list of requests. In this case, we'll standardize the hyphen character (-) as the wild card to indicate "across multiple parents."

Listing 18.5   HTTP request to create two resources with different parents

```
POST /chatRooms/-/messages:batchCreate HTTP/1.1
Content-Type: application/json

{
  "requests": [
    {
      "parent": "chatRooms/1",
      "resource": { ... }
    },
    {
      "parent": "chatRooms/2",
      "resource": { ... }
    }
  ]
}
```

> We rely on a wild card hyphen character to indicate multiple parents, to be defined in the requests.

> We define the actual parent in the list of requests to create the resources.

This same mechanism should be used for all the other batch methods that might need to operate across resources belonging to multiple parents. However, just like with the hoisted fields, this raises a question about conflicting values: what if a single parent is specified in the URL, yet some of the request-level parent fields conflict? What should be done?

In this case, the API should behave exactly as defined in section 18.3.4: if there is a conflict, we should reject the request as invalid and await clarification from the user in the form of another API call. This is for exactly the same reasons as noted before: the user's intent is unclear, and operating on a (potentially large) group of resources is certainly not the time to guess what those intentions might be.

With that, we can finally get to the good part: defining exactly what these methods look like and how each of them should work. Let's start by looking at one of the simplest: batch get.

18.3.6 Batch Get

The goal of the batch get method is to retrieve a set of resources from an API by providing a group of unique identifiers. Since this is analogous to the standard get method, and is idempotent, batch get will rely on the HTTP GET method for transport. This, however, presents a bit of a problem in that GET methods generally do not have a request body. The result is that the list of identifiers is provided in the query string like we saw with field masks in chapter 8.

Listing 18.6 Example of the batch get method

```
abstract class ChatRoomApi {
  @get("/chatrooms:batchGet")
  BatchGetChatRooms(req: BatchGetChatRoomsRequest):
    BatchGetChatRoomsResponse;

  @get("/{parent=chatRooms/*}/messages:batchGet")
  BatchGetMessages(req: BatchGetMessagesRequest):
    BatchGetMessagesResponse;
}

interface BatchGetChatRoomsRequest {
  ids: string[];
}

interface BatchGetChatRoomsResponse {
  resources: ChatRoom[];
}

interface BatchGetMessagesRequest {
  parent: string;
  ids: string[];
}

interface BatchGetMessagesResponse {
  resources: Message[];
}
```

Since ChatRoom resources have no parent, the batch get request doesn't provide a place to specify a parent.

All batch get requests specify a list of IDs to retrieve.

Since Message resources have parents, the request has a place to specify the parent (or provide a wild card).

The response always includes a list of resources, in the exact same order as the IDs that were requested.

As you can see, unless the group of resources are top-level resources without a parent, we'll need to specify *something* for the parent value in the request message. If we intend to limit the retrievals to be all from the same parent, then we have an obvious answer: use the parent identifier itself. If, instead, we want to provide the ability to retrieve resources across multiple different parents, we should rely on a hyphen character as a wild card value, as we saw in section 18.3.5.

Although it might be tempting to always permit cross-parent retrievals, think carefully about whether it makes sense for the use case. All the data might be in a single database now, but in the future the storage system may expand and distribute data to many different places. Since a parent resource is an obvious choice for a distribution key, and the distributed storage becomes expensive or difficult to query outside the scope of a single distribution key, providing the ability to retrieve resources across parents could become exceptionally expensive or impossible to query. In those cases, the only option will be to disallow the wildcard character for a parent, which is almost certainly a breaking change (see chapter 24). And remember, as we saw in section 18.3.5, if an ID provided in the list would conflict with an explicitly specified parent (i.e., any parent value that isn't a wildcard), the request should be rejected as invalid.

Next, as we learned in section 18.3.1, it's critical that this method be completely atomic, even when it's inconvenient. This means that even when just 1 out of 100 IDs is invalid for any reason (e.g., it doesn't exist or the requesting user doesn't have access to it), it must fail completely. In cases where you're looking for less strict guarantees, it's far better to rely on the standard list method with a filter applied to match on one of a set of possible identifiers (see chapter 22 for more information on this).

Additionally, as we learned in section 18.3.4, if we want to support partial retrieval of the resources, such as requesting only a single field from each of the IDs specified, we can hoist the field mask just as we did with the parent field. This single field mask should be applied across all resources retrieved. This should not be a list of field masks in order to apply a different field mask to each of the resources specified.

Listing 18.7   Adding support for partial retrieval in a batch get request

```
interface BatchGetMessagesRequest {
  parent: string;
  ids: string[];
  fieldMask: FieldMask;    ◁
}
```

To enable partial retrievals, the batch request should include a single field mask to be applied to all retrieved resources.

Finally, it's worth noting that despite the fact that the response to this request could become quite large, batch methods should not implement pagination (see chapter 21). Instead, batch methods should define and document an upper limit on the number of resources that may be retrieved. This limit can vary depending on the size of each individual resource, but generally should be chosen to minimize the possibility of excessively large responses that can cause performance degradation on the API server or unwieldy response sizes for the API clients.

18.3.7 *Batch Delete*

In a similar manner to the batch get operation, batch delete also operates on a list of identifiers, though with a very different end goal. Rather than retrieving all of these resources, its job is to delete each and every one of them. This operation will rely on an HTTP POST method, adhering to the guidelines for custom methods that we explored in chapter 9. And since the request must be atomic, deleting all the resources listed or returning an error, the final return type is void, representing an empty result.

> **Listing 18.8   Example of the batch delete method**

```
abstract class ChatRoomApi {
  @post("/chatrooms:batchDelete")
  BatchDeleteChatRooms(req: BatchDeleteChatRoomsRequest): void;

  @post("/{parent=chatRooms/*}/messages:batchDelete")
  BatchDeleteMessages(req: BatchDeleteMessagesRequest): void;
}

interface BatchDeleteChatRoomsRequest {

  ids: string[];
}

interface BatchDeleteMessagesRequest {
  parent: string;
  ids: string[];
}
```

For top-level resources, no parent field is provided on requests.

Just like batch get, batch delete operations accept a list of identifiers rather than any resources themselves.

Since Message resources are not top-level, we need a field to hold that parent value.

In most aspects, this method is quite similar to the batch get method we just went through in section 18.3.6. For example, top-level resources might not have a parent field, but others do. And when the parent field is specified, it must match the parent of the resources whose IDs are provided or return an error result. Further, just as is the case for batch get operations, deleting across several different parents is possible by using a wild card character for the parent field; however, it should be considered carefully due to the potential issues down the line with distributed storage systems.

One area worth calling out specifically again is that of atomicity: batch delete operations must either delete all the resources listed or fail entirely. This means that if 1 resource out of 100 is unable to be deleted for any reason, the entire operation must fail. This includes the case where the resource has already been deleted and no longer exists, which was the actual intent of the operation in the first place. The reason for this, explored in more detail in chapter 7, is that we need to take an imperative view of the delete operation rather than a declarative one. This means that we must be able to say not just that the resource we wanted deleted indeed no longer exists, but that it no longer exists due to the execution of this specific operation and not due to some other operation at an earlier point in time.

Now that we've covered the ID-based operations, let's get into the more complicated scenarios, starting with batch create operations.

18.3.8   *Batch Create*

As with all the other batch operations, the purpose of a batch create operation is to create several resources that previously didn't exist before—and to do so atomically. Unlike the simpler methods we've explored already (batch get and batch delete) batch create will rely on a more complicated strategy of accepting a list of standard create requests alongside a hoisted parent field.

Listing 18.9   Example of the batch create method

```
abstract class ChatRoomApi {
  @post("/chatrooms:batchCreate")
  BatchCreateChatRooms(req: BatchCreateChatRoomsRequest):
    BatchCreateChatRoomsResponse;

  @post("/{parent=chatRooms/*}/messages:batchCreate")
  BatchCreateMessages(req: BatchCreateMessagesRequest):
    BatchCreateMessagesResponse;
}

interface CreateChatRoomRequest {
  resource: ChatRoom;
}

interface CreateMessageRequest {
  parent: string;
  resource: Message;
}

interface BatchCreateChatRoomsRequest {
  requests: CreateChatRoomRequest[];
}

interface BatchCreateMessagesRequest {
  parent: string;
  requests: CreateMessageRequest[];
}

interface BatchCreateChatRoomsResponse {
  resources: ChatRoom[];
}

interface BatchCreateMessagesResponse {
  resources: Message[];
}
```

> **Rather than a list of resources or IDs, we rely on a list of standard create requests.** (pointing to `requests: CreateChatRoomRequest[];` and `requests: CreateMessageRequest[];`)

> **When the resource is not top-level, we also include the parent (which may be a wild card).**

Similar to the other batch methods, the parent fields are only relevant for non-top-level resources (in this case, the ChatRoom resource) and the restrictions remain the same (that if a non-wild card parent is provided, it must be consistent with all the resources being created). The primary difference is in the form of the incoming data. In this case, rather than pulling the fields out of the standard create request and directly into the batch create request, we simply include the standard create requests directly.

This might seem unusual, but there's a pretty important reason and it has to do with the parent. In short, we want to provide the ability to create multiple resources atomically that might have several different parents. Unfortunately, the parent of a resource isn't typically stored as a field directly on the resource itself when it's being created. Instead, it's often provided in the standard create request, resulting in an identifier that includes the parent resource as the root (e.g., chatRooms/1/messages/2). This restriction means that if we want to allow cross-parent resource creation without requiring client-generated identifiers, we need to provide both the resource itself along with its intended parent, which is exactly what the standard create request interface does.

Another similarity to the other batch methods is the ordering constraint. Just like other methods, the list of newly created resources absolutely must be in the exact same order as they were provided in the batch request. While this is important in most other batch methods, it is even more so in the case of batch create because, unlike the other cases, the identifiers for the resources being created may not yet exist, meaning that it can be quite difficult to discover the new identifiers for the resources that were created if they are returned in a different order than the one in which they were sent.

Finally, let's wrap up by looking at the batch update method, which is quite similar to the batch create method.

18.3.9 *Batch Update*

The goal of the batch update method is to modify a group of resources together in one atomic operation. And just as we saw with the batch create method, batch update will rely on a list of standard update requests as the input. The difference in this case is that the rationale for needing a list of requests rather than a list of resources should be quite obvious: partial updates.

In the case of updating a resource, we might want to control the specific fields to be updated, and it's quite common that different fields might need to be updated on different resources in the batch. As a result, we can treat the field mask similarly to how we treated the parent field when designing the batch create method. This means that we want the ability to apply different field masks to different resources being updated, but also the ability to apply a single blanket field mask across all the resources being updated. Obviously these must not conflict, meaning that if the batch request has a field mask set, the field masks on individual requests must either match or be left blank.

Listing 18.10   Example of the batch update method

```
abstract class ChatRoomApi {
  @post("/chatrooms:batchUpdate")
  BatchUpdateChatRooms(req: BatchUpdateChatRoomsRequest):
    BatchUpdateChatRoomsResponse;

  @post("/{parent=chatRooms/*}/messages:batchUpdate")
  BatchUpdateMessages(req: BatchUpdateMessagesRequest):
    BatchUpdateMessagesResponse;
}

interface UpdateChatRoomRequest {
  resource: ChatRoom;
  fieldMask: FieldMask;
}

interface UpdateMessageRequest {
  resource: Message;
  fieldMask: FieldMask;
}

interface BatchUpdateChatRoomsRequest {
  requests: UpdateChatRoomRequest[];
  fieldMask: FieldMask;
}

interface BatchUpdateMessagesRequest {
  parent: string;
  requests: UpdateMessageRequest[];
  fieldMask: FieldMask;
}

interface BatchUpdateChatRoomsResponse {
  resources: ChatRoom[];
}

interface BatchUpdateMessagesResponse {
  resources: Message[];
}
```

> Despite the standard update method using the HTTP PATCH method, we rely on the HTTP POST method.

> Just like the batch create method, we use a list of requests rather than a list of resources.

We can hoist the field mask for partial updates into the batch request if it's the same across all resources.

It's also worth mentioning that even though we use the HTTP PATCH method in the standard update method, to avoid any potential conflicts (and from breaking any standards) the batch update method should use the HTTP POST method as is done for all other custom methods.

18.3.10 *Final API definition*

With that, we can wrap up by looking at the final API definition for supporting batch methods in our example chat room API. Listing 18.11 shows how we might put all of these batch methods together to support a wide range of functionality, operating on potentially large groups of resources with single API calls.

Listing 18.11 Final API definition

```
abstract class ChatRoomApi {
  @post("/chatrooms:batchCreate")
  BatchCreateChatRooms(req: BatchCreateChatRoomsRequest):
    BatchCreateChatRoomsResponse;

  @post("/{parent=chatRooms/*}/messages:batchCreate")
  BatchCreateMessages(req: BatchCreateMessagesRequest):
    BatchCreateMessagesResponse;

  @get("/chatrooms:batchGet")
  BatchGetChatRooms(req: BatchGetChatRoomsRequest):
    BatchGetChatRoomsResponse;

  @get("/{parent=chatRooms/*}/messages:batchGet")
  BatchGetMessages(req: BatchGetMessagesRequest):
    BatchGetMessagesResponse;

  @post("/chatrooms:batchUpdate")
  BatchUpdateChatRooms(req: BatchUpdateChatRoomsRequest):
    BatchUpdateChatRoomsResponse;

  @post("/{parent=chatRooms/*}/messages:batchUpdate")
  BatchUpdateMessages(req: BatchUpdateMessagesRequest):
    BatchUpdateMessagesResponse;

  @post("/chatrooms:batchDelete")
  BatchDeleteChatRooms(req: BatchDeleteChatRoomsRequest): void;

  @post("/{parent=chatRooms/*}/messages:batchDelete")
  BatchDeleteMessages(req: BatchDeleteMessagesRequest): void;
}

interface CreateChatRoomRequest {
  resource: ChatRoom;
}

interface CreateMessageRequest {
  parent: string;
  resource: Message;
}

interface BatchCreateChatRoomsRequest {
  requests: CreateChatRoomRequest[];
}

interface BatchCreateMessagesRequest {
  parent: string;
  requests: CreateMessageRequest[];
}

interface BatchCreateChatRoomsResponse {
  resources: ChatRoom[];
}
```

```
interface BatchCreateMessagesResponse {
  resources: Message[];
}

interface BatchGetChatRoomsRequest {
  ids: string[];
}

interface BatchGetChatRoomsResponse {
  resources: ChatRoom[];
}

interface BatchGetMessagesRequest {
  parent: string;
  ids: string[];
}

interface BatchGetMessagesResponse {
  resources: Message[];
}

interface UpdateChatRoomRequest {
  resource: ChatRoom;
  fieldMask: FieldMask;
}

interface UpdateMessageRequest {
  resource: Message;
  fieldMask: FieldMask;
}

interface BatchUpdateChatRoomsRequest {
  parent: string;
  requests: UpdateChatRoomRequest[];
  fieldMask: FieldMask;
}

interface BatchUpdateMessagesRequest {
  requests: UpdateMessageRequest[];
  fieldMask: FieldMask;
}

interface BatchUpdateChatRoomsResponse {
  resources: ChatRoom[];
}

interface BatchUpdateMessagesResponse {
  resources: Message[];
}

interface BatchDeleteChatRoomsRequest {
  ids: string[];
}

interface BatchDeleteMessagesRequest {
  parent: string;
  ids: string[];
}
```

18.4 Trade-offs

For many of these different batch methods, we made quite a few very specific decisions that have some pretty important effects on the resulting API behavior. First, all of these methods put atomicity above all else, even when it might be a bit inconvenient. For example, if we attempt to delete multiple resources and one of them is already deleted, then the entire batch delete method will fail. This was an important trade-off to avoid dealing with an API that supports returning results that show some pieces succeeding and some failing, and instead focus on sticking to the behavior of transactional semantics in most modern database systems. While this might result in annoyances for common scenarios, it ensures that the API methods are as consistent and simple as possible while still providing an important bit of functionality.

Next, while there may be some inconsistencies in the format of the input data (sometimes its raw IDs; other times it's the standard request interfaces), the design of these methods emphasizes simplicity over consistency. For example, we could stick to a repeated list of standard requests for all batch methods; however, some of these methods (in particular, batch get and batch delete) would contain a needless level of indirection just to provide the identifiers. By hoisting these values into the batch request, we get a simpler experience at the cost of a reasonable amount of inconsistency.

18.5 Exercises

1 Why is it important for results of batch methods to be in a specific order? What happens if they're out of order?

2 In a batch update request, what should the response be if the `parent` field on the request doesn't match the `parent` field on one of the resources being updated?

3 Why is it important for batch requests to be atomic? What would the API definition look like if some requests could succeed while others could fail?

4 Why does the batch delete method rely on the HTTP `POST` verb rather than the HTTP `DELETE` verb?

Summary

- Batch methods should be named according to the format of `Batch<Method><Resources>()` and should be completely atomic, performing all operations in the batch or none of them.
- Batch methods that operate on multiple resources of the same type should generally target the collection rather than a parent resource (e.g., `POST /chatRooms/1234/messages:batchUpdate` rather than `POST /chatRooms/1234:batchUpdateMessages`).
- Results from batch operations should be in the same order as the resources or requests were originally sent.
- Use a wild card hyphen character to indicate multiple parents of a resource to be defined in the individual requests.

Criteria-based deletion 19

While the batch operations we learned about in chapter 18 provide the ability to delete several resources with a single API call, there's an underlying requirement that we must know in advance: the unique identifiers of the resource we want to delete. However, there are many scenarios where we're not so much interested in deleting a specific list of resources but instead are more interested in deleting any resources that happen to match a specific set of criteria. This design pattern provides a mechanism by which we can safely and atomically remove all resources matching certain criteria rather than by a list of identifiers.

19.1 Motivation

As is evident from chapter 18, it's not all that uncommon to want to operate on more than one resource at a time. More specifically, we might want to clear out a set of specific resources. However, compared to the other batch operations, deletion is by far the most straightforward, requiring no other information to perform an action: given an ID, remove the resource.

This is a wonderful piece of functionality, but it requires that we already know exactly which resources we want to delete. This means that if we don't yet know this information, we first have to investigate. For example, imagine we want to delete all ChatRoom resources that are flagged as archived. To make this happen, we need to discover which resources have this particular setting and then use those identifiers to remove the resources with the batch delete method.

Listing 19.1   Criteria-based deletion using standard list and batch delete methods

```
function deleteArchivedChatRooms(): void {
  const archivedRooms = ListChatRooms({        First we must find all
    filter: "archived: true"              ⟵    resources that are archived.
  });
  return BatchDeleteChatRooms({          Once we have the identifiers,
    ids: archivedRooms.map( (room) => room.id )   ⟵   we can delete all of them.
  });
}
```

Unfortunately, there are several problems with this design. First, and most obviously, it requires at least two separate API calls. And to make things even worse, as we'll learn in chapter 21, listing resources is unlikely to be a single request and is more likely to involve a long list of repeated requests to find all of the matching resources. Second, and most importantly, these two methods being stitched together lead to a nonatomic result. In other words, by the time we collect all of the IDs of archived resources, it's possible that some of them might have been unarchived. This means that when we're deleting these resources, we might be deleting resources that aren't archived anymore!

Because of these major issues, it's important we have an alternative that provides a single method allowing us to delete resources based on some set of criteria rather than exclusively based on a list of identifiers.

19.2 Overview

This pattern introduces an idea of a new custom method: purge. The purpose of the purge method is to accept a simple filter that can be executed, and any results matching that filter criteria are deleted. In essence, it's a combination of the standard list method with the batch delete method. However, rather than piping the output of one method into the input of another method (as seen in listing 19.1), we can use a single API call to accomplish our goal.

While the method and its purpose are straightforward, we also have to consider the obvious concern: this method is dangerous. As we'll see in chapter 25, users are not immune from mistakes, and we are often worried about users deleting data that they later regret having deleted. And in this case, rather than handing users a tool to delete a single resource (standard delete) or even a tool to delete lots of resources (batch delete), we're now handing them the biggest tool of all. The purge method allows users to delete resources without even being aware of the full extent of what they're deleting. Under the right conditions (e.g., a filter that matches all resources), we're able to wipe out all the data stored in the system entirely!

To avoid this potentially catastrophic result, we'll provide two specific levers that users can rely on as guard rails. First, we'll require an explicit Boolean flag be set on the request (`force`) before actually deleting anything. Second, in the case that this flag is not set (and therefore the request won't be executed), we'll provide a method to preview what would have happened if the request was actually executed. This will include both a count of the number of items that would be deleted (`purgeCount`) as well as a preview of some of the items that happen to match the list of results (`purge-Sample`). In some ways, this is a bit like having a `validateOnly` field on the request (see chapter 27), but with the opposite default: that a request is always for validation only unless explicitly requested.

19.3   Implementation

To see how this method works, let's start by looking at the typical flow of the purge method. As shown in figure 19.1, the process begins with a request providing the filter to be applied, but leaving the `force` flag set to `false` (or left unset). Because this is the equivalent of a validation request, no resources will actually be deleted, and instead the `purgeSample` field will be populated with a list of identifiers of resources that *would have been* deleted. Additionally, the `purgeCount` field would provide an estimate of the number of resources that match the filter and therefore would be deleted by the request.

With this new information from the validation request, we can double-check that the resources returned in the `purgeSample` field are indeed ones that match the intent expressed in the filter. And then, if we decide to follow through with deleting all the resources included, we can send the same request again, this time setting the `force` flag to `true`. In the response, only the `purgeCount` field should be populated with the number of resources deleted by executing the request.

Now that we have an idea of the overall flow, let's get into the tricky details of each of these fields and explore how they work together, starting with the `filter` field.

19.3.1 Filtering results

As you might expect, the `filter` field should work exactly as it does on the standard list method, as we'll see in chapter 22. The whole point of the purge method is that it provides almost identical functionality to the standard list method combined with the

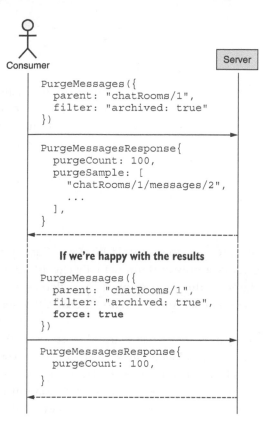

Figure 19.1 Interaction pattern for the purge method

batch delete method. This means that a filter specified and executed by the purge method should behave identically to that same filter having been provided to a standard list method.

One unusual, and scary, consequence of this is that just as an empty or unset filter on the standard list method returns all resources hosted by the API, this same behavior is therefore expected for the purge method. In other words, we're in a very tricky situation where if a user were to forget to specify a filter (or has a coding error resulting in the filter being set to undefined or an empty string), the method will match all existing resources and, if forced, delete all resources. While certainly dangerous, this is why the other fail-safes are built into this design.

Listing 19.2 Minor typos resulting in disastrous consequences

Unfortunately, a typo here (fliter instead of filter) will result in the filter being undefined and therefore will always match all resources.

```
function deleteMatchingMessages(filter: string): number {
  const result = PurgeMessages({
    parent: "chatRooms/1",
    filter: fliter,
```

This method accepts a filter string and deletes all Message resources matching the filter.

```
    force: true,
  });
  return result.purgeCount;
}
```

While it might be safer to prevent requests like these, the unfortunate reality is that users do have a need to perform this type action, and, further, the consistency with the standard list method is critical—otherwise users may start to think that filters work differently for different methods. As a result, we cannot simply reject requests with a missing filter, for example. That said, scenarios like these are the primary drivers behind the idea that, by default, the purge method acts as though we're asking for a preview only. In the next section, we'll explore this in more detail.

19.3.2   *Validation only by default*

As we'll learn in chapter 27, we can rely on a special validateOnly flag to make an API method validate the incoming request only and not actually execute the request itself. Purposefully, we chose the name of this field to push for a default value such that the method behaves normally unless explicitly asked to do otherwise (see section 5.2 for more discussion on this topic).

While this default is fine for those cases, as we just learned in section 19.3.1, it is exceptionally dangerous for the purge method as it allows a tiny mistake to result in deleting a potentially large amount of data from the API. If we rely exclusively on request validation, forgetting to specify that the request was for validation only will result in deleting data rather than providing some sort of preview as we might hope.

Listing 19.3   **An omission with the wrong default leading to disastrous results**

```
PurgeMessages({
  parent: "chatRooms/1",        If we rely on a validateOnly flag,
  filter: "...",                omitting it entirely can result in
  // validateOnly: true  ←───   accidentally deleting lots of data!
});
```

This is one of the few scenarios where we actually want to have a method crippled by default rather than the other way around. In other words, if a field is forgotten (perhaps a user didn't properly read the documentation), the default behavior should be safe for the user and not lead to catastrophic consequences.

To make this happen, we rely on a field called force, which does the exact same thing as the validateOnly field but is named to lead to a different default behavior. Thanks to this difference, forgetting to set this field (or leaving it set to false) leads to a completely safe result: no data is deleted at all. In addition to no data being deleted, we actually get a useful preview of the results had the request been actually executed. This preview is made up of two key pieces of information: a count of the number of matching resources as well as a sample set of those matching resources. In the next section, we'll start by looking at how this count of results works.

19.3.3 *Result count*

Regardless of whether a purge request is to be executed or is for validation only, one quite useful piece of information to have in mind is a count of how many resources happen to match the provided filter. To do this, purge responses should include a `purgeCount` field that provides this information.

There is a catch though: while the value should be an exact count of items actually deleted in a live request (`force: true`), when the request is for validation only this value can opt to provide a reasonable estimate rather than an exact count because in some cases it might be computationally intensive to find and count all the possible matches. And since we're not going through the process of deleting them all and would like to avoid wasting computing power, it's not really a big deal to rely on an estimate over a perfectly accurate count. That said, the goal is to be as realistic as possible, so it's important that the estimate be at least somewhat reflective of reality.

One thing to consider when relying on an estimated value for this field is that underestimates can be devilishly misleading and should be avoided as much as possible. To see why, consider the scenario where a response indicates that an estimated 100 resources match a given filter. This might give a user a false sense of confidence that the purge method won't remove that many resources. If, in truth, the number of matching resources is closer to 1,000, the user will first be shocked when the true results come in (showing 1,000 resources have been deleted compared to the estimate of 100) but will be exceptionally frustrated when they realize that they would have gone back and revised their filter expression had the estimate been more reflective of reality (say, 750 matching resources).

For this and a variety of other reasons, seeing the number of matching resources for a given filter is certainly useful information (both for live requests and validation requests), but there's an even more useful bit of data for validation-only requests that we could provide as well: a sample set of the resources that match and therefore will be deleted. In the next section, we explore how best to do this.

19.3.4 *Result sample set*

As we've seen, a preview of the number of resources matching a provided filter is useful but certainly not perfect. In fact, even when the count is an exact number rather than an estimate, we still have to accept that this is a single metric that simply counts all matching resources, and in many cases this type of aggregate can actually be misleading. For example, consider if 50 of 100 items match a filter. How do we know we're about to delete *the right* 50 items? Perhaps we meant to delete all 50 archived resources and instead are about to delete all 50 *unarchived* resources instead! Counts of matching items are often helpful for noticing glaring problems but fail when the issues are more subtle.

To address this problem, in addition to the count of matching resources, we can rely on a validation response providing a sample subset of items that would be deleted in a field called `purgeSample`. This field should contain a list of identifiers of matching resources, which can then be spot-checked for accuracy. For example, we could check a few of the resources returned and verify that they are indeed marked as archived and not the other way around.

Despite the fact that this requires some extra work, it is still quite useful. For example, in a user interface we might retrieve a few of these items using the batch get method and display them to a user for verification to be sure that the resources listed in the preview look like ones they intend to delete. If the user decides that none of these resources look out of place, they can proceed with executing the request by resending it with force set to true.

But this leads to an obvious question: how many items should be in this preview sample? In general, since the goal is to help catch any mistakes in the filter expression, it's important that the sample size be large enough for a user to notice if something looks out of place (e.g., if a resource that shouldn't match happens to appear in the sample set). As a result, a good guideline is to provide at least 100 items for larger data sets, while providing exact matches for smaller data sets that are relatively inexpensive to query.

19.3.5 *Consistency*

The final issue to worry about is quite a bit trickier and one that deserves at least a mention here: consistency. What happens if we send a validation-only purge request for few resources to be deleted, but by the time we send the actual request for execution later, the data has changed such that many more resources match the filter? In other words, is there a way to have any guarantee that the data returned during validation will match the data that will be deleted later during execution? Unfortunately, the short answer is no.

Even if we have the ability to perform queries over snapshots of data at a specific point in time, executing the purge request over data as it appeared in the past is unlikely to lead to the desired result. As a matter of fact, if this behavior is really the intent, then it's already supported by the combination of a standard list request and a batch delete request.

Additionally, while it is technically possible that we could require the purge method to fail in the case where data has changed between the time of a validation request and a live request, the method would become practically useless on any sufficiently large, concurrent, volatile data set. And in the world of APIs, this is not an uncommon occurrence.

19.3.6 *Final API definition*

Now that we have a full grasp on how the purge method works, let's look at a short example of a method to remove all Message resources provided a set of criteria to be specified in a filter string.

Listing 19.4 Final API definition

```
abstract class ChatRoomApi {
  @post("/{parent=chatRooms/*}/messages:purge")
```

```
  PurgeMessages(req: PurgeMessagesRequest): PurgeMessagesResponse;
}

interface PurgeMessagesRequest {
  parent: string;
  filter: string;
  force?: boolean;
}

interface PurgeMessagesResponse {
  purgeCount: number;
  purgeSample: string[];
}
```

19.4 Trade-offs

In case you haven't noticed, this is a dangerous method. It's a bit like handing a bazooka to users of an API, giving them the ability to destroy a lot of data very easily and very quickly. While the method as designed attempts to provide as many safety checks as possible, it still opens the door to the possibility that users will mistakenly destroy a large amount, if not all, of their data. As a result, unless this is an absolute necessity, it's generally a good idea to avoid supporting this functionality in an API.

19.5 Exercises

1 Why should the custom purge method be limited to only those cases where it's absolutely necessary?
2 Why does the purge method default to executing validation only?
3 What happens if the filter criteria are left empty?
4 If a resource supports soft deletion, what is the expected behavior of the purge method on that resource? Should it soft-delete the resources? Or expunge them?
5 What is the purpose of returning the count of affected resources? What about the sample set of matching resources?

Summary

- The custom purge method should be used to delete multiple resources matching a specific set of filter criteria but should be supported only if absolutely necessary.
- By default, purge requests should be exclusively for validation rather than actually deleting any resources.
- All purge responses should include a count of the number of resources affected (and a sample set of matching results), though this may be estimated for a validation request.
- The purge method should adhere to the same consistency guidelines as the standard list method.

Anonymous writes

This chapter covers

- What we mean by anonymous data
- How to ingest data into an API without relying on creating resources
- How to address consistency concerns with ingested data

So far, writing any new data into an API has involved creating resources, complete with their unique identifiers and schemas. Unfortunately, as much as we might want this to be the one and only way to create data, it sometimes does not quite fit with the realities of the world. Indeed, there are scenarios where data needs to be written but not uniquely identified after the fact, such as entries in a log file or time series data points to be aggregated into statistics. In this pattern, we address this idea of writing data rather than creating resources and how this new concept can still fit with our existing resource-oriented design principles.

20.1 Motivation

In all the discussion so far where we've written data to an API (either adding new data or updating existing data), we've thought and worked in terms of resources. Even in cases where we might bend the rules about what constitutes a resource,

278

such as in chapter 12, the underpinning has always been the concept of a resource. These resources have always acted as single, addressable, uniquely identifiable chunks of data that we can bring into existence, operate on, read, and then bring back out of existence when we're done with them, and they've served us well so far. Unfortunately, however, they aren't necessarily sufficient to cover all aspects and scenarios that might appear in the real world and therefore need to be considered in the world of API design.

Consider, for example, cases such as collecting time series statistics. One obvious way to store statistics like this is to have a `DataPoint` resource and rely on the standard create method to record an incoming data point. But this is a bit like individually wrapping and labeling each grain of rice rather than buying a 5-pound bag. In general, with systems like this users are more interested in aggregates than individual data points. In other words, it's far more likely that we'll ask for the average value of a data point for the month rather than requesting to view a specific single data point using a unique identifier. This is so common that many analytical data processing systems, time series databases, or data warehouses (e.g., Google's BigQuery [https://cloud.google .com/bigquery] or InfluxData's InfluxDB [https://www.influxdata.com/products/ influxdb/]) don't even support unique identifiers for data points being stored!

This leads to the obvious question: if we're using one of these systems for storing our analytical data, how exactly are we supposed to get data into the API in the first place? Should we pretend to have a unique identifier (storing a special field in the database) and just rely on the standard create method as usual? Should we modify the standard create method so that it inserts data into the database but doesn't return an addressable resource as a result, perhaps leaving the `id` field blank? Or should we try something else entirely? This pattern explores an alternative that aims to standardize how best to handle this type of non-resource-oriented data in our generally resource-oriented APIs.

20.2 Overview

This pattern works by presenting a special custom method called write. Similar to a standard create method, a custom write method's job is to insert new data into the API; however, it does this in such a way that the resulting data entry is anonymous (i.e., the data has no unique identifier). Generally, this is because the resulting data isn't addressable and cannot be retrieved, updated, or deleted after the fact.

Instead, rather than retrieving individual records, this type of data should only be explored on an aggregate basis. This means that rather than allowing users to request a single data point as they would with a typical resource, they can request an aggregate value based on these data points, such as the total number of entries or the average value of these entries. As you might guess, this manner of interaction is important for dashboard-style APIs that present lots of statistics about a system.

Since these data points have such a different access pattern from the resources we've grown accustomed to, it's almost certainly a good idea to use different terminology to describe the data being written. In this case, rather than referring to resources, we'll use the term *entry* for the data points that are being inserted into the API via this new write method.

To put this all together, an example of writing entries and reading aggregate data (e.g., a count) is shown as a sequence diagram in figure 20.1.

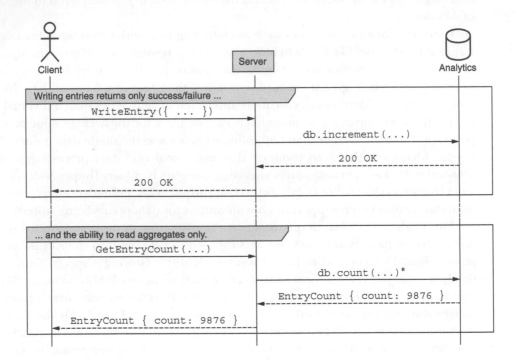

Figure 20.1   Sequence of events for the write method

In the next section, we'll explore the more nuanced details of the write method and how we can go about implementing it.

20.3   *Implementation*

While the write method is quite similar in nature to the standard create method, there are certainly a few differences worth exploring. First, let's look at the return type of the method. While the standard create method returns a newly created resource, the write method doesn't exactly have a resource to return. In fact, the write method involves data being added to a collection (either joining the group as another anonymous member) or being used in a streaming manner in order to increment a counter or update an aggregate (such as a moving average). This behavior is what makes the method special, but it also means that there's nothing useful that we could return other than a successful result or an error in case something went wrong. Due to this, the write method should return nothing whatsoever, or void.

The next question to answer is how exactly we transport the payload of data. The standard create method relies on a single field (resource) that accepts the resource value to be created. Again, unlike the standard create method, the write method doesn't deal in resources, and instead uses the concept of entries. Luckily, this leads us to an obvious and simple conclusion: treat a write request just like a create request, but rename the field from resource to entry.

Listing 20.1   Example write request

```
interface WriteChatRoomStatEntryRequest {
  parent: string;
  entry: ChatRoomStatEntry;          ←——| Here we use an entry field
}                                         rather than a resource field.
```

Finally, we have to wonder about what the right HTTP URL binding is for the write method. For example, imagine that we're trying to write some statistics about a Chat-Room resource. As we learned in chapter 9, specifically section 9.3.2, it's generally best to target the collection rather than the parent resource, which means that the write method should avoid a URL looking like /chatRooms/1:writeStatEntry, and should instead favor a URL looking something like /chatRooms/1/statEntries:write. While this might be a contentious choice (since statEntries isn't really an actual collection of resources), the fact remains that we will be able to interact with the collection of entries in the future through several other means. For example, we might be able to use a batch write method (chapter 18) to add multiple entries at once or use the purge method (chapter 19) to remove all entries.

Now that we have a good grasp on the basics, there's a more complex topic to cover: consistency.

20.3.1 *Consistency*

In general, when we insert data to an API (such as through the standard create method), we want to be able to see the results of that operation immediately. In other words, if the API says that our request to create some data succeeded, we should be able to read that data back from the API right away. In fact, this is so important that when we run into situations where an operation might take a while to complete, we rely on things like long-running operations (chapter 10) to help provide more insight into when the data will be available in the system.

Since the write method behaves a bit like a standard create method, we have some important questions to answer: Should it be consistent in the same way, with data being immediately readable after the operation completes? If not, should we rely on long-running operations to track the progress? If not, what should we do?

To answer these, we first must remind ourselves that the goal of the write method is to allow data that is not addressable to be added to a system. This means that the method by which we read the data is very different from the way we would read data added by the standard create method. In fact, since we almost always read this type of data through aggregates, it will be difficult—if not impossible—to know whether we're actually reading data that we ourselves added and not data that was added by someone else invoking the write method independently. In short, this means that it doesn't really make any sense to hold ourselves to a standard whereby all data must be readable by the time the method completes. In other words, it's perfectly fine for the write method to return immediately (as shown in figure 20.2), even before the data becomes visible to anyone using the API.

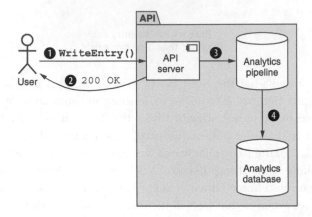

Figure 20.2   **Writing data gets an immediate response while data goes into an analytics pipeline.**

This happens to fit nicely with the majority of use cases involving large-scale analytics systems, as these tend to rely on eventual consistency and potentially long delays in data-processing pipelines. If we had to wait for all of the computation to complete before returning a result, we might run into some pretty serious request latency problems, rendering the method much less useful.

This, though, leads to an interesting option: if we want to respond before the data is visible, but we can't easily do so synchronously, what about using LROs (see chapter 10) to return right away and allow users to wait on the results to become visible? Unfortunately, there are two problems with this idea. First, it's often impossible to know when an individual piece of data becomes persisted as part of the aggregated statistical information. This is primarily due to the fact that a single entry should contain no unique identifier, so there's no way to track a single data point all the way through an analytics pipeline.

Second, even if we could track each data point through the system, one of the main points for relying on a write method rather than the standard create method was that we didn't want to store all of the entries individually. Instead we wanted to save space and compute time by aggregating data. If we then decide that each invocation of the write method should create a new Operation resource, we've basically shifted the problem from one place to another without really saving any space or energy.

Based on this, it's almost certainly a bad idea to return LROs as a result of the write method. If it's important to communicate to users that their data has been accepted into a pipeline but they should not expect it to be visible for quite some time, a good alternative is to simply return an HTTP 202 Accepted response code rather than the typical HTTP 200 OK response code. Further, if there's any concerns about duplicate entries being provided to the write method, the request deduplication pattern (chapter 26) should be a perfect fit to help avoid this problem.

With that, let's look at how we might apply this pattern and define an API supporting the write method.

20.3.2 Final API definition

Let's imagine that we want to start some arbitrary statistics about chat rooms. This might include things like how frequently users open a specific chat room, but we want to keep some flexibility for the future about the data points we add. To do this, we might craft a ChatRoomStatEntry interface that is a simple key-value pair of a string and a scalar value that we can then aggregate and analyze later on.

Further, we might want to support writing multiple ChatRoomStatEntry resources at once. To do that, we can rely on a batch write method (see chapter 18 for more on batch methods).

Listing 20.2 Final API definition

```
abstract class ChatRoomApi {
  @post("/{parent=chatRooms/*}/statEntries:write")        ◁─── As we learned
  WriteChatRoomStatEntry(req:                                   in section 20.3.1,
    ➡ WriteChatRoomStatEntryRequest): void;                    these custom
                                                               methods target the
                                                               collection, not the
  @post("/{parent=chatRooms/*}/statEntries:batchWrite")   ◁── parent resource.
  BatchWriteChatRoomStatEntry(req:
    ➡ BatchWriteChatRoomStatEntryRequest): void;          ◁── Similarly, even batch
}                                                              methods return nothing
                                                               as the result.
interface ChatRoomStatEntry {
  name: string;
  value: number | string | boolean | null;
}

interface WriteChatRoomStatEntryRequest {
  parent: string;
  entry: ChatRoomStatEntry;
}

interface BatchWriteChatRoomStatEntryRequest {
  parent: string;
  requests: WriteChatRoomStatEntryRequest[];
}
```

Rather than returning a resource, here we return nothing.

20.4 Trade-offs

Unlike many of the design patterns we've looked at so far, this one stands apart in that the use case is quite unique. In fact, this use case is almost exclusively for cases involving analytical data, whereas almost all of the data we've considered has been transactional in nature. As a result, there are not all that many alternatives for safely adding this type of analytical data to an API.

As we learned, it's certainly possible to rely on the standard create method and treat individual data points as full resources, each with their own unique identifier; however, this type of design is unlikely to work all that well with the majority of analytical storage and data-processing systems. Further, the data stored will almost certainly grow quite quickly and become difficult to manage. As a result, this is likely to be the best choice in the case where an API needs to support analytical data ingestion alongside more traditional resource-oriented design.

20.5   *Exercises*

1   If we're worried about ingesting duplicate data via a write method, what's the best strategy to avoid this?
2   Why should a write method return no response body? Why is it a bad idea for a write method to return an LRO resource?
3   If we want to communicate that data was received but hasn't yet been processed, what options are available? Which is likely to be the best choice for most APIs?

Summary

- When data needs to be ingested into a system (e.g., analytical data entries), we should rely on a custom write method rather than creating resources that will never be addressed individually.
- Data loaded into an API via a write method is a one-way street and cannot be later removed from the API.
- Write methods (and their batch versions) should return no response other than the resulting status codes. They should not return a resource at all—even an LRO resource—except in special circumstances.
- Rather than resources, the write method deals with entries, which are similar to resources but are not addressable and, in many cases, ephemeral.

Pagination

21

This chapter covers

- How pagination allows users to consume large data sets in bite-sized chunks
- The specific size of each page of data
- How API services should indicate that paging is complete
- How to define the page token format
- How to page across large chunks of data inside a single resource

In this pattern, we'll explore how to consume data when the number of resources or the size of a single resource is simply too large for a single API response. Rather than expecting all of the data in a single response interface, we'll enter a back-and-forth sequence whereby we request a small chunk of data at a time, iterating until there is no more data to consume. This functionality is commonly seen in many web interfaces, where we go to the next page of results, and is equally important for APIs.

21.1 *Motivation*

In a typical API, consumers may need to retrieve and browse through their resources. As these resources grow in both size and number, expecting consumers to read their data in a single large chunk becomes more and more unreasonable. For example, if an API offered access to 1 billion data entries using 100 GB of storage space, expecting a consumer to retrieve this data using a single request and response could be painfully slow or even technically infeasible. How best can we expose an interface that allows consumers to interact with this data? In other words, how can we avoid forcing consumers to bite off more than they can chew? The obvious answer is to split the data into manageable partitions and allow consumers to interact with these subsets of the data, but this leads to yet another question: how and where do we split the data?

We might choose to draw a dividing line between any two records, but this won't always be sufficient, particularly in cases where single records might grow to be unwieldy in size themselves (e.g., a single 100 MB object). In this case the question of splitting the data into reasonable chunks becomes even more fuzzy, particularly if that chunk is structured data (e.g., a 10 MB row in a database). Where should we split the data inside a single record? How much control should we provide to consumers over these split points?

On the other hand, there are some scenarios where consumers actually want all the records in the database delivered using a single request and response (e.g., backing up or exporting all data); however, these two scenarios are not necessarily mutually exclusive, so this doesn't change the fact that we still need a way of interacting with data in reasonably sized chunks. For this common scenario, there's a pattern that has become quite common on many websites and carries over nicely to APIs: pagination.

21.2 *Overview*

The term *pagination* comes from the idea that we want to page through the data, consuming data records in chunks, just like flipping through pages in a book. This allows a consumer to ask for one chunk at a time and the API responds with the corresponding chunk, along with a pointer for how the consumer can retrieve the next chunk. Figure 21.1 is a flow diagram demonstrating how a consumer might request multiple pages of resources from an API until there are no more left.

To accomplish this, our pagination pattern will rely on the idea of a cursor, using opaque page tokens as a way of expressing the loose equivalent of page numbers. Given this opacity, it will be important that the API responds both with the chunk of results as well as the next token. When it comes to handling large single resources, the same pattern can apply to each resource, where the content of a resource can be built up over multiple pages of data.

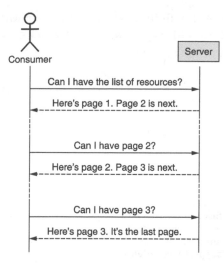

Figure 21.1   Flow of pagination

21.3   Implementation

At a high level, we really want a way of picking up where we left off, effectively viewing a specific window of the available data. To do this, we'll rely on three different fields to convey our intent:

1   `pageToken`, which represents an opaque identifier, meaningful only to the API server of how to continue a previously started iteration of results

2   `maxPageSize`, which allows the consumer to express a desire for no more than a certain number of results in a given response

3   `nextPageToken`, which the API server uses to convey how the consumer should ask for more results with an additional request

To see this more clearly, we can replace some of the text in figure 21.2 with these fields.

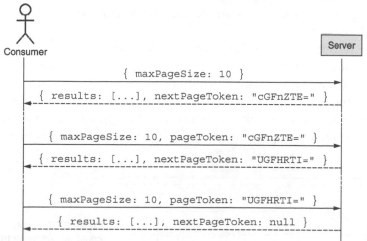

Figure 21.2   Pagination using these specific fields

If we were to translate this pattern into an API definition, we would end up with something that looks very similar to a standard list, with pageToken and maxPageSize added to the request and nextPageToken added to the response.

Listing 21.1   API specification for paginating in a standard list method

```
abstract class ChatRoomApi {
  @get("/chatRooms")
  ListChatRooms(req: ListChatRoomsRequest): ListChatRoomsResponse;
}

interface ListChatRoomsRequest {
  pageToken: string;
  maxPageSize: number;
}

interface ListChatRoomsResponse {
  results: ChatRoom[];
  nextPageToken: string;
}
```

Adding three new fields to the standard list method requests and responses to support pagination

This definition itself isn't all that interesting, but it turns out that each of these fields has some interesting hidden secrets. Let's first explore the harmless looking maxPageSize field.

21.3.1 Page size

At first glance, setting the size of the page you want (i.e., the number of results that should be returned) seems pretty innocuous, but it turns out that there's quite a bit more to it. Let's start by looking at the name of the field itself: maxPageSize.

MAXIMUM VS. EXACT

First, why do we use a maximum instead of just setting the exact size? In other words, why do we return up to 10 results instead of exactly 10 results? It turns out that in most cases an API server might always be able to return an exact number of results; however, in many larger-scale systems this simply won't be possible without paying a significant cost premium.

For example, imagine a system that stores 10 billion rows of data in a table, which, due to size constraints, has no secondary indexes (which would make querying this data more efficient). Let's also imagine that there are exactly 11 matching rows with 5 right at the start, followed by 5 billion rows, followed by the remaining 6, further followed by the rest of the data, as shown in figure 21.3. Finally, let's also assume that we have a goal of returning most responses (e.g., 99%) within 200 milliseconds.

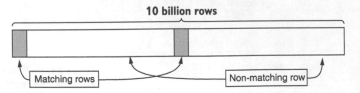

10 billion rows

Matching rows   Non-matching row

Figure 21.3   Matching rows could be widely distributed.

In this scenario, when a user asks for a page of 10 results, we have two options to choose between. On the one hand, we could return exactly 10 results (as there are enough to fill up the page), but it's unlikely that this query will be consistently fast given that it must scan about 5 billion rows in order to fill the page completely. On the other hand, we could also return the 5 matching rows that we find after having searched until our specific cut-off time (here this might be 180 ms) and then pick up where we left off on a subsequent request for more data.

Given these constraints, always trying to fill the entire page will make it very difficult to tell the difference between violations of our latency goal and simple variations in request complexity. In other words, if the request is slow (takes more than 200 ms), this could be because something is actually broken or because the request just searches a lot of data—and we won't be able to distinguish between the two without quite a bit of work. If we fill a page as much as possible within our time limit, we may often be able to return exactly 10 results (perhaps because we put them close together), but we don't paint ourselves into a corner in the case where our data set becomes exceedingly large. As a result, it makes the most sense for our interface contract to specify that we will return up to maxPageSize results rather than exactly that number.

DEFAULT VALUE

It's important to decide on reasonable defaults for any optional field so that consumers aren't surprised when they leave the optional field blank. In this case, choosing a default for the maximum page size will depend on the shape and size of the resources being returned. For example, if each item is tiny (e.g., measured in bytes rather than kilobytes), it might make sense to use a default of 100 results per page. If each item is a few kilobytes, it might make more sense to use a default of 10 or 25 results. In general, the recommended default page size is 10 results. Finally, it's also acceptable to require that consumers specify a maximum page size; however, that should be reserved for situations where a reasonable default simply can't be assumed by the API server.

While picking a default maximum page size is important, it's even more important to document this default value and remain consistent with it whenever possible across the rest of your API. For example, it's generally a bad idea to use a variety of default values for this field without a good reason for each value. If a consumer learns that your API tends to default to 10 results per page, it will be very frustrating if elsewhere in that API the default is 50 results for no good reason.

UPPER AND LOWER BOUNDS

Obviously a negative page size is meaningless to an API server, and as a result should be rejected with an error noting that the request is invalid. But what should we do if a request specifies a maximum page size of 3 billion? Luckily our previous design that relies on a maximum page size rather than an exact page size means that we can happily accept these values, return a reasonable number of results that our API server is capable of producing within some set amount of time, and remain consistent with the API definition.

In other words, while it's certainly acceptable to reject page sizes above a certain limit (e.g., over 1,000 results in a page), it's perfectly fine to consider them valid as we can always return fewer results than specified while sticking to our agreement with the consumer. Now that we've discussed the simple pieces, let's move onto one of the more complex ones: page tokens.

21.3.2 *Page tokens*

So far we've noted that a page token should be used as a cursor, but we haven't clarified the behavior of this token. Let's start by looking at one of the simplest, yet often confusing things about how page tokens work: how we know we're finished.

TERMINATION CRITERIA

Since there is no way to force a consumer to continue making subsequent requests, pagination can technically be terminated by the consumer at any point in time where the consumer simply decides they're no longer interested in more results. But how can the server indicate that there are no more results? In many systems we tend to assume that once we get a page of results that isn't full we're at the end of the list. Unfortunately, that assumption doesn't work with our page size definition since page sizes are maximum rather than exact. As a result, we can no longer depend on a partially full page of results that indicates pagination is complete. Instead, we'll rely on an empty page token to convey this message.

This can be confusing to consumers, particularly when we consider that it is perfectly valid to return an empty list of results along with a nonempty page token! After all, it seems surprising to get no results back but still be told there are more results. As we learned before when deciding to keep track of a maximum page size, this type of response happens when the request reaches the time limit without finding any results and cannot be certain that no further results will be found. In other words, a response of {results: [], nextPageToken: 'cGFnZTE='} is the way the API says, "I dutifully searched for up to 200 ms but found nothing. You can pick up where I left off by using this token."

OPACITY

So far, we've discussed how we use a page token to communicate whether a consumer should continue paging through resources, but we've said nothing about its content. What exactly do we put into this token?

Put simply, the content of the token itself should be anything the API server needs to pick up where it left off when iterating through a list of results. This could be something abstract like a serialized object from your code, or more concrete, like a limit and offset to pass along to a relational database. For example, you might simply use a serialized JSON object like eyJvZmZzZXQiOiAxMH0= which is {"offset": 10} Base64-encoded. What's more important though is that this implementation detail must remain completely hidden from consumers. This might seem unnecessary, but it's actually a very important detail.

Regardless of what you put into your page token, the structure, format, or meaning of the token should be completely hidden from the consumer. This means that rather than Base64 encoding the content, we should actually encrypt the content so that the content of the token itself is completely meaningless to consumers. The reason for this is pretty simple: if the consumer is able to discern the structure or meaning of this token, then it's part of the API surface and must be treated as part of the API itself. And since the whole point of using a page token was to allow us to change the implementation under the hood without changing the API surface for consumers, exposing this prohibits us from taking advantage of that flexibility. In essence, if we allow consumers to peek inside these page tokens, we're leaking the implementation details and may end up in a situation where we cannot change the implementation without breaking consumers.

FORMAT

Now that we've looked at what can go into a token, this notion of keeping the token opaque to consumers begs the question: why do we use a string type to represent the token? Why not use a number or raw bytes?

Given our need to store encrypted data, it becomes obvious that using a numeric value like an integer simply won't work. On the flip side, raw bytes tend to be a great way to store an encrypted value, but we use a string primarily out of convenience. It turns out that these tokens will often end up in URLs (as parameters in a GET HTTP request) as well as in JSON objects, neither of which handle raw bytes very well. As a result, the most common format is to use a Base64-encoded encrypted value passed around as a UTF-8 serialized string.

CONSISTENCY

So far, our discussion about paging through data has assumed that the data itself was static. Unfortunately this is seldom the case. Instead of assuming that the data involved is read-only, we need a way of paging through data despite it changing, with new results added and existing results removed. To further complicate the case, different storage systems provide different querying functionality, meaning that the behavior of our API may be tightly coupled to the system used to store our data (e.g., MySQL).

As you'd expect, this can often lead to frustrating scenarios. For example, imagine paging through data two results at a time and while this is happening someone else happens to add two new resources at the start of the list (figure 21.4). If you are using an *offset* count (where your next page token represents an offset starting at item 3), the two newly created resources added at the start of the list will cause you to see page 1 twice. This is because what is now the new page 2 has the offset from the start of the old page 1. Further, this scenario shows up again when a filter is applied to the request and results are modified such that they either join or leave the matching group. In that case, consumers may lose confidence in your API to deliver all the matching results as well as only matching results. What should we do?

Unfortunately, there is no simple answer to this question. If your database supports point-in-time snapshots of the data (such as Google Cloud Spanner or CockroachDB),

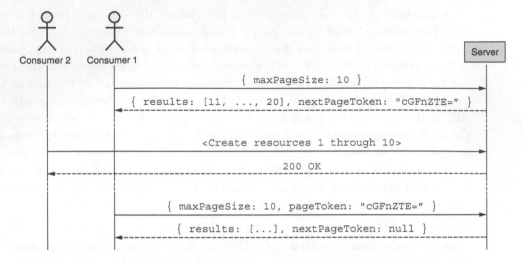

Figure 21.4   A consumer might see duplicate results if new data is added in the middle of paging.

it may make sense to encode this information in page tokens such that you can guarantee strongly consistent pagination. In many cases databases will not allow strongly consistent results, in which case the only other reasonable option is to note in the documentation of your API that pages may represent a "smear" of the data as underlying resources are added, removed, or modified (figure 21.5). As noted, it's also a good idea to avoid relying on a numeric offset and instead use the last seen result as a cursor so that your next page token really does pick up where things left off.

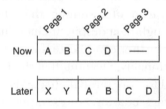

Page 1 now = page 2 later

Figure 21.5   Page numbers may change over time as the underlying data changes.

LIFETIME

When we think of consuming a large list of results, we tend to assume that the requests happen in some relatively short window of time, typically measured in seconds or minutes. But what if requests happen much more slowly (as seen in figure 21.6)? Obviously it might be a bit ridiculous to request a page of data and the next page 10 years later, but is 24 hours later all that crazy? What about 60 minutes? Unfortunately we rarely document the lifetime of page tokens, which can lead to some tricky situations.

Generally, APIs choose not to define limits of when page tokens might expire. Since paging through data should be an idempotent operation, the failure mode of

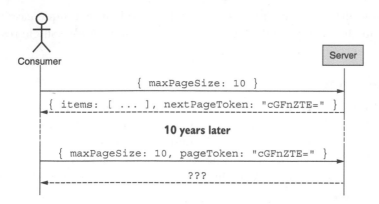

Figure 21.6 Using page tokens from 10 years ago might be unreasonable.

running into an expired token just requires a retry. This means that failure here is simply an inconvenience.

That said, we should clarify how long tokens should remain valid to set consumer expectations about their paging operations. In a classic case of setting the bar low, it's generally a good idea to set token expiration to be relatively short given your use case. For a typical API this is likely to be measured in minutes (or hours at the most), with a 60-minute expiration considered generous by most consumers.

21.3.3 *Total count*

Finally, a common question when paging through results is whether to include a total count of results, typically used when showing user interface elements like "Results 10–20 of 184." When this total count is relatively small (e.g., 184 as shown), it's an easy statistic to show. However, when this number gets much larger (e.g., 4,932,493,534), the simple act of counting those results could become so computationally intensive that it's impossible to return an accurate count quickly.

At that point we're left to choose between providing an accurate count very slowly, or an inaccurate count as a best guess relatively quickly. None of these options is particularly good, so APIs generally should not provide a total result count unless there is a clear need to consumers (i.e., without this count they cannot do their job) or the count can never become large enough that it lands in this situation. If, for some reason you absolutely must include the total count, it should be an integer field named `totalResults` attached to the response.

Listing 21.2 Response interface including the total number of results

```
interface ListChatRoomsResponse {
  results: ChatRoom[];
  nextPageToken: string;
  totalResults: number;
}
```

Use a totalResults field to indicate how many results would be included if pagination were completed.

Now that we know all about page tokens, let's look at a relatively unique case where single resources might be sufficiently large to justify pagination *inside* a single resource rather than across a collection of resources.

21.3.4 *Paging inside resources*

In some scenarios single resources could become quite large, perhaps to the point where consumers want the ability to page through the content of the resource, building it up into the full resource over several requests. In these scenarios, we can apply the same principles to a single resource rather than a collection of resources by breaking the resource up into arbitrarily sized chunks and using continuation tokens as cursors through the chunks.

> **Listing 21.3   API definition for paging through single large resources**
>
> ```
> abstract class ChatRoomApi {
>   @get("/{id=chatRooms/*/messages/*/attachments/*}:read")
>   ReadAttachment(req: ReadAttachmentRequest):
>     ReadAttachmentResponse;              ◁────  The custom read method allows
> }                                               us to consume a single resource
>                                                 in small bite-sized chunks.
>
> interface ReadAttachmentRequest {
>   id: string;
>   pageToken: string;       ◁────  The continuation token from a previous
>   maxBytes: number;        ◁────  response. If empty, it indicates a request
> }                                 for the first chunk of the resource.
>
>                                   Maximum number of bytes to return in
>                                   a given chunk. If empty, a default value
> interface ReadAttachmentResponse {  of, say, 1,024 bytes is used.
>   chunk: Attachment;
>   fieldMask: FieldMask;    ◁────  The list of fields with data
>   nextPageToken: string;   ◁────  provided in the chunk to be
> }                                 appended to the resource
> ```
>
> A single chunk of data belonging to the resource ⟶ (points to `chunk: Attachment;`)
>
> The token to use when requesting the next chunk of the resource. If empty, it indicates that this is the final chunk.

In this design, we assume that a read of a single resource can be strongly consistent, which means that if the resource is modified while we are paging through its data, the request should be aborted. It also relies on the idea of building up a resource over several requests where each response contains some subset of the data to be appended to whatever data has been built up so far, shown in figure 21.7. We also rely on the field mask to explicitly convey which fields of the ChatRoom interface have data to be consumed in this given chunk.

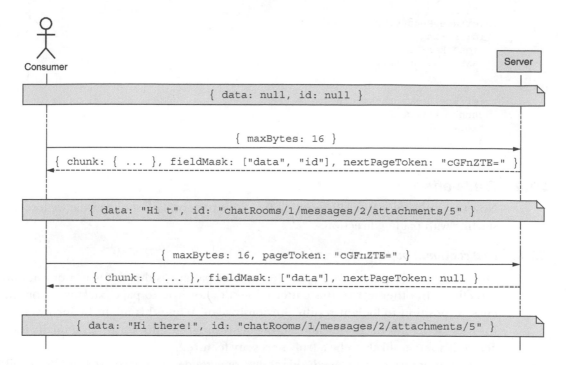

Figure 21.7 Example flow of paging through a single large resource

21.3.5 *Final API definition*

Now that we've gone through all of the nuances of this pattern, the final resulting API definition is shown in listing 21.4, covering both pagination across a collection of resources as well as inside a single resource.

> **Listing 21.4 Final API definition**

```
abstract class ChatRoomApi {
  @get("/chatRooms")
  ListChatRooms(req: ListChatRoomsRequest): ListChatRoomsResponse;

  @get("/{id=chatRooms/*/messages/*/attachments/*}:read")
  ReadAttachment(req: ReadAttachmentRequest): ReadAttachmentResponse;
}

interface ListChatRoomsRequest {
  pageToken: string;
  maxPageSize: number;
}

interface ListChatRoomsResponse {
  results: ChatRoom[];
  nextPageToken: string;
}
```

```
interface ReadAttachmentRequest {
  id: string;
  pageToken: string;
  maxBytes: number;
}

interface ReadAttachmentResponse {
  chunk: Attachment;
  fieldMask: FieldMask;
  nextPageToken: string;
}
```

21.4   Trade-offs

Now that we've seen the API resulting from this pattern, let's look at what we lose out, starting with paging direction.

21.4.1 Bi-directional paging

One obvious thing that is not possible with this pattern is the ability to work in both directions. In other words, this pattern doesn't allow you to page backward from the current position to look at results previously seen. While this might be inconvenient for user-facing interfaces that allow browsing through results, for programmatic inter-action it's very unlikely to be a truly necessary feature.

If a user interface truly needs this ability, one good option is to use the API to build a cache of results and then allow the interface to move arbitrarily through that cache. This has the added benefit of avoiding issues with paging consistency.

21.4.2 Arbitrary windows

Similarly, this pattern does not provide an ability to navigate to a specific position within the list of resources. In other words, there's no way to specifically ask for page 5 for the very simple reason that the concept of a page number doesn't exist. Instead of relying on page numbers, consumers should instead use filters and ordering in order to navigate to a specific matching set of resources. Again, this tends to be a feature required for user-facing interfaces that allow browsing rather than a requirement for programmatic interaction.

21.5   Anti-pattern: Offsets and limits

For the sake of completeness, let's look briefly at a simple (and quite common) imple-mentation of the spirit of this pattern that should generally be avoided. Given that most relational databases support the OFFSET and LIMIT keywords, it's often tempting to carry that forward in an API as a way of exposing a window over a list of resources. In other words, instead of asking for some chunk we choose a specific chunk by asking for the data starting at a certain offset and limiting the size of the result to a certain number, shown in figure 21.8.

When turned in an API surface, this results in two additional fields added to the request, both integers that specify the start offset and the limit. The next offset can

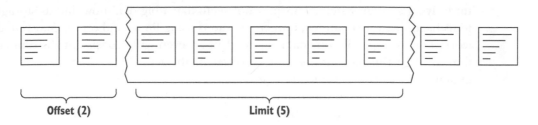

Figure 21.8 Defining a window using offets and limits

be easily computed by adding the number of results to the previously requested off-set (e.g., nextOffset = offset + results.length). Further, we can use an incomplete page as the termination condition (e.g., hasMoreResults = (results.length != limit)).

Listing 21.5   API surface using offset and limit

```
abstract class ChatRoomApi {
  @get("/chatRooms")
  ListChatRooms(req: ListChatRoomsRequest): ListChatRoomsResponse;
}

interface ListChatRoomsRequest {
  offset: number;
  limit: number;
}

interface ListChatRoomsResponse {
  results: ChatRoom[];
}
```

> **To support paging through resources, we include offset and limit parameters.**

When we translate this to our underlying database, there's basically no work to be done: we simply take the provided offset and limit parameters (e.g., a GET request to https://example.org/chatRooms/5/messages?offset=30&limit=10) and pass them along with our query.

Listing 21.6   Pagination using SQL LIMIT and OFFSET

```
SELECT * FROM messages
  WHERE chatRoomId = 5
  OFFSET 30
  LIMIT 10
```

> **The OFFSET modifier specifies the page number (in this case an offset of 30 with 10 results per page points to page 4).**

> **The LIMIT modifier specifies the page size (in this case, 10 results per page).**

The fundamental problem with this pattern is that it leaks the implementation details to the API, so this API must continue to support offsets and limits regardless of the underlying storage system. This may not seem like a big deal now, but as storage systems become more complex, implementations using limits and offsets may not always work. For example, if your data is stored in an eventually consistent distributed system, finding the starting point of an offset might actually become more and more expensive as the offset value increases.

This pattern also suffers from problems related to consistency. In this example, if some new results are added, they may cause the response to return results that were already seen in a previous page.

21.6   Exercises

1   Why is it important to use a maximum page size rather than an exact page size?
2   What should happen if the page size field is left blank on a request? What if it's negative? What about zero? What about a gigantic number?
3   How does a user know that pagination is complete?
4   Is it reasonable for page tokens for some resource types to have different expirations than those from other resource types?
5   Why is it important that page tokens are completely opaque to users? What's a good mechanism to enforce this?

Summary

- Pagination allows large collections of results (or large single resources) to be consumed in a series of bite-sized chunks rather than as a single large API response using three special fields: `maxPageSize`, `pageToken`, and `nextPageToken`.
- If there are more pages, a response will include a `nextPageToken` value, which can be provided in the `pageToken` field of a subsequent request to get the next page.
- We rely on a maximum page size rather than an exact page size as we don't know how long it will take to fill a page exactly and must reserve the ability to return even before a page of results is fully populated.
- Paging is complete when a response has no value for the next page token (not when the results field is empty).

Filtering

This chapter covers

- Why standard list methods should support filtering resources
- How to communicate a filter expression as part of the standard list request
- Guidelines for behavior when filtering resources
- Functionality that should and should not be supported in filter conditions

While the standard list method provides a mechanism to iterate through a complete set of resources in an API, so far we really don't have a way to indicate an interest in only a subset of those resources. This pattern will explore using a special field on the standard list request as a way to filter the full data set to return only a matching result set. Additionally, we'll get into the details of how to structure input values for this special filtering field.

22.1 *Motivation*

So far, the typical way of retrieving lots of resources has been pretty straightforward: use the standard list method. Similarly, if we're looking for a specific resource and happen to know its identifier, we have an equally straightforward tool at our disposal: the standard get method. But what if our goals fall somewhere in between? What if we want to browse through resources that happen to match a specific set of criteria? We're neither looking for an individual resource, nor are we aiming to browse through all resources, but we do have some idea of the resources we're searching for. How can we handle this?

Unfortunately, so far there's no good way to express this middle ground. Instead, the best we can technically do is build on the standard list method and apply a set of filtering criteria over the list of resources as they're returned.

Listing 22.1   Example of filtering resources on the client side

```
async function ListMatchingChatRooms(title?: string):
    Promise<ChatRoom[]> {
  let results: ChatRoom[] = [];
  let response: ListChatRoomsResponse;
  while (response === undefined ||
         response.nextPageToken) {
    response = await ListChatRooms({
      pageToken: response.nextPageToken
    });
    for (let chatRoom of response.resources) {
      if (title === undefined ||
          chatRoom.title === title) {
        results.push(chatRoom);
      }
    }
  }
  return results;
}
```

Loop on the first iteration as long as there's a next page of resources to view

Fetch the page of resources from the API.

Loop through each resource and check for a match of the title field.

As you might imagine, this design is far from ideal. The most glaring issue is that in order to be certain we've found all matching results, the client must fetch, iterate, and evaluate the filter criteria against the entire set of resources stored in the API. This is particularly frustrating with edge cases where there are no matches, as we must filter through the resources only to discover that none of them meet the filter criteria. But in data transportation consumption alone, it's obvious that this is excessively wasteful. How do we address this issue?

22.2 *Overview*

Luckily, the solution to this conundrum is pretty obvious. Rather than retrieving all the resources available and filtering those we're not interested in, let's flip things around instead and push this responsibility onto the API server itself. In other words, all we have to do is declare to the API server the criteria to match against and then the result set will contain only the matching resources.

Listing 22.2 Additional filter field on the standard list request

```
interface ListChatRoomsRequest {
  filter: any;
  maxPageSize: number;
  pageToken: string;
}
```

This is listed as any right now because we haven't decided how we'll implement this.

These fields relate to the pagination pattern (chapter 21).

While this design concept might be obvious, the implementation itself is a bit more complicated. It's easy to state that we should communicate some sort of filtering criteria to the server when listing resources, but what should that filter data actually look like? Should it be a simple string resembling a SQL query? Or a more complex structure for matching fields like a MongoDB query filter document?

Once we've chosen an acceptable format for communicating the query, we then have to consider what functionality should be supported. For example, should we allow matches on resource fields only (e.g., matching a ChatRoom resource's exact title)? Or should we expand this further with wildcards (e.g., matching a keyword anywhere in the title)? Or even arbitrary text searches, like a search query (e.g., a keyword appearing in any of the fields)?

What about querying things that aren't specifically stored on the resource? For example, should we allow querying based on metadata about fields, such as the number of members of a ChatRoom? And does this open the door to queries extending into related resources? For instance, should a filter provide a way to limit ChatRoom results to only those who have a member named Joe? Or only those with a member named Joe who is a member of another ChatRoom with a member named Luca? If so, how far does this ability extend?

As these examples hopefully make clear, this could quickly become a very deep cave to explore, with many different twists and turns, not all of which are worth supporting in a filtering specification. The goal of this pattern will be to address these key concerns, particularly how to specify a filter and exactly what functionality is worth supporting.

22.3 *Implementation*

The first thing we need to do is decide how best to communicate a filter representing the user's intent to the API server for execution. In other words, there are lots of different ways in which we can represent the same filtering intent, but it's important that we settle on a single way to use consistently across standard list methods that support filtering. What format is best?

22.3.1 *Structure*

Just as we have lots of different choices for the serialization format in an API (such as JSON [https://www.json.org/json-en.html] versus protocol buffers [https://developers .google.com/protocol-buffers] versus YAML [https://yaml.org/]), we similarly have many different choices for how we'll represent filters when listing resources. Generally, these choices fall into two distinct categories: structured and unstructured.

On the unstructured side of the spectrum we have things like SQL queries, where a filter is represented as a string value, which just so happens to conform to a very specific syntax. This string value is then parsed by the API server and evaluated to ensure only matching resources are returned to the user.

Listing 22.3   Example SQL query for filtering ChatRoom resources

```
SELECT * FROM ChatRooms WHERE title = "New Chat!";
```

On the unstructured side, we push some of the responsibility away from the API server and back onto the client, effectively requiring the client to parse the query ahead of time into a special schema and then send this complex interface directly to the API server for evaluation (requiring little or no parsing of the content). While less common than the ubiquitous SQL-style string value, there are still many systems, such as MongoDB, that rely on these structured interfaces for filtering.

Listing 22.4   Example MongoDB structured query for filtering ChatRoom resources

```
db.chatRooms.find( { title: "New Chat!" } );
```

But this brings us to a fundamental question: which of these two is right? Before we get deep into discussion over the benefits and drawbacks of each of these options, it's important to remember that this decision is, in many ways, superficial. In other words, the end result of each option might look different, but each should be capable of accomplishing the same things. In fact, it should actually be simple and straightforward to transform from one format to another, sort of how it's easy to translate from a JSON-serialized resource to a YAML-formatted resource. In this case, however, the transformation relies on *serialization* when converting from a structured representation to a string and *parsing* when going in the other direction, a bit like `JSON.stringify()` and `JSON.parse()` in Node.js, shown in figure 22.1.

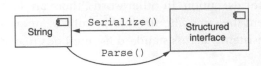

Figure 22.1   Relationship between string queries and structured queries

Since these two options are functionally equivalent, making a choice between the two really becomes a question of usability and future flexibility. In other words, since both options can be made to satisfy the same functional requirements, we have to ask: which will be easier for clients to use and which will better survive the test of time?

As API designers, our first instinct in this scenario is almost always to attempt a reusable, flexible, and simple design for representing filters. And while this is a valiant goal, unfortunately even the best design possible will still suffer from a few key drawbacks due to the fact that the input must adhere to a structured schema.

The main issue to consider is that, ultimately, these filters are no different from any other code we might write in any programming language. A filter itself is certainly more limited and sandboxed than some arbitrary code, but if we look closely at what we're doing here, at a fundamental level we're really just filling in a specific function definition with user-provided code. This code might then be used in a `filter()` function on an array of resources to determine which to include and which to exclude.

> **Listing 22.5 An example of how filter expression code should be evaluated**

```
function resourceMatchesFilter(resource: Object): boolean {
  if (/* user-provided code here! */) {
    return true;
  } else {
    return false;
  }
}
```

To see why it doesn't quite make sense to try to define a structured representation for filtering, let's imagine that, instead of accepting a small filter expression that might act as the condition of the if-statement in listing 22.5, we actually accepted an arbitrary function to be evaluated. In this case, where we're evaluating user-provided code, does it really seem like a good idea to define a schema for this arbitrary input? Or would it make more sense to accept some bytes as input and do as most compilers do: apply syntax rules over the contents to validate that it is, indeed, valid code? There's a reason we still define functions using text-based files and not some structured schema to represent what our programs should do—and filters are no different. But the story doesn't end there. String filters stand out as the better choice for a few more reasons.

First, when using a string value, the syntax rules are enforced and validated exclusively by the API server. This means that any changes or improvements (e.g., new functionality) are managed by the API server itself and therefore won't require changes by the client. As we'll learn in chapter 24, the ability to make improvements without requiring any changes or work from the client can be a very powerful tool.

Second, string queries are generally well known and understood by those who will be using the API, particularly if they've ever used a relational database that speaks some flavor of SQL. This means that a string query is likely to be much easier for a user to understand right off the bat, as it relies on concepts they're already familiar with.

Finally, it might be surprising, but even the best designed structures tend to get a bit difficult to follow as the filtering criteria become more complicated. To see how this plays out in a real-world example, table 22.1 shows how a variety of different filter conditions might be represented as strings in SQL compared to a structured filter object in MongoDB.

Table 22.1   SQL string queries versus MongoDB filter structures

SQL query	MongoDB filter
`title = "New Chat!"`	`{ title: "New Chat!" }`
`userLimit >= 5`	`{ userLimit: { $gt: 5 } }`

`title = "New Chat!"`
`AND`
`admin = "1234"`
	`{ title: "New Chat!", admin: "1234" }`

`title IN ("New Chat!", "Old Chat!")`	`{ title: { $in: [`
	`    "New Chat!",`
	`    "Old Chat!"`
	`] } }`

`title = "New Chat!"`
`OR`
`title = "Old Chat!"`
	`{ $or: [`
	`    { title: "New Chat!" },`
	`    { title: "Old Chat!" }`
	`] }`

`(title = "new chat!"`
`AND userLimit >= 5)`
`OR`
`title = "old chat!"`
	`{ $or: [`
	`    { title: "New Chat!",`
	`      userLimit: { $gt: 5 } },`
	`    { title: "Old Chat!" }`
	`] }`

As you can see, while both options are capable of expressing the same Boolean conditions, the SQL-style strings tend to be a bit easier to follow and mentally process for many of us. This is probably because these strings actually look quite a lot like the Boolean expressions we might write in a typical programming language. In other words, we're relying more and more on things that users are already familiar with rather than expecting and requiring them to learn something new specifically for our API.

So while a structured interface for representing filter criteria would certainly work, it is far more likely to result in a more brittle API definition that suffers as time goes on. Additionally, custom structured interfaces almost always come with a steeper learning curve, and without much benefit over a serialized string representation. As a result, even though it might be tempting to try designing a fantastic structure for representing these filters, it's almost always safer to rely on a string field that can grow with your API as the service itself evolves and changes over time.

Now that we've made the case for why an unstructured value (e.g., a string) is the better choice to represent a filter, let's dig into the underlying syntax we should use for that string.

22.3.2 *Filter syntax and behavior*

Just because we're calling a string the unstructured option doesn't mean that these string values come with no rules whatsoever. On the contrary, the unstructured nature of a string refers to the data type and schema rather than the format of the value itself, which must conform to a specific set of rules in order to be valid. But what are these rules? What is the proper syntax for a filter string?

As fun as it might be to design and specify a complete language for filtering resources, that might be getting a bit too far outside the scope of this book. In fact, there are quite a few language specifications out there that accomplish this goal, such as Common Expression Language (CEL; https://github.com/google/cel-spec/blob/master/doc/langdef.md), JSONQuery (https://www.sitepen.com/blog/jsonquery-data-querying-beyond-jsonpath), RQL (https://github.com/persvr/rql), or Google's Filtering specification (https://google.aip.dev/160). And in some (but not all) cases it might even make sense to attempt to rely on the underlying storage system's querying abilities, for example enforcing that the query syntax adheres to a specific subset of the equivalent of a SQL WHERE clause, with quite a few restrictions on allowed functionality.

Instead of potentially reinventing the wheel from scratch, or even stipulating a particular "correct" syntax, let's instead go through some of the characteristics and restrictions that are most likely to lead to the best results, regardless of the specific implementation and syntax.

EXECUTION TIME

Even though filtering expressions should be made up of nothing more than simple comparisons (e.g., title = "New Chat!"), it turns out that these simple comparisons can actually get quite complicated. If you pick up a book on SQL syntax and functionality of various databases, it can be surprising to see just how complex these types of simple statements can get. For example, what if we change the right side of a comparison from a literal value (e.g., a specific string like "New Chat!") to another variable (e.g., title = description)? Or what if we go even further and involve a different resource (e.g., something like administrator.employer.name = "Apple")? Where do we draw the line between a simple filter condition and something that's too complex for our filtering language?

The first thing we consider when deciding what functionality to support is much more practical than exciting: the run time of executing the evaluation function. This means we must think back to our days as undergraduate computer science students being quizzed on big-O notation and determining the worst-case scenarios for running functions. And in this case, we're concerned about whether there are given filter strings that might cause an evaluation function to be extraordinarily slow or computationally intensive. For an absurd example, imagine that we provided a way to filter against data fetched from a server on the moon or data that required a full scan of all rows in a very large database. Obviously this would lead to extremely slow filtering, which leads to a poor experience overall. Luckily, there's a simple strategy to ensure that the run time of the evaluation function remains reasonable: limit the data available as inputs.

A general guideline to follow is that filters should only ever require the context of a single resource to evaluate a filter condition successfully. This means that if we were to consider the filter evaluation function, it would take as input parameters only two things: the filter string itself and the resource that may or may not match the filter criteria. This means there's no way to include any extra data that isn't part of the resource (e.g., data fetched from the moon).

Listing 22.6   An evaluation function with just a filter and a potential match

```
function evaluate(filter: string, resource: ChatRoom): boolean {
  // ...
}
```

If, instead, we permitted more than just a single resource for evaluation (shown in listing 22.7), we'd have quite a few additional questions to answer. For example, should we allow unlimited numbers of additional resources for comparison or limit the number to something else (e.g., five)? How do we load this information into the context? Should we allow resources of different types or restrict them to only the same type as the resource being evaluated? We also have more complicated performance implications such as whether to prefetch or cache resource information that might be used for evaluation, as well as new problems related to resource freshness and data consistency.

Listing 22.7   An evaluation function that supports additional context

```
function evaluate(filter: string, resource: ChatRoom, context: Object[]):
    boolean {
  // ...
}
```

While it's certainly possible to solve for all of these problems, it's unlikely that the value gained by doing so would be worth the effort. In other words, while expanding the scope of variables available for comparison in a filter expression might come in handy from time to time, it's far from the most common thing necessary if we stick to the true goal of filtering, which is to limit results based on simple conditions about the target resources themselves. As a result, it's almost always the best option to avoid having to answer these questions at all. Instead we can simply require that the filter conditions only accept as input two pieces of information: the filter expression itself and a single resource that may or may not match the expression.

While that's a good start, it doesn't address all the potential concerns. Even though we've decided the filter syntax should require that only a single resource is involved in the evaluation, we haven't said anything about what that filter expression might actually do during the evaluation. For example, what's stopping a filter expression from referencing another resource, using a relationship from the starting resource to do so? Put a bit differently, should we allow a filter expression to refer to other resources and retrieve these from elsewhere (e.g., a database) in order to evaluate the expression?

The answer is a hard no. And we'll take this even further: a filter expression should generally not have the ability to communicate with other external systems at all; instead, it should remain *hermetic* and isolated from the outside world. This means that a filter expression should not be able to refer to a related resource's data unless it's already embedded in that resource. For example, if we want to filter based on the name of the administrator of a `ChatRoom` resource, this should only be possible if the `administrator` field embeds the information directly. If the `administrator` field is a string identifier referring to another resource, then filters expecting the system to de-reference that string field should fail (e.g., `administrator.name = "Luca"`).

If filter evaluation functions were not hermetic and were able to communicate with the outside world (e.g., request new resource data from a database), we would open quite a large can of worms, leading to more questions, similar to those we just went through. For example, how far away can we navigate into related resources? What if the data stored in one of the fields is actually in a system that has poor uptime or high latency when retrieving information (e.g., the server on the moon)? Ultimately, keeping the function isolated and able to rely on only the data provided as parameters reduces the likelihood that it will lead to exceptionally long or computationally expensive executions. As a result, it's generally a good idea to keep filter evaluation hermetic and isolated from other services, where all data needed is already present on the resource being evaluated.

ARRAY INDEX ADDRESSING

When filtering resources, most of the time these filter conditions are based on specific fields (e.g., `title = "New ChatRoom!"`), and specifying the field in question is pretty straightforward. However, there are some cases in which indicating which field should be used for comparison is a bit more complicated. An obvious example of this is specific keys in map fields. These can be tricky primarily because they might have reserved characters that require any filter syntax to support some form of escaping, which would make it clear when a reserved character is meant to be operative or to be taken literally. But there's another important issue that is less about the manner in which we specify the value and more about the implications of doing so: values in an array.

When a field stores an array of values rather than a single value and we intend to filter based on these individual values, we're necessarily required to decide how exactly we'll address these individual values in a filter expression. In other words, how would we filter resources based on the first item in an array field matching a specific value?

While it's certainly possible in many languages to express this type of thing (e.g., `tags[0] = "new"`), this is very rarely a good idea due to the implied requirement that the order of items in the array is static. Addressing individual items in an array necessarily requires that the items are kept in a strict order. This tends to appear simple but often leads to quite a lot of confusion when operating on these values, as changing the order of the items in the array value effectively leads to a completely different value rather than a slightly augmented value. For example, if we're enforcing strict ordering rules, does that mean that new values must always be appended to the end of the array? Or inserted at the beginning? Or added based on a specified index? These questions might seem simple, but they add up and quickly become difficult to manage.

Instead, it's actually far more likely that users will want to test for the presence of a value (in any position) in an array rather than a value at a specific index. As a result, it's much more convenient to provide a mechanism for checking whether a field contains a test value (e.g., `tags: "new"` or `"new" in tags`) rather than addressing items in a specific position in an array. In other words, it's often best to treat array fields as unordered or having an indeterminate order, where items are never at any specific position but instead are either present or not present in the array. And when ordered lists of items are required, rely on a special field to indicate the priority or order of the item in question and perform filters based on that (e.g., `item.position = 1` and `item.title = "new"`).

It might be tempting to make the argument that filters are only reading data, so it's not all that big of a deal to handle this—after all, the failure case is that you just end up with different filtered results; it's not like we'll accidentally erase all the data in the API. This is certainly true, but one of the key goals of a good API is that it is consistent and predictable. And subtle ordering requirements leading to false negatives (e.g., where we expect a resource to match a filter but due to the order of items it doesn't) can be far more frustrating than they seem. As a result, it's generally best to fight the urge to support this feature and instead focus on only supporting testing for the presence of items in arrays.

STRICTNESS

As with any syntax that we might define, there naturally comes the question of how strict the syntax rules truly are. For example, in some programming languages there's quite a bit of flexibility (e.g., Javascript with sometimes optional semicolon characters), while others are extraordinarily rigid (e.g., C++ in many instances). Ultimately, this comes down to how much guessing the interpreter is willing to do when processing some input. The obvious question then becomes how strict should filter expressions be? Should they be flexible and make lots of guesses about the true user intent when it's not clear? Or should these expressions be required to be rigid and make no assumptions about what a user might have meant? In general, the best strategy is to avoid making any guesses, only allowing flexibility when the intent is clear and unambiguous. For example, when specifying field masks, we require escaping and back-tick characters for strings with special characters such as spaces or dots, but not when using the standard letters A through Z.

Often, it can be tempting to allow lots of flexibility into filter expressions because they are primarily reading data. In other words, since the failure scenario for a misinterpreted filter expression doesn't do anything all that catastrophic, why not allow a bit more guesswork into the process? While this is certainly true, it doesn't necessarily make it the right choice.

First, we have the obvious case of the purge custom method, which accepts a filter of items that match a particular filter (chapter 19). In this case, the failure scenario is indeed catastrophic and may result in resources being deleted when they shouldn't (false positive matches) as well as resources being left around when they should have been deleted (false negative mismatches). That pattern, while generally discouraged, is at the mercy of the strictness of the filter expression syntax, and a misinterpretation of the user intent due to a lack of specificity could be very problematic.

Next, it's worth noting that mismatches (either false positives or false negatives) might not be catastrophic in the read-only cases, but that doesn't make them any less frustrating. For example, imagine we attempt to filter a resource based on a field value (e.g., filtering `ChatRoom` resources with `title = "New"`) but accidentally mistype the field name (e.g., "ttile" instead of "title"). Obviously the filter expression isn't capable of figuring out which field we truly intended, but we must ask ourselves, "Should that filter result in an error?"

On the one hand, we might do as we have seen with field masks, which would attempt to retrieve the value of this oddly named field ("ttile") and come back with a missing value (e.g., `undefined` in Javascript). This would clearly not match with the value we're testing (`New`), and the result would filter all the resources possible. In other words, the value of this retrieval will always resolve to `undefined` and never equal `New`, so we've effectively just filtered all possible results.

Another option is quite simple: throw an error when a field reference is invalid. This would ensure that rather than going through the frustration of finding a typo in a filter expression, the API service itself can specify exactly where the typo is (e.g., `Error: Invalid field specification at position 0 ("ttile")`). And even though we all hate seeing these types of errors, it's far more frustrating to have subtle mistakes that end up causing downstream problems.

This same strategy applies to other subtle scenarios such as coercing values between types for proper comparison (e.g., 1234 as a string being converted to 1234 as a numeric value or vice versa). Whereas a loose interpretation might simply return a nonmatching result for a given condition, being strict and returning an error in the case of lack of clarity is far more useful to those attempting to filter resources. For example, if a condition compares a numeric field with a string value (e.g., `userCount = "string"`), there's obviously no way for this condition to evaluate to `true`. However, rather than simply returning `false` the filtering system should instead return an error result for the obviously mistaken condition.

CUSTOM FUNCTIONS

Finally, since APIs always have their own set of unique requirements, it's almost guaranteed that there will be times where users will need to "break the glass" around these restrictions for things that aren't natively supported by the basic filtering syntax. For example, while we generally don't want to provide the ability to perform resource-intensive computation in a filter expression, there may be one unique case where a user really needs this ability. While we don't want to open the floodgates to things like arbitrarily complex computation, we do need a way to allow these types of actions on a narrowly scoped basis. How can this work?

The common solution to allowing users to bend or break the rules in unique circumstances is to rely on special function calls in expressions. In other words, we don't want to allow running arbitrary code, connecting to external data sources, or fancy data manipulation by amending the native syntax, so instead we can provide helper functions to perform these actions in a well-controlled manner.

To see how this might work, consider the example of performing more advanced matches on strings, such as matching based on prefixes or suffixes rather than simple exact matches. We could augment the filter syntax to handle this, perhaps by supporting wild cards (e.g., `title = "*(new)"`), but this introduces a whole pile of new problems (e.g., now we need escape characters to match on the literal asterisk character). Instead, we could use a special `endsWith` function call that would perform the same behavior (e.g., `endsWith(title, "(new)")`). We might even provide a simpler utility function for manipulating strings, such as a way to retrieve a substring of a string. This might lead to prefix filtering that looks something like `substring(title, 0, 5) = "(new)"`.

And these special functions shouldn't be limited to just simple string manipulation. If an API has a way of performing some advanced machine learning analysis on data, we might expose that as a special function. For example, if `User` resources have a `profilePhoto` field and we have an API for recognizing things in images (e.g., faces, landmarks, or common objects), it is possible to provide a function that will allow checking for the presence of some of these things (e.g., `imageContains(profile-Photo, "dog") = true`).

The point to consider in this case is not what these functions might be capable of doing, but that they are a way to break basic syntax rules. This way, the syntax for filtering resources remains simple and straightforward, while those using the API still have the ability to perform more advanced filtering if the API decides it's critically necessary for the use case in question.

22.3.3 *Final API definition*

In this case, the API definition for filtering resources is quite simple and involves only updating the standard list request to include a filter field. However, the decision to make this field take a string type is an important one.

Listing 22.8   Final API definition

```
abstract class ChatRoomApi {
  @get("/chatRooms")
  ListChatRooms(req: ListChatRoomsRequest): ListChatRoomsResponse;
}
```

```
interface ListChatRoomsRequest {
  filter: string;
  maxPageSize: number;
  pageToken: string;
}

interface ListChatRoomsResponse {
  results: ChatRoom[];
  nextPageToken: string;
}
```

22.4 Trade-offs

The most obvious trade-off is between supporting filtering and not. While providing the ability to filter resources in a standard list request is often more resource intensive, the benefits provided to users almost certainly outweigh any additional short-term cost. Further, if users are forced to roll their own filtering by fetching all resources, these users aren't just wasting their own time, they're wasting the computing resources of the API in order to retrieve and transport quite a lot of information that could've been filtered out ahead of time. As a result, while there are cases where filtering isn't critically necessary, the standard list method for most resources should support the functionality, particularly if the number of resources being fetched could grow to be sufficiently large (e.g., measured in the several hundreds into the thousands).

Additionally, perhaps the biggest trade-off, as discussed in section 22.3.1, is the choice between a structured filter and an unstructured filter string. While they both are technically representative of the same thing, using a string means that changes to the format of the structure over time are easier to manage without communicating any new technical API specifications (e.g., open API specification documents). Instead, with a string the documentation can be updated and the new format supported without much else needed to be communicated back to users.

22.5 Exercises

1 What is the primary drawback of using a structured interface for a filter condition?
2 Why is it a bad idea to allow filtering based on the position of a value in an array field?
3 How do you deal with map keys that may or may not exist? Should you be strict and throw errors when comparing against keys that don't exist? Or treat them as missing?
4 Imagine a user wants to filter resources based on a field's suffix (e.g., find all people with names ending in "man"). How might this be represented in a filter string?

Summary

- Providing filtering on standard list methods means that users aren't required to fetch all data in order to find only those they're interested in.
- Filter specifications should generally be strings adhering to a specific syntax (akin to a SQL query) rather than a structured interface to convey the same intent.
- Filter strings should only require a single resource as the context for evaluation to avoid unbounded growth in execution time.
- Filters should not provide a way to compare items on a resource based on their position or index in a repeated field (e.g., an array).
- Errors discovered during a filter evaluation should be surfaced immediately rather than hidden or ignored.
- If basic comparisons are insufficient for users' intentions, filters should provide a set of documented functions that can be interpreted and executed while filtering.

Importing and exporting 23

This chapter covers

- Specific definitions for *import* and *export*
- Interacting directly with remote storage systems
- Converting serialized bytes into API resources
- Handling consistency for exporting volatile data sets
- How unique identifiers should be processed when importing and exporting
- What to do about related resources being imported or exported
- Handling failures during import or export operations
- How import and export differ from backup and restore
- Filtering data on input and output data

In this pattern, we'll explore how to safely and flexibly move resources in and out of an API via custom import and export methods. More importantly, this pattern relies on the API communicating directly with the external storage system rather than through an intermediary client. We'll make all of this work by defining several loosely coupled configuration structures to cover the various aspects of these resources on their journey between the API and the underlying storage system, maximizing both flexibility and reusability.

23.1 *Motivation*

In any API that manages user-supplied data (which is almost every API), we've already defined several ways to get resources in and out of the system. Some of these work on individual resources (e.g., the full suite of standard methods), while others operate on groups of them (e.g., the group of batch methods), but all of them have one important thing in common: the data is always transferred from the API service back to the client directly.

Let's consider the case where we have some serialized data we want to load into an API, such as a bunch of `Message` resources to be created inside a `ChatRoom` resource. One way to do this is to write an application server that retrieves the data from the storage system, parses the serialized bytes into actual resources, and then uses traditional methods to create the new resources in the API. While this might be inconvenient, it will certainly get the job done.

There's one key aspect of this plan that might turn out to be a problem: the route the data is required to take. In this case, the data must take quite a long route, going from the storage system to the application code that will do the loading, and then finally to the API, as shown in figure 23.1.

Figure 23.1   Importing data requires an intermediate data loader application.

If the data happens to be on the same machine as the application server (or even nearby), this is not a horrible proposition. But what if the infrastructure arrangement isn't so friendly? For instance, what if the data and API live near one another, but the application server is not permitted to live nearby? This means that the custom function to load the data will be transporting the entire data set all the way to the application server and then all the way back to the API server. It's sort of like going to the store every time you need a glass of milk rather than buying a carton and keeping it in your fridge: both consume energy, but one is far more efficient.

This problem carries over for data flowing in the other direction as well. If, instead of loading new resources into the system, we want to take existing resources out of the system, using custom code to do so requires the data flow through this intermediary application server. And as the amount of data grows for either scenario (as data tends to do nowadays), this problem only gets worse.

Because of this, there's a pretty strong case to be made for having data flow directly between the API and a remote storage system. Not only would it minimize the amount of custom code users would need to write, it would also reduce wasted bandwidth and user-managed compute resources necessary to get data from one place to another. In the next section, we'll outline a solution to this inefficient process.

23.2 Overview

In this pattern, we'll rely on two special custom methods for moving resources in and out of an API: import and export, outlined in figure 23.2. Since the overall goal is to allow the API to interact directly with an external storage system, each of these methods will take on the responsibility of transporting all data between the API service and the storage system. Further, since it's unlikely that any external storage system stores data in the exact same way as any API service, these methods will also need to take on the responsibility of converting API resources into raw bytes (and vice versa) that the storage system understands.

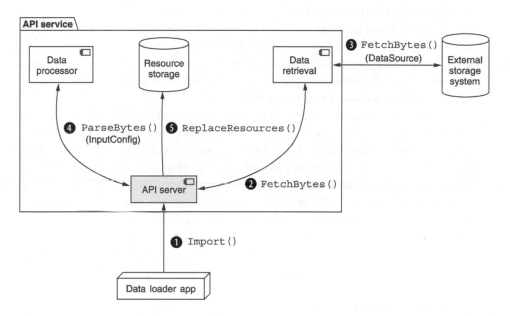

Figure 23.2 An `import` operation combines data retrieval and processing into the API service.

The problems arise in sheer variety on both of these configuration aspects. There are an enormous number of storage systems out there, so it's critical that we structure the request messages for these custom methods in such a way that we can easily introduce new ones as the users of the API demand them. Further, there is a similarly vast collection of different serialization formats available that can be used to transform API resources into raw bytes, so it's important that the request structure be flexible enough to support any of those in existence today, but also grow to support any new ones that might appear in the future.

And if this wasn't complicated enough, after data has been serialized into a bunch of bytes, there may be a need to perform further transformations. For example, it's not unusual for data to be compressed or encrypted before being stored on a disk. And since these custom methods must communicate directly with the external storage system, they're also responsible for allowing users of the API service to configure these additional parameters.

To make all of this work, we'll rely on an overarching configuration interface as the primary input to the import and export custom methods. These configuration interfaces (`InputConfig` for import and `OutputConfig` for export) are responsible for storing all of the relevant information for both transforming data between resources and bytes as well as transporting those bytes to and from the external storage system.

Since the number of storage systems is immense, varies widely, and is constantly changing, we'll rely on structures that allow us to keep the configuration for data transportation separate and independent from that of data transformation. In other words, we'll separate configuration for how to access external storage separate from the configuration for how to serialize API resources or deserialize raw bytes. For this, we'll use generic `DataSource` and `DataDestination` interfaces, such that each extending interface will include all the configuration necessary for transporting bytes to or from the intended source or destination.

Once we've addressed the structural concerns and decide on how to arrange all of these configuration details, we're left with some complicated questions to answer about the behavior of each of these custom methods. For example, how do we handle failures and decide on whether it's safe to retry requests? What about the underlying consistency of the data? When we export data, do we take a full snapshot of the data and export that, or is it allowed to be a smear? Similarly, when we import data, how do the new resources interact with the existing ones? And how do we handle identifier collisions? Should these be stripped before exporting data?

In the next section, we'll explore these behavioral questions as well as all of the structural concerns in quite a bit more detail.

23.3   *Implementation*

Now that we've outlined the high-level problems, it's time to start digging into the details. Let's start by looking at the custom import and export methods themselves, and then we'll explore how their respective request interfaces are structured.

23.3.1 *Import and export methods*

Since our goal is to import and export data directly to and from an external storage system, the first thing we need to do is define the custom import and export methods that will manage all of the complexity of these operations. Even though we've been talking about these methods generically, it's important to note that these custom methods, like those we saw in chapter 9, will be anchored to a specific resource in an API. In other words, each custom import or export method will be responsible for a single resource type (e.g., ImportMessages or ExportMessages).

The next (potentially obvious) property about these methods worth highlighting is the return type. As we learned in chapter 10, when API methods are not immediate or might take a while, it's best to make these return a promise of sorts to complete the actual work. While it's possible that these custom methods could complete relatively quickly, they run the risk of taking quite a bit of time and, as a result, definitely fit the guidelines for returning an LRO and an eventual result rather than a result synchronously.

By putting these two pieces together and following the other guidance from chapter 9, we can pretty easily come up with two example methods to import Message resources into a given ChatRoom resource.

Listing 23.1 Example of custom import and export methods

```
abstract class ChatRoomApi {
  @post("/{parent=chatRooms/*}/messages:export")      ◁──────┐ We're importing
  ExportMessages(req: ExportMessagesRequest) :               │ many resources
    Operation<ExportMessagesResponse, ExportMessagesMetadata>; │ into a collection
                                                               │ belonging to a
  @post("/{parent=chatRooms/*}/messages:import")      ◁───────┘ parent resource.
  ImportMessages(req: ImportMessagesRequest) :
    Operation<ImportMessagesResponse, ImportMessagesMetadata>;
}
```

It's also important to note that these two custom methods are focused on importing multiple resources into a collection, but that's not the only option available. We might also want to import data that isn't represented by a set of API resources and is, instead, just many data points which, after being imported, are individually addressable. For example, if our chat API included a virtual assistant trained with a fancy machine learning algorithm, we might have a way to import training data points into a single VirtualAssistant resource, resulting in the custom method.

Listing 23.2 Example of importing non-addressable data points into a resource

```
                              Rather than importing into a collection, we might
                          import non-addressable data into a specific resource.
abstract class ChatRoomApi {
  @post("/{id=virtualAssistants/*}:importTrainingData")      ◁──────
  ImportTrainingData(req: ImportTrainingDataRequest) :
    Operation<ImportTrainingDataResponse, ImportTrainingDataMetadata>;
}
```

As we can see, these are pretty ordinary-looking custom methods that return LROs that will eventually resolve to standard responses. The tough part, as we'll learn in the next section, is how we should structure the request methods.

23.3.2 *Interacting with storage systems*

Since connecting to external storage systems is a key component of our design to import and export data, it only makes sense that we'll need a place to put all the possible configuration options for each of these storage systems. Often, it can be tempting to simply throw in all the various configuration options together, such that you have a single configuration schema that's capable of talking to all the storage systems out there. Then, when we need to add support for a new one, we might just add some new fields to this configuration interface and call it a day.

Besides being quite messy, this design is problematic because it can lead to quite a bit of confusion. First, when we have a single interface with a large number of options all right next to each other, it can become challenging to decide which ones are required under which circumstances. This leads to unnecessary back and forth with the API server rejecting the various import or export requests because of missing configurations for the data source or destination.

Second, when we continue adding more and more configuration options to a flat structure, our next temptation is to reuse existing fields on the interface such that they might apply to multiple different storage systems. In other words, rather than having a `sambaPassword` field along with a `s3secretKey` field, we might just have one `password` field and attempt to use it for both the S3 secret key issued by Amazon Web Services as well as the password for a specific user on a Samba network share. This looks like a good idea at first but leads to even more confusion when a single field is used for more than one purpose, just because it happens to have a similar-sounding name.

A more straightforward solution is to have a single polymorphic field that then has specific interfaces for each different storage system supported. In other words, we might have a `S3DataSource` for loading data from Amazon's Simple Storage Service as well as a `SambaDataSource`, which is capable of interacting with Samba network shares.

Listing 23.3   Example using S3 as a data source

```
interface DataSource {
  type: string;                          ◁───── The type is a static string
}                                                for the final interfaces
                                                 with the identifier of the
The specific   ┌─▷ interface S3DataSource extends DataSource {   storage system.
DataSource     │     type: 's3';          ◁─────
interfaces     │     bucket: string;
extend the     │     glob: string;        ◁───── Here we store a glob expression (e.g., archive-*.gzip)
base.          │   }                              of matching objects to treat as a data source.
```

This same pattern applies for storage services as destinations for data flowing out of the API, leading to a modular, reusable concept for the API, such that connections to external storage systems can be reused when importing or exporting a variety of resources. But this leads to an interesting question: if these interfaces are just about how to connect to a storage system, why do we need separate interfaces for data being read than for data being written?

While these two concepts are closely related (after all, they're both about interacting with external storage systems and transporting data), they're not identical. For example, when we are using Amazon's S3 as a source of data, we want to apply a pattern (in this case, a glob expression [https://en.wikipedia.org/wiki/Glob]) to select which S3 objects (just like files on a disk) to retrieve. On the other hand, when exporting data, we're more likely to have either a single output file or potentially several different files, but all placed inside the same directory (which in S3, is expressed by using a prefix to the file name, such as exports/2020/).

> **Listing 23.4 Example using S3 as a data destination**

```
interface DataDestination {
  type: string;
}

interface S3DataDestination extends DataDestination {
  type: 's3';
  bucket: string;
  prefix: string;      ◄──┤  In this case, rather than a glob expression,
}                              we'd have a prefix to determine how
                               written objects would be named.
```

In other words, while these two concepts are very similar, they are not identical and don't represent the same thing. There may be many overlapping fields, but this is by design to allow the two interfaces to change independently. And this type of loose coupling is the type of design that remains flexible even in the face of immense volatility.

Now that we have a way to configure the way an API should retrieve bytes from (or send bytes to) an external storage system, we can get to the next piece: figuring out how to convert between API resources and those bytes.

23.3.3 *Converting between resources and bytes*

It's interesting to note that by the very nature of building a web API, we already have a mechanism to turn the underlying API resources into a serialized chunk of bytes. Typically this relies on a format like JSON; however, every API needs a way to send data over the internet, and as a result must have a way of serializing data for users. While this pre-existing mechanism will come in handy, serializing lots of resources for export (or deserializing for import) is not quite the same thing. For example, we might use JSON to serialize a single resource, but when exporting data we might rely on a modified format (e.g., new line separated JSON rather than a JSON array of resources) or a different format entirely (e.g., CSV or TSV with a header row). We won't go into all of the details of resource serialization, but an example of serializing some Message resources to CSV is shown in listing 23.5. (If you're wondering why the identifier is missing, look at section 23.3.5.)

Listing 23.5   Sample CSV serialized Message resources

```
sender, type, content                    ◄──┐  In data exported as CSV, the first row is
"users/1", "text", "hi"                  ◄──│  typically a header row defining the columns.
"users/2", "text", "hi back"                │
                                            │  Each row stores the fields to be imported.
```

Further, even after we've serialized the data, we might want to perform further transformations before storing it for export (and similarly in the other direction). This might be something as simple as compressing or encrypting the data with some user-provided secret key, or it might be a bit more complicated than that, such as chopping the data up into several different files to be stored on the external storage service.

Regardless of what we might want to do with the data, we certainly need a place to put all of this configuration, and for that we'll use an `InputConfig` interface (or an `OutputConfig` interface for exporting data). And just like the custom import and export methods, these interfaces will be on a per-resource basis, leading to interfaces like `MessageInputConfig`.

Listing 23.6   Example input and output configuration for Message resources

```
interface MessageInputConfig {                    ◄──┐
  // The content type of the input.                    │
  // Choices: "json", "csv", undefined (auto-detected) │
  contentType?: string;                                │   These two are quite
                                                       │   similar but not identical,
  // Choices: "zip", "bz2", undefined (not compressed) │   as they have different
  compressionFormat?: string;                          │   responsibilities.
}                                                      │
                                                       │
interface MessageOutputConfig {                   ◄──┘
  // The content type for serialization.
  // Choices: "json", "csv", undefined for default.
  contentType?: string;

  // Use ${number} for a zero-padded file ID number.
  // Content type will be appended with file extension (e.g., ".json").
  // Default: "messages-part-${number}"
  filenameTemplate?: string;

  maxFileSizeMb?: number;

  // Choices: "zip", "bz2", undefined (not compressed)
  compressionFormat?: string;
}
```

Hopefully, this should all look quite boring and innocuous. The real value isn't in the specific configuration parameters for importing and exporting data, but instead in the separation of concerns for retrieving raw data versus processing that data. This loose coupling ensures that we can reuse data sources and destinations for importing and exporting a variety of resource types across the API.

Now that we've covered the structural aspects, let's switch gears and start digging into the behavioral nuances of this pattern, starting with how we should address underlying resource consistency in the API.

23.3.4 Consistency

When it comes to exporting data, we're obviously required to read the entire collection of resources that are intended for export. And as much as we wish we could read any number of resources instantaneously, that's typically only the case with sufficiently small numbers of resources. For collections that might be larger, reading all of the data will clearly take some nonzero amount of time. This on its own is not necessarily a problem, but there's no guarantee that this export operation will have exclusive access to the system. This leads to an important question: what should we do about resources that might be changing during the course of an export operation?

There are two simple options to address this issue. One is to rely on the snapshot or transactional capabilities provided by the underlying resource storage system. For example, we might read all the resources at a specific point in time, ensuring that we have a consistent picture of the resource collection we're exporting. If we do this, any changes made concurrently while the export operation is running will not be reflected in the data being exported.

Unfortunately, not all storage systems support this type of snapshotting functionality. And even worse, the systems capable of handling exceptionally large data sets tend to be less likely to do so. What can we do?

The other option, which is perfectly acceptable for an export operation, is to acknowledge that the best we can do with the storage system we have is to provide a smear of the data being exported. This means that the resources we export might not be an exact representation of the data at any single point in time but a best effort attempt of the collection of resources in the API for the duration that the export operation is running. While this is certainly not ideal, in many cases it will be the only option available and thus is the best we can do.

If this idea of a smear of data is a bit unclear, let's consider an example. In table 23.1, the first two columns show the actions of an export operation as well as a user concurrently manipulating the data in the system. The final two columns show both the current state of the data (which resources exist) as well as the data that's been exported.

Due to the unique interleaving of the actions of both parties (the user and the export operation), we actually end up with a set of resources that looks a bit strange. This specific group of resources (A, B, and D) never existed together (check the Stored data column to see that this combination of resources was never present at the same time). This type of smear is certainly unusual, but is a necessary evil when we don't have the ability to operate on a consistent snapshot of the data.

Table 23.1   Export scenario with a smear of data

User action	Export action	Stored data	Exported data
Create A, B, C		**A, B, C**	
	Export A	A, B, C	**A**
Delete A		B, C	A
	Export B	B, C	A, **B**
Create D		B, C, **D**	A, B
Delete C		B, D	A, B
	Export D	B, D	A, B, **D**

If the storage system of the API doesn't support consistent snapshots for reading data but this inconsistent export data is completely unacceptable, one other option to consider is to disable modifying resources in the API while an export is in process. While this is certainly an inconvenience (and involves system-wide operational downtime during an export), it's sometimes the only safe option available (and is, in fact, how Google Cloud Datastore recommends consumers export a consistent view of data stored in that storage system).

If there's one key takeaway from this section it should be the critical idea that exporting data is *not* the same as backing up data. Whereas backups imply a snapshot of the data, including all sorts of uniquely identifying information, an export of the data is really about retrieving data through traditional means, routing that data directly to an external storage service. In the next section, we'll look at what exactly we should do with unique identifying information in resources being exported, because it's a bit more complicated than it seems.

23.3.5 *Identifiers and collisions*

So far we've been operating under the assumption that when we serialize a given resource, it should include all the fields for that resource, including the identifier. Even though this might seem like a tiny detail, it turns out that this single field leads us to quite a few interesting questions. For example, when importing resources into a collection, what should we do if we come across a resource in the source data that has an ID already in use in the API?

Another interesting case comes up when we export resources with specific identifiers but then attempt to import those same resources back into the API but into a different parent resource. In other words, what if we export a `Message` resource with an ID set to `chatRooms/1234/messages/2` and we want to import that resource into `ChatRoom` #5678? Should it be created as `chatRooms/5678/messages/2` or be given an entirely different identifier?

Finally, we have to wonder about the case where the API doesn't permit user-specified identifiers in resources. What should we do with the identifiers of the resources we're trying to import? Ignore them? As we'll see in section 23.3.7, this becomes quite important when we start exploring what happens when we need to retry a previously failed import.

Luckily, we can fall back on our original definition of importing and exporting to answer this question. The custom import and export methods are intended to provide a way to bridge the gap between the API and an external storage system, cutting out the application code as the middleman when shuffling data from one place to another. This means that the functionality should be equivalent to taking data from an external storage location and using the batch create method to create a bunch of new resources based on the data provided. Anything beyond this simple (and naive) functionality is, quite frankly, out of scope.

The result of this definition is pretty powerful: if user-specified identifiers are not supported (which should generally be the case, as we learned in chapter 6), then the custom import method should ignore any identifiers provided (e.g., the id field) when creating new resources in the API. That said, it makes sense to keep the identifiers when exporting data in the scenario where we need to determine the source of the data later on.

But doesn't this mean that we might be able to create lots of duplicate resources if we import the same data twice? Absolutely, but that's by design.

The import and export methods are emphatically not intended to be a mechanism for backing up and restoring data into an API. That special functionality requires far stricter guarantees about the data, such as consistency of the snapshots when backing up data (as we saw in section 23.3.4), and full replacement of a collection when importing data. And these custom methods make no such guarantees.

23.3.6 *Handling related resources*

So far, both the custom import and export methods have been focused exclusively on a single resource at a time, but that's a bit of an oversimplification. After all, given our discussions on resource layout and hierarchy (see chapter 4), it's pretty reasonable to expect that we may want to import or export resources that also have child or other related resources. Taking a very simple example, what if we wanted to export a collection of ChatRoom resources? Should that include all of the child Message resources as well? Obviously the chat information itself is important, but an empty ChatRoom probably isn't what we have in mind when we think of importing or exporting chat rooms.

While we might be eager to attempt twisting this pattern to accommodate operation on multiple different resource types in a single API call, this is, quite simply, not what this pattern is about. As we learned in section 23.1, the goal of this pattern is to bridge the gap between an API service and an external storage system, avoiding the middleman to shuffle data between the two. It is not intended to introduce new, more advanced functionality about how data is retrieved from or loaded into the API itself. Due to this, just as we restrict other API methods to a single resource type (e.g., the standard list or batch create methods), the custom import and export methods should be similarly restricted.

This means that importing and exporting data is almost always limited to resources that have no children and are likely to be useful without any additional related resources. For example, while it probably doesn't make sense to import or export ChatRoom resources, it is still quite useful to be able to import or export the Message resources contained in a given ChatRoom resource.

Put a bit differently, when we are importing or exporting Message resources, the focus is on moving useful, semi-independent data into and out of an API. When we do the same with a ChatRoom resource, our focus appears to have shifted away from the simple shuffling and routing of data and into the world of backup and restore functionality, where we want to preserve a specific state of the data and potentially restore the system back to that state at a later point in time. While this idea of preservation and restoration is certainly an important one, and it happens to have quite a bit of overlap with the idea of importing and exporting, these two are most certainly not the same thing.

Let's change topics and consider how we might deal with the unexpected as it inevitably arises in any API.

23.3.7 *Failures and retries*

Just as any system is likely to run into problems from time to time, those that involve two systems transferring potentially large amounts of data are almost guaranteed to do so. Additionally, since the behavior expected by the custom import and export methods is inherently about writing data in one place or another, we have a more complicated scenario: if a failure occurs in the middle of reading or writing data (either resources in the API or bytes in external storage system), the failure will almost certainly be more difficult to recover from.

Failures from either of these methods can come in two flavors, oriented around which way the data is flowing. When importing data, a failure might arise when the storage system is unable to provide raw bytes to the API service or if the API service is unable to create new resources. When exporting data, the failures are similar but in the other direction, arising from an inability to read resources from the API or to transport and write raw bytes into the external storage system. How do we address these failures? And more importantly, how can we know whether it's safe to retry an operation if it happens to fail? Let's address the easier of the two first.

EXPORT FAILURES

While failures of any kind are inconvenient, the good news about an export failure is that it's generally safe to retry. The reason is that another attempt at exporting the data from an API is completely independent from an earlier (potentially failed) attempt.

This doesn't mean this type of failure is without complications, though; there are a few potential issues that need to be addressed.

First is the most obvious: the data of one export attempt is not guaranteed to be identical to that of a later attempt. Particularly in volatile data sets with many concurrent users interacting with the system, it's very unlikely that the two attempts will yield similar results. Luckily, the goal of the export method is to transport data out of the API, and it already may make no guarantees about the consistency of the data being exported. On the contrary, as we learned in section 23.3.4, the data is likely to be a smear of resources rather than a single consistent snapshot, so a repeat export attempt shouldn't result in any meaningful problems with the resulting data.

Next, we have to wonder what to do with the data from a previous failed export attempt. Should we attempt to delete it or leave it around to be manually cleaned up later? As wasteful as it might seem, the best practice is generally to leave the data alone, regardless of where in the process the failure occurred.

The reason for this is two-fold. First, there's no guarantee that the API will even have permission to delete data from the external storage system (and it's best practice to deny that permission in this case). Second, we have no idea whether the data that was actually exported is valuable or worthless to the user requesting the export.

This might seem counterintuitive, but the bottom line is that we aren't in a position to judge how much data being exported is sufficient for the user's purposes. Obviously 100% is useful and 0% is not, but everything in between is a complete gray area. For example, imagine we're exporting a very large 10 terabyte data set. How much data needs to be exported before we judge it to cross the line from worthless to valuable? If the export operation fails on the very last resource, is it really worth deleting entirely? Maybe that one resource wasn't all that important in the grand scheme of things. The bottom line is that deleting export data is outside the scope of exporting data, and it should be left to the owner of the storage system to decide what to do with the data.

Given this, we have a new problem: what if the storage system runs out of space? Unfortunately, given the previous discussion about leaving the decision to the user, this is a problem we're just not in a position to solve. Even worse, this might lead to cascading failures where a repeated export operation will fail due to a lack of storage space. That said, given the constraints and principles we've established thus far, this is simply a case we have no choice but to live with, as the alternative is fundamentally worse for API users.

Now that we've covered failures when exporting data, let's switch directions and look at what to do about failures when data flows the other way.

IMPORT FAILURES

Unlike export failures, a failure when importing data isn't something we can simply retry and assume all is well. First, it's possible that the failure might have arisen due to a validation error rather than a transient networking or data transport error. If this is the case, no amount of retrying will resolve the problem and we should report the entries that failed validation in the LRO results.

Even if the failure is the result of something transient, we have to be cognizant of the fact that a previously failed attempt to import data may have still created some resources. This is a big problem because, unless the import failed immediately, a future attempt to retry the import operation is practically guaranteed to result in duplicate resources being created. What can we do?

One obvious solution is to execute the import operation inside a transaction, rolling back the transaction at the sign of any sort of failure. While this is a quick and simple fix for the problem, the unfortunate fact is that not every storage system will support full transactional semantics. And even those that do may have trouble with excessively large amounts of data, leading to monstrous numbers of resources being created inside a single transaction.

For the cases where we cannot simply fall back on a valuable piece of database functionality, we'll clearly need another solution. For this, we can take a page out of chapter 26 and protect our API from the perils of duplicate API requests.

While there's quite a lot to read and understand about request deduplication, the simple overview is that for each record that will be imported, we can assign a single globally unique identifier called an import request identifier. This `importRequestId` will be assigned to each individual resource that will be created during an import operation, and the API service can cache the identifier when it's created the first time, discarding any future attempts to import this same record.

Listing 23.7   Some sample JSON resources with import request IDs for deduplication

```
{ importRequestId: "abc", sender: "users/1", content: "hi" }      ◁
{ importRequestId: "def", sender: "users/2", content: "hi back" }
```
The import request ID is used by the API to disambiguate and avoid creating duplicate resources for a given data entry.

To make this friendlier for those who might want to re-import data after it's been exported, we might even consider adding a configuration option in the `MessageOutput-Config` interface to support whether these `importRequestId` values should be injected into the serialized data during an export operation. Regardless of whether we do that, the point is that if we want to ensure that duplicate resources are not imported when retrying failed import operations, there must be a way to tell the difference between a resource entry we've seen before and one we haven't. Since the resource ID is already being ignored for some very good reasons, as we learned in section 23.3.5, this leads us to introduce something new for just this purpose. This means that if this special field is not present on input, retrying a failed import request in a system that doesn't have support for transactions in the underlying storage system will ultimately lead to the retried import operation creating duplicate resources.

23.3.8 *Filtering and field masks*

As we saw in chapter 22, the ability to filter a collection of resources is a valuable piece of functionality that enables us to interact more efficiently with the data stored in an API. But does this idea of filtering resources apply just as well to the custom import and export methods as it does to the standard list method? The answer, in this case, is both yes and no.

FILTERING OUTPUT

When it comes to exporting data, recall that the goal was nothing more than providing a way to connect a storage system directly to the API. In other words, the export method should be doing nothing different from a standard list method. Therefore, it stands to reason that the custom export method should most certainly support filtering items before exporting them. And, as you'd expect, the API definition for this is no more complicated than adding a filter field on the export request interface.

> **Listing 23.8　Example of adding a filter to an export request**

```
interface ExportMessagesRequest {
  parent: string;
  outputConfig: MessageOutputConfig;       We can filter the
  dataDestination: DataDestination;         exported resources
  filter: string;                       ◄─  with a filter string field.
}
```

You may be wondering why the filter is placed next to (rather than inside of) the `OutputConfig` interface. The answer is simply that the output configuration is focused exclusively on the way we take a bunch of resources and turn them into a bunch of bytes. Filtering, on the other hand, is something that happens before this stage and focuses on selecting which resources will be serialized, compressed, and so on. While it might be tempting to put this configuration inside the `OutputConfig`, the separation of concerns here is critical, ensuring that each piece is responsible for one (and only one) thing.

FILTERING INPUT

Unlike exporting data, where we apply a filter on the data being selected by the API, filtering data on the way in the door is a bit more unusual. It involves transporting the bytes from the external storage system to the API service, then the API service applying the details stored in the `InputConfig` to the serialized bytes (e.g., decompressing, decrypting, and deserializing), and only then applying a filter to decide whether to throw away the resource or create it in the API.

To throw another wrench into the mix, it's also possible that there may be some derived data on the resources being imported that are only be available for filtering after they've been loaded into the API. For example, how would we go about filtering incoming data based on an output-only field such as `createTime` or any other service-computed property? To do so effectively, we'd need to run the data through the business logic of the API itself, which would result in even more complexity and potentially wasted effort.

As you might guess, while it's certainly not impossible to support filtering of ingress data during an import operation, it is one of those things we generally should not do in an API. Even if the API doesn't run into the problems listed currently, there's no guarantee that this fact will remain true in the future. And if we ever do make changes that lead to this scenario, we're now stuck figuring out how to continue supporting filters on imports in some potentially tricky situations. Instead, the user should be responsible for any data transformation (including filtering) before executing an import operation.

23.3.9   *Final API definition*

The following API definition covers how we might import and export `Message` resources in our chat API. There are two example sources and destinations covering a Samba (https://en.wikipedia.org/wiki/Samba) storage system and Amazon's S3 (https://aws.amazon.com/s3/).

Listing 23.9   **Final API definition**

```
abstract class ChatRoomApi {
  @post("/{parent=chatRooms/*}/messages:export")
  ExportMessages(req: ExportMessagesRequest):
    Operation<ExportMessagesResponse, ExportMessagesMetadata>;

  @post("/{parent=chatRooms/*}/messages:import")
  ImportMessages(req: ImportMessagesRequest):
    Operation<ImportMessagesResponse, ImportMessagesMetadata>;
}

interface ExportMessagesRequest {
  parent: string;
  outputConfig: MessageOutputConfig;
  dataDestination: DataDestination;
  filter: string;
}

interface ExportMessagesResponse {
  chatRoom: string;
  messagesExported: number;
  // ...
}

interface ExportMessagesMetadata {
  chatRoom: string;
  messagesExported: number;
  // ...
}

interface MessageOutputConfig {
  // The content type for serialization.
```

```
  // Choices: "json", "csv", undefined for default.
  contentType?: string;

  // Use ${number} for a zero-padded file ID number.
  // Content type will be appended with file extension (e.g., ".json").
  // Default: "messages-part-${number}"
  filenameTemplate?: string;

  // Undefined for no maximum file size.
  maxFileSizeMb?: number;

  // Choices: "zip", "bz2", undefined (not compressed)
  compressionFormat?: string;
}

interface DataDestination {
  // A unique identifier of the destination type (e.g., "s3" or "samba")
  type: string;
}

interface SambaDestination extends DataDestination {
  // The location of the Samba share (e.g., "smb://1.1.1.1:1234/path")
  type: 'samba';
  uri: string;
}

interface S3Destination extends DataDestination {
  type: 's3';
  bucketId: string;
  objectPrefix?: string;
}

interface ImportMessagesRequest {
  parent: string;
  inputConfig: MessageInputConfig;
  dataSource: DataSource;
}

interface ImportMessagesResponse {
  chatRoom: string;
  messagesImported: number;
}

interface ImportMessagesMetadata {
  chatRoom: string;
  messagesImported: number;
}

interface MessageInputConfig {
  // The content type of the input.
  // Choices: "json", "csv", undefined (auto-detected)
  contentType?: string;

  // Choices: "zip", "bz2", undefined (not compressed)
  compressionFormat?: string;
}
```

```
interface DataSource {
  type: string;
}

interface SambaSource extends DataSource {
  type: 'samba';
  uri: string;
}

interface S3Source extends DataSource {
  type: 's3';
  bucketId: string;
  // One or more masks in glob format (e.g., "folder/messages.*.csv")
  mask: string | string[];
}
```

23.4 *Trade-offs*

Even though it might have seemed a bit like this pattern would cover everything related to getting data in and out of an API, perhaps the most confusing thing is that it's actually a very specific and narrowly focused design, covering a distinct way of moving data around and trying to solve a simple goal: bridge the gap between the API service and an external storage system. The result of this specificity and narrow focus leads us to two major drawbacks.

First, the pattern is not designed to handle more than one resource type. This means it's not here to help you with exporting big chunks of related resources, parent and child resources, or anything in general that results in multi-resource relationships. This pattern is, quite simply, about taking lots of self-contained data points and helping to shuffle them between an API service and an external storage system without an application server acting as the middleman. If you do indeed need the ability to connect multiple resources together and manipulate those resources in any meaningful way, this middleman is no longer just a middleman; it's become an important piece of business logic. The custom import and export methods are not intended to contain or implement any special business logic; they're designed to be simple data movers.

This leads us to the next major drawback: it's easy to confuse import and export with backup and restore functionality (after all, they both typically involve shuffling data between an API and a storage system). As we saw in section 23.3.4, these custom methods are not at all designed to address the task of atomic preservation of data or complete restoration of data from a previous snapshot. Instead, they operate with no consistency guarantees and, if not fully understood, can lead to some pretty confusing results.

23.5 *Exercises*

1 Why is it important to use two separate interfaces for configuring an import or export method? Why not combine these into a single interface?
2 What options are available to avoid importing (or exporting) a smear of data? What is the best practice?

3 When a resource is exported, should the identifier be stored along with the data? What about when that same data is imported? Should new resources have the same IDs?

4 If an export operation fails, should the data that has been transferred so far be deleted? Why or why not?

5 If a service wanted to support importing and exporting, including child and other related resources, how might it go about doing so? How should identifiers be handled in this case?

Summary

- The custom import and export operations allow us to move data directly between an API service and an external storage system.
- These methods are not intended to act like backup and restore functionality and have several consequences arising from this key difference.
- The API definitions focus on two orthogonal configuration interfaces: one for moving bytes in and out of the external storage system and another for converting those bytes to and from API resource representations.
- Unless the system supports point-in-time data loading, it's very possible that the custom import and export methods will lead to a smear of data stored in the system.
- Importing and exporting data should generally be limited to a single resource type at a time, relying on backup and restore functionality to handle child and other referenced resources.

Part 6

Safety and security

It's easy to forget that users will occasionally make mistakes when using an API. Since these mistakes are unfortunately inevitable, it's important to design an API that allows users to help minimize the damage when they happen. In the next several chapters we'll look at design patterns aimed at doing just that.

In chapter 24, we'll explore the high-level concepts of versioning and compatibility and the strategies available for versioning an API. In chapter 25, we'll look at the idea of an API recycle bin of sorts to prevent accidental deletion. In chapters 26 through 28, we'll look at various strategies for preventing duplicate work, testing requests before executing work, and keeping a history of changes to resources in case users ever need to undo their changes.

In chapter 29, we'll explore when and how to safely retry requests in the event of network failures or other issues. And finally, in chapter 30, we'll explore how an API service can safely authenticate requests.

24

Versioning
and compatibility

This chapter covers

- What versioning is
- What compatibility means
- How to define backward compatibility
- The trade-offs involved in choosing a versioning strategy
- An overview of a few popular versioning strategies for web APIs

The software we build is rarely static. Instead, it tends to change and evolve frequently over time as new features are created and new functionality is added. This leads to a problem: how do we make these improvements without seriously inconveniencing users who have come to depend on things looking and acting as they did before? In this chapter, we'll explore the most common mechanism for addressing this problem: versioning.

24.1 Motivation

Not only is software development rarely static, it is also rarely a continuous process. Even with continuous integration and deployment, we often have *checkpoints* or *launches* where some new functionality "goes live" and is visible to users, which holds especially true for web APIs. This need is exacerbated by the fact that APIs are both rigid and public, meaning changes are difficult to make safely. This leads to an obvious question: how can we make changes to a web API without causing damage to those using the API already?

The default option of "users will deal with it" is clearly not acceptable. Additionally, the alternative of "just never change the web API" is practically impossible, even when we never plan to add new functionality. For example, if there were a security or legal issue (e.g., a lawyer notifies you that the API call in question is somehow breaking the law), the change would be unavoidable. To address this, this pattern will explore how to introduce the concept of versions to an API along with a variety of different strategies that suit the wide spectrum of requirements for web APIs.

24.2   Overview

In order to ensure that existing users of an API are unaffected by subsequent changes, APIs can introduce checkpoints or versions of their API, maintaining separate deployments for each different version. This means that new changes that might typically cause problems for existing users of the API would be deployed as a new version rather than as changes to the existing version. This effectively hides changes from the subset of users that is not ready for these changes.

Unfortunately, there's far more to this than just labeling different deployments of a web API as separate versions and calling the problem solved. We also have to worry about the different levels at which versioning can be implemented (e.g., client libraries versus wire protocol) as well as which versioning policy to choose out of the many available options. Perhaps the most challenging aspect is that there's really no right answer. Instead, choosing how to implement versioning in a web API will vary with the expectations and profiles of those building the API, as well as those using it on the other side.

There is, however, one thing that remains invariant: the primary goal of versioning is to provide users of an API with the most functionality possible while causing minimal inconvenience. Keeping this goal in mind, let's start by exploring what we can do to minimize inconvenience by examining whether changes can be considered compatible.

24.2.1   What is compatibility?

Compatibility is the distinction of whether two different components can successfully communicate with one another. In the case of web APIs, this generally refers to communication between a client and a server.

This concept might seem elementary, but it gets far more complicated when we consider the temporal aspects of compatibility. When you launch a web API, any client-side code will, clearly, be compatible with the API, but, unfortunately, neither APIs nor clients tend to be static or frozen in time. As things change and we start seeing more combinations of clients and servers, we have to consider whether these different combinations are able to communicate with one another, which is not as simple as it sounds. For example, if you have three iterations of an API client and three different API server versions available, you actually have nine total communication paths to think about, not all of which are expected to work.

Since API designers don't have the ability to control client-side code written by users of the API, we instead must focus on whether changes made to the API server are compatible with existing client code. In other words, we'd call two API server versions compatible with one another if you could swap out one for the other and any existing client-side code wouldn't notice the difference (or at least wouldn't stop functioning).

For example, let's imagine that a user of a web API has written some code that talks to the API (either directly or through a client library). Let's now imagine that we have a new version of the web API service (in this case, v1.1), shown in figure 24.1. We'd say that these two versions are compatible if the client code continues working after traffic is shifted away from v1 and over to v1.1.

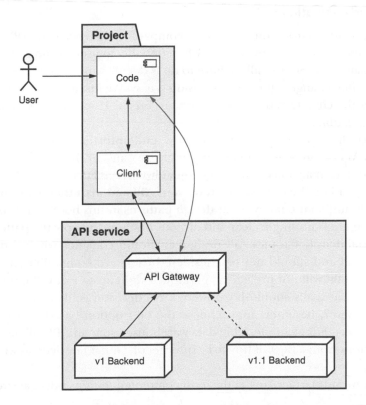

Figure 24.1 Experiment to determine whether two versions are compatible

So why do we care about compatibility? If you recall earlier in this section, we learned that versioning is a means to an end: to provide the maximum amount of functionality to our users while causing as little inconvenience as possible (and ideally no inconvenience at all). One way we do this is by deploying new versions alongside existing ones so that users can access new functionality without causing any previously written code to break for others. This works because we effectively create a whole new world with a new API version, but is this really the best we can do? What if there was an even better way to get more functionality into the hands of existing users without causing any inconvenience?

It turns out that we can do better by injecting new functionality into an existing version in such a way that the API itself is close enough to how it looked before. The modified version would be so close, in fact, that a client may not even be able to tell the difference between the API before and after adding the new functionality. This means that if we only ever make changes to an API that are compatible, all existing code will continue functioning in blissful ignorance of our changes.

But now this leads us to a very complicated and intricate problem: how do we decide whether a given change is backward compatible? In other words, how do we decide whether or not a change will be noticeable or break existing client-side code?

24.2.2 *Defining backward compatibility*

As we just saw, the ability to make only backward compatible changes to an API means that we have the mystical power to provide new functionality to users without the need to do any work whatsoever. So now all we have to do is decide what exactly constitutes a backward compatible change. Often, this decision is easy. We just ask ourselves a simple question: does the change cause existing code to break? If so, then it's breaking, or backward incompatible.

It turns out that that's not quite the whole story, and, unfortunately, this is one of those scenarios in API design where there is no single easy answer. Instead, what we're left with is lots of different answers that are all arguably correct. Further, the degree of correctness will depend on the users who rely on your API and what their expectations are. In other words, unlike the many other design patterns in this book, this is one of those cases where there is no single clear and obvious best way to apply the pattern.

There are certainly a few topics API designers should consider when setting a policy of what should and should not be considered backward compatible. In other words, while this section will not provide a guaranteed right answer, it will pose a few different questions that really should be answered. No decision is likely to be purely right or wrong; however, designers must choose the best option based on what the users of the API expect. For example, a big data warehouse using an API will have very different expectations from a fleet of tiny IoT (Internet of Things) devices, as we'll see a bit later.

Let's dive right in and start looking at the most common questions worth answering.

ADDING FUNCTIONALITY

The most obvious place to start is whether you want to even consider this ability to augment existing versions as a way of providing new functionality. In other words, are the users of your API so strict on their stability requirements that they want every single version frozen in time forever? If the main users of an API are banks, this might be a very reasonable expectation. They might want any new versions to be explicitly opt-in, such that they have to actually change their code to take advantage of any new features. And that's perfectly fine. On the other hand, if the users of an API are a bunch of small tech startups, they might care a lot more about getting new functionality than the stability of a single API version.

If you do decide that new functionality should be permitted inside an existing version, you may need to think more closely about how that new functionality appears to API users. For example, new functionality could be represented as new fields on existing resources, as entirely new resources, or as new actions that can be performed. And each of these has different effects on the users.

In the case of new fields on existing resources, this could have a meaningful effect on any users that have very strict resource requirements. For example, imagine an API used by an IoT device with very limited memory available. If a new field is added to an existing resource, a previously working HTTP GET request could actually cause the device to run out of memory and the process to crash. This might seem far-fetched when retrieving a single resource, but imagine adding a field that might contain a lot of information and the IoT device listing all the resources. Not only might the amount of data per resource increase beyond the expected boundaries, but the problem is magnified based on the number of resources showing up in response to listing the items.

In the case of adding new resources or new API methods, it's unlikely (if not impossible) that existing code will be aware of these new aspects of the API; however, this doesn't mean we're completely free from any issues. For example, imagine client-side code to back up all resources from an API. If a new resource is created and the existing code has no knowledge of the new resource, it will obviously be missing from the backup output. While in many cases it's best to avoid taking on responsibility for these types of problems, there are scenarios where it might be reasonable to prohibit adding new resources for cases like these.

Things get a bit dicier in cases where the newly added resource introduces some sort of new dependency or relationship with the existing resources or fields. For example, imagine that an API introduces a new MessagePolicy sub-resource belonging to a ChatRoom resource (and includes a primitive policy by default). If we can only delete a ChatRoom resource after we've first deleted the MessagePolicy resource, we're effectively forcing existing users to learn about this new change rather than allowing them to live in ignorance of this new functionality, which could be a bad choice.

As we discussed before, these are certainly not firm rules that must be followed. Instead, these are potential scenarios that any API designer should consider and decide on when launching a new API. Ultimately, deciding whether it's safe to add new functionality to an existing API is a bit more art than science, so the least that can be expected is consistent and clear policies articulated on the topic.

Even if you decide that adding new functionality in any form isn't something you want to consider safely backward compatible, there's an even more difficult topic to cover: how to handle bug fixes.

FIXING BUGS

When writing software, we rarely get things perfectly right on the first try. It's far more common that we make a mistake, have that mistake pointed out by someone else when they find it, and then we simply go back and fix the mistake. But, as you might be seeing now, isn't that change just another form of improved functionality? If so, do we have to fix our mistakes in a separate version? Or can we safely inject that change into the existing version and call it a backward compatible change? As you might guess, the answer to this question is, "It depends."

Some bugs will present themselves very obviously. When a client makes a specific API request, the service has an error and returns the dreaded HTTP `500 Internal Server Error` response code. In these cases, fixing the bug will usually be backward compatible because there should never be client-side code that assumes a given request will result in an internal error on the API server and then fail when it stops crashing.

But what about more subtle issues? What if a specific API request succeeds, returning a nonsensical result when it should instead have returned an error (e.g., a `400 Bad Request` error)? It's far more likely that someone has come to depend on this erroneous but mistakenly successful behavior. And if we "fix the bug," client code that previously returned a successful result will start seeing an error result instead.

Taking this even further, consider the case where this bug is buried deep inside some calculating code and fixing it means that result numbers change. One day, when we make an API call like `Add(0.1, 0.2)` it might return `0.30000000000000004`; then the next day we fix the bug with floating point arithmetic and it starts returning `0.3`. Is this something we want to consider backward compatible?

Listing 24.1   **Example of an API implementation with floating point arithmetic problems**

```
class AdditionApi {
  Add(a: number, b: number): number {
    return a + b;          ⭠⎯  This simply adds two floating point
  }                                numbers together, resulting in a
}                                  floating point bug.
```

Listing 24.2   **Example where we fix the floating point issues using fixed-point math**

```
const Decimal = require('decimal.js');

class AdditionApi {
  Add(a: number, b: number): number {
    return Number(Decimal(a).plus(Decimal(b)));    ⭠⎯ By relying on a fixed-
  }                                                   point construct, we avoid
}                                                     the floating point error.
                                                      But is this a backward
                                                      compatible change?
```

Unfortunately, yet again, there is no right answer. In general, fixing API calls that throw errors is pretty safe for most users. Making an API call suddenly start throwing errors is probably not a great idea, particularly if the users of the API care a lot about stability and would rather not have their code start breaking for no obvious reason.

For the even more subtle fixes it really depends on the profile of the typical user and the impact of the bug. For example, if the bug really is just about adding two numbers together and having something that's pretty close but has some weird floating point error, then perhaps it's not all that important to fix. If the calculation is being used for rocket launch trajectories and the precision is critically important, then it probably makes sense to have a policy of fixing the bug, even if it leads to a change in results from one day to the next.

This leads us to a similar though not quite identical issue worth discussion: mandatory changes.

HANDLING MANDATORY CHANGES

Almost always, the decision to add new functionality or make changes to a web API is our own. In other words, the typical course of events is that we, the creators of this web API, decide we want to make a change and get to work putting that into action. Occasionally though, we may have some work forced on us by others. For example, when the European Union (EU) passed their privacy law (General Data Protection Regulation; GDPR; https://gdpr-info.eu/), there were many new changes that were required in order to serve users residing in the EU. And since many of these requirements were focused on data retention and consent on the web, it's certainly possible that there were API changes that needed to be made to accommodate the new regulations. This leads to the obvious question: should those changes be injected into an existing version or should they be deployed as a new, isolated version? Put differently, should we consider the changes made to adhere to the rules set out in the GDPR to be backward compatible?

Ultimately, this decision depends on what, exactly, the changes are and what the law says, but it's still open to discussion whether the change would be considered backward compatible given who is using and relying on the API itself. In the case of the GDPR, you might follow their timeline and deploy a new version with the new changes while leaving the existing, noncompliant API available to everyone up until the date at which the GDPR comes into effect. At that point, you might begin blocking any requests coming from customers that have a registered address in the EU (or made from an IP address located in the EU), requiring these EU-based customers to use the new version of the API that is GDPR compliant. Or it might make more sense to simply shut down the noncompliant API entirely given the potential risks and fines involved in GDPR violations. It should go without saying that security patches and other changes in that category are often mandated, although not always by lawyers.

While there are cases that it's simply impossible to be completely compliant with all laws (e.g., it's rumored that the bitcoin blockchain has metadata storing material that's illegal in most countries, and blockchains are built specifically so that you cannot alter past data), it's almost always possible to make changes to comply with relevant laws. The question, really, is one of how best to make these mandated changes (often coming from lawyers or other primarily nontechnical people) without causing undue amounts of stress on API users. In other words, when these types of changes come up it's almost impossible to insulate API users from the changes you're mandated to make. The question is one of how to minimize the impact on those users by providing advance notice when possible and minimizing the work required of existing users.

UNDER-THE-HOOD CHANGES

Diving further down the rabbit hole, we can start to look at other subtle types of changes that might or might not be considered backward compatible. This generally includes deeper changes such as performance optimizations or other general subtle functionality changes that are neither bug fixing nor necessarily new functionality but are still modifications of the underlying system that responds to API requests and result in different results in some way or another.

One simple example of this is a performance optimization (or regression) that makes an API call return a result faster (or slower) than it did previously. This type of change would mean that the API response is completely identical, but it would show up after a different amount of computing time on the API server. This is often considered a backward compatible change; however, the argument could be made in the other direction.

For example, if an API call currently takes about 100 milliseconds to complete, it's pretty difficult to notice a change that causes that same call to take 50 milliseconds (if performance improved) or 150 milliseconds (if performance degraded). On the other hand, if the API call suddenly takes 10 seconds (10,000 milliseconds) to complete, this difference in timing is enough to justify a change in programming paradigm. In other words, with an API call that slow, you might prefer to use an asynchronous programming style so that your process can do other things while waiting for the API response in the meantime. In cases like that, you might consider this a backward incompatible change, or potentially even a bug introduced that causes such a severe degradation in performance.

Another example of a deeper change might be if you rely on a machine learning model to generate some results in an API call, such as translating text, recognizing faces or items in an image, or labeling scene changes in a video. In cases such as these, changing the machine learning model that's used might lead to drastically different results for these types of API calls. For example, one day you might have an image that the API call says contains pictures of a dog, and the next it might say that's actually a muffin (this is more common than you might think; try searching for "Chihuahua or Muffin" to see an example).

This kind of change might be an improvement to one API user and a regression to another given the different results. And, depending on the profile of API users, there may be a need for stable results from a machine learning model. In other words, some users might really rely on an image providing consistent results unless they explicitly ask for an upgrade of sorts. In cases like these, this type of change might actually be considered backward incompatible.

CHANGING SEMANTICS

The last category to consider is probably both the broadest and most subtle: general semantic changes. This refers to general behavioral changes or the meaning of the various concepts in an API (e.g., resources or fields).

These types of changes cover a broad range of possibilities. For example, this might be something large and obvious (such as the behavioral changes resulting from the introduction of a new permission model in an API), or it might be something much more subtle and difficult to notice (such as the order of items returned when listing resources or items in an array field). As you might guess, there is no blanket best practice policy for handling these types of changes. Instead, the best we can do is explore the effect it would have on existing users and their code, consider how accepting of instability those users might be, and then decide whether the change is disruptive enough to justify injecting the change into an existing version or deploying a new, isolated one.

To see what this means, let's imagine an example Chat API with `ChatRoom` and `User` resources, where users can create messages inside chat rooms. What if we decide we want to introduce a new concept of a message policy that determines whether users are able to create messages inside chat rooms based on a variety of factors such as the rate at which users are sending messages (e.g., you can't post more than once per second) or even the content of the messages (maybe a machine learning algorithm determines whether a message is abusive and blocks it). Would a change introducing this resource be backward compatible? As you might guess, the answer is, yet again, "maybe."

First, the decision might depend on the default semantics of existing `ChatRoom` resources (e.g., do existing `ChatRoom` resources automatically pick up this new behavior? Or is this only reserved for newly created `ChatRoom`s?). Regardless, we have to look at the impact to existing users. Does the new message policy concept cause existing code to break? This also depends. If someone has a script that attempts to send two messages in quick succession, that existing code might stop functioning correctly due to the restriction of only allowing a single message per second.

Listing 24.3 Code that may fail after new semantic changes introduced

```
function testMessageSending() {
  const chatRoom = GetChatRoom(1234);
  chatRoom.sendMessage("Hello!");                      ◁─  This sendMessage() call
  chatRoom.sendMessage("How is everyone?");      ◁─      will succeed as usual.
}
```

This sendMessage() call
will succeed as usual.

This sendMessage() call might fail
if new rate limiting is enforced.

But how does that scenario play out? Does the user get an error response when they previously would have gotten a successful one? Or does the message simply go into a queue and show up one second later? Neither of these is necessarily right, but they are certainly different. In the first, the user will see an error immediately, which would clearly cause them to think the change has caused their existing code to break. In the latter, the error might not be noticed until later down the line (e.g., if they send two messages quickly and then verify they have both been received, the verification step will fail because the message has been delayed for a full second).

Listing 24.4   Code that may fail in a different place after changes

```
function testMessageSending() {
  const chatRoom = GetChatRoom(1234);
  chatRoom.sendMessage("Hello!");                      These two sendMessage()
  chatRoom.sendMessage("How is everyone?");            calls will succeed as usual.
  const messages = chatRoom.listMessages();
  if (messages.length != 2) {          ◄────┐  This check for the messages being posted will fail
    throw new Error("Test failed!");         │  unless there is a full one-second pause between
  }                                          │  the sending and the check for the message results.
}
```

As we've learned, ultimately the decision of whether this change is backward compatible or not is dependent on the expectations of the existing users. Almost always there will be a user somewhere who will have code that manages to demonstrate that an API change is breaking. It's up to you to decide whether a user could reasonably expect that particular bit of code would be supported over the lifetime of a specific version of an API. Based on that, you can determine whether your semantic change is considered backward compatible.

Now that we have at least some sort of grasp on the different issues that we'll need to consider when deciding on a backward compatibility policy, we need to move on and look at some of the considerations that go into deciding on a versioning strategy. To do this, we need to understand the various trade-offs that will go into our decision.

24.3   *Implementation*

Assuming you've made some choices about what changes you'll consider backward compatible, you're only about halfway through the journey of deciding how to manage versioning. In fact, the only case where you're already done is if you decide that absolutely everything will be backward compatible because you'll only ever need one single version forever. In all the other cases though, we'll need to explore and understand the many different options available on how to handle the new versions when you do happen to need them. In other words, if you make a change you consider backward incompatible and intend to create a new version, how exactly does that work? For example, what should we use as a name for the new versions? Ideally, there's some sort of pattern to make it easy for users to understand. How long should these versions live before being deprecated? One possible answer for this is forever, but for every other choice, you'll need a deprecation policy to convey to users when they should expect old versions to disappear and stop working.

With these types of issues in mind, let's take a moment to explore a few popular versioning strategies. In these, we'll explain how they work, their benefits and drawbacks, and how they compare to one another based on the trade-offs we considered in section 24.2. Keep in mind that these strategies might hint at or imply a set of policies for determining backward compatibility, but they don't always prescribe a single policy for making this determination. In other words, each strategy should have some flexibility when it comes to choosing some policies on whether to consider a change backward compatible.

24.3.1 *Perpetual stability*

One of the most popular versioning strategies happens to be the one many people often end up using accidentally. Far more than anyone would care to admit, many APIs are created with no versioning scheme or strategy in mind at all. It's only when the need arises to make a very big, scary, and (most importantly) backward incompatible change that we start to think about versioning. In that scenario, our next step is to decide that everything as it exists today will become "v1" and the API with the new changes will be called "v2." At this point, we often might start considering what else can fit into v2. For example, maybe that other field we've been wanting to change for a while can be fixed in v2.

This strategy is often referred to as *perpetual stability* primarily because each version is typically left stable forever, with all new potentially backward incompatible changes being reserved for the next version. Even though this strategy tends to come about accidentally, there is nothing preventing us from using the same strategy in an intentional way. In that case, how might it work?

The general process we follow with this strategy is as follows:

1 All existing functionality is labeled "Version N" (e.g., the first version is Version 1").
2 Any changes that are backward compatible are added directly into Version N.
3 Any new functionality that might fall afoul of our compatibility definitions is built as part of "Version N+1" (e.g., anything that is backward incompatible for Version 1 is saved for "Version 2").
4 Once we have enough functionality to merit a new version, we release Version N+1.
5 Optionally, at some point in the future, we might deprecate Version N to avoid incurring extra maintenance costs or because no one appears to be using the version anymore.
6 At this point, we go back to step 1 and the cycle begins again.

This process works well in a few scenarios, with the trade-offs shown in figure 24.2. First, in cases where you don't introduce many backward compatible changes, the majority of changes can be rolled into the existing version without causing much trouble for users and leaving most changes happily stuck on step 2. Assuming the compatibility policy maintains a reasonably high bar of what is backward compatible, this will likely lead to a very stable API in exchange for deploying lots of new functionality rapidly.

Additionally, and again assuming a reasonably high bar for what passes as a backward compatible change, this strategy tends to maximize the number of people who

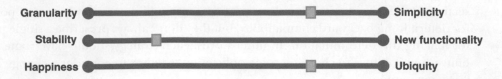

Figure 24.2   Trade-offs for perpetual stability versioning strategy

can reasonably use the API based on the versioning strategy. It might not be perfect, but the majority of users are likely to be in the "okay" bucket of the distribution.

This strategy is unlikely to work well in cases where users absolutely require an extreme level of granularity. For example, an IoT device as an API client using this versioning strategy would probably struggle because it encourages lots of changes rolling into the existing version whereas IoT devices typically need the ability to freeze an API at an exact version to avoid some tricky edge cases such as memory overflows.

In cases where the bar for backward compatibility is excessively high (i.e., all changes are considered incompatible), you may end up in a world with an exceeding large number of versions (v1, v2, . . ., v100, and on). Obviously, this can become unwieldy for both the service managing all of those versions and clients deciding which version is right for them to use.

Regardless of these issues, many popular APIs rely on this versioning mechanism and have made it work well over the years. For example, many Google Cloud Platform APIs use this strategy for a variety of reasons, and while it certainly isn't perfect, it does seem to work quite well for many customers.

24.3.2 *Agile instability*

Another popular strategy, sometimes referred to as *agile instability,* relies on a sliding window of active versions in order to minimize the maintenance overhead for API designers while still providing new functionality in a timely manner to customers. While far from perfect, this strategy can be quite effective with active and engaged API users who are involved enough in product development to cope with frequent deprecations of previous versions in exchange for the new functionality provided.

This strategy works by pushing each version through a steady life cycle, going from birth (preview), where all functionality might change at any time, all the way to death (deleted), where the version itself is no longer accessible. An overview of the different states is shown in table 24.1, but to see how this works, let's go through an example scenario of a few versions in a demo API.

When first starting out, an API is certainly not stable enough to show anyone. Most importantly, developers want the freedom to change it at the drop of a hat. In this scenario, it's simply easiest to put all work into version 1. In this case, we'd label version 1 as "Preview" as it's not really ready for real users. Any users who are accepting of the

Table 24.1 Overview of different version states

State	Description	Change policy
Preview	An unstable and still-in-progress preview of functionality users should expect to exist in the next current version	All changes permitted
Current	A very stable set of functionality that should not change and can be expected to continue running for some pre-decided amount of time	Only mandatory changes
Deprecated	A prior current version that is scheduled for impending removal according to the deprecation policy	Only mandatory changes
Deleted	A prior deprecated version that has been removed or otherwise made inaccessible to users	N/A

fact that there are no stability guarantees for this stage are free to use it, but they should be certain they understand the hard truths here: code they write today will probably be broken tomorrow.

Once version 1 is looking more mature, we might want to allow real users to start building against this API. In this case, we promote version 1 to "Current." While in this stage, we want to ensure that client code continues working, so the only changes that should be made are mandatory requirements (e.g., security patches) and potentially critical bug fixes. In short, by promoting version 1 to current, we're freezing it exactly as it is and leaving it alone unless absolutely necessary.

Obviously feature development shouldn't simply stop, though. So where do we put all the new hard work? The simple answer is that any new features or other noncritical changes that we would've liked to make to version 1 would simply be put into the next version: version 2. And it just so happens that version 2 is labeled as the new preview version. As you might expect, the rules for version 2 are the same rules we used to have for version 1 when it was in the preview stage.

At some point this cycle will repeat and version 2 will become more mature to the point that we'll want it to be promoted to become the new current version. When that happens, we have a new problem: what do we do with the existing current version? We shouldn't maintain two current versions, but we also don't want to delete a version entirely just because there's something newer and shinier available to users. In this strategy, our answer is to mark this version as "Deprecated." While in the deprecated state, we'll enforce the same rules about changes as we did when the version was current; however, we start a ticking clock for when the version will ultimately go away—after all, we don't want to maintain every version that ever existed until the end of time!

Once the clock timer expires, we remove the deprecated version in question entirely and it can be considered deleted. The exact timing of how long it takes for a version to go from deprecated to deleted depends on API users' expectations; however, the most important thing is to have some specific amount of time declared ahead of time, shared with the users of the API, and stick to the timeline. A summary of this timeline is shown in table 24.2 with a monthly release cadence (and a two-month deprecation policy).

Table 24.2   Example timeline of versions and their states

Date	Version 1	Version 2	Version 3	Version 4	Version 5
January	Preview				
February	Current	Preview			
March	Deprecated	Current	Preview		
April	Deprecated	Deprecated	Current	Preview	
May	Deleted	Deprecated	Deprecated	Current	Preview

There are quite a few interesting things about this strategy, with a summary of the different trade-offs shown in figure 24.3. First, note that while there may be lots of different deprecated (and deleted) versions, there is only ever a single current version and a single preview version. This is a critical piece of the strategy in that it acts as a forcing function to move toward continual improvement while keeping the number of active versions to an absolute minimum. In other words, this strategy tends to see new versions as improvements on top of the existing versions rather than alternative views that happen to be equally good. By deprecating versions in order to make way for the latest and greatest new version, we ensure that new functionality doesn't take too long to get in front of API users.

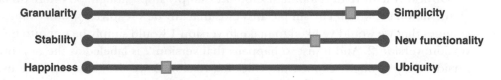

Figure 24.3   Trade-offs for agile instability versioning strategy

Additionally, notice that this benefit of rapid cycling through versions can also be a drawback: any code written against a current version is virtually guaranteed to stop working eventually. At the very least, there is absolutely no guarantee that it will continue to function, so if it does that might be a pure coincidence. This means that any users who expect to be able to write code and then forget about it for a couple of years will likely find this versioning strategy completely unusable. On the other hand, anyone who is actively updating and changing their code and has a great appreciation for new functionality will find this strategy quite welcoming given their attitude toward software development.

Overall, this strategy can work well when users are active and engaged in development and need small windows of stability followed by quick upgrades to new versions with new functionality. Any users who require longer-term stability in exchange for having less access to new functionality over time will almost certainly find this model very difficult to use. And while it's possible to coincidentally have code continue to work, the lack of a guarantee can be quite off-putting to anyone who would much rather have a stronger promise that their code will continue to function as intended for more than a fixed, relatively short window of time.

24.3.3 *Semantic versioning*

Probably the most popular form of versioning out there today, *semantic versioning* (or SemVer; https://semver.org), is a very powerful tool that allows a single version label to convey quite a lot of meaning in three simple numbers. Most importantly, this meaning is practical: it can tell a user about the differences between two APIs and whether code written against one should continue to work with another. Let's take a moment to look at how exactly this works.

A semantic version string (illustrated in figure 24.4) is built up of three numbers separated by dots (e.g., 1.0.0 or 12.5.2), where each number increases as changes are made to an API and carries a different meaning about the change that was made to bring about this increase. The first number of the version string, called the *major version*, is increased in scenarios where the change is consid-

Figure 24.4   The different version numbers in a semantic version string

ered backward incompatible according to the compatibility policy defined, which we explored in section 24.2.2. For example, changing a field name is almost always considered a backward incompatible change, so if we were to rename a field, the version string would increment the major version (e.g., from **1**.0.0 to **2**.0.0). In other words, you can assume that any code written for a major version N is almost certainly not going to function as expected for a major version M. If it happens to actually work, it's entirely coincidental and not at all due to any sort of guarantee by design.

The next number in a semantic version string is the *minor version*. This number is incremented when a backward compatible change is made according to the rules defined in the compatibility policy that is some new functionality or change in behavior. For example, if we were to add a new field to the API and we've defined this action as being backward compatible in our policy, then we would increment the minor version rather than the major version (e.g., from 1.**0**.0 to 1.**1**.0). This is powerful because it allows you to assume that any code written for a specific minor version is guaranteed not to be broken when targeted at future minor versions, as each subsequent minor version is only making backward compatible changes (e.g., code written for version 1.0.0 will not crash when run against both 1.1.0 and 1.2.0). While this older code will not be able to take advantage of the new functionality provided in the newer minor versions, it will still function as expected when run against any of the newer minor versions.

The third and final number in a semantic version string is the patch version. This number is incremented when a change is made that is both backward compatible and primarily a bug fix rather than new functionality being added or behavior being altered. This number should, ideally, convey no obvious implication regarding compatibility. In other words, if the only difference between two versions is the patch version, code written against one should work with the other.

Semantic versioning, when used with web APIs, simply follows these rules as new changes come out. Making a change that would be backward incompatible? That change should be released as the next major version. Adding some backward compatible functionality to the API? Keep the same major version but increment the minor version. Applying a backward compatible bug fix? Keep the same major and minor version and release the patched code with an incremented patch version. As we explored in section 24.2.2, your compatibility policy will guide you to decide which category your change falls into; so as long as you follow it, semantic versioning works quite well.

One major issue with semantic versioning, though, is the sheer number of versions available to the user (and to be managed as separate services). In other words, semantic versioning provides a huge number of versions to choose from, each with a varying set of functionality, to the point where users might end up quite confused.

Additionally, since users will want to be able to pin to a specific, very granular version for as long as possible, this means that the web API must actually maintain and run lots of different versions of the API, which can become an infrastructural headache. Luckily, since versions are almost completely frozen after they are made available to users we can often freeze and continue to run a binary, but the overhead can still be quite daunting. That said, modern infrastructure orchestration and management systems (e.g., Kubernetes; https://kubernetes.io/) and modern development paradigms (e.g., microservices) can help to alleviate much of the pain brought about by this problem, so relying on these tools can help quite a bit.

That said, it's not necessarily required that versions always live forever. On the contrary, there's nothing wrong with defining a deprecation policy and stating from the time a version is made available how long it's expected to be maintained and continue running. Once that clock runs out, the version is removed from service and simply disappears.

This deprecation policy aside, one of the best things about relying on semantic versioning is the balance between stability and new functionality, effectively giving us the best of both worlds. In a sense, users are able to pin to specific versions (all the way down to which bug was fixed) while at the same time having access to new functionality if needed. There is the clear issue that it might be hard to pick and choose specific features (e.g., someone might want to use version 1.0.0 but get access to some special functionality that was added in version 2.4.0), but that's simply an issue with any chronologically based versioning strategy.

Lastly, this strategy also finds a balance between being satisfactory to everyone and making quite a few people happy (summarized in figure 24.5). In short, because there is so much choice available, and assuming a reasonable deprecation policy, most use cases, ranging from the small startups who want the ability to quickly explore new

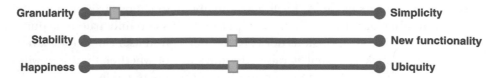

Figure 24.5   Trade-offs for semantic versioning strategy

functionality to large corporate customers who want stability, are able to get what they want out of this versioning scheme. Most importantly, this doesn't come at the cost of a strategy that frustrates users. It might be a bit overwhelming in the number of version options available, but overall this strategy allows users to get what they want from an API, assuming it's been built and put into a specific version.

Keep in mind that these are just a few popular strategies for versioning web APIs and not at all an exhaustive list. As you've seen, each has their own benefits and drawbacks, and therefore none is guaranteed to be a perfect fit for all specific scenarios. As a result, it's important to understand all the different options available and think carefully about which option is likely to be the best choice for your web API given the constraints, requirements, and preferences of your unique set of users.

24.4 Trade-offs

As we can see, defining a policy on what types of changes should be considered backward compatible is complicated. But more importantly, the choices we make on these topics will almost certainly be our way of striking a balance between two different ends of a spectrum. While there is typically never a perfect choice on these topics, the least we can do is understand the trade-offs we're making and ensure that these choices are made consciously and intentionally. Let's take a moment to understand the various spectrums we should consider when deciding on the compatibility policy for each unique situation.

24.4.1 Granularity vs. simplicity

The first, very broad, spectrum that many of our choices will lie on is one of choice. In the book *The Paradox of Choice* (Harper Perennial, 2004), Barry Schwartz discusses how more choice for consumer products doesn't always lead to happier buyers. Instead, the overwhelming number of choices can actually cause increased levels of anxiety. When designing an API, we're not really buying a product at a shopping mall; however, the argument may still carry some weight and is worth looking at. When it comes to choosing a versioning policy, this trade-off has to do with striking a balance between lots of granularity and choice versus a simpler, one-size-fits-all single option.

To see how this works, consider the case where we decide that our customers care about stability so much that any change at all should be considered backward incompatible. The result is that each and every change will be deployed as an entirely new version, and users of the API will have the ability to choose from a potentially enormous number of versions for their application. It's certainly true that this extensive collection of potential versions does ensure that a given user can choose a very specific version and stick to it, but it raises the question of whether that user will be overwhelmed or confused by the sheer number of options available.

Further, it's also likely that versioning schemes behaving this way will tend to follow a temporal flow, resulting in a steady stream of changes over time. This means that a user isn't able to pick and choose specific aspects of an API but instead is only given a time machine of sorts where they can pick a specific version representing how the API looked at a specific point in history. If that user wants some behavior from two years ago as well as some feature from today, they'll typically be forced to accept all changes in behavior between those two points as well. In short, the cost for pinning to a version is that it must include all changes made up until the launch of that specific version.

Now consider the other end of the spectrum: every single change is always considered backward compatible no matter what the effect on existing users of the API happens to be. In this scenario, the resulting API would have only one single version, always and forever, meaning there is no choice at all for the users. While no one could ever argue that this choice doesn't provide enough of a choice, it probably skews too far toward oversimplification. In other words, one choice is clearly the easiest thing to understand, but it's rarely a practical choice given the typical audience of an API, particularly those who have specific stability requirements.

Obviously there is no right answer, but the best answer is almost certainly somewhere in between these two ends of the spectrum. This might mean finding a set of policies for what changes are backward compatible such that they result in a reasonable number of versions (the definition of reasonable here will certainly vary), or it might mean finding a deprecation policy where you delete old versions at some point in time. Either way, the trade-off will depend on the users and how big their appetite for choices is (as well as how big yours is for managing all of these different versions).

24.4.2 *Stability vs. new functionality*

The next trade-off worth discussion is probably the most obvious: how much new functionality do API users really need? In other words, if you simply make fewer changes to your API, then you have fewer chances to even decide whether a change is backward compatible. This trade-off is really more about short-circuiting the compatibility policy entirely at the cost of API users having less access to new features, bug fixes, or behavioral changes.

To put this into perspective, on one end of this spectrum we have perfect stability: never make any changes, ever. This scenario means that once the API is launched and available to users, it will never change ever again. While this might sound easy (after all, how hard can it be to just leave it alone?) it's actually far more complicated than that. To truly remain perfectly stable, you'd also need to ensure that you never applied any security patches or upgraded the underlying operating system for the servers that are powering your API, and that the same remains true of any of your suppliers. If any of those things change, it's very easy for something subtle to make its way into the users' view, resulting in, technically, a change. And that means you'd need to decide whether that merits a new version.

On the other end of the spectrum, you might decide that any and all functionality is critically important to launch. All bugs are critically important to fix. And operating system and library upgrades, security patches, and other underlying changes should be pushed out to API users as quickly as possible. In this scenario, the choices made when defining backward compatibility will be as important as ever.

As usual, there's no best choice for where you should fall on this spectrum; however, APIs that don't make the choice of where on the spectrum best suits their users (and instead just make it up on the fly) tend to anger and frustrate users far more. And, as always, the best choice almost certainly lies somewhere in between. For less accommodating users (e.g., a large government organization) the desire of new features might not be as important as stability. And the opposite might be true if the typical user is a startup. But it's important to identify the expectations of those who will be using the API and decide where on this spectrum best suits those users.

24.4.3 *Happiness vs. ubiquity*

The final, and possibly most important, trade-off has to do with how your policy is received by the various users of your API. So far we've thought of users as one single group that will either be happy or not with your policies on which changes might be considered backward compatible. Unfortunately, this type of homogeneity across all of your users is relatively rare. In other words, it's very unlikely that your policies will be well received by every single customer for the simple reason that users are different from one another and have different opinions on the topics we're deciding on. While some APIs may skew toward homogeneous groups of users (e.g., a set of APIs built for central banks or municipal governments may all want stability far more than new functionality), many APIs attract a diverse group of users and we can no longer assume that all users fall into the same bucket. What do we do?

As you might guess, this is yet another trade-off. To understand this, we need to think of API users as falling into one of four groups with different levels of satisfaction with our policies. The spectrum goes from those who would refuse to use the API given the circumstances (cannot use), to those who can use it but are not at all happy with it (mad), to those who are fine with the policy but not thrilled either (okay), and finally those who are completely satisfied with the policy (happy). While typically the majority of users should land in the okay bucket, some policies may alienate a big group of potential users. For example, if an API had a policy of considering all changes backward compatible, that policy might alienate quite a few people and force them to look elsewhere for their API needs (e.g., lots of users in the cannot use bucket). Given this distribution, let's look at the trade-off we're considering.

On one end of the spectrum we have maximum happiness for users, where our decision is aimed at maximizing the number of users who are in the happy bucket with our policy on backward compatibility. While we certainly can't make all users happy, we can always try. However, keep in mind that this means we are choosing a policy without any consideration for the other buckets. This can lead to the situation shown in figure 24.6, where we might maximize the number of happy users, but because we're not thinking about the other buckets, we end up with quite a lot of users falling into the cannot use bucket.

Figure 24.6   We might maximize the number of happy users at the cost of a lot of users who cannot use the API.

On the other end of the spectrum is the maximum usability across all users, where our decision tries to maximize the number of users who can definitely use the API. Put another way, this end of the spectrum is aimed at minimizing the number of users in the cannot use bucket and thus obviously suffers from a similar problem: it doesn't consider which bucket the other users are in so long as they're not in the cannot use bucket. In figure 24.7, we can see a potential distribution of users categorized by these buckets, where we certainly have a minimal number of people in the cannot use bucket. However, it's pretty obvious that this is unlikely to be a good situation as the overwhelming majority of users, while able to use the API, are not at all happy with it and fall into the mad bucket.

Figure 24.7   We might minimize the number of users who cannot use the API but at the cost of lots of mad users.

As always, the best choice probably lies somewhere in the middle of this spectrum and will obviously depend on the profile of these users. This might try to balance the need for maximizing happiness with minimizing those who simply cannot use the API entirely. Ideally, it might also minimize the mad users and search for a solution that maximizes the number of users in either the okay or happy buckets. This might lead to the user distribution of buckets shown in figure 24.8. One thing we can be certain of is that it's typically impossible to find a policy that makes all people happy all the time. The next best thing we can do is figure out whether we will aim for a solution that prioritizes ubiquitous access to the API by minimizing those who cannot use it entirely or prioritize the most happiness.

Figure 24.8 A balanced distribution minimizes the number of users who cannot use the API and still maintains a respectable number of users who are happy with the policy.

24.5   *Exercises*

1   Would it be considered backward compatible to change a default value of a field?
2   Imagine you have an API that caters to financial services with a large commercial bank as an important customer of the API. Many of your smaller customers want more frequent updates and new features while this large bank wants stability above all else. What can you do to balance these needs?
3   Right after launching an API, you notice a silly and embarrassing typo in a field name: port_number was accidentally called porn_number. You really want to change this quickly. What should you consider before deciding whether to make this change without changing the version number?
4   Imagine a scenario where your API, when a required field is missing, accidentally returns an empty response (200 OK in HTTP) rather than an error response (400 Bad Request), indicating that the required field is missing. Is this bug safe to fix in the same version or should it be addressed in a future version? If a future version, would this be considered a major, a minor, or a patch change according to semantic versioning (semver.org)?

Summary

- Versioning is a tool that allows API designers to change and evolve their APIs over time while causing as little detriment and providing as many improvements to users as possible.
- Compatibility refers to the property where code written against one version of an API will continue to function against another version.
- A new version is considered backward compatible if code written for a previous version continues to function as expected. The question that is left to interpretation is how an API designer defines user expectations.

- Often things that might seem harmless (e.g., fixing bugs) can lead to backward incompatible changes. The definition of whether a change is backward compatible is dependent on API users.
- There are several different popular versioning strategies, each with their own benefits and drawbacks. Most come down to trade-offs between granularity, simplicity, stability, new functionality, individual user happiness, and ubiquity of usability.

Soft deletion

As we learned in chapter 7, the standard delete method has one goal: remove a resource from the API. However, in many scenarios this permanent removal of data (a so-called *hard deletion*) from the API is a bit too extreme. For the cases where we want the equivalent of our computer's "recycle bin," where a resource is marked as "deleted" but still recoverable in the case of a mistake, we need an alternative. In this pattern, we explore *soft deletion*, where resources are hidden from view and behave in many ways as though they have been deleted, while still providing the ability to be undeleted and restored to full view.

25.1   *Motivation*

Starting with Windows 95, Microsoft introduced the Recycle Bin, a temporary storage area for files that a user requested to be deleted but were not yet permanently removed from the system. The problem was simple: too many people deleted files from their computer and then realized later they shouldn't have done that. It could have been an accident (clicking on the wrong file), or a mental mistake (thinking it was the right file but realizing it wasn't), or even just a change of heart later (thinking they're done with a file but realizing later they actually needed it), but the point remains the same: they needed a delete action that was recoverable and separate from a permanent deletion. This same issue pops up in APIs quite often.

We might write code that deletes all resources with a specific set of properties, but perhaps we do a comparison incorrectly and end up deleting a bunch of resources that shouldn't have matched the criteria. We might have a script that deletes data and realize that we ran it accidentally when we shouldn't have, or ran it when we thought it was okay to delete some resources and realized later we actually needed them. This gets even worse with large data sets. Can you imagine accidentally deleting a petabyte of user data from a storage system? (It's for this reason that you can't delete an entire bucket in the Google Cloud Storage service.)

In this case, it'd be wonderful if our deletions, even if only for certain resource types, could be partial or soft, such that the data isn't necessarily erased from the face of the earth but is instead only hidden from view when we're exploring our data (e.g., with the standard list method). And to make this form of soft deletion actually useful, we'll need a way to undelete resources just as easily as we can delete them. Finally, we'll need a way to perform the original permanent deletion on resources.

25.2   *Overview*

Luckily, the mechanism to accomplish our goal of soft deleting resources is pretty simple: store the deleted status on the resource itself, either through a simple deleted Boolean flag or, if the resource uses a state enumeration, a deleted state. This field will serve as a marker throughout the lifetime of the resource to indicate we should treat it differently from the other non-deleted resources.

Once we have this new way of storing the deleted status of resources, we'll have to modify the standard delete method to update this status rather than remove the resource entirely. To handle complete removal, we'll rely on a special custom expunge method that will take over this responsibility. Finally, we'll need a way to restore soft-deleted resources, leading us to a custom undelete method. The new life cycle of a resource supporting soft deletion might look something like figure 25.1.

In the next section, we'll explore the details of this pattern and all the changes needed and edge cases we'll need to cover to support soft deletion.

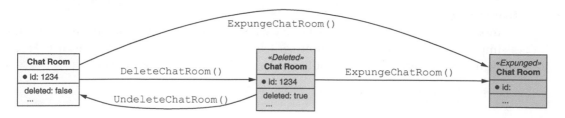

Figure 25.1 Life cycle of a resource being soft deleted and expunged

25.3 *Implementation*

As is the case in most topics in API design, the details of this pattern constitute the majority of the work we have cut out for us. In this case, all of the work stems from our one simple choice of relying on an additional field to indicate whether a resource is deleted. Once we've decided how this extra field should look, we have quite a bit more to cover.

First, we'll need to adjust several of the standard methods to behave slightly differently from how they were defined in chapter 7. For example, rather than deleting the resource entirely, the standard delete method now needs to act a bit more like a standard update method, modifying the resource to mark it as deleted. Additionally, the standard list method will need to ignore deleted resources. After all, if it automatically included deleted resources, then it defeats the purpose of marking resources as deleted in the first place! Finally, we'll need new custom methods to cover each of the new special behaviors: one for undeleting a resource that we've soft-deleted, and another for permanently removing a resource (as the standard delete method used to do).

As usual, these new methods and behaviors will lead to other complicated questions to answer. For example, what happens if we attempt to soft delete a resource that's already marked as deleted? And do we need to enforce any referential integrity rules when other resources reference those that are marked as deleted? What about other methods that are similar to the standard delete method, such as the batch delete method? Should these types of methods adopt this new behavior or continue behaving exactly as they have so far?

This is quite a lot to unpack, so let's start by covering how we might store the new deleted status on resources.

25.3.1 *Deleted designation*

In order to enable this pattern on a resource type, we'll need a way to indicate that a resource should be considered deleted by the rest of the system. In this case, there are two clear contenders: a simple Boolean flag field and a more complex state field. Let's start by looking at the simpler option.

BOOLEAN FLAG

In most cases, the best way to indicate that a resource has been soft deleted is to define a simple Boolean field on the resource. Obviously this field would default to `false`, since newly created resources should not begin their life cycle as deleted.

Listing 25.1   Soft-deleted resource with a Boolean flag

```
interface ChatRoom {
  id: string;                    This flag defines whether
  // ...                         the resource should be
  deleted: boolean;      <——    considered soft deleted.
}
```

The more interesting aspect of this field is the fact that it should be treated as output only. This means that if someone attempts to set this field (for example, using the standard update method), the value itself should be ignored. Instead, as we'll see later, the only way to modify this field is by using the standard delete method (to change from `false` to `true`) or the custom undelete method (to go in the opposite direction). This means that code that attempts to update just the deleted field on a resource would still succeed, but the resource would remain unmodified.

Listing 25.2   Example of interacting with an output-only field

```
let chatRoom = GetChatRoom({ id: "1234" });        We start by retrieving
assert(chatRoom.deleted === false);                a resource using the
chatRoom.deleted = true;                            standard get method.
chatRoom = UpdateChatRoom({
  resource: chatRoom,
  fieldMask: ['deleted']        Here we manually set the
});                             resource's deleted field to true.
assert(chatRoom.deleted === false);

                                Notice that this doesn't return
Despite the successful result,  an error result, but instead
the resource is still not deleted!  simply ignores the output-only
                                fields (such as deleted).
```

With this simple yes-or-no Boolean field, we can enable all the other complicated behavior we'll explore in section 25.3.2 and beyond. However, before we do that let's look at one other alternative: a state field.

STATE FIELD

In some cases, resources can be in one of several states with a well-defined life cycle that can be represented by a proper state machine. Consider a world where new chat rooms need to be approved by a system administrator and then might still be suspended later if the participants don't follow the rules. In this case, we might have a state diagram that looks something like figure 25.2, with three states: pending approval, active, and suspended.

In cases where we already have a state field that keeps track of the state of a given resource, rather than adding a Boolean flag to store whether the resource has been

Figure 25.2 Life cycle of a resource with state changes

soft deleted, we can opt to reuse the state field by introducing a new deleted state. This leads to a state diagram that looks something like figure 25.3.

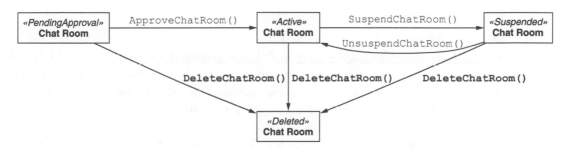

Figure 25.3 Adding deleted as a new state option

While this might look quite clean at first, it turns out that it suffers from a big problem: when we go to undelete a resource, how do we know what the target state is? In this case, we can assume that a ChatRoom resource that's been restored should always go back to requiring approval, treating it the same as if it was just re-created (see figure 25.4). However, this assumption might not hold in all scenarios. In other words, it's perfectly fine to use a state field to keep track of the state of a resource, and then rely on a Boolean field to keep track of this single orthogonal aspect of the resource (whether it is soft deleted or not).

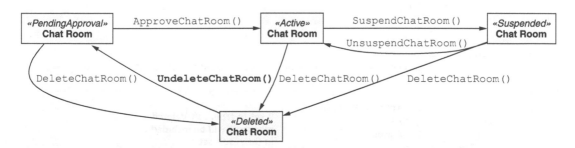

Figure 25.4 Adding support for the custom undelete method

Now that we've covered the different ways to indicate whether a resource is deleted, we have to look at the effect this new indicator will have on the existing methods. Let's start by looking at the collection of standard methods we'll need to adjust.

25.3.2 *Modifying standard methods*

Now that we have a new place to keep track of whether a resource is deleted (a Boolean field or possibly a state field), we'll need to do something with this designation. In particular, we'll need to make resources with this special attribute appear deleted, but only to an extent. In some cases, methods won't need to change at all. For example, since the deleted indicator is output only and cannot be manually set, both the standard create and update methods have no meaningful changes. Let's start looking through those that do need to be modified a bit.

GET

When it comes to soft-deleted resources, the standard get method should behave exactly as it does with any other resource: return the resource as requested. This means that retrieving a resource immediately after deleting it would not return a 404 Not Found HTTP error, but instead would return the resource as though it wasn't deleted at all. As we'll see, in other cases it makes sense to require additional work to access soft-deleted resources, but when we know the identifier of a resource, retrieving it using that identifier is a clear indication that we might want to determine whether it's soft-deleted; not that we're sure it's deleted and want to view the data anyway.

LIST

The standard list method is one of the methods that needs to be changed to remain useful in the face of soft-deleted resources. In this case, we want to provide a mechanism to view only non-deleted resources, but also the ability to include the soft-deleted resources in the result set if the user explicitly requests.

To make this work, we need to do two things. First, the standard list method should automatically exclude any soft-deleted resources from the result set. Second, we need to augment the request interface to include a new field that allows a user to express an interest to have soft-deleted resources included.

Listing 25.3   Including deleted results in the standard list methods

```
abstract class ChatRoomApi {
  @get("/chatRooms")
  ListChatRooms(req: ListChatRoomsRequest): ListChatRoomsResponse;
}

interface ListChatRoomsRequest {
  pageToken?: string;
  maxPageSize?: number;
  includeDeleted?: boolean;      ⤺ If set to true, soft-deleted
  filter?: string;                 resources will be included
}                                   in the result set.
```

```
interface ListChatRoomsResponse {
  resources: ChatRoom[];
  nextPageToken: string;
}
```

This definition raises an obvious question: why not use the `filter` field to include the soft-deleted resources? There are a few reasons for this. First, there's no guarantee that all standard list methods will support filtering. In the case that they don't, we'll still need a mechanism to support including soft-deleted resources in the result set, and in that case we'll have to choose between a Boolean flag as shown or a filter that only supports a *very* limited grammar for caring only about soft-deleted resources.

Second, while these two concepts are closely related, they are actually orthogonal to one another. The `filter` field is responsible for taking a set of possible results and whittling those results down to only those matching a specific set of criteria. The `includeDeleted` field is responsible for doing the opposite: enlarging the potential result set before even applying the filter.

This combination does mean that we have a bit of a confusing way for *only* showing the soft-deleted resources, but it also means that the API remains consistent and clear in the purpose of each of the different fields.

Listing 25.4 Example to view all soft-deleted resources

```
let softDeletedChatRooms = ListChatRooms({          To show only soft-deleted resources,
  filter: "deleted: true",                          we need to limit results using a filter.
  includeDeleted: true,
});                            To ensure that soft-deleted resources are included
                              in the result set (and then filtered), we first need
                              to indicate that by including them explicitly.
```

DELETE

As we've already learned, the standard delete method needs to be augmented so that now, rather than actually removing a resource, it should mark the resource as deleted using the indicator discussed in section 25.3.1. It should also return the newly modified resource.

Listing 25.5 Definition of the modified standard delete method

```
abstract class ChatRoomApi {
  @delete("/{id=chatRooms/*}")
  DeleteChatRoom(req: DeleteChatRoomRequest): ChatRoom;          
}

interface DeleteChatRoomRequest {          The augmented standard delete
  id: string;                              method now returns the resource
}                                          rather than void as before.
```

The new question is what exactly should happen when you attempt to soft delete a resource that's already been soft deleted? That is, if a resource is marked as deleted, should the standard delete method leave it as is? Or throw an error? Or do something else entirely?

The answer follows the same principles we learned about in chapter 7 about repetitive deletion: it's important to be able to distinguish between the imperative (that this request caused the resource to be deleted) and the declarative (that the resource is deleted, whether or not it was the result of this request). Because of this, it's important that the new standard delete method return an error result (e.g., a 412 Precondition Failed HTTP error) to indicate that the resource has already been soft deleted and therefore the request cannot be executed as expected.

Now that we've covered the relevant standard methods, let's start looking at the new custom methods we'll need to implement, starting with the custom undelete method.

25.3.3 *Undeleting*

One of the main benefits of supporting soft deletion is the fact that data isn't permanently deleted by the standard delete method. Instead, by marking the resource as deleted but leaving the underlying data intact, we're somewhat insulated from the variety of possible mistaken API calls. To make this insulation really worthwhile though, we need a way of undoing our mistakes. In other words, if we delete a resource and decide later that we should not have done so, there must be a way to restore or undelete a resource. As you might guess, we can do this with a custom method.

Listing 25.6   Definition of the custom undelete method

```
abstract class ChatRoomApi {
  @post("/{id=chatRooms/*}:undelete")
  UndeleteChatRoom(req: UndeleteChatRoomRequest):      ⟵──┐ Just like a standard update
    ChatRoom;                                              │ method, we return the
}                                                          │ resource itself.

interface UndeleteChatRoomRequest {
  id: string;
}
```

The custom undelete method is simple. Given an identifier of a soft-deleted resource, unmark the resource so that it no longer appears deleted. The question then becomes yet another about idempotence and repetition: what if the resource we're trying to undelete is not currently soft deleted? In this case, just as in the case of the changes we made to the standard delete method, the response should be an error result (e.g., a 412 Precondition Failed HTTP error). The purpose is, yet again, to make sure users can tell the difference between a request causing a result (imperative) or a result being true but not necessarily caused by a specific request (declarative).

25.3.4 *Expunging*

With all this talk of new functionality provided by soft deletion, we've kind of glossed over the old functionality of full deletion. But just because we want to be protected from our mistakes with our API recycle bin doesn't mean we never want the ability to actually empty it. Unfortunately, we've repurposed the standard delete method to do only soft deletion, so how do we handle the old style of full deletion?

To address this gap, we have two options: provide an extra parameter on the standard delete method or rely on a custom method. While the extra parameter on the standard delete request might result in fewer interfaces and custom methods, it has a couple of drawbacks. The first is that the HTTP DELETE method doesn't typically accept a request body. This means that our special new parameter will have to be provided in the query string. Ultimately, this means that the behavior of a typical HTTP request to delete a resource (DELETE /chatRooms/1234) will do something drastically different from the same request with an additional query parameter (DELETE /chatRooms/1234?expunge=true). In general, additional parameters, particularly those in a query string, should not drastically alter the behavior and result of the request. Otherwise, why have multiple methods to delete versus create? Why not just a single request with ?action=create as a parameter?

The other drawback of relying on a parameter in the standard delete request is that, due to permissions and access control, in general, it's easier to control access to specific API methods than it is to control the same method with different sets of parameters. In this case, if we wanted to prohibit a user from permanently deleting resources while allowing that same user the ability to soft delete resources, we would have to allow access to the standard delete method, but only if the special flag on the method was set to false. While possible, this is certainly more complex to implement.

Because of these reasons, it's probably better to rely on a separate method to handle the responsibility of completely removing resources from the system.

Listing 25.7   Definition of the custom expunge method

```
abstract class ChatRoomApi {
  @post("/{id-chatRooms/*}:expunge")
  ExpungeChatRoom(req: ExpungeChatRoomRequest): void;        ⟵
}

interface ExpungeChatRoomRequest {
  id: string;
}
```

> **Just like the old standard delete method, expunging should return an empty result.**

Since we had to worry about preconditions and error results with the modified standard delete method and the custom undelete method, it's worth asking the same question regarding the expunge method. In this case, since the result is a fully deleted resource, the question is slightly different: can we call this method on any resource, whether or not it's already been soft deleted? Or do we need to first soft delete a resource and only then remove it permanently?

While there may be some reasons for going through the intermediate step of first soft deleting a resource, this is likely to become nothing more than an API speed bump in the long run. In other words, it'll mostly be an inconvenience and turn what should be a single API request into two, without really doing much else. As a result, it should almost always be possible to call the custom expunge method on any resource, whether or not it's already been soft deleted.

25.3.5 *Expiration*

While often soft deletion and explicit permanent deletion are sufficient, there may be cases where we want to have the recycle bin emptied every so often. For example, when we delete a message in Gmail, it goes into the trash (i.e., soft deleted). However, after 30 days in the trash, a message is permanently deleted. This pattern, which we saw a bit of in chapter 10 with the behavior of LROs, is not unusual for soft-deleted resources. The only issue is determining how best to implement it.

Just as with LROs, soft-deleted resources should also have an expiration time. This means we'll need a new field on any resource that supports soft deletion in addition to the designation alone, described in section 25.3.1. This new field should be called `expireTime` and should be set immediately when a resource is deleted, calculating the expected expiration time according to some predefined policy (e.g., expires after 30 days). If a resource is ever marked as anything other than deleted, the expiration time should be set to an explicit `null` value. This means that if we undelete a resource, it's expiration time should be reset.

Listing 25.8   Adding a new expiration time field to a resource

```
interface ChatRoom {
  id: string;
  // ...
  deleted: boolean;
  expireTime: Date;     <──┐   This field keeps track of when a
}                               resource should expire and be
                                permanently removed.
```

This puts the burden of determining when things expire on the method doing the expiring (in this case, the standard delete method), but also has the nice side effect of allowing any policy changes to only affect newly soft-deleted resources by default. For example, if we change the policy from 30 days to 45 days, all of the already soft-deleted resources will still be deleted 30 days from their soft-deletion date, but any newly soft-deleted resources will fall under the new policy.

This policy also ensures the code for handling this expiration of resources is simple and to the point. In essence, we can rely on two simple conditions: if a resource is flagged as deleted (e.g., `resource.deleted == true`) and the expiration time is after or equal to now (e.g., `resource.expireTime >= Date.now()`), we should simply remove the resource entirely.

25.3.6 *Referential integrity*

Another topic worth addressing with soft deletion is that of referential integrity. In short, we have to decide whether soft-deleted resources can still be referenced by other resources. We went through these types of issues in quite a lot of detail in chapter 13, with the main takeaway being that different APIs have different patterns when it comes to referential integrity. Some of them might restrict the ability to break a reference. Others might simply cascade the change (e.g., if a related resource is deleted, it might delete the other resources involved). Others still might leave the reference alone, like a ticking time bomb for anyone attempting to use the reference in the future.

In the case of soft deletion, the scenarios are quite similar. As a result, the rules should remain the same. This means that whatever pattern was enforced by the normal standard delete method, changing to enable soft deletion shouldn't alter that portion of the behavior. So if deletion used to be prevented to maintain referential integrity, soft deletion should have the same restrictions, regardless of the fact that technically the reference wouldn't be broken.

While this does present some complications when it comes to our original goal of being able to undo a mistaken deletion (as now we can't just restore a resource exactly as it was before in some cases), the additional complexity of changing behavior, only to have it change at the time where a resource is expired or expunged, is simply not worthwhile.

25.3.7 *Effects on other methods*

Even though we've covered the various changes needed for the existing standard methods, we've said nothing about other related methods. For example, if we support batch methods, the batch delete method presents a bit of a quandary. Should that method continue behaving as it always has, permanently deleting resources in bulk? Or should it likewise be modified to soft delete by default? And if it should be modified, should there also be a batch expunge method?

The simple answer is that it should be modified, and there should be a batch expunge method if that type of behavior is required. In general, when we alter standard method behavior (in this case, the standard delete method), we should consider other related methods almost as if they used those newly altered methods.

Listing 25.9 Example implementation of the batch delete method

```
abstract class ChatRoomApi {
  @post("/chatRooms:batchDelete")
  BatchDeleteMessages(req: BatchDeleteMessagesRequest): void {
    for (let id of req.ids) {
      ChatRoomApi.DeleteMessage({ id: id });      ⟵┐  The soft-delete behavior
    }                                                │  of a batch delete method
  }                                                  │  will be inherited.
}
```

As a result, the batch delete method should be defined as the standard delete but in bulk, and therefore will inherit the new behavior from the modified standard delete method to support soft deletion.

25.3.8 *Adding soft delete across versions*

Finally, as we very rarely get things right on the first try, we should address the concern of how to safely add soft-deletion support to an API that previously didn't have it. As we learned in chapter 24, it's critical to have a policy on what constitutes a backward compatible change, and implementing soft deletion in an API that previously only supported hard deletion is certainly a change we need to examine.

As with almost all issues related to versioning, the answer is pretty unappealing: it depends. Generally, changing the behavior of a method is unlikely to be a safe change to make, but in many cases, this type of change to soft deletion might be perfectly fine. For example, if we implement soft deletion with a 24-hour expiration window on resources, is it really such a huge deal that resources aren't immediately deleted but instead are removed 24 hours later? This is especially true if the information being deleted isn't particularly important (e.g., there are no laws governing the disposal of such data).

As a result, whether or not soft-delete functionality can be added to an existing API in a non-breaking way is really open for interpretation. It will almost certainly depend on the end result (e.g., whether expiration is implemented as well), but most definitely will require a solid understanding of the purpose of the data as well as the expectations and regulations related to the privacy and security of that data. To be on the safe side, it's generally a good idea to assume that it might be considered backward incompatible in some sense. As a result, incrementing the major version number (or equivalent) when implementing soft deletion is perfectly acceptable.

25.3.9 *Final API definition*

Putting everything together, listing 25.10 shows how we might define an interface for supporting soft deletion in our chat API.

Listing 25.10   Final API definition

```
abstract class ChatRoomApi {
  @delete("/{id=chatRooms/*}")
  DeleteChatRoom(req: DeleteChatRoomRequest): ChatRoom;

  @get("/chatRooms")
  ListChatRooms(req: ListChatRoomsRequest): ListChatRoomsResponse;

  @post("/{id=chatRooms/*}:expunge")
  ExpungeChatRoom(req: ExpungeChatRoomRequest): void;
}

interface ChatRoom {
  id: string;
```

```
  // ...
  deleted: boolean;
  expireTime: Date;
}

interface ListChatRoomsRequest {
  pageToken?: string;
  maxPageSize: number;
  filter?: string;
  includeDeleted?: boolean;
}

interface ListChatRoomsResponse {
  resources: ChatRoom[];
  nextPageToken: string;
}

interface ExpungeChatRoomRequest {
  id: string;
}
```

25.4 *Trade-offs*

Soft deletion in general is a trade-off between permitting users to remove specific information permanently from the API and preventing them from shooting themselves in the foot. As a result, it really depends on the circumstances of your API to decide whether soft deletion is a good idea.

For example, if the data being stored is regulated in some way, it might be far more important that the standard methods do exactly as expected, removing information permanently exactly when requested. In cases like these, it might make sense to work on a more thorough data backup strategy as a way of preventing accidental data loss. This way, users requesting data be removed get what they want, but data is still preserved with a policy that is likely acceptable according to any relevant regulations.

And this cuts in the other direction as well. Some regulations might focus on ensuring that data is never permanently deleted. In cases like these, we may want to avoid implementing resource expiration or the custom expunge method to avoid running afoul of those regulations.

25.5 *Exercises*

1 When does it make sense to use a Boolean flag versus a state field to represent that a resource has been soft deleted? Does it ever make sense to have both fields on the same resource? Why or why not?

2 How should users indicate that they wish to see *only* the soft-deleted resources using the standard list method?

3 What should happen if the custom expunge method is called on a resource that hasn't yet been soft deleted? What about calling the custom undelete method on the same resource?

4 When does it make sense for soft-deleted resources to expire? How should the expiration deadline be indicated?

5 In what circumstances might we consider adding support for soft deletion to be a backward compatible change? What about a backward incompatible change?

Summary

- Soft-deletion refers to the ability to mark a resource as deleted without actually removing it from the API service's storage systems.

- Typically resources are marked as being deleted using a Boolean flag field called `deleted`, but they may also add a new deleted state in an already existing state field.

- Standard method behavior for resources supporting soft deletion require a few minor changes (e.g., the standard get method should not return a `404 Not Found` error when a soft-deleted resource is requested).

- Soft-deleted resources may be restored using a custom undelete method and permanently removed using a custom expunge method.

- Whichever referential integrity guidelines were in place for the standard delete method (e.g., cascading deletes of referenced resources) should similarly apply for soft deleting resources.

Request deduplication

This chapter covers

- How to use request identifiers to prevent duplicate requests
- How to manage collisions with request identifiers to avoid confusing results
- Balancing caching and consistency of requests and responses

In a world where we cannot guarantee that all requests and responses will complete their journeys as intended, we'll inevitably need to retry requests as failures occur. This is not an issue for API methods that are idempotent; however, we'll need a way to safely retry requests without causing duplicated work This pattern presents a mechanism to safely retry requests in the face of failure in a web API, regardless of the idempotence of the method.

26.1 Motivation

Unfortunately, we live in a very uncertain world, and this is especially so in anything involving a remote network. Given the sheer complexity of modern networks and the variety of transmission systems available today, it's a bit of a miracle that we're able to reliably transfer messages at all! Sadly, this issue of reliability is just as prevalent in web APIs. Further, as APIs are used more frequently over wireless networks on smaller and smaller devices, sending requests and receiving responses over longer and longer distances means that we actually have to care about reliability more than we would on, say, a small, wired, local network.

The inevitable conclusion of this inherent unreliability of networks is the scenario where a request sent by the client might not always arrive at the server. And even if it does, the response the server sends might not always arrive at the client. When this happens with idempotent methods (e.g., methods that don't change anything, such as a standard get method), it's really not a big deal. If we don't get a response, we can always just try again. But what if the request is not idempotent? To answer this question, we need to look a bit closer at the situation.

In general, when we make a request and don't get a response, there are two possibilities. In one case (shown in figure 26.1), the request was never received by the API server, so of course we haven't received a reply. In the other (shown in figure 26.2), the request was received but the response never made it back to the client.

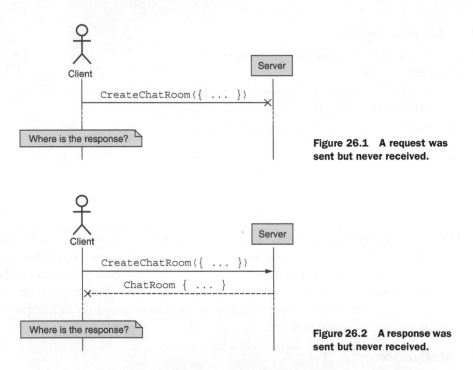

Figure 26.1   **A request was sent but never received.**

Figure 26.2   **A response was sent but never received.**

While both of these scenarios are unfortunate, the first one (where a request is never even received by the API server) is a completely recoverable situation. In this case, we can just retry the request. Since it was never received, it's basically as though the request never happened at all. The second case is far scarier. In this scenario, the request was received, processed by the API server, and the response was sent—it just never arrived.

The biggest problem though is that we can't tell the difference between these two scenarios. Regardless of whether the problem happened when sending the request or on receiving the response, all the client knows is that there was a response expected and it never showed up. As a result, we have to prepare for the worst: that the request made it but we haven't been informed about the result. What can we do?

This is the main goal of this pattern: to define a mechanism by which we can prevent duplicate requests, specifically for non-idempotent methods, across an API. In other words, we should be able to safely retry methods (even ones that launch missiles) without knowing whether the request was received, and without worrying about the method being executed twice as a result of retrying.

26.2 Overview

This pattern explores the idea of providing a unique identifier to each request that we want to ensure is serviced once and only once. Using this identifier, we can clearly see whether a current incoming request was already handled by the API service, and if so, can avoid acting on it again.

This leads to a tricky question: what should we return as the result when a duplicate request is caught? While returning an error stating that this request was already handled is certainly sufficient, it's not all that useful in practical terms. For example, if we send a request to create a new resource and never get a response, when we make another request we're hoping to get something useful back, specifically the unique ID of the resource that was created. An error does prevent duplication, but it's not quite what we're looking for in a result.

To handle this, we can cache the response message that went along with the request ID provided that when a duplicate is found, we can return the response as it would have been returned when the request was first made. An example of this flow using request IDs is shown in figure 26.3.

Now that we have an idea of how this simple pattern works at a high level, let's get into the implementation details.

26.3 Implementation

The first thing needed to make this pattern work is a definition of a request identifier field so that we can use it when determining whether a request has been received and processed by the API. This field would be present on any request interfaces clients send for any methods that require deduplication (in this case, that's generally just the methods that are not idempotent). Let's begin by looking more closely at this field and the values that will end up stored in it.

26.3.1 Request identifier

A request identifier is nothing more than a standard ID field; however, rather than living on a resource interface, this field lives on certain request interfaces (see listing 26.1). Just as an ID field on a resource uniquely identifies the resource across the entire API, a request identifier aims to accomplish the same goal. The catch here is that while

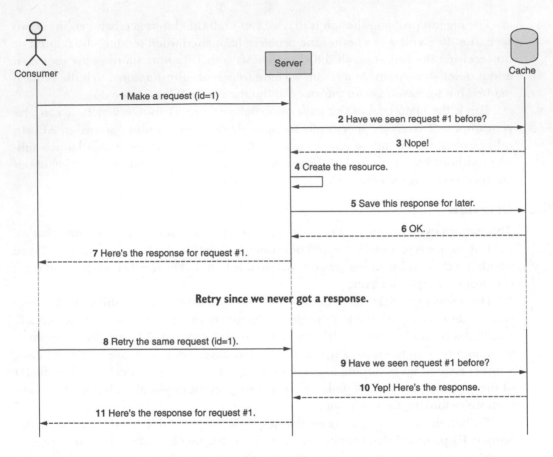

Figure 26.3   Overview of the sequence of events for deduplicating requests

resource identifiers are almost always permanent (chapter 6), request identifiers are a bit more like single-use values. And because they're something a client uses to identify their outgoing requests, it's absolutely critical that they be chosen by the client itself.

Listing 26.1   Definition of a request with an identifier field

```
interface CreateChatRoomRequest {
  requestId?: string;
  resource: ChatRoom;
}
```

Defining the request identifier as an optional string field on the request interface

Unfortunately, as we learned in chapter 6, it's usually a bad idea to allow clients to choose identifiers, as they tend to choose poorly. Since it's a necessity, though, the best we can do is specify a format, recommend that the identifier be chosen randomly, and enforce the indicated format (e.g., we really wouldn't want someone sending a request with its ID set to 1 or "abcd"). Instead, request identifiers should follow the same standards for resource identifiers (discussed in chapter 6).

Even though request identifiers are not as permanent as those for resources, this doesn't make them any less important. As a result, if the API server receives an incoming request with an invalid request ID, it should reject the request and throw an error (e.g., a 400 Bad Request HTTP error). Note that this is different from leaving a request identifier blank or missing. In that case, we should proceed as though the request is never going to be retried, bypassing all the caching discussed in section 26.2, and behaving as any other API method would.

AVOIDING DERIVED IDENTIFIERS

One question that often comes up is, "Why not just derive an identifier from the request itself?" At first glance this seems like quite an elegant solution: perform some sort of hash on the request body and then ensure that whenever we see it again we know it shouldn't be processed again.

The issue with this method is that we cannot guarantee that we won't actually need to execute the same request twice. And instead of an explicit declaration from the client ("I definitely want to ensure this request is only processed once"), we're implicitly determining the intended behavior without providing a clear way to opt out of this deduplication. Obviously the user could provide some extra headers or meaningless query string parameters to make the request look different, but this has the defaults swapped around.

By default, requests should not be deduplicated, as we cannot know for sure the user's intent. And a safe way to allow a user to clearly express the intent of their request is to accept a user-chosen identifier, not deriving one implicitly from the request content.

Finally, given what we'll learn in section 26.3.5, this ultimately will not be a true case of never duplicating work. Since cache values almost certainly expire at some point, this would act more as a rate limit mechanism, ensuring the same request wouldn't be executed twice within some time period.

While we're on the topic of how caching works, let's briefly discuss what will be cached and the rationale behind these choices.

26.3.2 *Response caching*

In figure 26.4, we can see that every request that has a request identifier will have the result stored in a cache somewhere. The process begins by checking the cache for the provided request ID, and if a value is present we return the result that was cached the first time around when the request was actually processed by the server. If the request ID isn't found in the cache, we process the request and then update the cache with the result value before sending the response back to the user as requested.

One thing that might seem worrisome with this pattern is the fact that the entire response value is being stored in the cache. In this case, the storage requirements can grow out of control pretty quickly; after all, we're technically caching the results of every non-idempotent API call. And what if these responses are quite large themselves? For example, imagine a batch create method with 100 resources provided. If we receive that request and are using this pattern for request deduplication, we'll need to cache quite a bit of data, and that's only a single request.

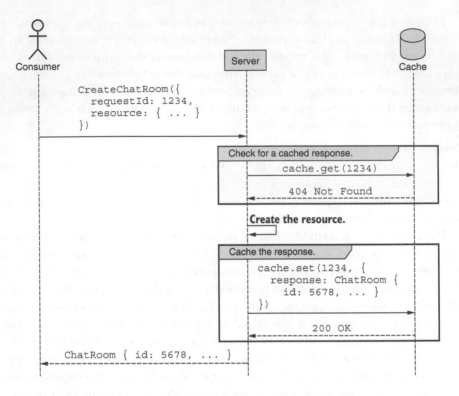

Figure 26.4   Sequence of caching responses for nonduplicate requests

The bottom line, for all the clever engineers out there, is that even though we could design a more complicated system that avoids caching all this data and instead tries to recalculate the response without processing the request again, it's still not a good idea. At the end of the day, an engineer's hourly rate for debugging and managing a complex system far outweighs the costs for more RAM or a larger caching cluster in the cloud. As a result, caching the responses is just the safe bet in the long term, as you can always throw more hardware at a problem pretty quickly, but it's not nearly as easy to throw more brain power.

26.3.3 *Consistency*

Hidden in this requirement to cache the responses from requests that have been processed is a key question of consistency. In other words, cached values can very easily become stale or out of date as the data is updated over time and these updates are not reflected in the cached value. The question, then, is whether this is important when it comes to request deduplication.

To illustrate the problem more clearly, let's imagine that two clients (A and B) are both performing updates on a resource, shown in figure 26.5. And in this case, let's

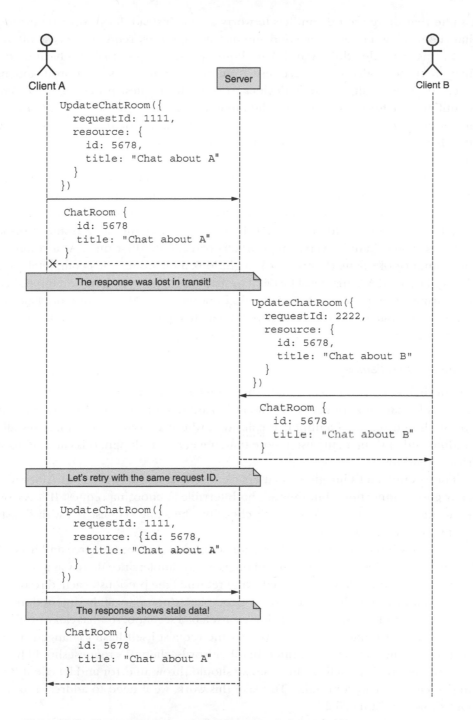

Figure 26.5 It's possible to see stale data when retrying requests.

assume that there are no conflicts to worry about. Instead, let's worry about the fact that client A has a poor connection and may need to retry requests every so often.

In this example, while A and B are both updating a resource and having no conflicts in those updates, the response from A's update is lost in transit and never received. As a result, A simply decides to retry the request using the same request identifier as before to ensure that the modifications are repeated twice. On this second attempt, the server responds with the cached value of the resource, showing A the title that was originally set in the request. There's one problem though: that's really not how the data looks right now!

In general, stale or inconsistent data like this can be an enormous problem, but it's critical to recall the purpose of this pattern. The primary goal is to allow clients to retry requests without causing potentially dangerous duplication of work. And a critical part of that goal is to ensure that the client receives the same result in response that they would have if everything worked correctly the first time. As a result, while this sequence of events (figure 26.5) might look a bit strange, it's completely reasonable and correct. As a matter of fact, it'd probably be more confusing and unpredictable to return anything else besides this result. In other words, the cache should absolutely not be kept up-to-date as the underlying data changes, as it would lead to even more confusion than the stale data we see in this case.

26.3.4 Request ID collisions

An inevitable consequence of allowing users to choose their own identifiers for requests is that they are generally bad at it. And one of the most common results of poorly chosen request identifiers is collisions: where a request ID is not really all that random and ends up being used more than once. In our design, this can lead to some tricky situations.

For example, let's imagine two users (A and B) interacting with our API, with perfectly good connections, but they are both terrible at choosing request IDs. As we can see in figure 26.6, they end up each choosing the same request ID, with disastrous (and very strange) consequences.

Somehow it seems that client B attempted to create a `User` resource and instead got back a `ChatRoom` resource. The cause of this is pretty simple: since there was a collision on the request ID, the API server noticed it and returned the previously cached response. In this case, it turns out that the response is completely nonsensical, having nothing to do with what client B is trying to do. This is clearly a bad scenario, so what can we do?

The correct thing to do is ensure that the request itself hasn't changed since the last time we saw that same identifier. In other words, client B's request should have the same request body as well—otherwise, we should throw an error and let client B know they've clearly made a mistake. To make this work, we'll need to address two things, both shown in listing 26.2.

First, when we cache the response value after executing a request that doesn't yet have a cache value, we need to also store a unique fingerprint of the request body

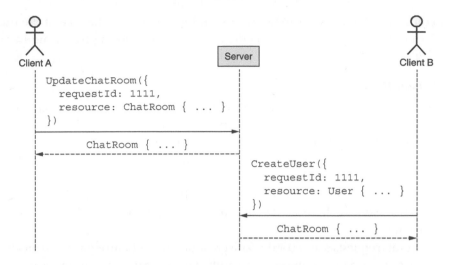

Figure 26.6 Confusing results happen due to request identifier collisions.

itself (e.g., a SHA-256 hash of the request). Second, when we look up a request and find a match, we need to verify that the request body on this (potential) duplicate matches the previous one. If they match, then we can safely return the cached response. If they don't, we need to return an error, ideally something along the lines of a 409 Conflict HTTP error.

Listing 26.2 Example method to update a resource with request identifiers

```
function UpdateChatRoom(req: UpdateChatRoomRequest): ChatRoom {
  if (req.requestId === undefined) {                     ◄─── If there's no request ID provided,
    return ChatRoom.update(...);                               simply perform the update and
  }                                                            return the result.
  const hash = crypto.createHash('sha256')
    .update(JSON.stringify(req))
    .digest('hex');                                           If there's no cached value for
  const cachedResult = cache.get(req.requestId);              the given request ID, actually
  if (!cachedResult) {                                   ◄─── update the resource.
    const response = ChatRoom.update(...);
    cache.set(req.requestId, { response, hash });  ◄──┐  Update the cache
    return response;                                     with the response
  }                                                      and the hash value.

  if (hash == cachedResult.hash) {            ◄──┐  If the hash matches, we can
    return cachedResult.response;                  safely return the response.
  } else {
    throw new Error('409 Conflict');       ◄──┐  If the hash doesn't
  }                                             match, throw an error.
}
```

By using this simple algorithm, whenever we see a request ID that has already been serviced, we can double-check that it really is a duplicate of the same request and not a collision. This allows us to safely return the response in the face of the unfortunately common scenario where users do a poor job of choosing truly unique request identifiers.

26.3.5 Cache expiration

Now that we've covered most of the complicated bits of this pattern, we can move onto one final topic: how long to keep data around in the cache. Obviously, in a perfect world, we could keep all data around forever and ensure that any time a user had to retry a request, even if it was several years after the request was made, we could return the cached result exactly as we would have when we first responded. Unfortunately, data costs money to store, and is therefore a limited commodity in our API. Ultimately, this means we have to decide on how long we want to keep things in the request cache.

In general, requests are retried relatively soon after a failure occurs, typically a few seconds after the original request. As a result, a good starting point for a cache expiration policy is to hang onto data for around five minutes but restart that timer every time the cached value is accessed, because if we have a cache hit it means that the request was retried. If there is further failure, we want to give subsequent retries the same expiration policy as first attempts.

To make this decision easier, there's some good news. Since caching, by its very nature, results in data expiring after some amount of time, whatever we decide can always be fine-tuned later based on how much capacity there is compared to how much traffic there is. In other words, while five minutes is a good starting point, this decision is extraordinarily easy to reevaluate and adjust based on user behavior, memory capacity available, and cost.

26.3.6 Final API definition

The final API definition is quite simple for this pattern: just adding a single field. To clarify the details of the pattern once more, a full example sequence is shown in figure 26.7.

Listing 26.3   Final API definition

```
abstract class ChatRoomApi {
  @post("/chatRooms")
  CreateChatRoom(req: CreateChatRoomRequest): ChatRoom;
}

interface CreateChatRoomRequest {
  resource: ChatRoom;
  requestId?:string
}
```

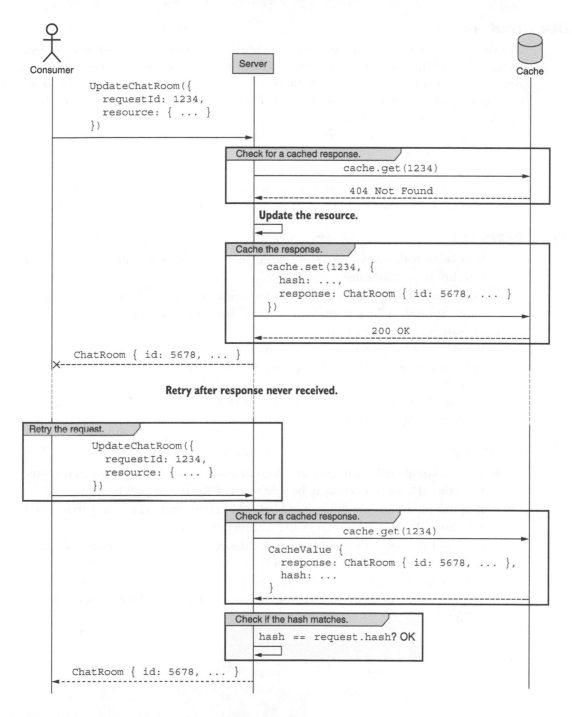

Figure 26.7 Sequence of events for request deduplication

26.4   *Trade-offs*

In this pattern, we use a simple unique identifier to avoid duplicating work in our APIs. This is ultimately a trade-off between permitting safe retries of non-idempotent requests and API method complexity (and some additional memory requirements for our caching requirements). While some APIs might not be all that concerned about duplicate request scenarios, in other cases it can be critical—so critical, in fact, that request identifiers might be required instead of optional.

At the end of the day, the decision of whether to complicate certain methods with this mechanism for request deduplication really does depend on the scenario. As a result, it likely makes sense to add it on an as-needed basis, starting with some particularly sensitive API methods and expanding over time to others.

26.5   *Exercises*

1   Why is it a bad idea to use a fingerprint (e.g., a hash) of a request to determine whether it's a duplicate?
2   Why would it be a bad idea to attempt to keep the request-response cache up-to-date? Should cached responses be invalidated or updated as the underlying resources change over time?
3   What would happen if the caching system responsible for checking duplicates were to go down? What is the failure scenario? How should this be protected against?
4   Why is it important to use a fingerprint of the request if you already have a request ID? What attribute of request ID generation leads to this requirement?

Summary

- Requests might fail at any time, and therefore unless we have a confirmed response from the API, there's no way to be sure whether the request was processed.
- Request identifiers are generated by the API client and act as a way to deduplicate individual requests seen by the API service.
- For most requests, it's possible to cache the response given a request identifier, though the expiration and invalidation parameters must be thoughtfully chosen.
- API services should also check a fingerprint of the content of the request along with the request ID in order to avoid unusual behavior in the case of request ID collisions.

Request validation

APIs can be confusing. Sometimes they can be confusing to the point where it's unclear what a result will be for a given API call. For safe methods, we have a simple solution to figure out the result: just give it a try. For unsafe methods, though, that solution will obviously not work. In this pattern, we'll explore a special `validateOnly` field we can add to request interfaces, which will act as a mechanism by which we can see what would have happened if the request was executed, without actually executing the request.

27.1 Motivation

Even the most straightforward APIs can be somewhat confusing—after all, APIs are complicated (otherwise there wouldn't be a book like this). And no matter how many times we read the documentation, double-check our source code, investigate the permissions granted to us, and review the outbound requests we're about to send to an API, we very rarely get everything right on the first attempt. Perhaps on the next attempt. Or the one after that. The key point is that there will be many attempts and it's okay if some of them don't succeed, or do succeed but in the wrong way.

While this method of poking and seeing what happens works quite well when we're just getting started, it can cause serious problems when it involves a production system. This is sort of the same reason most people take their cars to the mechanic when somethings wrong: they could poke at it, but this runs the risk of breaking it. And it's not a toy car, it's a critical tool to get to and from work, school, or the grocery store.

At first, we can get around this danger by poking only at the safe methods that don't change any data or have any scary side effects, but what about the others? For example, we probably don't want to experiment with a method named `DeleteAll-DataAndExplode()`. It's not as though we have less of a need to experiment with these methods; we simply don't have a good way of doing so.

This is critically important when we realize just how much human error is involved in checking something as simple as whether we have access to execute a given API method. For example, consider the case where we want to verify whether we can call the `DeleteAllDataAndExplode()` method. As shown in figure 27.1, we could look at the documentation to see what permissions are required, then check which credentials we're using to send the API call, and then check in the system whether those credentials have the permission listed by the documentation. But what if there was a mistake anywhere along that chain of dependencies?

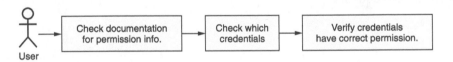

Figure 27.1   Requests might involve human error in all the various checks in the system.

At the end of the day, humans make mistakes whereas computers just do *exactly* as they're instructed to (even when we might mean to instruct them differently). So while we might be 99% sure that everything will go smoothly, we won't know for certain until we try. There must be a better way to experiment with all API methods—even the dangerous ones.

27.2   Overview

Since our goal is to allow users to get preview responses to their API calls, we can accomplish this with a single field specifying that the request should be treated as for validation purposes only. When an API method sees that a request is to be validated and not executed, it can perform as much of the actual work as is feasible without causing any true changes to occur to the underlying system. In a way, requests specified as only needing validation should be a bit like executing the work inside a transaction that's automatically rolled back and never committed.

Listing 27.1   Example of a standard create method supporting validation requests

```
interface CreateChatRoomRequest {
  resource: ChatRoom;
  validateOnly?: boolean;
}
```

> We rely on a simple Boolean flag to indicate whether a request is for validation only.

The reason for this is simply that users should get as much validation as possible. This means that requests should be checked for permission to perform the action, for conflicts with existing data (e.g., perhaps a unique field requirement would not be satisfied), for referential integrity (e.g., perhaps a request refers to another resource that doesn't exist), and for any other server-side form of validation on the request. In general, if the request would throw an error when it was actually executed, it should throw that same error when being validated.

While valiant, this is not always possible. This could be due to many different things (e.g., connections to external services or other dependencies, as discussed in section 27.3.1), but the goal remains the same: try to make validation responses as close to the real thing as possible. In the next section, we'll explore all of the details of how validation-only requests should be handled as well as various tricky scenarios that need to be addressed.

27.3   *Implementation*

As we saw in listing 27.1, we can allow a user to specify that a request is for validation only by setting the `validateOnly` field to an explicit Boolean `true`. Otherwise, by default, the request will be nothing more than a regular request. This default is important because if we chose the other way around (defaulting to always validate requests only), we'd be inadvertently crippling all requests from doing actual work by default. To get anything resembling normal behavior in this case, we'd always need to set a flag, which is likely a big mistake for any API.

Since the goal is to provide a realistic preview of a response to a request, validation requests should strive to validate as many aspects of the request as possible, which may involve talking to other remote services (just not actually modifying any data). For example (as shown in figure 27.2), we might talk to an access control service to determine whether the user has access to perform the action requested. We might check that a resource exists if there are questions of referential integrity to worry about. We might validate some parameters for correctness, such as ensuring a string SQL query is in a valid format.

In addition, the response to the request should be representative of what a response to a regular (non-validation) request would be. This means that if the request would cause an error for any reason, we should return that error exactly as we would otherwise.

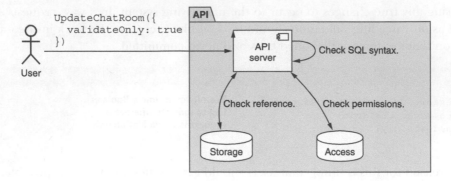

Figure 27.2   Validation requests might still connect to other internal components.

For example, if we don't have access to execute the request, we might get a 403 Forbidden HTTP error.

On the other hand, if the request would have been successful, the response should be as close to a real response as is possible. This means that whatever fields can be reasonably filled in for the response type should be populated. Some fields simply cannot be filled in (e.g., a server-generated identifier) and should be left blank or filled in with a realistic-looking (but certainly not valid) value. Ultimately though, the result fields are mainly intended to confirm that the request will execute successfully, so it shouldn't be a hard requirement that all information is returned in the response. For that, users should execute a real request rather than a validation request. It also should go without saying that it's perfectly reasonable to support validation requests on some methods and not others—after all, it simply might not make sense on some methods.

The most important thing in all of this is that any validation request should result in a method that is completely safe and idempotent. That means that no data should be changed, no side effects should manifest in any way, and any requests marked as "validate only" should be re-runnable each time and get the same result (assuming no other changes are happening in the system).

This might get confusing when an API method is read-only but not necessarily free. For example, consider an API method to query a large data warehouse. Running a SQL query of a large set of data technically doesn't change any data, but it certainly could cost quite a lot of money. And in some cases, the cost is related to the amount of data that happens to match the query itself. In this case, even though it might seem like a validateOnly parameter might be unnecessary, it's actually quite critical. Otherwise, how can a user know for sure whether their SQL query contains only valid syntax? While we might not be able to verify all aspects of the query, we can at least return an error result in the case where the query is invalid.

With all that said, the unfortunate truth is that some aspects of a request will cause us to violate these rules about always being completely safe and idempotent, so we have a big question to answer: what do we do when providing full fidelity with the behavior of the method results in a violation such as a non-idempotent method? In the next section, we'll look at external dependencies and how to work with them in the context of validation requests.

27.3.1 External dependencies

One obvious place that presents a problem to validating requests is dependencies on external services or libraries. The reason is simple: since we don't control those externalities, we can't explain that we're only communicating with them for validation purposes. For example, if our API sends email messages whenever ChatRoom resources are updated, we could validate whether we can send email to a particular recipient by sending them a test email (shown in figure 27.3), but this would be a pretty big side effect for a validation request. As a result, we have to make a choice: avoid validating certain aspects or break our rules about side effects, safety, and idempotence.

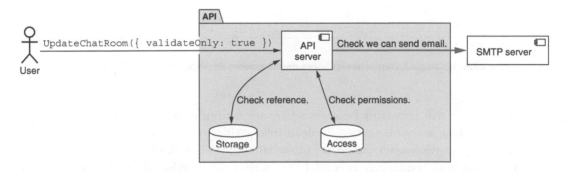

Figure 27.3 External dependencies make validation requests difficult or impossible.

Luckily, the choice is simple: stick to the rules. If an external dependency supports validation requests like this, then we can happily rely on those to provide us with the information we need to do true validation of this downstream service; however, if this is not available, we should skip it entirely. The importance of having a safe, idempotent, and side effect–free validation process is far more important than validating each and every tiny issue.

This might mean taking a bit of extra time to perform other related validation when it's clear that an external resource will not support the use case necessary. For example, while we might not be able to test sending an email with an external service, we can likely perform some sort of email address format validation to at least catch obvious invalid data (e.g., an email with no "@" symbol present). It's certainly not a perfect replacement, but it is better than performing no validation at all.

27.3.2 *Special side effects*

Even when we control the entire system and maintain no external dependencies, there's still a chance that providing a useful preview response to a validation request can be confusing. Consider an example of a special chat room lottery feature, with a method that returns a special winning response randomly (shown in figure 27.4). Assuming the request is valid, what should the response be when we send a validation request to this method? Or what if we had something a bit more deterministic rather than purely random, but still dependent on the behavior of others in a chat room? For example, what if instead of a randomly selected winner it's more like a radio show contest where every 100th call to an API method results in a special response? Does this change our opinion on the possible response?

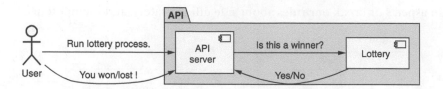

Figure 27.4   Example lottery requests with internal random dependencies

Since there will inevitably be cases where we cannot omit information and instead have to make a choice (e.g., a Boolean field saying whether we won the lottery), it's important to remember the goals of this validation method. First, we need to validate a request and return any potential errors that might arise. Second, assuming the request is indeed valid, we should return a plausible result that is not necessarily real but is instead representative of reality.

If we follow these guidelines, the answers to our earlier questions are much more straightforward: we should feel free to return a winning lottery result some of the time and a losing result other times. The percentages of these wins do not necessarily need to be reflective of the true lottery odds, so long as the result is one that could plausibly have been returned if the result had been real. The same thing goes for the more deterministic radio contest style: sometimes we might win, and others we might not, so the response value can be either one; both are representative of reality. In short, anything that is passable as a real response should be considered an acceptable response for a validation request.

27.3.3 *Final API definition*

In this case, the API definition itself is fairly simple: a simple (optional) Boolean field that allows users to specify that a request is for validation only, thereby making the request completely safe and idempotent.

Listing 27.2   Final API definition

```
abstract class ChatRoomApi {
  @post("/chatRooms")
  CreateChatRoom(req: CreateChatRoomRequest): ChatRoom;
}

interface CreateChatRoomRequest {
  resource: ChatRoom;
  validateOnly?: boolean;
}
```

27.4   Trade-offs

In general, validation requests are a simple answer to a nagging problem. By providing a simple flag, these users can get some amount of certainty in the face of a massive amount of complexity that comes with all of the details present in APIs. That said, they're rarely a hard necessity and much more of a convenience, primarily for users.

While users are the ones gaining the most value, there are still benefits to the APIs themselves. For example, in cases where API methods are expensive (either monetarily, computationally, or both), if that expense is not passed onto the user, supporting validation requests will certainly minimize waste for the simple reason that users can express their intent to simply validate a request and never execute it.

27.5   Exercises

1   Why should we rely on a flag to make a request "validate only" rather than a separate method that validates requests?

2   Imagine an API method that fetches data from a remote service. Should a validation request still communicate with the remote service? Why or why not?

3   Does it ever make sense to have support for validation requests on methods that never write any data?

4   Why is it important that the default value for the `validateOnly` flag is false? Does it ever make sense to invert the default value?

Summary

- Some API requests are sufficiently dangerous that they merit supporting a way for users to validate the request before actually executing it.
- API methods that support this functionality should provide a simple Boolean field (`validateOnly`) indicating that a request is to be validated only and not actually executed. These requests should be considered safe and should not have any effect on the underlying system.
- There will often be scenarios where API methods supporting validation requests will interact with external services. In these cases, these methods should validate those externalities to the best of their ability, acknowledging that it is not possible to validate safety for some aspects.

Resource revisions

This chapter covers

- How to safely store multiple revisions of a single resource as it changes over time
- How to identify individual revisions
- Strategies for creating revisions, either implicitly or explicitly
- How to list the available revisions and retrieve specific revisions
- How restoration to previous revisions works
- What to do about child resources of revisable resources

Though resources change over time, we typically discard any changes that might have occurred in the past. In other words, we only ever store what the resource looks like right now and completely ignore how the resource looked before changes were made. This pattern provides a framework by which we can keep track of multiple revisions of a single resource over time, thereby preserving history and enabling advanced functionality such as rolling back to a previous revision.

28.1 Motivation

So far, all of our interactions with resources in an API have focused exclusively on the present state of the resource and ignored previous states. While we do occasionally consider topics like consistency (e.g., when we looked at what happens as resources change while paginating through a list), there's always been a big assumption about resources: they only exist at a single point in time, and that time is right now.

This assumption has served us well so far, but it's not uncommon for certain resources to require a bit more than just one snapshot at a time. For example, we often keep track of revision history in a Microsoft Word or Google document. Likewise, if our API involves resources that represent contracts, purchase orders, legal filings, or even advertising campaigns, it's not a crazy thought that users might benefit from being able to view the history of the resource over time. This means that if a problem were to occur it would be much easier to diagnose which change was the cause.

The goal of this pattern is to provide a framework that enables storing multiple revisions for a single resource and also allow other more complex functionality such as deleting revisions that aren't necessary anymore or rolling a resource back to a previous revision, effectively undoing previous changes.

28.2 Overview

To solve these problems, this pattern will rely on a new concept called a *resource revision*. A resource revision is simply a snapshot of a resource that's labeled with a unique identifier and timestamped with the moment at which it's created. These revisions, though simple in nature, provide quite a lot of interesting functionality.

For example, if we can browse all revisions of a given resource and retrieve individual revisions directly, we've technically gained the ability to look into the past and see the evolution of a resource over time. More importantly, we can undo previous changes by rolling back to a specific revision, making a resource look exactly as it did at the time of a prior revision.

But what does a resource revision look like? Will we have to keep two separate interfaces synchronized over the lifetime of an API? Luckily the answer is no. A resource revision is not a separate interface at all; instead it's a concept brought about by simply adding two new fields to an existing resource: a revision identifier and a timestamp of when the snapshot was taken to create this revision.

> **Listing 28.1 Adding support for revisions to a Message resource**

```
interface Message {
  id: string;
  content: string;
  // ...

  revisionId: string;
  revisionCreateTime: Date;
}
```

By adding two fields, we can now represent multiple revisions of a resource with the same interface.

In short, this works by storing multiple records with the same identifier (`id`); however, each of these records has a different revision identifier (`revisionId`) and represents the resource as it looked at some point in time. And now, when we retrieve a resource by its identifier, the result will be a resource revision that just happens to be the latest one. In a sense, the resource identifier becomes an alias of sorts for the latest resource revision, and "latest" is defined as the revision with the most recent value for the `revisionCreateTime` field.

As always, however, there are many questions about the details that need answering. First, how do we decide when to create a new revision? Should it be automatic or require specific user intervention? How do we implement the functionality to list revisions or retrieve a resource at a specific revision? And what about rolling back to a previous revision? In the next section, we'll go into all of these questions in detail.

28.3   *Implementation*

How do resource revisions work? As we've seen, there are two new fields necessary to make a resource revisable, but is that all? Definitely not. There is a whole pile of additional topics we need to explore. This includes a variety of custom methods we need to create and existing standard methods we need to modify to fit with this pattern. In short, we need to define new API methods for every new behavior we want to support (e.g., retrieving an individual resource revision, listing revisions, rolling back to a previous revision, etc.).

Before we can do any of that, we need to explore what exactly will go into this new revision identifier field and how it will work. In the next section, we'll start digging into this pattern by deciding what makes for a good revision identifier and how it might differ from our typical resource identifiers.

28.3.1 *Revision identifiers*

When it comes to choosing a revision identifier, there are a few options. First, we could go with a counting number, sort of like an incremented version number (1, 2, 3, 4, . . .). Another option is to use a time-based identifier like a simple timestamp value (e.g., 1601562420). And yet another option is to use a completely random identifier, relying on the principles we learned about in chapter 6.

These first two options (counting numbers and timestamps) imply a chronological ordering of revisions in their identifier, separate and apart from the `revisionCreateTime` field, which can become a bit problematic. If we use incremental revision numbers, it might be confusing if a revision is ever deleted (see section 28.3.6), as this would leave a gap in the revision history (e.g., 1, 2, 4). Since the goal of deleting something is to remove all traces of it, using incremental numbers for the revision string is certainly not ideal as it leaves a gap, making it obvious that a revision was deleted.

Timestamps, on the other hand, are immune to this problem, as they convey chronological ordering with a tolerance for gaps in the data. With timestamp identifiers, we instead need to worry about collisions on identifiers. It is very unlikely we'll run into this issue (typically only likely to occur in cases of extremely high concurrent access to the system), but this doesn't mean we can write off the problem entirely. In other words, if there are no better options, then timestamps are a fine compromise; however, there is a better option that adheres to the principles explored in chapter 6: a random identifier.

Unlike the other two options, a random identifier serves one and exactly one purpose: it's an opaque chunk of bytes that uniquely identifies a single revision. But should revision identifiers be completely identical to resource identifiers? While we should opt to use identifiers consistently throughout an API, there is one question worth exploring in the case of revisions: how big do we need the identifier to be?

While a 25-character identifier in Crockford's Base32 format (120 bits) might be critical when creating billions of resources and beyond, the question is whether we really need to support as many revisions of a single resource as we do resources of a given type. Generally, we have far fewer revisions than we do resources, so we almost certainly don't need the full 120-bit key space. Instead, it probably makes sense to rely on a 13-character identifier (60 bits) as a close approximation for the same key space size provided by a 64-bit integer.

Another question to consider is whether it still makes sense to rely on a checksum character in the identifier, as described in section 6.4.4. While it might seem extraneous, remember that the goal of the checksum character is to distinguish between something not being present (i.e., a valid identifier with no underlying data) and something not able to ever have been present (i.e., an invalid identifier entirely). It stands to reason that just as it's important to make this distinction for a resource, it's equally important for a single revision of a resource. As a result, we should almost certainly keep the checksum character part of a resource revision identifier.

We can reuse much of the same code shown in chapter 6 to generate an identifier but with a shorter identifier.

Listing 28.2 Example code to generate random resource revision identifiers

```
const crypto = require('crypto');
const base32Decode = require('base32-decode');

function generateRandomId(length: number): string {
  const b32Chars = '012345689ABCDEFGHJKMNPQRSTVWXYTZ';
  let id = '';
  for (let i = 0; i < length; i++) {
    let rnd = crypto.randomInt(0, b32Chars.length);
    id += b32Chars[rnd];
  }
  return id + getChecksumCharacter(id);
}

function getChecksumCharacter(value: string): string {
  const bytes = Buffer.from(
    base32Decode(value, 'Crockford'));
```

Here we generate an ID by randomly choosing Base32 characters.

Finally, we return the ID along with a calculated checksum character.

We start by decoding the Base32 string into a byte buffer.

```
const intValue = BigInt(`0x${bytes.toString('hex')}`);
const checksumValue = Number(intValue % BigInt(37));

const alphabet = '0123456789ABCDEFG' +
                 'HJKMNPQRSTVWXYZ*~$=U';
return alphabet[Math.abs(checksumValue)];
}
```

Then we convert the byte buffer into a BigInt value.

Calculate the checksum value by determining the remainder after dividing by 37.

Here we rely on Crockford's Base32 checksum alphabet

Now that we've had a refresher on generating unique identifiers for revisions, let's look at how exactly these revisions come into existence.

28.3.2 *Creating revisions*

Obviously, being able to identify revisions is important, but it's basically useless unless we know how exactly these revisions get created in the first place. When it comes to creating new revisions, we have two different options to choose from: create revisions explicitly (where users must specifically ask for a new revision to be created) or create them implicitly (where new revisions are automatically created without any specific intervention).

While each of these strategies is perfectly acceptable, it's important that the same strategy be used across all resources that support resource revisioning because if we use different revision strategies across different resources, it can often lead to potential confusion where users expect one strategy and are surprised when their expectations are broken. As a result, mixing and matching should be avoided if at all possible and clearly documented in the cases where there's a critical reason for using a different strategy.

There is one caveat to all of this. Regardless of which strategy we choose, if a resource supports revisions, when that resource is first created it must populate the revisionId field no matter what. Without this, we might end up with resources that aren't actually revisions, which would cause quite a few problems with the interaction patterns that we explore in the following sections.

Let's start exploring the different mechanisms for creating revisions by looking at how implicit creation works.

IMPLICIT REVISIONS

The most common mechanism for creating resource revisions in any API that supports this functionality is to do so implicitly. This simply means that rather than a user specifically instructing the API to create a new revision, the API itself decides when to do so. This isn't to say that users have no ability to influence when a revision is created. For example, the most common mechanism for creating new revisions is to have the API do so automatically every time the data stored in a resource changes, shown in figure 28.1. In fact, there are many real-world systems that rely on this mechanism, such as Google Docs' revision history or GitHub's issue tracking, both of which keep track of all history of the resource in question (either a document or an issue).

While this is the most common and certainly the safest option (preserving the most history), there are many other implicit revision-tracking strategies available.

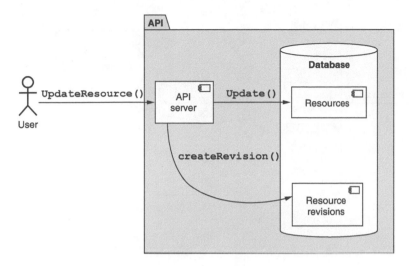

Figure 28.1   Flow diagram of implicitly creating revisions when updating.

For example, rather than creating a new revision for every modification, a service might do so on a schedule, where a new revision is created at the end of each day so long as some changes have been made, or perhaps skipping a certain number of changes, creating a new revision after every third modification rather than each individual modification.

Further, we can base revisions on milestones rather than intervals. This means that rather than creating a new revision each time a resource is updated, we might create a revision every time a single specific field is modified or perhaps whenever a specific custom method is executed. For example, perhaps we create new revisions for a `Blog-Post` resource only when the custom `PublishBlogPost()` method is executed.

All of these are perfectly acceptable, and as lovely as it'd be to prescribe a single one-size-fits-all answer to how revisions should be created, that's simply not possible here. The reason is simple: each API is different and with different business or product-focused constraints come different best-fit strategies for creating resource revisions.

A good general guideline is to err on the side of keeping more revisions rather than fewer (we explore space-saving techniques in section 28.3.7), and one of the simplest and most predictable strategies is to simply create new revisions each time a resource is modified. This strategy is easy to understand and use and creates a very useful result for most cases where users need to rely on resource revisions.

EXPLICIT REVISIONS

In many cases, however, implicitly creating revisions might be completely unnecessary and overly wasteful. This leads us to an obvious alternative: allow users to explicitly state exactly when they want to create a new resource revision using a special custom method, shown in figure 28.2. This explicit mechanism allows a user to control exactly

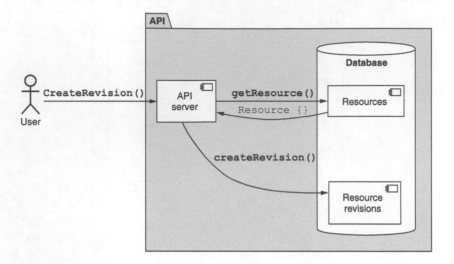

Figure 28.2   Flow diagram of explicitly creating resource revisions

when revisions are created, pushing the responsibility of deciding on a policy for revision creation from the API itself back onto the user.

To do this, we can create a new custom method that, in many ways, resembles the standard create method. Rather than creating a new resource under an existing parent, this custom create revision method has a single responsibility: take a snapshot of the revision as it exists at that exact moment and create a new revision to represent that snapshot. This new revision should have a randomly generated identifier (as described in section 28.3.1), and the creation timestamp of the revision should be set to the time at which the revision is finally persisted.

Listing 28.3   API definition for creating a resource revision

```
abstract class ChatRoomApi {
  @post("/{id=chatRooms/*/messages/*}:createRevision")
  CreateMessageRevision(req: CreateMessageRevisionRequest):    ⟵
    Message;
}

interface Message {
  id: string;
  content: string;
  // ...
  revisionId: string;
  revisionCreateTime: Date;
}

interface CreateMessageRevisionRequest {
  id: string;     ⟵
}
```

The custom create revision method creates a new revision and returns the newly created revision (which is just the resource with special fields set).

We can make the Message resource revisable by adding the two fields we learned about in section 28.2.

The method needs to know only the identifier of the resource.

Now that we've seen the ways in which we can create new resource revisions, let's look at how we can actually interact with those revisions, starting by how we can look back in time by retrieving specific revisions.

28.3.3 *Retrieving specific revisions*

As we learned in section 28.2, one of the most valuable features provided by resource revisions is the ability to look backward and read the data of a resource as it appeared in the past. But this leads to an interesting question: how exactly do we ask for a past revision of a resource? Technically, the revision identifier (section 28.3.1) is stored as a field on the resource itself; so should we rely on the standard list method with a special filter? While that technically would work, it certainly is quite cumbersome and feels a little odd to use the standard list method to retrieve a single resource (and not for its main purpose of browsing through resources). Luckily, there's a much better way to go about this, involving two pieces.

First, since retrieving single items is definitively the responsibility of the standard get method, this mechanism should certainly rely on extending that method to support this new revision-oriented use case. Second, it follows that we'll need a clear and simple way of providing the revision identifier in the request to the method. To do this, we can rely on a new special separator character to divide the entire resource identifier into two pieces: the resource ID and the revision ID. For this purpose, we'll rely on the "@" symbol as the divider, leading to complete resource revision identifiers such as /chatRooms/1/messages/2@1234 to represent revision 1234 of the given Message resource.

The benefit of using this special dividing character is pretty wonderful: the standard get method does not need to change at all. Since we're just sending a slightly more detailed identifier, we can rely on the same id field in the standard get request and allow the API service to interpret it as a resource at a given revision.

This does lead to an interesting question: when the resource responds with a specific revision, what should go in that resource's ID field? In other words, if we request a resource at revision 1234, would the ID match what was provided in the request exactly (e.g., rcsources/abcd@1234) or should we fall back to just the resource identifier alone (e.g., resources/abcd) and put the revision into the revisionId field?

The answer is pretty simple: the resource returned should have an identifier equivalent to exactly what was asked for (and the revisionId field should always be populated with the identifier of the revision returned) because it's important that we can easily assert we were given exactly what we asked for.

Listing 28.4   The invariant of you get what you ask for

```
assert(GetResource({ id: id }).id === id);
```
⮜ **Retrieving something by its ID should always return a result with that same ID.**

This means that when we ask for a resource without specifying the revision ID, the id field of the resource returned would have only the resource ID (with no "@" symbol and no revision ID), but the `revisionId` field should still be populated. If we then made a request for that same resource revision (based on `revisionId` field), the result would have the same data, but the `id` field would include the revision ID as well.

Listing 28.5   **Client-side interaction showing different identifiers for retrieved resources**

The revisionId field is always populated with the correct value.

```
> GetMessage({ id: 'chatRooms/1/messages/2' });
{ id: 'chatRooms/1/messages/2',
  // ...,
  revisionId: 'abcd' }

> GetMessage({ id: 'chatRooms/1/messages/2@abcde' });
{ id: 'chatRooms/1/messages/2@abcd',
  // ...,
  revisionId: 'abcd' }
```

When we request a resource with no revision ID, the result has an identical ID (without a revision ID).

When we request the same resource but also provide a revision ID, the revision is included in the result's ID.

Now that we've looked at how to retrieve a single resource revision, let's look at how to browse through all revisions, similarly to how we might browse through all resources of a given type.

28.3.4 *Listing revisions*

Luckily for us, we have quite a bit of experience with listing resources based on our exploration of the standard list method (see section 7.3.4). In this case, however, we're listing revisions that are tied to a single resource rather than child resources of a different parent. In other words, while we can draw on most of the same principles for this functionality, we can't simply copy and paste the standard list method and make it work for resource revisions.

What do we have to change about the standard list method? For starters, rather than using a HTTP `GET` method on a collection of resources, we'll rely on something that looks much more like a custom method, mapping to `GET /resources/*:list-Revisions`. Further, since the target isn't a parent itself but instead the actual resource on which the revisions are kept, we'll use a field called `id` rather than a field called `parent`. Other than that, the method should work in all the same ways, even supporting pagination, as we saw in chapter 21.

Listing 28.6   **API definition for listing resource revisions**

```
abstract class ChatRoomApi {
  @get("/{id=chatRooms/*/messages/*}:listRevisions")
  ListMessageRevisions(req: ListMessageRevisionsRequest):
    ListMessageRevisionsResponse;
}

interface ListMessageRevisionsRequest {
  id: string;
  maxPageSize: number;
```

```
    pageToken: number;
}

interface ListMessageRevisionsResponse {
  results: Message[];
  nextPageToken: string;
}
```

This custom list revisions method also supports pagination like any other list method.

Note that the response includes the resources themselves with varying revision identifiers.

This custom list revisions method gives us the ability to browse through the history of a given resource's previous revisions, relying on many of the same principles as the standard list method. Now that we've got a good grasp on creating, retrieving, and browsing revisions, let's try doing something more interactive with these revisions: rolling back to previous ones.

28.3.5 *Restoring a previous revision*

While having a historical record of the changes made to a resource over time is a useful feature, one of the most valuable bits of functionality we can provide based on revision history is the ability to restore a resource to the way it looked at some point in the past. To do this, we'll rely on a custom restore revision method, which has the responsibility of creating a *new* revision of a resource using a specific existing revision as the source of the resource's data. Since this new revision is the newest (and therefore has the most recent revisionCreateTime value), it becomes the current representation of the resource. In a way, it's sort of like going through a file for an old version of a document, making a photocopy of that document, and putting the new one at the top of the stack. In this case, the photocopy becomes the latest revision despite it being older data.

Listing 28.7   API definition for restoring resource revisions

```
abstract class ChatRoomApi {
  @post("/{id=chatRooms/*/messages/*}:restoreRevision")
  RestoreMessageRevision(req: RestoreMessageRevisionRequest): Message;
}

interface RestoreMessageRevisionRequest {
  id: string;
  revisionId: string;
}
```

To restore a previous revision, we use a custom method attached to the resource.

The restore revision request must also indicate the revision that should be restored.

It's important to remember that even though we're creating a new custom method, this functionality is currently available with the existing building blocks (it's just not atomic or nearly as convenient).

Listing 28.8   Client-side implementation of restoring a prior revision

```
function restoreMessageRevision(messageId: string, revisionId: string):
  Message {
```

```
const old = GetMessage({
  id: `${messageId}@${revisionId}`
});
UpdateMessage({
  resource: Object.assign(old, { id: messageId })
});
return CreateMessageRevision({ id: messageId });
}
```

We start by retrieving an older revision of the resource.

After that, we update the resource with the older data (ensuring that we target the message itself and not the old revision).

If a new revision isn't created automatically, we should explicitly create one and return the result.

Why not just allow users to implement this functionality themselves? As is the concern with many of these do-it-yourself API methods, we have to worry about concurrency, atomicity, and convenience. This function as implemented requires three full back-and-forth lines of communication, any of which might fail, be delayed, or be interrupted by other users interacting with the same resource. By providing the same functionality as a custom method, we give users an atomic way to perform this restoration to previous revisions.

The critical thing to remember about this method is that it does not remove or alter the history of the resource. It doesn't take an old revision and move it to the front of the line (e.g., by changing the creation timestamp to appear as the newest). Instead, it creates an entirely new revision, copied from an old one, and puts that duplicate at the top of the pile, though with a different revision identifier. This ensures that when we're browsing history, we can clearly see the progression of data changes over time and not get confused with revisions being moved into different positions.

There may come a time when we do need to rewrite history, as unfortunate as that may seem. In the next section, we'll explore how we can alter the historical record by removing revisions.

28.3.6 *Deleting revisions*

Unfortunately, we all make mistakes. And while resource revisions are powerful for letting us look back at the history of changes to a resource, they also make it so that our mistakes live on forever and simply cannot be forgotten. This might seem like a minor inconvenience, but imagine if we were to accidentally store some sensitive data (Social Security numbers, credit card numbers, health information) in a resource that supports revisioning. When we go to remove the offending data, it's never actually gone since it would presumably still be present in a previous revision. As you can guess, this can become a very big problem.

To address this, in many systems it will be critical to support a method by which we can delete revisions of resources. This method, like several others we've discussed, relies on the same principles as the standard delete method, removing a resource by its unique identifier, which in this case is the resource identifier combined with the revision identifier.

Listing 28.9 API for deleting a resource revision

```
abstract class ChatRoomApi {
  @delete("/{id=chatRooms/*/messages/*}:deleteRevision")      ◄──────┐
  DeleteMessageRevision(req: DeleteMessageRevisionRequest): void;     │
}                                                                     Just like the standard
                                                                     delete method, we
interface DeleteMessageRevisionRequest {                             map to the HTTP
  id: string;      ◄──┐                                              DELETE method.
}                      All we need to provide is the
                       full resource revision identifier
                       (including the resource identifier).
```

While this method looks quite simple and straightforward, there are a couple of questions worth exploring in more detail. A good place to start is why this method should exist at all.

OVERLOADING THE STANDARD DELETE METHOD

Didn't we just argue in section 28.3.3 that we can reuse the existing standard method to perform similar work if the only difference is the identifier? Why not just reuse the standard delete method and accept revision identifiers also?

The answer is pretty short: it's easy to mix these up. Since deleting data is something that can do quite a bit of damage, it's important to make the distinction between deleting a resource and deleting a single revision of a resource exceedingly obvious. If we don't separate these API methods from one another, a mistaken variable substitution could be the difference between removing a single revision of a resource and removing all revisions (and the resource itself). It's far safer to rely on a separate custom method rather than overloading the existing standard delete method.

DELETING THE CURRENT REVISION

What happens if a user wants to delete the current (most recent) revision of a resource? If we were to allow this, we'd effectively be providing a way to delete a revision and restore another revision in a single API method, as the next most recent revision would become the new "current" revision. While this is certainly a tempting proposition, it would expand the scope of the custom delete revision method beyond its original intent. If a client attempts to delete the most recent revision, the request should fail with a `412 Precondition Failed` HTTP error or equivalent. Luckily, this behavior also ensures that we don't have to deal with the scenario where a user is trying to delete the sole remaining (and therefore current) revision.

SOFT DELETION

Finally, we have to consider how we address the topic of soft deletion (chapter 25) with regard to revisions. Should revisions be able to be soft deleted? If so, should the revisions also be the same way? Revisions should generally not be considered eligible to be soft deleted. In fact, even if the resource itself can be soft-deleted, it's important that we have the ability to restore a previous revision, which may jump from a soft-deleted state to a non-deleted state! As a result, when we delete revisions, they should be hard deleted only and disappear from the system.

28.3.7 *Handling child resources*

Thus far, we've made a pretty big assumption: that resource revisions are snapshots of a single resource and its directly embedded data. But what if that resource is a parent to other resources? For example, what if we want to support resource revisions for ChatRoom resources? Should the child Message resources be kept together as part of the ChatRoom revision? Or should these resource revisions only store the data directly about a ChatRoom such as the title of the room?

This is a complicated topic. On the one hand, if we truly wanted to have a snapshot of a ChatRoom resource, it would certainly make more sense that restoring to a previous revision would revert to the messages as they existed when the revision was created. On the other hand, this would mean quite a bit more work, more storage space, and ultimately more complexity for users who want to restore only the data embedded directly.

Unfortunately, this is one of those scenarios where there is no one-size-fits-all solution. In general, keeping revisions focused on a single resource and not its entire child hierarchy is a perfectly fine solution. It also happens to be a much more straightforward proposition. In other more unique scenarios, it may be required to keep track of the child hierarchy alongside the resource itself.

In short, if required, it's perfectly acceptable to expand beyond the resource itself, but be certain that it's a firm business requirement and that other options (such as an export method, as seen in chapter 23) aren't available. If hierarchical-aware revisions can be avoided, then complexity alone should be enough reason to avoid them.

28.3.8 *Final API definition*

In listing 28.10, we can see an example of all the revision-specific API methods to handle revisions on individual Message resources.

Listing 28.10   Final API definition

```
abstract class ChatRoomApi {
  @get("/{id=chatRooms/*/messages/*}")
  GetMessage(req: GetMessageRequest): Message;

  @post("/{id=chatRooms/*/messages/*}:createRevision")
  CreateMessageRevision(req: CreateMessageRevisionRequest): Message;

  @post("/{id=chatRooms/*/messages/*}:restoreRevision")
  RestoreMessageRevision(req: RestoreMessageRevisionRequest): Message;

  @delete("/{id=chatRooms/*/messages/*}:deleteRevision")
  DeleteMessageRevision(req: DeleteMessageRevisionRequest): void;

  @get("/{id=chatRooms/*/messages/*}:listRevisions")
  ListMessageRevisions(req: ListMessageRevisionsRequest):
    ListMessageRevisionsResponse;
}
```

```
interface Message {
  id: string;
  content: string;
  // ... more fields here ...
  revisionId: string;
  revisionCreateTime: Date;
}

interface GetMessageRequest {
  id: string;
}

interface CreateMessageRevisionRequest {
  id: string;
}

interface RestoreMessageRevisionRequest {
  id: string;
  revisionId: string;
}

interface DeleteMessageRevisionRequest {
  id: string;
}

interface ListMessageRevisionsRequest {
  id: string;
  maxPageSize: number;
  pageToken: string;
}

interface ListMessageRevisionsResponse {
  results: Message[];
  nextPageToken: string;
}
```

28.4 Trade-offs

While resource revisions are incredibly powerful, they also lead to significantly more complexity, both for the API designer and API users. Further, they can lead to much larger storage space requirements due to the extra data that's tracked as resources are modified over time and revisions are created. In particular, even if resource revisioning is a critical piece of functionality for an API, hierarchy-aware revisions (where a single revision encompasses both a resource and all its child resources) are even more complex and come with even more extreme storage requirements.

As a result, if resource revisioning can be avoided in an API, it certainly should be. That said, sometimes revisions are the best fit for the job (e.g., if an API is tracking legal documents) and we need to store the history of the resource forever. In cases like these, resource revisioning provides a safe and straightforward way to support this functionality for API users.

28.5 *Exercises*

1 What types of scenarios are a better fit for creating revisions implicitly? What about explicitly?

2 Why should revisions use random identifiers rather than incrementing numbers or timestamps?

3 Why does restoration create a new revision? Why not reference a previous one?

4 What should happen if you attempt to restore a resource to a previous revision but the resource is already equivalent to that previous revision?

5 Why do we use custom method notation for listing and deleting resources rather than the standard methods?

Summary

- Resource revisions act as snapshots of resources taken as they change over time.
- Revisions should use random identifiers like any other resource even though it might seem to make sense to rely on something like an incrementing number or timestamp as an identifier.
- Revisions can be created both implicitly (e.g., whenever a resource is modified) or explicitly (e.g., on request by a user).
- Retrieving resources at specific revisions can be done by using an "@" character to indicate the revision (e.g., GET /chatRooms/1234@5678). However, both listing and deleting revisions should be done using a custom method attached to the resource in question.
- Resources may be restored to a previous revision's state using a custom method that creates a new revision equal to the previous one and marks it as the active revision.

Request retrial

This chapter covers

- How to decide which failed API requests are safe to retry
- Advanced exponential back-off strategies for retry timing
- How to avoid stampeding herds
- Ways APIs can dictate retry timing for clients

When errors occur in web APIs, some of them are due to client mistakes, while others are due to issues outside the client's control. Often the best solution to this second group of errors is to retry the same request at a later time in hopes of a different result. In this pattern, we'll explore a mechanism by which clients can have clear direction in both how and when they retry requests that have previously failed due to errors on the API server.

29.1 Motivation

It's an inevitable fact of web APIs that some requests will fail—hopefully not the majority, but some nonetheless. Many of these failed requests will be due to client-side errors such as invalid request messages, while others might be due to failed preconditions and constraints being enforced on the API server. All of these types of errors share an important attribute: the problem is with the request itself violating some constraints or going against the API's business logic. Put differently, if we replayed the same invalid request again, we should get the same error response. After all, the business logic typically doesn't change from one moment to another.

An entire other category of errors is quite different. Sometimes a request leads to an error response that is completely transient. This type of error has absolutely nothing to do with the request itself and is instead the result of some problem internal to the API. Perhaps the API server is overloaded and wasn't able to handle the incoming request, or maybe the system or a necessary subcomponent was undergoing scheduled downtime and was not available when processing the request. Regardless of the problem, there's a clear and obvious way to address the issue: retry the request.

The point is that the error response wasn't really caused by the specific request made. On the contrary, the response was due to things that were at best tangentially related to the request and far more likely to have nothing to do with the request. This means that if we were to simply try the same request again at some point in the future, there's a good chance that the retrial will succeed (or, at the very least, result in a different error).

The big question then becomes how exactly we can determine the difference between a request that should be retried and one that shouldn't. In general, HTTP errors are numbered to communicate what went wrong, with certain errors more likely to be retriable than others. For example, 400-level errors (e.g., 400 Bad Request, 403 Forbidden, 404 Not Found, etc.) are likely problems with a particular request, whereas 500-level errors (e.g., 500 Internal Server Error or 503 Service Unavailable) are more likely to represent problems with internal services. Of these two categories, the 500-level errors are more likely to be retriable, but that's more of a guideline than an actual rule, so this certainly needs some more discussion. Further, while these error codes might hint at whether a request can be retried, they don't really say much about when a client should retry a failed request, leaving the client guessing at how long to wait before trying the same request again.

In this pattern, we'll explore how API services can define a retry policy for both determining which requests are eligible to be retried as well as the timing algorithm to determine how long to wait before retrying. We'll also cover how the API service might inform a client of exactly when to retry in the case that the service is aware of some additional information.

29.2   *Overview*

The goal of this pattern is simple: respond to as many requests as possible while retrying as few as possible. To accomplish this, we need to address two issues. First, we must provide the clients with an algorithm to follow in order to minimize the number of requests being retried across the system. Second, if the API service knows something the client does not, and this information would lead to a specific time at which a request could be retried successfully, the service should have a mechanism to provide the client with an explicit instruction of when to retry a request. Let's start by looking at the algorithm for determining the timing delay between retrying requests.

29.2.1 *Client-side retry timing*

When we run into a failure that's retriable, we should almost certainly try to send the same request again in the hopes that the service has become available. But should we do so right away? Or should we wait a bit? If we should wait, then how long should we wait?

It turns out that this is a very old problem, going back to the beginning of the internet when we needed an algorithm to know when we should retry sending TCP packets over a potentially congested network. It's particularly tricky because we have no idea what's happening once the request is sent, leaving us to simply make guesses about when the request is more likely to be handled successfully on the other side. Based on these constraints, the most effective, battle-tested algorithm for this problem is *exponential back-off.*

The idea of exponential back-off is pretty simple. For a first retry attempt, we might wait one second before making the request again. After that, for every subsequent failure response we take the time that we waited previously and double it. If a request fails a second time, we wait two seconds and then try again. If that request fails, we wait four seconds and try once more. This would continue doubling (8, 16, 32 seconds) until the end of time or until we decide to give up. We'll introduce some extra pieces to this algorithm, but the core concept will remain unchanged.

As we noted, this algorithm is great when the system on the other side is a complete black box. In other words, if we know nothing else about the system, exponential back-off works quite well. But is that the case with our web API? In truth, this is not the case and, as we'll see in the next section, there is actually a better solution for a unique subset of scenarios.

29.2.2 *Server-specified retry timing*

While exponential back-off is still a reasonable algorithm, it turns out that there are certain cases in which there is a better option available. For example, consider the scenario where a request fails because the API service says that this request can only be executed once per minute. In this case, the server actually knows exactly how long to wait before retrying the request (in this case, about 60 seconds).

In general, whenever the server can provide some authoritative guidance about when a request should be retried, this information should be communicated back to the client. After all, even a partly informed guess is better than a blind guess. And while these types of scenarios are not common, they are certainly not rare enough to disregard entirely.

We'll rely on a parameter designed specifically to address this scenario. This parameter, when present, instructs the client to disregard the exponential back-off algorithm they would typically use and instead retry the request based exclusively on the value provided to determine when to retry. By doing so, we can override the blind guessing for some slightly more informed guessing in most cases and absolute certainty in the rare case.

29.3 *Implementation*

As we learned in the previous section, this pattern will rely on exponential back-off for most cases and a special field for other cases where the server can instruct the client exactly how long to wait before retrying requests. However, before we get into the details of these topics, there's a bit of an elephant in the room to discuss. How do we determine whether a given request should be retried at all?

29.3.1 *Retry eligibility*

It might be tempting to assume that all errors are eligible to be retried, but unfortunately that's a dangerous assumption. The biggest concern is that this might lead to some unintended consequences such as duplicating results (e.g., creating the same resource twice). How do we know what types of requests can be retried and which cannot?

In general, there are three categories of error responses: those that definitely cannot be retried, those that might be able to be retried but should be looked at carefully, and those that can probably be retried without any issues. In addition, the ability to retry also depends on the API method itself, particularly whether it is idempotent and safe. In this section, we'll look at these categories and summarize the HTTP error codes that fall into each one.

GENERALLY RETRIABLE

Unfortunately, the list of error codes that is considered probably retriable is relatively short, summarized in table 29.1.

Table 29.1   Sample of response codes that are generally retriable

Code	Name	Description
408	Request Timeout	The client didn't produce a request fast enough.
421	Misdirected Request	The request was sent to a server that couldn't handle it.
425	Too Early	The server doesn't want to try handling a request that might be replayed.
429	Too Many Requests	The client has sent too many requests in a given period of time.
503	Service Unavailable	The server cannot handle the request because it's overloaded.

In the case of codes 408, 421, 425, 429, and 503, the server never actually even began addressing these requests. The conclusion we can draw is that it's almost certainly acceptable to retry requests that receive these error responses.

DEFINITELY NOT RETRIABLE

In general, if a server receives and processes a request but determines that the request was invalid in some fundamental way, it's usually not retriable. For example, if we try to retrieve a resource and get a `403 Forbidden` error, retrying the request won't lead to a different result unless something else changes in the API (such as permissions being adjusted). These types of errors (a few of them are shown in table 29.2) are pretty easy to spot as they are errors about the requests themselves or server errors stating violations of intrinsic rules.

Table 29.2 Sample of response codes that are definitely not retriable

Code	Name	Description
403	Forbidden	The request was fine, but the server is refusing to handle it.
405	Method Not Allowed	The method specified is not allowed.
412	Precondition Failed	The server does not meet the conditions of the request.
501	Not Implemented	The server cannot recognize or handle the request.

In general, all of these response codes indicate something permanent about the situation such that retrying the request in the future will not lead to a different response. (Obviously this assumes that nothing else changes in the system.)

MAYBE RETRIABLE

The trickiest category is the set of error codes where retrying the request may be acceptable, but it will depend on some more details about the request and the API method. For example, a `504 Gateway Timeout` error indicates that the API request was passed off to a downstream server and that server never replied. As a result, we don't know for sure whether the downstream server actually received and began working on the request. Based on this uncertainty, we can only retry the request if we're certain a repeated attempt wouldn't cause any problems. A sample of requests that fall in this category is shown in table 29.3.

Table 29.3 Sample of response codes that might be retriable

Code	Name	Description
500	Internal Server Error	An unexpected failure occurred on the server.
502	Bad Gateway	The request was passed to a downstream server that sent an invalid response.
504	Gateway Timeout	The request was passed to a downstream server that never replied.

As always, the best mechanism for ensuring that we can indeed retry requests is to rely on the request identifiers as a way to allow the server to deduplicate requests and avoid unwanted behavior, as discussed in chapter 26.

Now that we have an idea of the various requests and whether they're retriable (and in what circumstances), let's switch topics and start looking at the cases where we've decided it's acceptable to retry a request. In particular, let's look at the way we'll decide on how long to wait before retrying a request.

29.3.2 *Exponential back-off*

As we learned earlier, exponential back-off is an algorithm by which the delay between requests grows exponentially, doubling each time a request returns an error result. Perhaps the best way to understand this would be by looking at some code.

Listing 29.1   Example demonstrating retrial with exponential back-off

```
async function getChatRoomWithRetries(id: string): Promise<ChatRoom> {
  return new Promise<ChatRoom>(async (resolve, reject) => {
    let delayMs = 1000;                          ← We define the initial delay as
    while (true) {                                 1 second (1,000 milliseconds)
      try {
        return resolve(GetChatRoom({ id }));     ← First, attempt to retrieve the
      } catch (e) {                                resource and resolve the promise.
        await new Promise((resolve) => {         ←
          return setTimeout(resolve, delayMs);     If the request fails, wait
        });                                        for a fixed amount of time,
        delayMs *= 2;       ← Finally, double the  defined by the delay.
      }                        amount of time
    }                          we'll need to wait
  });                          next time.
}
```

While this implementation is a good starting point, it could use a few improvements. Let's start by looking at some maximums.

MAXIMUM DELAYS AND RETRIES

As we noted earlier, exponential back-off generally will continue retrying a request until the end of time or the request succeeds. And even though we might admire the algorithm's persistence, this is generally not a good strategy, as it means that there are no bounds on how long it might take a request to finish.

To address this, we can add in some limits. First, we can add a limit to the number of retries we want to attempt. Then we can add a limit to the maximum amount of time to wait between requests being retried.

Listing 29.2   Adding support for maximum delays and retry counts

```
async function getChatRoomWithRetries(
    id: string, maxDelayMs = 32000, maxRetries = 10): Promise<ChatRoom> {
  return new Promise<ChatRoom>(async (resolve, reject) => {
    let retryCount = 0;              ← We track the number of retries
    let delayMs = 1000;               (loop iterations) by incrementing
    while (true) {                    the value and rejecting if we go
      try {                           past the maximum allowed.
        return resolve(GetChatRoom({ id }));
```

We track the
number of retries
(loop iterations) by
incrementing the
value and rejecting
if we go past the
maximum allowed.

```
      } catch (e) {
        if (retryCount++ > maxRetries) return reject(e);
        await new Promise((resolve) => {
          return setTimeout(resolve, delayMs);
        });
        delayMs *= 2;
        if (delayMs > maxDelayMs) delayMs = maxDelayMs;
      }
    }
  });
}
```

If the new delay time
is longer than the
maximum, we
change it to the
maximum.

With these new limits, we have a way to ensure the function will eventually fail, effectively saying, "We tried and tried but couldn't get a successful response." Now that this is covered, there's one other topic to address: stampeding herds.

STAMPEDING HERDS

A *stampeding herd* does not refer to literal animals running across the plains. In technology, a stampeding herd refers to a case where a bunch of remote clients all make the same request at the same time, overloading the system on the receiving end. In short, the system might be able to handle each of the requests individually, but certainly not all at the same time as the massive concurrency overwhelms the system. But what does this have to do with exponential back-off?

To understand the connection, let's consider the case where we might have 100 different clients all sending a request at the same time—a stampeding herd, so to speak. When each of these clients sees that their request has returned an error, they'll immediately begin retrying in the hope that a subsequent request will be successful. The problem, however, is that they'll all do so according to the same exponential back-off algorithm. The result is that each of these 100 requests will continue to arrive at the server at the same time, just with larger gaps in between each stampede. In other words, because the clients happened to land in a situation where they're accidentally synchronized, the requests keep getting in the way of each other to the point where none of them succeed. In a sense, the deterministic nature of the algorithm leads to its downfall.

What can we do about this? A simple solution is to introduce something that differs from one client to another rather than perfectly following the exponential back-off algorithm. To do this, we'll rely on the concept of *random jitter* in the delay timing between requests. In other words, all we have to do is add some random amount of time to wait in addition to the time delays dictated by the exponential back-off algorithm.

Listing 29.3 Adding jitter to avoid stampeding herds of requests

```
async function getChatRoomWithRetries(
    id: string, maxDelayMs = 32000, maxRetries = 10): Promise<ChatRoom> {
  return new Promise<ChatRoom>(async (resolve, reject) => {
    let retryCount = 0;
    let delayMs = 1000;
    while (true) {
```

```
        try {
          return resolve(GetChatRoom({ id }));
        } catch (e) {
          if (retryCount++ > maxRetries) return reject(e);
          await new Promise((resolve) => {
            return setTimeout(resolve,
              delayMs + (Math.random() * 1000));     ◁──┐ Add up to 1,000
          });                                             milliseconds of jitter to
          delayMs *= 2;                                   avoid stampeding herds.
          if (delayMs > maxDelayMs) delayMs = maxDelayMs;
        }
      }
    });
}
```

Note that the random jitter introduced here is not additive. In other words, it's not included in the delay that is continually doubled by the back-off algorithm.

Now that we have an idea of how the exponential back-off algorithm works in depth, let's switch gears and consider the scenario where an API server might know how long a client should wait.

29.3.3 *Retry After*

Exponential back-off (with the enhancements in section 29.3.1) is a great option for determining when to retry a given request, but our preference for this algorithm is generally predicated on the assumption that we have basically no additional information that could help us do anything smarter. In some cases, however, we know this isn't the case. The most common example of this is an error due to rate limiting, where the client is sending requests too frequently and we are in control of when the next request is allowed. In other words, since the API server knows exactly when this service-imposed limit will be reset, it also is in a unique position where it can say exactly when a request should be retried such that it will no longer violate the rate-limit rules.

What's the best way to instruct a client that they should skip the exponential back-off routine and instead just do as instructed? It turns out that there is an Internet Engineering Task Force (IETF) standard for just this topic, in the semantics and content specification of HTTP: RFC-7231 (https://tools.ietf.org/html/rfc7231). This RFC specifies a "Retry-After" HTTP header (section 7.1.3), which indicates how long a client "ought to wait before making a follow-up request." In short, this HTTP header is the perfect place for an API server to send more specific instructions about when a request should be retried.

This leads to the next question: how do we format our delay instructions in this HTTP header?

FORMAT

The specification explicitly states the Retry-After header can contain either a date value (e.g., Fri, 31 Dec 1999 23:59:59 GMT) or a duration of seconds to delay before making the retry (e.g., 120). Despite the fact that the specification (and most modern

HTTP servers) will support both formats, it's almost always a better choice to rely on the duration rather than a timestamp.

The reason for this is time is a tricky thing. If we rely on a duration, it is generated by the server and then sent over the network back to the client. This means that the total duration that a client will end up waiting is slightly longer than the duration specified. For example, if a server puts a value of 120 in the Retry-After header, and it takes 100 milliseconds for the response to travel from the server back to the client, then the client will actually end up delaying for 120.1 seconds in total.

Compare this to the much scarier scenario involving *clock synchronization*. If the server informs the client about a specific time after which it should retry the request, this assumes that the server and the client both agree on the current time . Not only does that suffer from the same types of transit delays that are present in the duration format (120), it could lead to far larger differences in time if the client's clock happens to be out of sync with the server's clock. For example, if the server thinks it's noon and the client thinks it's 1:00 p.m., when the server says "Don't retry until 1:00 p.m.," the client would actually retry immediately rather than the 60-minute delay intended by the server.

While all of this might seem a bit far-fetched, clocks have been the downfall of many systems over the years. With leap seconds, time zone complexity, and clock synchronization problems, it's rarely a good idea to assume that two systems have clocks that agree with one another (and even worse to depend on this fact for proper behavior). The safest bet is to always rely on durations rather than a specific time value, if possible.

Now that we've clarified what value should go in the Retry-After header, we can see just how easily we're able to implement support for this.

> **Listing 29.4 Adding support for dictated retry delay durations**

```
async function getChatRoomWithRetries(
    id: string, maxDelayMs = 32000, maxRetries = 10): Promise<ChatRoom> {
  return new Promise<ChatRoom>(async (resolve, reject) => {
    let retryCount = 0;
    let delayMs = 1000;
    while (true) {
      try {
        return resolve(GetChatRoom({ id }));
      } catch (e) {
        if (retryCount++ > maxRetries) return reject(e);
        await new Promise((resolve) => {
          let actualDelayMs;
          if ('Retry-After' in e.response.headers) {      // If the Retry-After value is provided, we use that as a delay duration.
            actualDelayMs = Number(
              e.response.headers['Retry-After']) * 1000;
          } else {
            actualDelayMs = delayMs + (Math.random() * 1000);   // Otherwise, we fall back to the standard exponential back-off algorithm.
          }
          return setTimeout(resolve, actualDelayMs);
        });
```

```
            delayMs *= 2;
            if (delayMs > maxDelayMs) delayMs = maxDelayMs;
        }
    }
  });
}
```

29.3.4   *Final API definition*

Putting everything together, listing 29.5 shows an example demonstrating how clients should ideally retrieve a resource, including retries with exponential back-off and rate-limit awareness.

Listing 29.5   Final API definition

```
async function getChatRoomWithRetries(
    id: string, maxDelayMs = 32000, maxRetries = 10): Promise<ChatRoom> {
  return new Promise<ChatRoom>(async (resolve, reject) => {
    let retryCount = 0;
    let delayMs = 1000;
    while (true) {
      try {
        return resolve(GetChatRoom({ id }));
      } catch (e) {
        if (retryCount++ > maxRetries) return reject(e);
        await new Promise((resolve) => {
          let actualDelayMs;
          if ('Retry-After' in e.response.headers) {
            actualDelayMs = Number(
              e.response.headers['Retry-After']) * 1000;
          } else {
            actualDelayMs = delayMs + (Math.random() * 1000);
          }
          return setTimeout(resolve, actualDelayMs);
        });
        delayMs *= 2;
        if (delayMs > maxDelayMs) delayMs = maxDelayMs;
      }
    }
  });
}
```

29.4   *Trade-offs*

The unfortunate thing about this design pattern is that it relies on clients doing as instructed. This might be following instructions to use exponential back-off or to retry after an exact amount of time, but the point remains that the decision is ultimately left to the client, over whom we have no control.

The upside about this pattern is that there really isn't anything we give up by relying on it. Exponential back-off is a common standard that has been used for many years, with great success across the world. And we only ever dictate a specific retry time when the server has some special information and can therefore lead to fewer retry requests if the instructions are followed. In other words, this pattern is generally without drawbacks.

29.5 Exercises

1   Why isn't there a simple rule for deciding which failed requests can safely be retried?

2   What is the underlying reason for relying on exponential back-off? What is the purpose for the random jitter between retries?

3   When does it make sense to use the Retry-After header?

Summary

- Errors that are in some way transient or time related (e.g., HTTP `429 Too Many Requests`) are likely to be retriable, whereas those that are related to some permanent state (e.g., HTTP `403 Forbidden`) are mostly unsafe to retry.

- Whenever code automatically retries requests, it should rely on some form of exponential back-off with limits on the number of retries and the delay between requests. Ideally it should also introduce some jitter to avoid the stampeding herd problem where all requests are retried according to the same rules and therefore always arrive at the same time.

- If the API service knows something about when a request is likely to be successful if retried, it should indicate this using a Retry-After HTTP header.

Request authentication

30

This chapter covers

- Requirements of a request authentication system
- Overview of digital signatures
- Credential generation, registration, and signing
- Fingerprinting HTTP requests
- Communicating the details of a signature
- Verifying signatures and authenticating HTTP requests

In this pattern, we'll explore how and why to use public-private key exchange and digital signatures (https://en.wikipedia.org/wiki/Digital_signature) to authenticate all incoming API requests. This ensures that all inbound requests have guaranteed integrity and origin authenticity and that they cannot be later repudiated by the sender. While alternatives (e.g., shared secrets and HMAC; https://en.wikipedia.org/wiki/HMAC) are acceptable in the majority of cases, these fail when it comes to introducing third parties where nonrepudiation is required.

30.1 Motivation

So far, we've simply assumed that all API requests are guaranteed to be authentic, leaving security to be dealt with later on. As you might guess, now is the time where we need to explore a fundamental question: given an inbound API request, how can we determine that it came from an actual authorized user?

Ultimately the decision to honor a given request comes down to a yes or no answer, but there are several different requirements we need to consider to make this binary decision. First, we need to know whether a request originated from the same user as it claims. In other words, if the request states it was sent by user 1234, we need to be able to tell for sure that it did indeed come from user 1234 (for our definition of what it means to be user 1234). Next, we need to be sure that the request content hasn't been corrupted or tampered with. Finally, it may become important down the line that a disinterested third party is able to verify, with no doubt, that a request undeniably came from a specific user. In other words, if we find a request claiming to have been sent from user 1234 (and this is verifiable), user 1234 must not be able to later claim that the request was actually forged by someone else. Let's take a moment to explore each of these aspects in more detail, starting with the origin of a request.

30.1.1 Origin

The first and most important ability we need is establishing where a request originated. In this case, we're not concerned with a geographical origin but with the user who sent the request, leading us to the concept of identity.

Unlike the concept of identity in the real world, we're not interested in drivers' licenses or birth certificates. Instead, all we actually care about is that if a request claims to come from user 1234, then that request also has some sort of proof that can only be supplied by the same party that registered with our service as user 1234. There are many ways to accomplish this, which we'll discuss in section 30.2, but for now let's move on to discussing what we mean by integrity.

30.1.2 Integrity

Integrity refers to the certainty that the content of a request as received is exactly as it was when sent, and it's a critical piece of the API security puzzle. Without it, even though we can be sure of the origin of a request (e.g., that a request claiming to be from user 1234 has the credentials for user 1234), we can't be certain that the content of the request was never tampered with after it was sent. And if we can't be sure that the request is the same as it was when sent, it's not really all that useful to know where it came from.

While uncommon, requests can certainly be altered in transit. This might range from an unintentional mistake (e.g., some networking infrastructure is faulty and messed with the data) all the way to the malicious (e.g., someone intercepted the request and deliberately tampered with it), but the point remains: it's critical that we're able to ascertain whether a request's content has been modified in any way after it was sent and reject any requests that have been modified in transit.

Additionally, even though we can often rely on network-layer security (e.g., TLS), doing so means taking incoming requests at face value rather than verifying the request itself, and assuming that the request was transported in the correct way. And while it would be lovely if we could assume that everyone always does the right thing with network security, it turns out that our other requirements lead to this aspect coming along for free.

30.1.3   *Nonrepudiation*

Nonrepudiation refers to the idea that once we've verified the origin of a request, that origin can't then deny that they were the origin. At this point, you might be thinking, "But why is this even an issue? If we can verify the origin, then this requirement is implied already!" It turns out that this is almost right, but there's a bit more to it.

The real concern is that it's very easy to design a credential system that is symmetrical, where the credentials needed to prove that you are user 1234 are the same ones needed to verify that a request came from user 1234, sort of like a shared secret between the two parties. This idea of a symmetric credential would not have been an issue until now because of the key assumption that API requests should never originate from an API server. But what happens when someone else (not user 1234 and not the API server) needs to verify that user 1234 was the true origin of the request? How can this third party tell the difference between a request with a true origin of user 1234 and one forged by an API server misusing its shared credential that was only intended to be used for verifying user 1234?

This requirement pretty plainly dictates that the mechanism by which a user proves that they are the true origin of a request must not also be shared with an API server. In other words, the credentials used to prove and verify the origin of an API request must be asymmetrical, with different credentials for each party. By doing this, we ensure the user is the only party with access to the credential, and a third party looking at a request from the user can be sure it originated with that user and was not forged by the API server.

30.2   *Overview*

While there are many design contenders, one option stands out: digital signatures. We'll dive into the details about how digital signatures work in the next section, but it's important to cover the basics of what they are and why they're a good fit given these requirements.

Fundamentally, a digital signature is nothing more than a chunk of bytes. That said, these bytes represent a value that, beyond a reasonable doubt, can only be generated and verified using a special pair of credentials. This means that a signature generated with one credential is effectively impossible to recreate without possessing that credential.

However, the most important distinguishing property of these cryptographic digital signatures has to do with the asymmetry of the credentials. This asymmetry means that the credential used for generating the signature is not the same as the one used for verifying it. In other words, each credential in the pair has a single role: one is used to generate a signature and the other is used to verify the signature.

When it comes to authenticating API requests, digital signatures happen to fit the requirements quite nicely. First, their cryptographic nature means that it's inherently simple to prove that the signature was generated by someone possessing the correct credentials. Next, the fact that the signature is dependent on the message being signed means that a signature is invalid if the message was changed in any way whatsoever. Finally, because there is one and only one party capable of generating digital signatures, there is no way that party can later claim that a signature has been forged. In other words, this mechanism meets all three of the key criteria listed in section 30.1.

But how exactly do these signatures work? And how can we integrate them into a web API? The process of using digital signatures for request authentication involves three distinct stages. First, the user creates a public-private keypair. Next, we allow users to register with the API service, establishing an identity with the system based on the public half of the pair. From that point on, the user can simply digitally sign all requests with their private key and the API server can verify those signatures using the previously associated public key.

If this sounds a bit simplistic, don't worry; in the next section, we'll cover these concepts in much more detail.

30.3 Implementation

As we learned in section 30.2, using digital signatures for request authentication is a multistage process on the part of both the user and the API server. We'll begin our journey at the foundation of this entire system: generating the proper asymmetric credentials.

30.3.1 Credential generation

Before a user can do anything, they first need to generate a keypair. This keypair is a special type of credential that consists of two pieces: a private key and a public key. It's critical that the private key be kept absolutely secret because, as we learned earlier, possession of the correct credential is the definition of identity. In other words, possessing the right credential is proof enough and there's no photo on the credential to compare with the person presenting it as a secondary check.

But why does the user have to be responsible for generating this pair of credentials? Why can't the server generate them and then simply give the user the private key for use later on? As we learned with the requirement of nonrepudiation, the entire point of having an asymmetric pair of credentials (rather than a shared secret) is to prevent the user from denying that they signed a request. This works because the credential used to sign requests is only ever in the hands of the user and isn't shared with the API server. In this case, if we allow the API server to generate the credential, we have nothing but their guarantee that they haven't kept a copy of that key for themselves. Further, we have to worry about the private key being transmitted over the internet, which runs the (small, but real) risk of being intercepted. As a result, if we truly want to meet the requirement for nonrepudiation, the private key can never leave the hands of the user.

How can we generate this key? There are many tools out there, such as ssh-keygen on most Linux systems, but the following TypeScript code shows how you can do so programmatically.

Listing 30.1   Generating a set of credentials

```
const crypto = require('crypto');

interface KeyPair {
  publicKey: string;
  privateKey: string;
}

function generateCredentials(size = 2048): Promise<KeyPair> {
  return new Promise<KeyPair>( (resolve, reject) => {
    crypto.generateKeyPair('rsa', { modulusLength: size },
      (err, pub, priv) => {
      if (err) { return reject(err); }        ⟵  If any errors arise, simply
      return resolve({                            reject the promise.
        publicKey: pub.export({ type: 'pkcs1', format: 'pem' }),   ⟵
        privateKey: priv.export({ type: 'pkcs1', format: 'pem' })
      });                              Use the string serialized
    });                                data for the public and
  });                                    private key values.
}
```

After clients execute code like this, they'll be left with a public key that serializes to a string we can share with others. Now we need to somehow transfer this public key over to the API server in a way that we can establish our identity.

30.3.2   *Registration and credential exchange*

As we learned in section 30.1.1, identity is an important concept in general, but when it comes to request authentication, the specific interpretation of this concept is a bit different from what we've come to expect in our day-to-day lives. In particular, there is simply nothing absolute about identifying a user. In other words, the API server is never going to verify something intrinsic about a user (e.g., their fingerprints), but instead defines an identity as anyone holding the credential that established that identity. Put simply, proving you possess a secret assigned to an identity is enough to prove that you are that identity.

This makes the idea of registration simpler. In this case, we can allow a new user to register with the API by providing the public key credential, and we will generate a unique identifier for this user. This sequence of events is shown in figure 30.1.

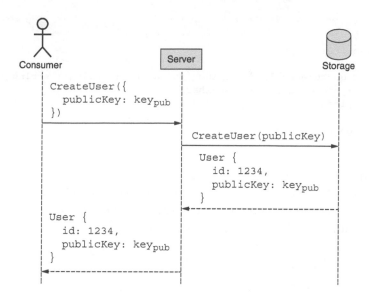

Figure 30.1 Sequence of registering an account with a public key

Using this simple, atomic standard create method, we've made a single API call and now have a unique identifier to use in future requests (e.g., user 1234), and the public key credential can be used to verify signatures before accepting requests. Note that this also avoids the requirement to authenticate with the service using a more traditional method such as a username and password. Instead, this scheme relies entirely on digital signatures from the very beginning.

Now that we've covered how to generate credentials and safely share them with the API server to establish a shared understanding of identity, how exactly do we use these keys?

30.3.3 *Generating and verifying raw signatures*

Without going into too much detail on cryptography or number theory, the important thing to remember about a digital signature is that it's a special number that can be easily computed using a private key but is almost impossible to compute without that key. Similarly, this special number can be quickly and easily verified using a public key, but that same public key can't be used to generate the same signature value. In a way it's a bit like a secure glass box: only the person with the key can put something inside, but once they have anyone can see the item and know that it was placed there only by someone possessing the key.

To calculate a signature, we combine the request body along with the private key, and we can rely on standard libraries such as Node.js's `crypto` package to handle the actual hard mathematical work of generating the signature.

Listing 30.2   Signing an arbitrary string

```
const crypto = require('crypto');

function generateSignature(payload: string, privateKey: string): string {
  const signer = crypto.createSign('rsa-sha256');
  signer.update(payload);
  signer.end();
  return signer.sign(privateKey);
}
```

Verifying a signature is equally straightforward. We take the signature, the payload that we expect to have been signed, and the corresponding public key and combine these three using standard library functions. The result of the function will be a simple Boolean value stating whether the signature checks out.

Listing 30.3   Verifying an arbitrary signature

```
const crypto = require('crypto');

function verifySignature(
    payload: string, signature: string, publicKey: string): Boolean {
  const verifier = crypto.createVerify('rsa-sha256');
  verifier.update(payload);
  verifier.end();
  return verifier.verify(publicKey, signature);
}
```

One thing that might seem surprising about both of these examples is the fact that the payload parameter is a string rather than, say, an object or some other representation of an API request. But this actually brings us to an important question: what exactly should we be signing?

It turns out that this question is a lot more complicated than it sounds. In the next section, we'll talk about how to determine what to put into the payload parameter when generating or verifying a digital signature.

30.3.4 *Request fingerprinting*

So far we've sort of waved our hands around and said we must sign the request but haven't really been all that specific about how this works. Let's take a moment to explore some of the aspects we need to consider when deciding what should be signed before sending the request to the API server.

As tempting as it might be to just sign the request body, it turns out that even this is a bit trickier than it seems because the request body requires us to serialize data (e.g., using JSON.stringify() in TypeScript), and there are actually lots of different ways to serialize things, even relying on the same serialization format. For example, there are a variety of character encodings and normalization forms, leading to many strings that might be semantically equivalent but still have different byte representations.

Further, with most formats, including JSON, there are typically no rules about the order in which properties appear in various map-like structures. For example, while {"a": 1, "b": 2} is semantically the same as {"b": 2, "a": 1}, the byte representations of these values are completely different.

Since calculating a digital signature operates on the raw, opaque bytes, this means that the low-level byte representation of the content is actually incredibly important. If, for instance, the party verifying a signature uses a different byte representation of the same semantic message, this would result in a failed signature when, in truth, the content hasn't actually changed. Instead, the byte representation is simply being computed differently.

To make things even more complicated, we have to remember that the API request may involve far more than just the request body. For example, when deleting a resource using HTTP as the transport mechanism, the HTTP request body is empty (and not something like {"id": "chatRooms/1"}). Instead, the intended action is encoded in the HTTP verb (DELETE) and the target to delete is represented in the URL (/chatRooms/1). Additionally, there may be other pieces of information in the HTTP headers that are important to the meaning and integrity of the request (e.g., the time at which the request was sent) and really should be included in calculating the signature. Each of these factors makes it all the more important that we have some way of computing a request fingerprint that can uniquely represent a given request and ultimately act as the payload when computing a digital signature with a private key.

But how do we define this fingerprint? To figure that out, we need to consider which pieces of the HTTP request need to be included in the signature. Luckily, the answer to this is pretty simple. First, we need to incorporate the HTTP method, URL (host and path), and request body. Additionally, if present, we should include an indication of the time at which the request was sent; most often this is present in a HTTP header called "Date," in order to support rejecting requests that might be too old (a summary of these fields is shown in table 30.1).

Table 30.1 Components necessary for fingerprinting a HTTP request

Field	Location	Description
Method	First line	Action of the request
Path	First line	Target resource of the request
Host	HTTP header	The destination host for the request
Content	HTTP body	Payload of the request
Date	HTTP header	When the request is created

As we can see, the data comes from a variety of locations, which makes our job a bit more complicated. To simplify this, we can do two things. First, we can treat the first line of the HTTP request as something special, often called the *request target*, including both the HTTP method (e.g., POST) and the path (e.g., /chatRooms/1). Second, rather than relying on signing the request body, which could get excessively large, we can calculate a hash of the body and store that in a separate HTTP header (in Base64 format) called "Digest." By relying on this derived field, we can maintain the integrity and security of the fingerprint while limiting its size.

Listing 30.4   Generating the hash value for a digest header

```
const crypto = require('crypto');

function generateDigestHeader(body: string): string {
  return 'SHA-256=' + crypto        ◁—— We prefix the hash with a
    .createHash('sha256')               specification of the hash algorithm
    .update(body)                       used (in this case, SHA-256).
    .digest()
    .toString('base64');      ◁—— The hash should be
}                                  Base64-encoded.
```

Once we've done these things, we need to assemble the pieces. To do this, we can use an ordered list of the components (e.g., request target, host, date, and then digest), format them appropriately (e.g., convert headers to lowercase characters), and place each one in a string with newline characters between each one.

Listing 30.5   Generating a fingerprint given a HTTP request

```
const HEADERS = ['(request-target)', 'host', 'date', 'digest'];

function generateRequestFingerprint(
    request: HttpRequest, headers = HEADERS): string {     The "(request-target)"
  return headers.map((header) => {                         field should include the
    let value;                                             lowercase HTTP method
    if (header === '(request-target)') {        ◁———       and the path.
      value = `${request.method.toLowerCase()} ${request.path}`;
    } else if (header === 'digest') {
      value = generateDigestHeader(request.body);     All other values should
    } else {                                     ◁——  be just as specified in the
      value = request.headers[header];                header of the request.
    }
    return `${header.toLowerCase()}: ${value}`;     ◁——  Finally, return a set of key-
  }).join('\n');                                          value pairs, separated by a
}                                                         colon (just like headers are).
```

The "digest" field should generate a hash of the request body.

Listing 30.6   Example fingerprint used for signing HTTP requests

```
(request-target): patch /chatRooms/1     ◁——  The special "(request-target)" field
host: example.org                              is treated like any other header.
date: Tue, 27 Oct 2020 20:51:35 GMT
digest: SHA-256=HV9PltG0QPRNsl1FB7ebQA8XPasvPyRg6hhU0QF2l4M=     ◁——

                                         We also include the additional digest header.
```

This canonical format of key-value pairs is sufficient as a fingerprint of the request and, more importantly, is something we could eventually use as the payload for computing a digital signature. It has all the information about the request's target resource (/chat-Rooms/1), action (PATCH), destination (example.org), time (Oct. 27), and the body (in the form of a SHA-256 hash digest) in order to uniquely identify the request later.

The next problem is that we need to somehow inform the API server of exactly how we came to compute this fingerprint. In the next section, we'll explore how we can communicate these parameters with the server to ensure it's able to properly come up with the same fingerprint for the request.

30.3.5 *Including the signature*

After we've computed the request fingerprint, we can't just sign it and call it a day. In order to ensure that the API server is capable of verifying the signature correctly, it must be able to compute the same fingerprint value given the inbound request. And to do that, we need to include a few bits of metadata about both the fingerprint and the signature.

First, we need to be clear about which headers were included in the fingerprint and, critically, in what order. Only having the list of headers is insufficient because rendering them in a different order will result in a different fingerprint. Next, we need to somehow tell the API server which public key should be used to verify the signature. This ID can be equivalent to the user ID created during registration since each user has exactly one public key. Finally, we should also include the algorithm used to generate the signature so that the API server can verify it using the same algorithm. A summary of these fields is shown in table 30.2.

Table 30.2 **Components necessary to define a signature**

Field	Description
headers	Ordered list of headers used to generate the request fingerprint
keyId	Unique ID used to choose the public key for verification
signature	Digital signature content to be verified
algorithm	Algorithm used to generate the signature

Once we have all this information, we can assemble it and pass the generated value along with the request in a special signature header.

Listing 30.7 **Generating a signature header given a fingerprint and other components**

```
const HEADERS = ['(request-target)', 'host', 'date', 'digest'];

interface SignatureMetadata {
  keyId: string;
  algorithm: string;
  headers: string;
```

```
    signature: string;
}

function generateSignatureHeader(
    fingerprint: string, userId: string,
    privateKey: string, headers = HEADERS): string {
  const signatureParts: SignatureMetadata = {        ◄──
    keyId: userId,                                         Specify a list of the different
    algorithm: 'rsa-sha256',                               signature components.
    headers: headers.map((h) => h.toLowerCase()).join(' '),
    signature: generateSignature(fingerprint, privateKey)
  };

  return Object.entries(signatureParts).map(([k, v]) => {   ◄──
    return `${k}="${v}"`;
  }).join(',');                        Combine parts into comma-
}                                      separated quoted key-value pairs.
```

The output of this function should end up being a comma-separated string of each of the different fields we need to adequately define a signature.

Listing 30.8   Example of the value for a signature header

```
keyId="1234",algorithm="rsa-sha256",headers="(request-target)
➡  host date digest",signature="mgBAQEsEsoBCgIOBiNfum37y..."
```

Now that we have all the pieces, all that's left is to assemble everything. This means that we need to take an HTTP request and attach two new headers: a digest header and a signature header. We can use our helper methods defined earlier to do the heavy lifting.

Listing 30.9   Function to sign a request (assigning relevant headers)

```
const HEADERS = ['(request-target)', 'host', 'date', 'digest'];

function signRequest(
    request: HttpRequest, userId: string,
    privateKey: string, headers = HEADERS): HttpRequest {
  request.headers['digest'] =
    generateDigestHeader(request.body);
  const fingerprint =
    generateRequestFingerprint(request, headers);    ◄──
  request.headers['signature'] = generateSignatureHeader(
    fingerprint, userId, privateKey, headers);    ◄──
  return request;         ◄──
}
```

Update the digest header. → (points to `generateDigestHeader(request.body);`)

Generate the request fingerprint needed for the signature.

Update the signature header.

Return the augmented request.

The output of this function is a request that should include both a digest header set to a hash of the request body as well as a signature header that not only includes the digital signature, but also all the information necessary for the API server to verify the signature value itself.

Listing 30.10   Example of a complete signed HTTP request

```
PATCH /chatRooms/1
Host: example.org
Digest: SHA-256=HV9PltG0QPRNsl1FB7ebQA8XPasvPyRg6hhU0QF2l4M=
Signature: keyId="1234",algorithm="rsa-sha256",headers="
           (request-target) host date digest",
           signature="mgBAQEsEsoBCgIOBiNfum37y..."
Date: Tue, 27 Oct 2020 20:51:35 GMT

{"title":"New title"}
```

Note that the order of the headers in the actual request is not important. This is because we've specified the order in which headers should be used to generate the fingerprint when verifying the signature. The next thing we need to consider is how exactly an API server can go about verifying a signature and ultimately authenticating a request. Let's look at this in the next section.

30.3.6 *Authenticating requests*

As you'd expect, we can rely on the same algorithm to verify a signature and, therefore, authenticate a request. But what exactly do we need to validate?

First, we need to ensure that the digest header is actually a true representation of the content in the request body. If not, this means that the request body has changed since the hash was calculated and the request should be rejected. Next, we need to recompute the fingerprint of the request using the schema provided in the signature header. After that, we need to use the key identifier provided in that header to look up the public key that should be used to verify the signature. Finally, we should use the public key and fingerprint to verify that the signature is correct.

While this might sound like a lot, we've already written the majority of the code that will do the heavy lifting..

Listing 30.11   Verifying a signature given a request object

First we need a function to parse a signature header into separate components.

```
function parseSignatureHeader(signatureHeader: string):     ⏎
    SignatureMetadata {
  const data = Object.fromEntries(         Split the
    signatureHeader                        k="v",k="v" pairs.
    .split(',')                      ⏎
    .map((pair) => pair.split('='))       ⏎  Split the k="v" pair.
    .map(([k, v]) => [k, v.substring(1, v.length-1)]));   ⏎  Remove
  data.headers = data.headers.split(' ');     ⏎  Split       quotes.
  return metadata;                               just the
}                                                headers.

async function verifyRequestSignature(request: HttpRequest):
    Promise<Boolean> {
  if (generateDigestHeader(request.body) !==
```

```
                         request.headers['digest']) {          ◁─┐   Verify that the request body
                  return false;                                  │   matches the digest header.
     Parse the  │  }
     signature  │  const metadata = parseSignatureHeader(
  header into  ├─▷   request.headers['signature']);                Determine the payload
  a bunch of  │  const fingerprint = generateRequestFingerprint(   that was signed based
     pieces.   │    request, metadata.headers);              ◁─   on the headers.
                  const publicKey = (await database.getUser(
                    metadata.keyId)).publicKey;              ◁──   Figure out the public key for
                  return verifySignature(                          the provided ID (stored in the
              ┌─▷    fingerprint, metadata.signature, publicKey);   database somewhere).
              │  }

  Verify the signature against the
  fingerprint with the public key.
```

And with that, we now have the ability to generate and register some credentials with the API server, digitally sign an outbound request, and authenticate an inbound request from a user.

30.3.7 *Final API definition*

The final API definition for this pattern is pretty straight forward, involving just the method for creating new users with the associated public keys and retrieving those users by their ID later. The implementations for how to sign requests and verify signatures were explored earlier, so this section won't reproduce that same code.

Listing 30.12   Final API definition

```
abstract class ChatRoomApi {
  @post("/users")
  CreateUser(req: CreateUserRequest): User;

  @get("{id=users/*}")
  GetUser(req: GetUserRequest): User;
}

interface CreateUserRequest {
  resource: User;
}

interface GetUserRequest {
  id: string;
}

interface User {
  id: string;
  publicKey: string;
  // ...
}
```

30.4 *Trade-offs*

Since there are so many different authentication methods available, there are obviously trade-offs when choosing one over the others. And even though digitally signing requests is almost certainly the most secure option available, this doesn't make it the right choice in all scenarios. In fact, the most common objection to this type of design is that it's overkill for the scenario.

For instance, there are many cases where nonrepudiation is more of a "nice to have" than a true requirement. The argument for insisting on nonrepudiation is when you might provide signed requests for others to execute later (involving third parties that may or may not be fully trusted), or when the API requests themselves are particularly sensitive (e.g., updating health or financial records). In these cases, nonrepudiation is important for the API server to protect itself from accusations of impropriety (e.g., a user claiming they never made those requests) that might arise during a future audit of historical logs.

While these things are not impossible, they are certainly not incredibly common. After all, when we update our data on Facebook or Twitter, we're not really planning to repudiate API requests after the fact. As a result, other systems (such as using HMAC with a shared secret) are certainly worth exploring. While we won't go into detail of using HMAC or other standard authentication mechanisms using short-lived access tokens (e.g., OAuth 2.0; https://oauth.net/2/), these are almost certainly valid options for any API that has slightly less stringent requirements and can expect to rely on proper security protocols implemented at the transport layer.

But why not just rely on the safest option when it's available to you? One common answer is that this type of cryptography is more computationally intensive and ultimately is handled by the API server itself rather than at a lower level in the stack. In fact, even in the common usage of public-key cryptography, such as SSL, the system only uses the asymmetric system up front to exchange a temporary symmetric key, relying on the less intensive symmetric algorithms from then on. As a result, systems that are concerned about available compute resources may opt for an alternative that is more efficient.

30.5 *Exercises*

1 What is the difference between proving the origin of a request and preventing future repudiation? Why can't the former dictate the latter?

2 Which requirement isn't met by a shared secret between client and server?

3 Why is it important for the request fingerprint to include the HTTP method, host, and path attributes?

4 Are the digital signatures laid out in this pattern susceptible to replay attacks? If so, how can this be addressed?

Summary

- There are three requirements for successful request authentication: proof of origin, proof of integrity, and prevention of repudiation.
- Origin is the proof that a request came from a known source, without any uncertainty.
- Integrity is focused on ensuring that the request itself has not been tampered with from the time it was sent from the known origin.
- Nonrepudiation refers to the inability of the requester to later claim the request was actually sent from someone else.
- Unlike real-world identity, authentication relies on identity being defined as possession of a secret key, sort of like a bearer bond.
- When signing a request, the actual content being signed should be a fingerprint of the request, including the HTTP method, path, host, and a set of content in the HTTP body.

index

RELATED MANNING TITLES

Design of Web APIs
by Arnaud Lauret
Foreword by Kin Lane

ISBN 9781617295102
392 pages, $44.99
October 2019

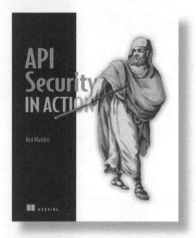

API Security in Action
by Neil Madden

ISBN 9781617296024
576 pages, $69.99
November 2020

Microservices Patterns
by Chris Richardson

ISBN 9781617294549
520 pages, $49.99
October 2018

For ordering information go to www.manning.com